Cross-cultural Marketing

Cross-cultural Marketing

Edited by
Robert Rugimbana
and
Sonny Nwankwo

THOMSON

Australia • Canada • Mexico • Singapore • Spain • United Kingdom • United States

THOMSON

Cross-cultural Marketing

Copyright © Thomson Learning 2003

The Thomson logo is a registered trademark used herein under licence.

For more information, contact Thomson Learning, High Holborn House, 50/51 Bedford Row, London, WC1R 4LR or visit us on the World Wide Web at: http://www.thomsonlearning.co.uk

British Library Cataloguing-in-Publication Data
A catalogue record for this book is available from the British Library

ISBN 1–86152–801–9

First edition 2003

Typeset by Photoprint, Torquay, Devon
Printed in Italy by G. Canale & C.

Contents

Preface

As we move into the 21st century propelled by the globalization wave, there is an increasing awareness of a striking reality building up around the world. Multiculturalism as an alternative worldview is assuming greater significance largely because of the potential effects of culture are pervasive in all markets, 'consumer' or 'industrial'. Unlike globalization, multiculturalism focuses on cultural diversity and therefore cross-cultural issues present different challenges to all marketers and in so doing encourage critical and analytical thinking and discovery from a different international stance. This edited book acknowledges both worldviews by including and integrating a wide range of works that demonstrate cultural differences and similarities between and within countries. In the process the book brings together works that highlight the diversity and depth of thought that characterizes modern debate on globalization and cultural diversity.

The acknowledgement of both worldviews is consistent with observations by many scholars that whilst the world has become a much smaller place and business today does take place in a global market, business activities, however, still take place through and with people. Such scholars make the point that although European and US academics have taken quite different approaches to the study of culture, providing unique perspectives, together they provide a greater understanding of why the differences arise and how successful adaptation can occur. Clearly such an integrated approach is necessary if practitioners are to successfully manage the paradox of how to employ effective marketing strategies in the face of growing globalization and increasing acknowledgement of cultural diversity with its emphasis on cultural identity.

This edited book is characterized by an integrated cultural approach to international as well as intra-national or *domestic* marketing. It is arguable that the challenges of practicing marketing can become more complex as companies move from a single domestic market to an international market and ultimately to several international or global markets. This is due to the requirements to adapt to the needs and preferences of customers who have different cultures, varying purchasing powers, and who reside in environments that are different in terms of patterns of competition and ways of doing business between nations as well as between regions within nations. Despite this reality, there are also important underlying similarities across borders nationally and domestically.

Goals

This edited book has been advanced on the premise that cross-cultural planks should be a central discourse in contemporary marketing literature and that cross-cultural marketing is a distinct area for scholarly inquiry that cannot be subsumed within the 'amorphous' field of International Business (IB) or general management. The text's integrated approach offers readers a framework for the development and implementation of both global and domestic marketing programmes in different marketing contexts. It is anticipated that readers will also be able to develop marketing strategies that are relevant to contemporary areas of marketing and that reflect on the future of globalization within diversity. To enable a clearer understanding of the themes in the book, we adopt a particular conceptualization of the cultural process which views cross-cultural marketing as the process of *marketing to global villages* – entities that are as global as they are diverse. The basic assumption adopted is that just as world cultures share many common features, they also display important unique characteristics that must be attended to. It is an assumption that characterizes more modern approaches to understanding cross-cultural marketing. After reading this book, the reader should be better equipped to understand how the firm can manage challenges of diversity in local, regional, global or international marketing settings. The book has the underlying objective of preparing readers for the realities and complexities of diversity. Readers will benefit from a subject that challenges limited ethnocentric and excathedra perspectives of the real world; in so doing it will also expand their capacity to apply marketing strategies to a given situation involving specific kinds of consumers.

Target Audience

This book has been prepared for people who wish to develop effective market responsive strategies in global yet diversified markets. It is also expected to be an essential and valuable resource to academics and students from related subjects such as International Business. In addition the book will have special appeal to anyone involved in, or interested in, any international interactions involving cross-cultural disciplines such as cross-cultural management, international buyer behaviour, developing country developments, global or international marketing, or deeper perspectives and applications of marketing knowledge to business management, planning and implementation in a world that is as diverse as it is global.

Key Features

An important competitive feature of this work over other publications such as those that address cross-cultural management and international marketing, is that it attempts to shift focus away from internal organizational issues to deal directly with external and practical 'consumer issues' in the marketplace. As such the book is positioned to address the cultural contexts of marketing. It is robust in its development and is written for an audience wishing to more directly capture the temporal, spatial and deeply embedded cultural antecedents and artefacts relating to cross-cultural marketing. In addition the book attempts to tailor works so that they are presented as teaching materials, without being overly conceptual and therefore more suitable for classroom usage at both undergraduate and MBA levels.

This has been achieved through: (a) *clearer positioning*, that is, a more market-oriented approach in terms of focusing the needs of the target readership; (b) *tightening pedagogical elements* by specifying learning objectives of each chapter, defining and explaining new terms and concepts appropriately as well as providing real-life illustrations/short cases, relevant end of chapter review questions, and useful further readings; and (c) ensuring *consistency* in both structure and content.

Outline

As this book has a clear cross-cultural marketing implementation orientation, it is broadly structured to cater for key decisions which cross-cultural marketers face when doing business in an environment that is both global and diverse. The eighteen chapters are divided into four parts. The schematic outline shows how these parts fit together. Examples of the practice of cross-cultural marketing are sprinkled throughout the book as discussed in the key features above.

- Part 1 – Cross-cultural marketing environment.
- Part 2 – Developing a cross-cultural marketing strategy.
- Part 3 – Implementing a cross-cultural marketing strategy.
- Part 4 – Contemporary issues in cross-cultural marketing.

Acknowledgements

We have great pleasure in acknowledging a heavy debt of gratitude to all the distinguished authors whose highly significant contributions comprise this work. We are grateful to the publisher, Thomson Learning, for believing in the worth of this book and supporting it. Throughout this enterprise we have had the pleasure of working with several editors who have seen this work through to its completion in an admirable fashion. We would therefore like to thank Commissioning Editor, Jennifer Pegg, and Development Editor, Melody Woollard. We would also like to extend our gratitude to Byron Keating for his tireless efforts in assisting with the preparation of the manuscripts and for providing various assistance throughout the review process. We also extend our greatest gratitude to all of our colleagues whose works have been cited or referred to in different ways and have made this book possible. Finally, we wish to thank our families for their support throughout the revision and editing process.

Robert Rugimbana and Sonny Nwankwo
2002

Contributors

Chandrama Acharya
College of Business Administration
National University of Singapore
Email: chandrama@nus.edu.sg

Laura Ancilli
School of Business
Swinburne University of Technology, Australia
Email: LAncilli@groupwise.swin.edu.au

Poul Houman Andersen
Aarhus School of Business
Aarhus University
Email: poa@asb.dk

Charles Blankson
Seidman School of Business
Grand Valley State University, 410C DeVos Centre, Fulton Street
Grand Rapids, Michigan, USA
Email: Blanksoc@gvsu.edu

Dawn Burton
Leeds University Business School
Leeds University
Email: d.b@lubs.leeds.ac.uk

Michael Callow
School of Business & Management
Morgan State University
Email: mcallow@moac.morgan.edu

Susan Carley
Kennesaw State University
Email: susan_carley@coles2.kennesaw.edu

Jamie Carlson
Newcastle Business School
The University of Newcastle, Australia
Email: c/o LAncilli@groupwise.swin.edu.au

Constant Cheng
School of Marketing, International Business & Asian Studies
University of Western Sydney
Email: c.cheng@uws.edu

Val Clulow
School of Business
Swinburne University of Technology, Australia
Email: VClulow@groupwise.swin.edu.au

Michael Dailey
New Moon Research
Email: mdailey@futuresguild.com

William Darley
IMES Department
University of Toledo
Email: wdarley@utoledo.edu

Isobel Doole
Sheffield Hallam University
Email: I.doole@shu.ac.uk

Frances Ekwulugo
Westminster Business School
University of Westminster
Email: ekwuluf@wmin.ac.uk

Greg Elliott
Graduate School of Management
Macquarie University
Email: greg.elliott@mq.edu.au

Jacqueline Flint
Central Coast School of eBusiness and Management
The University of Newcastle, Australia
Email: jacqueline.flint@newcastle.edu.au

Byron Keating
University of Newcastle in Australia
Email: byron.keating@newcastle.edu.au

Anton Kriz
Central Coast School of eBusiness and Management
The University of Newcastle, Australia
Email: Anton.Kriz@newcastle.edu.au

Dawn Lerman
Graduate School of Business
Fordham University
Email: dlerman@fordham.edu

Andrew Lindridge
Manchester School of Management
UMIST
Email: a.lindridge@umist.ac.uk

Robin Lowe
Sheffield Hallam University
Email: r.lowe@shu.ac.uk

Denise Luethge
School of Management
University of Michigan Flint
Email: dluethge@umflint.edu

Frank Manu
School of Business & Management
Morgan State University
Email: fmanu@moac.morgan.edu

Li-Wei Mai
Westminster Business School
University of Westminster
Email: maid@wmin.ac.uk

Paul Matthyssens
University of Antwerp
Email: paul.matthyssens@luc.ac.be

Sonny Nwankwo (co-editor)
East London Business School
University of East London
Email: S.Nwankwo@uel.ac.uk

Ogenyi Omar
South Bank Business School
South Bank University, 103 Borough Road, London SE1 AA
Email: Omaroe@sbu.ac.uk

John Paynter
Department of Management Science and Information Systems
The University of Auckland, New Zealand
Email: J.Paynter@auckland.ac.nz

Guilherme Dias Pires
School of Management
University of Newcastle in Australia
Email: mggp@alinga.newcastle.edu.au

Nathalie Prime
Paris School of Management
ESCP-EAP
Email: prime@escp.eap.net

C. P. Rao
Department of Marketing
University of Kuwait
Email: cprao@cas.kuniv.edu.kw

Phillip J. Rosenberger III
Newcastle Business School
The University of Newcastle, Australia
Email: mgpjr@mail.newcastle.edu.au

Robert Rugimbana (co-editor)
School of Management
University of Newcastle in Australia
Email: mgror@cc.newcastle.edu.au

Ven Sriram
School of Business & Management
University of Baltimore
Email: vsriram@ubmail.ubalt.edu

John Stanton
School of Management
University of Newcastle in Australia
Email: ecjcs@alinga.newcastle.edu.au

Ian Wilkinson
School of Marketing, International Business & Asian Studies
University of Western Sydney
Email: i.wilkinson@unsw.edu.au

Huib Wursten
Business Culture & International Training
Email: huib@itim.org

PART 1

Cross-cultural marketing environment

The global marketing literature provides a vacillating view of marketing thought. On one hand is the view that the world is becoming increasingly interdependent. International markets and international exchanges are becoming so accessible that the notion of a global village is a reality. On the other hand, the literature suggests that due to the enduring nature of the cultural variable and cultural diversity, it is far more realistic to imagine the existence of numerous global villages for localizing marketing strategies.

Part 1 of this book introduces key concepts in the cultural process that have great influence on the understanding of the cross-cultural marketing environment, international or domestic, and the design of appropriate *international* marketing strategies that take both views into account.

Chapter 1 offers an introduction to the basic explicit and implicit dimensions of culture, with the view of highlighting the risk of ethnocentrism in cross-cultural marketing activity. In the process the chapter presents two important and complementary facets of doing business in a culturally diverse setting. The first is *external diversity* as it relates to diverse consumption behaviours. The second is *internal diversity* as it relates to the internal dynamics of organizations interested in their various subsidiaries being able to cooperate with teams working in different countries. The chapter introduces the notion of a value orientation model in order to address the issue of cultural unity within diversity.

Chapter 2 presents a series of concepts of the cultural process from the point of view of domestic or individual nation-states. The author outlines the importance of ethnic markets and 'international marketing at home' strategies to effectively deal in these local markets. The rationale for this topic is to enable readers to appreciate the fallacy and dangers of equating cultural boundaries with national boundaries. The limitations of such assumptions are presented. Finally, the chapter reviews how the roles of race, ethnicity and multiculturalism influence the development of certain forms of social representations or ethnicity and how the latter can be incorporated into viable marketing strategy formulation.

CHAPTER 1

Cultural value

Nathalie Prime

LEARNING OBJECTIVES

At the end of this chapter readers will be able to:

▶ Develop cultural sensitivity to implicit cultural dimensions (norms, values, social representations) underlying consumption and managerial behaviours around the world.

▶ Understand that globalization does not mean standardization: cultures can simultaneously converge and remain unique.

▶ Use the *value orientation model* in order to address the issue of cultural unity within diversity.

▶ Cope better with ethnocentrism when designing and executing cross-cultural marketing programmes.

1.1 Introduction

Doing business abroad involves managing corporate activities in a multicultural environment. Given its boundary role nature, international marketing must manage two different sources of cultural diversity:

■ *External diversity*: marketing managers are faced with numerous obvious and less obvious effects of cultural determinants on buying and consumption processes (who? what? where? how? why?), as well as the cultural traits characteristic of 'marketing by agreement' (McCall and Warrington, 1984) and more generally in doing business with partners abroad (negotiation and relationship management with suppliers, distributors, and others).

■ *Internal diversity*: marketing managers working in the different subsidiaries of multinational companies have to cooperate with teams operating in different countries on key issues ranging from strategic decision-making to the implementation and execution of marketing programmes (such as designing advertising campaigns and conducting local marketing research). Marketing departments are increasingly multicultural, especially in Europe, but also more generally in multinational companies located in the Triad economies. In European countries, it is not rare for international marketing managers to work on a daily basis in the same department with a dozen expatriates from different countries.

In spite of the emergence of standardized consumption patterns across countries for culture-free products in general (such as high tech B to B products or expensive luxury products targeting the 'elite' transnational segment worldwide and especially in the 15-country European regional market), products are ultimately bought and consumed in a specific environment where local cultural determinants cannot be avoided (Solomon *et al.*, 1999; Usunier, 2000). Similarly, the globalization of managerial cultures in terms of principles of marketing management and organizational behaviour does not mean standardization: ultimately marketing is about satisfying consumer needs better than the competition by providing the best value for money, but marketing is always carried out within the constraints of a given environment (either local, multilocal or global). Managers carry their cultures with them when managing, as do consumers when consuming (Hofstede, 2000).

The aim of this chapter is to highlight the risk of ethnocentrism in cross-cultural marketing activities, i.e., what works at home (a market approach or a marketing mix) does not always work abroad; what constitutes value for money to home customers and partners does not always meet with foreigners' expectations. In other words, 'what is good for us may not be good for others'. The risk of ethnocentrism, though it exists in every professional sphere, is particularly pronounced in international business situations. The assumption that the spread of (a few) Western consumption patterns around the world is creating a universal civilization is based on a kind of universalism and the wishful thinking of global companies (de Mooij, 1998). This is reinforced by the spread of American marketing and management philosophies, exported via business schools and academic and professional publications (Usunier, 2000).

In the first section, we present a theoretical framework that can be used to understand the impact of the implicit and generally unconscious cultural diversity in norms, values and representations. Starting with the theoretical background of the value orientation model (Kluckhohn and Strodbeck, 1961), we elaborate on a few universal core dimensions of cultures that greatly impact on the success of marketing operations abroad. These universals pertain to the relationship of cultures to nature, others, power, rules, action, affect, space and time. They are universal domains of human experience that are always given meaning by social communities. This set of value orientations shapes a conceptualization of reality and ultimately defines the most efficient ways of doing things in different cultures. Examples in international marketing and international business are presented to show how one can learn to better overcome (as far as that is possible) ethnocentrism when designing marketing programmes and executing them abroad.

1.2 Value Orientations: Cultural Solutions to Universal Human Problems

As individuals, we are all exposed to several cultural influences depending on the different 'in-groups' we belong to: the nation, the state, the family, the region, the profession, the company, the industry or sector, the ethnic group, the religious group, the age group, or the gender. As they become successively or simultaneously members of these groups, individuals can be considered to be fundamentally multicultural.

When adapting to the multicultural nature of the specific environments where international marketing strategies will be effectively executed, the influence of culture is often presented in terms of broad descriptions of explicit behavioural differences: how people usually do things (customs, usages, traditions, habit clusters in relation to communication, eating, hygiene, housing, etc.), or how people are usually organized in social institutions (family, education, government, justice, religion). Differences are often described by means of descriptive anecdotes that do not allow a deep understanding of cultures in the sense of 'why' people behave this way or that way. As pointed out by Geertz (1973), understanding cultures requires a 'thick description' approach. In this chapter, we focus on the more implicit level of cultural norms, values and social representations which underlie consumption and business cultures and which are of some relevance to cross-cultural marketing issues and activities.

It is these more implicit elements of cultures that are less easily grasped because they are less easily observable than languages, customs or institutions. The implicit cultural elements are located below the surface of the cultural iceberg of societies as well as in the back of the minds of individuals. Generally unconscious, implicit cultural elements are more stable than explicit elements; they occupy a central position in a person's cognitive system. Hence, there is a need for managers who are involved in cross-cultural marketing to understand the diversity of norms, values and social representations that deeply shape behaviours. Because 'markets are people, not products' (de Mooij, 1998: 3), culture impacts on marketing managers, their customers, the other employees and the external partners of the firm doing business abroad.

In order to find a certain unity within cultural diversity, several studies have been conducted to identify what the different cultures of mankind have in common. These common denominators of cultures were first identified by Murdock (1945) in a list of 73 'cultural universals', such as the universal existence of age categories, training, cooking, arts, division of labour, etiquette rules, language, mourning or trade. Though very useful for understanding that different cultures share similar domains of concern, this initial approach was further developed by other studies focusing on the *meanings* attached to such universal activities or concepts. Especially at the level of implicit cultural elements, cultures may share the existence of a certain value, but still differ in the underlying meaning ascribed to that value and in the consequent explicit behaviours resulting from its operationalization. This is best illustrated by the difference between hunger and appetite: everyone needs food to survive (and human beings are biologically omnivores), but we don't all have a taste for the same kinds of food. What is emphasized here is that understanding cultural universals is ultimately a matter of understanding the underlying meanings attached by a given community to those universal concepts and activities and to the consequent behaviours of individuals in these domains.

In the field of cross-cultural value research, the value orientation model developed by anthropologists Kluckhohn and Strodbeck (1961) is particularly powerful in addressing the issue of cultural unity within diversity in the psyche of social life. They discuss the following set of assumptions (p. 10):

- There is a limited number of common human problems for which all peoples at all times must find some solution (cultural universals in the sense of Murdock's list).

- While there is variability in solutions of all the problems, it is neither limitless nor random but definitely variable within a range of possible solutions (e.g. the different possible foods to satisfy the need for eating)

- All alternatives of solutions are present in all societies at all times, but are differentially preferred. Every society has, in addition to its dominant profiles of value orientations, numerous variant or substitute profiles (e.g. the diversity of methods for curing disease that range from surgery to prayer).

In both the dominant profile and variations, there is a ranking of preferences for alternatives: cultures do not vary in essence (people spend their time trying to solve similar problems) but in their preferences for certain solutions. In societies undergoing change, the ordering of preferences will not be clear-cut. People will make different choices depending on the situation.

It is important first to understand that this approach based on universal value orientations is not meant to refer to the behaviour of all people all of the time, nor to the behaviours of any particular person. Instead, it refers to broad norms that guide most people most of the time. Second, especially for societies that are undergoing change (in an age of increasing globalization, this in fact means all societies), the ordering of preferences may change depending on the situation: young people in Japan have become more self-centred in their consumption patterns, but are still traditional when it comes to relationships with their families. Third, one can often observe what are called 'value paradoxes' (De Mooij, 1998), suggesting that cultures may simultaneously ascribe worth to opposing values, such as the French valuing of independence and equality as well as dependence and hierarchy, or the American valuing of both freedom and belonging, or the Japanese valuing of tradition and innovation. Value paradoxes are statements that seem contradictory but are actually true. They exist in all cultures and reflect the contradiction between the desirable and the desired. In the next sections we describe eight core value orientations and the related possible cultural preferences (see Table 1.1). Managerial implications are emphasized using examples from international marketing and international business situations.

Nature	Domination	Harmony	Subjugation
Others	Individualism		Communalism
Power	Equality		Hierarchy
Rules	Universalism		Particularism
Activity	Doing		Being
Affect	Expression		Neutralization
Space	Private		Public
Time	Economic time		Eventual time
	Monochronism		Polychronism
	Past	Present	Future

Table 1.1
Universal problems, cultural preferences.

Sources: Adapted from Kluckhohn and Strodbeck, 1961; Hofstede, 1980; Hall, 1983; Trompenaars, 1993; Prime, 1994; Adler, 1999 and Usunier, 2000.

1.3 The Relationship to Nature

One of the first fundamental problems human societies must deal with is the meaning attributed to nature. Three options can be observed: domination, harmony and subjugation. The domination orientation is based on the feeling that it is possible to dominate nature in order to submit it to human requirements. This vision is based on the idea of an internal locus of control. It is prevailing in the Judeo-Christian world where the sacred book says that human beings should multiply and rule over the Earth and the animals for their own benefit. The domination orientation also is consistent with the industrialized world, where scientific and technical advances to a certain extent have allowed humankind to bring natural forces under control (as in vaccination, birth control, genetics, biotechnologies or space exploration); however, this orientation is more characteristic of Western cultural traditions. In the domination world, agriculture is industrialized and based on mass utilization of sophisticated scientific and technical means for increasing yields (agribusiness). This domination orientation is often implemented on a short-term basis. Consequently, nature, the environment and ultimately people may suffer from the dangers of excessive domination over nature (witness global ecological issues or the numerous food crises in Europe – mad cow disease, the foot and mouth epidemic, etc.).

The second type of relationship to nature is called harmony and is cosmocentric, as opposed to anthropocentric. In a global systemic vision, humanity is conceived as just one component of nature among others, and its role therefore consists in being in harmony within nature. In the 'harmony world' the farmer plants the right crop in the right place at the right time. Traditionally, the harmony vision is characteristic of traditional cultures everywhere, and more specifically of Asian cultures that ascribe positive value to the idea of balance and harmony, inside as well as outside the self. This vision is observable in all traditional medicines (e.g. Chinese and Indian) which are based on a systemic conceptualization of human beings in which the body, the mind and the rest of the world are inseparable. In industrialized societies, the quest for harmony is observable in a large variety of product categories, from 'green' products (food, hygiene, clothes, medicine) to 'green' activities which provide a feeling of harmony with the natural environment (in sorting household rubbish for recycling, leisure activities and the like).

The last possible value orientation towards nature is called subjugation. It describes humans as part of nature, but submitted to external forces and accepting them: what predominates is the feeling of an external locus of control. This type of relationship to nature is characteristic of societies that are self-sufficient, have little contact with the rest of the world, are resistant to modernity and are less educated (in the Western sense). In the subjugation world, the farmer hopes that there will be no natural disasters, but if one occurs, it is because 'it was destined to be so'. From the point of view of the domination world, subjugation is equal to fatalism. By contrast, people from the subjugation world see domination-oriented people as 'fools' who claim that the uncontrollable can be controlled.

Subjugation is often religious, as in Hinduism where the theory of Karma accounts for the conditions of present human life, or in Islam where the expression 'Inch'

Allah' ('if God wills') is systematically pronounced at the end of a sentence, which implies an option on the future (for an appointment, a forecast etc.). Subjugation is also seen in the belief in the forces of magic, especially in black Africa (Zadi Kessy, 1998): many Africans believe that success in life, in projects or in one's career is dependent upon the action of secret magical forces (like those resulting from the powers of the medicine man over the hierarchical manager). In the subjugation world observable in India, there are sacred cows instead of mad cows: serving the cow is like serving God (see Vignette 1.1).

VIGNETTE 1.1: Maharajah Burger: mad cows, sacred cows

The domination relationship to nature prevailing in the industrial world is perfectly illustrated by the mad cow crisis in Europe. This started in the United Kingdom where, in order to increase the milk production of cows, they were given more proteins in a cheap food made out of dead sheeps' bodies. In other words, meat was given to herbivores. By contrast, in India the image of the cow is sacred and provides an example of a subjugation relationship to nature. Cows have been worshipped by Hindus for more than 2000 years. They are taken care of in specialized 'hospitals for cows', the *gauchala*. There are about 6000 *gauchala* all over India, including a dozen in Vrindavan where Lord Krishna, the protector of cows, was born. In essence, serving the cow is like serving God. Besides, the cow is often presented as the mother who provides everything – milk that is necessary for healthy development, butter, excrements (which serve as a cheaper fuel than wood for household heating and crematoriums), urine (used in agriculture). When responding to the mad cow crisis, Indians quite simple cannot believe that meat was given to cows and that millions of British cows in particular were to be slaughtered. McDonald's recently established a few restaurants in India targeting the urban and high social classes. But is is the only market in the world where beef is not offered and most of the menu is vegetarian ('veggie'). (*Maharajah Burger, Vaches folles, Vaches sacrées*, a film by Thomas Balmès, Canal + – TBC production – Quark production, 1997).

When marketing across cultures it is of crucial importance to take into account the relationship to nature. For example, in the domain of eating habits; it would be difficult for most Hindus to eat beef, and it would be difficult for most Europeans to eat foods containing snakes or cockroaches or to drink 'snake juices' as some do in Taiwan. In the domain of medical habits, exports of Western allopathic medicines produced by large Western pharmaceutical companies cannot compete with local traditional practices for the treatment of a large number of ailments. The latter are not only more accessible (financially and physically) than modern Western treatments, but have proved their efficacy in the past. This does not mean that a Chinese person or an Indian would reject modern medical techniques (for surgery in particular) if they were accessible. From a general point of view, rural marketing in developing countries (where urbanization has not taken place on a large scale) is highly conditioned by the sacred relationship to nature for the sale of 'domination products' in many product categories, such as industrial agriculture, hygiene, medicine or insurance.

1.4 The Relationship to Others

This dimension describes the relationship between the individual and his or her community, and the cultural definition of identity (Triandis, 1989). Numerous studies have compared individualistic and communalistic cultures: are individuals to be defined in isolation from their in-group or in relation to it? Who is considered to belong to the family (the extended family composed of dozens of direct and indirect members, or the typical Western nuclear family)? What is the influence of the community on the daily activities of its members? How does the group impact on buying behaviour? Korea (Crane, 1978), India (Jain, 1988), China (Hsu, 1981) and Japan (Barnlund, 1989) have been described as countries that are characterized by a communalistic orientation. In Asia, communalism has been shown to influence consumer behaviour to a great extent, as evidenced in the adoption of innovations (see Vignette 1.2 below).

VIGNETTE 1.2: Communalism and diffusion of innovations in Asia

From a cultural point of view, Asia is far more culturally diverse than Europe or Latin America. Moreover, India, China, South East Asian countries, Korea and Japan have cultural roots dating back such a long time (several thousand years) that the assumption that modernization leads to universal values is seen as wishful thinking. Communalism, in particular, finds its expression in many aspects of consumer behaviour. Belonging is more important than individual desires, reciprocity contributes to the social positioning of individuals in their relationship networks, status is expressed in language and behaviours, and group conformity limits the opportunities available for individuals to be different from their in-groups. Consequently, the Western theory of diffusion of new products is modified: there is a smaller proportion of innovators (who run the risk of social marginalization), but also of late majority adopters and laggards (who take the same risk, but for an opposite reason, the fear of being 'out of date'). The need for conformity explains that once risk aversion is managed, the speed of diffusion can be exceptional, especially in Japan where the life cycle of a product can be very short (H. Assael, *Consumer Behaviour and Marketing Action*, 6th edition, International Thomson Publishing Company, 1998).

Communalism is also observable in Latin-American cultures or in Arabic cultures (Nydell, 1987). In communalistic cultures, identity is primarily defined in relation to the main reference group (such as family, clan or firm), and the linkages between the individual and the community are seen as permanent. Members' obligations towards the group grow with age or success, the latter of which is generally shared with the group.

Standing in contrast to this communalistic orientation is the individualistic orientation, which places emphasis on an autonomous conception of the self and on the self-actualization of the individual. It is the modern man or woman born in the Western world, where the individual stands for his/her individuality. For historical reasons, individualism is particularly dominant in the United States, where early immigrants could rely only on themselves to make things happen (Stewart, 1972). But also France

(Zeldin, 1996) and all Western countries (although to different degrees, the south of Europe being more family-orientated than the north), can be said to share this vision of the relationship between the individual and others. Hofstede (1980) found a high positive correlation between level of individualism and Gross Domestic Product. In general, urbanization tends to have an impact on the development of individualism because individuals become more isolated from their original communities and commitments towards the in-groups may diminish.

An important question in looking at the relationship dimension relates to the definition of the relevant in-group in a communalistic culture. Two cultures can have a high degree of communalism but still operate on a communalistic logic of a different kind. For example, individualism is higher in Korea than in Japan because the main emotional commitment of the Korean is directed towards his family (filial piety). In Japan, loyalty is given rather to the company or to the country. Professional mobility is traditionally less frequent in Japan, where it tends to be perceived as a lack of loyalty to the company, whereas in Korea mobility is more socially accepted.

Similarly in India, although following a different tradition, the Joint Hindu Family (also called the Hindu Undivided Family) can be seen as the archetypical form of communalism: it is composed of individuals with a common ancestor and is unlimited in size and in time. It is a community of patrimony (Coparcenary), of eating practices (from the same kitchen), and of religious rituals. Contrary to Western legal systems where the individual is the primary unit defined by the law, the Indian legal system is based on the Joint Hindu Family. Black African countries, which are considered low in individualism (Blunt and Jones, 1992; Jackson, 1999) tend to exhibit another type of communalism. Black African communalism is opposed both to individualism (and the cult of individual competition) and to Asian communalism (and the kind of de-personalization of the individual, who tends to melt into the group) (Khoza, 1994).

The cross-cultural marketing implications of the concept of value orientation are crucial in the management of people from different countries working together. In general (e.g. Adler, 1999; Barsoux and Lawrence, 1997), one can note that in communalistic (individualistic) societies:

- The relationship to power is more hierarchical (egalitarian).
- The relationship to rules is more particularistic (universalistic).
- The relationship to space is more public for the in-group (private).
- Communication is more implicit (explicit).
- The decision-making process is more collective (individual).
- Leadership is more authoritarian (participative).

International business negotiations provide an excellent opportunity to observe the differences in strategies used by teams from individualistic versus communalistic cultures. Whereas the former usually negotiate in small teams composed of decision-makers in the various fields of negotiation, the latter negotiate in groups and report to their hierarchy before any decision is made or whenever some new information is brought to the negotiation table. For instance, Japanese negotiators work in teams and also negotiate among themselves. Decisions are analyzed collectively even if made by a senior manager. Any decision-making tends to take more time than in individualistic cultures, but execution is lightning-quick because everyone has already been involved. In the West, the opposite often happens: decision-making is fast because it requires the input of fewer people, but execution can be terrible because each and every person involved in the decision has to be independently convinced.

This dimension also has much impact in the field of consumer behaviour. It defines the identity of the consumer (individual versus collective), it impacts on the buying process and on the value attached to consumption (especially for those products to be used in social contexts in communalistic societies), it emphasizes the role of certain marketing mix levers (such as place, which is crucial in communalistic cultures where clients prefer to buy from people they know well and who know them well). In highly industrialized multicultural societies, such as the United States, ethnic marketing has been developed to target specific communities with adapted marketing strategies (including Hispanic American communities, African Americans and Chinese Americans).

1.5 The Relationship to Power

Understanding the relationship to power and its distribution in society is important for understanding the behaviour of people. Many studies have identified this dimension using various concepts, such as the relationship to authority (Inkeles and Levinson, 1969) or power distance (Hofstede, 1980). Two main options have been observed in the way cultures define power relationships between members of the society: distribution of power can be hierarchical (vertical) or egalitarian (horizontal).

Hierarchical cultures do not see members of the society as equal and power distance is said to be large (Hofstede, 1980). The important thing is that everyone has a place and is treated according to this particular place in a hierarchical system. Social differentiation can be on the basis of assigned or real characteristics, and it is important to identify the criteria of hierarchy which are prevalent, such as age (social system based on seniority), gender, qualifications, money, name and birth, and occupation. Such differentiations separate individuals socially and psychologically, each position being associated with a given set of roles, expectations and norms of behaviour.

Western and non-Western cultures are frequently contrasted as far as the relationship to power is concerned. Among Western cultures, Anglo-Saxon and Scandinavian cultures are more egalitarian than the Latin cultures. In the rest of the world, most societies have a social system based on hierarchical relationships that shape a large part of individuals' behaviours in different social situations. Status will impact on the way people deal with others, starting with language; for example both verbal and non-verbal nuances define the relative place of each party to the interaction and the specific relationship which must be respected.

Confucianism in Eastern Asia has spread a hierarchical vision of society, as seen in Japan or Korea, where there is always one who is more powerful than, older than, or inferior to the other, and should therefore be treated accordingly. Respect and loyalty towards superiors is an absolute rule in Korea (Kim, 1989). Social interactions are governed by hierarchical relationships and the concept of equality in daily interactions is not relevant. African cultures are also very hierarchical and the opportunities for climbing up the social ladder are often restricted (when they exist) to certain social origins, such as belonging to certain social categories of age, gender, ethnicity or caste. Qualifications play a great role as well and define the tasks to be done (or rejected). Seniority is absolute: a newly-graduated African manager will have difficulties trying to make use of an authority based on expertise when working with older collaborators. Moreover, that manager will not be able to learn the practicalities of the job very quickly because he or she will not be able to question subordinates without the risk of losing status (Camilleri, 1995).

In India, the social organization (which is based on religion) is structured according to the different caste distinctions (Dumont, 1970). It still plays an important role even after reference to castes was outlawed by the Indian Constitution in 1948. The caste system is still very much alive inside the mind of individuals and is largely internalized. Names usually reveal a geographic or caste affiliation, primarily dependent on birth (*jati*) and occupation. Caste defines status and rules for appropriate interpersonal communication. Weddings are organized within the same caste or with related castes, and food and water are usually not shared with outsiders. Bypassing these rules can lead to exclusion from the community.

In Western cultures, the principle of equality between human beings is a declared value, defined in the Universal Declaration of Human Rights. Of course, this does not mean that inequality does not exist, but rather that the ideal of equality is more of a reality for individuals and for society. In the United States, where the social structure is less hierarchical than in Europe (in spite of the existence of real social classes in North American society), the style of communication between interlocutors is not so different depending on the social status of the parties involved (Stewart, 1972). Scandinavian countries are perhaps the cultures which value the principle of equality the most, especially equality between men and women. Latin countries in Europe are more hierarchical, especially France where the positioning of individual managers within organizations is dependent primarily on qualifications – the most valued educational background being an engineering degree from the best Parisian 'grandes écoles' (Barsoux and Lawrence, 1997). In Germany, many more senior managers actually gained an apprenticeship diploma first (*die Lehre*) and only after some years of company experience went back to school to obtain an advanced degree in engineering.

Orientation to social stratification and power distribution in society has an impact on numerous managerial variables. Among these are intra- and intercultural communication, which condition not only who can talk to whom, about what, in which situation, but the expectations of the parties to an interaction, such as parent–child, husband–wife, teacher–student, buyer–seller, superior–subordinate, and local–foreigner. The buying process is also dependent on the power dimension, which influences the selection of the decision-maker, the product category and the speed of the decision-making process.

As for the management of relationships with foreign collaborators in the workplace, the relationship to power impacts on many aspects of organizational behaviour (Adler, 1999; Schneider and Barsoux, 1997), such as the preference for flat (where equality is valued) versus vertical (where hierarchy is valued) organization structure. The power dimension also impacts on preferred promotion schemes (internal or external, promotion based on criteria such as performance, seniority, social origin, or a combination of these), or on preferred leadership style (participative, authoritarian, or a combination of these) (see Vignette 1.3).

VIGNETTE 1.3: **The 'nurturant-task' leader in India**

Effectiveness of leadership in India is contingent on two main factors: effectiveness in doing tasks (assertiveness) and effectiveness in meeting the social needs of collaborators in the workplace. It combines two different sets of roles usually seen as separated. An effective leader will be required to incorporate Indian meta-values while designing his or her action strategies for meeting the objectives of the organization. The 'nurturant-task' leader (Sinha, 1980) combines the two aims of performance and the development of people. Using the analogy of a mother nurturing her child, an effective leader (and by extension an effective organization) will often provide collaborators with a combination of physical nurturing (such as food, clothing and medical care), of emotional nurturing (by providing encouragement, support and appreciation in order to build self-confidence), of intellectual nurturing (by providing knowledge of do's and dont's and training to make people autonomous) and more generally of spiritual nurturing. When leaders combine these aspects, subordinates put a lot into their tasks and this results in high quality and productivity. The famous Indian business leaders (the founders of the major industrial and trading companies in India, such as Tata, Birla, Godrej, Ambani and Bajaj) are often presented as highly respected 'fathers'. Their projects involve developing their business as well as the welfare of their community, as reflected in the saying that 'What is good for Tata is good for India, and vice-versa'.

1.6 The Relationship to Rules

Rules are formalized norms, explicit or implicit, concerning methods or procedures. They are numerous and affect all domains of social behaviour, from respect for the law (e.g. speed limit on the motorways or payment of taxes) to norms of politeness (e.g. when queuing at the bank or in public transport, when invited for dinner or during a business meeting). The need for regulation of individual and collective behaviours is universal, but cultures have been observed to favour either a particularistic or universalistic orientation (Trompenaars, 1993).

Particularism is based on the premise that rules are applied differently depending on the quality of people; that is, the focus is on relationships and situations. For example, the attitude towards rules will differ according to whether or not the person concerned belongs to the in-group. For the group, protecting the individual will take priority over respecting a universal rule perceived to be external, and when behaviour has to be sanctioned this will be done by the in-group. There is an association between particularism and communalism such that communalistic cultures tend logically to be more particularistic vis-à-vis their in-group members.

Universalism is based on the idea that rules must be applied to each and every person in the same fashion, regardless of other positioning characteristics of the individual in the society. It is prevalent in Anglo-Saxon and Scandinavian cultures and especially in business and political communities in the United States where the rationale of transactions (and the overwhelmingly powerful legal body that goes with it) defines the regulation system. In the case of a violation of a rule, law will sanction behaviours. In Latin cultures, such as France, universalism is strong, but there often is a wider gap between speech and action than there is in the north of Europe. The need for universalistic regulation (through a well developed legal body) is strong, but so is the need for particularism when behaviours are concerned (through the typical tendency to try to bypass the rules whenever it is possible without 'being caught').[1]

The relationship to rules is not separable from the relationship to power, which will be translated into the production and execution of rules. In egalitarian cultures, where individuals generally are more involved in the production of rules, these are more often implemented, which in turn serves to enhance the sense of equality. On the other hand, hierarchical societies produce individuals who are mostly submissive to rules, in the creation of which they have not been involved. Moreover, rules are more strictly applied to the powerless than to the powerful (or to the more intelligent), the latter being 'above' the rules applicable to ordinary people.

The implications of this value orientation are important in all domains of management where regulation is concerned. Regulation of individual behaviour may be achieved via shame in communalistic and particularistic societies, whereas guilt is prevalent in individualistic and universalistic societies (Benedict, 1946). Value orientation also impacts on the regulation of business behaviour, especially regulation by means of 'contracts'. Signing contracts may be a universal phenomenon, but the concrete execution of contractual duties varies across different cultures. In Asia, contracts usually evolve in step with the relationship. A contract is not seen as the final point of agreement for a given transaction, but rather as the beginning of a relationship that will necessarily change over time. The quality of a (good) partner is therefore very much linked to their capacity to adjust to the legitimate expectations of the other partner over time. Loyalty is paramount in relationships.

The relationship to rules also impacts on the notion of trust, whereby universalistic people tend not to trust particularistics because 'they always look after their own' (particularistic people tend not to trust universalitics for the opposite reason, that is because 'they don't even look after their own'). Finally, conflict management in international contracts between business partners is linked to the relationship to rules. For example, mediation is preferred by cultural tradition in communalistic and particularistic societies.

1.7 The Relationship to Action and Activity

Action or activity relates to the capacity to act – to show the will to accomplish something (to carry out activities) that will lead to change, however minimal. The relationship to activity can be defined on the basis of two opposite value orientations: doing or being. The psychoanalyst E. Fromm (1976) describes the doing orientation as connected with having; that is, with the external component of activity. The doing–having orientation is characteristic of industrial societies around the world where the most important thing in life is money, and where (perceived) happiness is measured according to the number of material possessions.[2]

In contrast, the being mode implies a certain kind of independence vis-à-vis the material conditions of life. However, being is not synonymous with passive behaviour. It involves activity, but activity which creates value for the person, which nourishes the self for its own sake, in qualitative terms, in order to develop being qualities such as wisdom, social intelligence, humility, strength, creativity, serenity, loyalty or patience. In Western industrialized societies, this relationship to activity tends to disappear, so that being is confounded with idleness (so-called 'workoholics' are often simply not capable of idleness) or worse, with boredom.

The being qualities count a lot in many cultures that have not yet been submitted to massive industrialization, or that have developed economically on the basis of a large network of relationships (such as the Chinese *guanxi*). Who are you in the social network? Who do you know? With whom did you previously work? What is the number of 'relationship assets' that you can bring to a deal?

The difference that can be observed between doing-having and being orientations is thus not simply an opposition between Western and non-Western cultures, but more accurately between societies focusing on people versus societies focusing on things. The doing orientation is also associated with a relationship to nature based on an internal locus of control that favours problem-solving attitudes with a doing approach.

This action–activity dimension plays an important role when it comes to human resources management. Are collaborators recruited and promoted on the basis of competencies (doing orientation) or on intrinsic qualities attached to their person and which create cultural obligations (such as seniority in Africa, India or Japan)? Last, but not least, the value orientation towards action and activity impacts on the cultural indicators of trust (see Vignette 1.4).

VIGNETTE 1.4: The language of trust

Looking at how trust is expressed in different languages is extremely important for understanding which aspects of the concept are emphasized by the corresponding cultures. The English concept of trust is based on reliance on, and confidence in, the truth and reliability of a person, a word, or a thing. This explains why the legal institution of trust has been highly developed in the common-law tradition of Anglo countries, whereas it was non-existent in the Roman-Germanic tradition until very recently. The German concept is based on two verbs, *trauen* and *vertrauen,* both of which literally mean 'to trust'. However, *trauen* is mostly used in a negative sense, as in '*Ich traue Dir nicht*' (I do not trust you), and *vertrauen* in the positive sense, as in '*Ich vertraue Dir*' (I trust you). The prefix *ver* indicates a transformation: the initial position is distrust, and trust can be established only after a favourable change has occurred. Trust is inseparable from distrust. In French (as in other Roman languages), *confiance* comes from the Latin *confidentia* which is a compound of *cum* (with, shared) and *fides* (faith, belief). Hence, the emphasis in the Latin concept of trust is placed on sharing common beliefs, religion, and possibly education or group membership (adapted from J-C. Usunier, *International and Cross-Cultural Management Research*, Sage Publications, 1998, pp. 107–8).

1.8 The Relationship to Affect

Before undertaking marketing operations in a multicultural environment, one should understand the relationship to affect. Human beings are emotional, but cultures do not value emotional states and their expression in the same way (see Table 1.2). Two

Cultures that . . .	Mix business with feelings	Separate business and feelings
Express emotions	Latin cultures Semitic cultures Slavonic cultures	Anglo-Saxon cultures
Neutralize emotions	Asian cultures African cultures	Scandinavian cultures

Table 1.2 Relationship to affect across cultures.

basic dimensions of the way affect and emotions may be handled in society are reflected in the following questions:

- Is it better to show emotions or to keep them inside whilst maintaining a 'mask' in front of others?

- Is there a preference for doing business with people one knows and possibly likes, or a preference for a 'business is business' attitude?

The cultural clusters presented in Table 1.2 are extremely general, and empirical reality is full of all sorts of nuances. For example, among Latin cultures, Italians and Brazilians tend to be far more extroverted than the French. In addition, the situation may impact on the emotional commitment of individuals towards others. In Japan, Doi (1988) notes that there are three main circles of affect for a Japanese mind: (1) the intimate world (the world of *amae*, or indulgence); (2) the circle of kinship and professional relationships (the world of compromise and the search for harmony, the world of reciprocity, debt and obligations which predominate over the expression of personal feelings); and (3) the circle of affect that is composed of the 'others' towards whom the individual has no obligation, no feeling, and from whom he expects nothing. These three circles rarely coincide.

The implications of this value orientation are extremely important in the field of international negotiation and communication. To what extent is the affect used (becoming friends first, and then eventually the business will come)? Is it better to show emotions or to hide them (especially in leadership)? What are the limits for mixing affect and business? Can friends be used for business purposes? To what extent can affect be used to motivate collaborators? What are the different options for delegating organizational objectives to teams (and controlling the execution of tasks), according to whether one is working in an affect-expressive or an affect-neutralizing environment?

1.9 The Relationship to Space

In addition to time, the relationship to space is a second dimension along which human consciousness is able to project. Like that of time, the social meaning of space is different in different cultures. Two main conceptions of space have been observed depending on whether it is seen as public or private. In individualistic cultures, public space is not occupied by everyone, and private space is generally not shared easily by a large number of persons, except close family (if not the so-called 'nuclear family'). In communalistic cultures, space is more public for the in-group members, such as in homes inhabited by people from three generations. Working space is not distributed in the same way everywhere – it is more often fully open in Asia, partially-open in the United States, and closed in Latin countries.

The relationship to space also covers the issue of how space is used in communication, and especially how interpersonal distances are manipulated and invested with specific meanings (Hall, 1959; 1976). This distance can be very short (as in Middle Eastern cultures or in Slavonic cultures), or very large (as in Japan), while a full range of intermediate preferred distances can be observed (e.g. Morris, 1995).

Finally, the relationship to space addresses several key questions, including the following: What is the appropriate place in which to do business? What are the boundaries between working space and non-working space? Where is business actually done? Is a restaurant a suitable place to develop business relationships? (It is very much so in China and in France, especially as compared to Anglo-Saxon–Scandinavian cultures). Is having a drink after work actually *part of work* as it is in Japan? Such questions call for specific attention from international managers and, above all, in communication. It is important to respect non-verbal codes involving the use of space as in greeting rituals (which are all non-verbal) and in negotiation behaviours.

1.10 The Relationship to Time

Time talks, with an accent (Levine, 1997: xi). Studies of temporal representations in the great civilizations that have arisen throughout human history reveal a great deal of variability in those representations (e.g. Gurevitch, 1976). The temporal elements of culture are shared neither by contemporaries nor across history. The links that humanity maintains with time have evolved in step with other aspects of human development and each temporal representation has created its own vision of the world, its origins and its destiny.[3]

Our concepts of time are always 'culturally-bound' (Hallowell, 1955), but numerous anthropological studies allow us to define a representation of time as a fundamental dimension of all cultures (e.g. Hall, 1983; Munn, 1992). It is a 'quintessential dimension' (Spengler, 1991), a common denominator in all cultures that is accorded various meanings (Eliade, 1968; Hall, 1983; Kluckhohn and Strodbeck, 1961) as a function of the collective experience of time (Hallowell, 1955).

From a functional viewpoint, the representation of time contributes to the stability and the longevity of the social system; socially shared, it allows for the synchronization of activities and relationships in a manner that makes them efficient for the group's long-term functioning (Hallowell, 1955). The representation of time finds its foundation in the necessary collaboration of different members of society and serves to 'weave' the social fabric. Finally, it conditions the meanings of actions and of social situations; the same social action can have different meanings in different temporal contexts (Zerubavel, 1981). For example, eating has a different meaning according to whether it is a festive occasion or an ordinary day; arriving late or being on time for an official ceremony – or drinking alcohol – have different meanings for an adult or a child.

Three dimensions are useful to structure the relationship to time (see Table 1.3):

Dimensions	Preferences for . . .		
Conceptualization of time	Economic time 'time is money' – digital clock time – Newtonian time – machine-time – time to do and to have – time is a scarce economic resource (industrial time)	Eventual time 'time is events' – auspicious time of 'what happens' – natural time – human time – time to be – time is an abundant relational resource (human time)	
Allocation of time to activities	Monochronism 'one thing at a time' – rigid planning – activity is subordinated to time – task-orientated – high psychological commitment to digital time – work regularly at a measured and sustained pace – low context communication	Polychronism 'several things at one time' – flexible planning – time is subordinated to activity – people-orientated – low psychological commitment to digital time – work intensely but in a less sustained manner – high context communication	
Collective temporal orientation	Past 'traditions/golden age'	Present 'immediate conditions'	Future 'progress'

Table 1.3 Time representations across cultures.

Source: Adapted from several authors by Prime (1994), *Culture, Temps et Négociation Commerciale Internationale*, thèse de doctorat, Ecole Supérieure des Affaires, Université Pierre Mendès France, Grenoble.

■ The conceptualization of time: a monetary vision ('clock time') versus an event-based vision ('auspicious time').

■ The allocation of time to activities: monochronic (one thing at a time) or polychronic (several things at one time).

■ The overall collective temporal orientation: towards the past, present and future.

The Conceptualization of Time

The social construction of managerial time – a nexus of assumptions, beliefs and values which specify time as linear, continuous and economic – was promoted by Western industrial development and the horological disciplines associated with mechanical clock design and manufacture contributed to it (Mumford, 1963; Thompson, 1967). This form of time has also been called 'Anglo-time' (Graham, 1981) because of its close association with North American society; it underlies much of the current managerial literature. In fact, this economic conceptualization is that of the modern 'technological' world, which was dominant from the beginning in the Western Anglo-Saxon and Scandinavian industrial world. However, it is also manifest outside the West in more recently industrialized nations such as Japan, especially in professional contexts and in interactions with Westerners (Hall and Hall, 1987). Latin industrialized cultures, like France, tend to resist (often unconsciously) a pure economic conceptualization of time: time is more flexible (depending also on 'unexpected occurrences').

The event-based conceptualization of time characterizes the functioning of two types of cultures. On the one hand, ancient cultures and non-industrialized countries, for which a natural and often sacred representation of time is quite common; on the other hand, industrialized nations, whose deep cultural bases were not originally founded on a primarily monetary vision of time. The latter cultures are in the process of integrating the quantitative representation of time as a response to the constraints of the modern global environment, which is marked by international exchanges and where American 'standards' are often imposed. Latin European cultures, like France (Hall and Hall, 1990) or, more recently, East Asian cultures (Hall, 1983), for which industrialization is a more recent phenomenon than in the Anglo-Saxon world, tend to have a traditional (sincere), qualitative representation of time.

In order to be efficient abroad, it is particularly important to be aware of the polysemy of time in international business contexts. Expatriates often consider that after learning the language, adjusting to a new social tempo is the second most difficult thing to master. The 'time cultures' associated with foreign partners and consumers have many implications for marketing. How much time does one have to do what? Consumers in industrialized countries see a significant benefit in time-saving products and services that allow them to 'save' time, from microwave ovens to ready-to-eat food, from cosmetics (2-in-1 products) to scratch cards (Mermet, 1998). From a managerial point of view, the priority of collaborators in cultures where 'time is money' will be to optimize time, which is seen as a scarce economic resource. They will show a preference for precise and rigid planning, for punctuality, and for the rapid completion of tasks rather than the management of relationships or adjustment to unplanned events.

The Allocation of Time to Activities

Cultures have been described as monochronic or polychronic depending on the way in which they allocate time to activities (Hall, 1983). Monochronic cultures have a preference for doing one thing at a time and activity is subordinated to time. If a task is not finished during the planned slice of time, it will be postponed instead of postponing the schedule. Monochronic time is the traditional Anglo-Saxon and Scandinavian model of allocating time to activities. It underlies most of the normative time management techniques that have been imposed almost worldwide, even though this use of time did not always fit with indigenous cultures. This is especially true in traditionally polychronic cultures (the Latins, the Africans, the Asians) where people tend to do several things at the same time and more readily accept flexibility in planning. Punctuality varies according to the situation (to hierarchical relationships and to the stakes involved) and time is subordinated to activity. The French are considered to be intellectually monochronic (this resulting from a long tradition of Cartesianism and scientific and technical achievements), but polychronic in their behaviours (this being typical of Latin cultures in general). The Japanese (and perhaps most non-Western, newly-industrialized countries) are polychronic among themselves, but monochronic (and sometimes 'over-monochronic') when interacting with foreigners.

The marketing implications of monochronic versus polychronic cultures are very important when it comes to planning international operations with foreign collaborators or when negotiating a delivery date. Moreover, monochronic collaborators will usually work methodologically at a regular pace, whereas polychronic people are more prone to work intensely but in a less sustained manner. The temporal organization of a typical working day will be very different. Anglo-Saxons and Scandinavians usually start working at around 8 a.m. to finish at around 5 p.m., but the Latins start later and finish later (7 p.m. is common in large urban areas). In Latin cultures, people accept that they will be interrupted in their work all day long, and therefore it usually takes more (economic) time to do the same thing than it would in Anglo-Saxon–Scandinavian cultural environments. In Europe, coordinating the different 'social tempo' can be a real headache (see Vignette 1.5).

VIGNETTE 1.5: Social tempo in European countries

There is no single European lunchtime: people eat at 3 p.m. in Spain, at noon in Germany, or at 1 p.m. in the U.K. In Greece, no one uses the phone between 2 and 5 p.m. Hence, Greeks dealing with Norwegians have to call them in the morning, because the latter start leaving work from about 4 p.m. Norwegians come to work at 8 a.m., have lunch at 11 a.m. and sometimes have dinner at 5 p.m. Foreign visitors are often surprised to find all restaurants ready to close at 9 p.m. In the same vein, there is no single market in terms of opening hours for retail, where retail outlets stay open long hours in France, between 8 and 13 hours a day from Monday to Saturday (with some stores opening on Sunday, too), whereas they are open from 7 a.m. to 6:30 p.m. from Monday to Friday in Germany (and only in the morning on Saturdays) due to legal restrictions.

Finally, the expected degree of personalization in business relationships with distributors and the various partners of the international company will be affected by the monochronism–polychronism dimension. Building a relationship is important for polychronic people, whereas for the others it takes second place to task-orientation.

Collective Temporal Orientation

Cultures do not project themselves with the same intensity along temporal horizons. To value the past, it is first necessary to have one, and cultures with a past are usually proud of it. It represents for them the world of traditions and the idea of the 'golden age'. For example, Japan, China, Middle Eastern countries, Thailand, India and most European countries give importance to their past. An extreme example of past orientation is in cultures that worship ancestors, especially in sub-Saharan Africa where *le passé s'assure d'avance de l'avenir* (the past has already determined the future) (Kamdem, 1990).

An orientation towards the present can be observed amongst the lower social classes in rich countries and in most countries 'in transition' (where it is not possible either to rely on reference points from the past, or to project clearly into an uncertain future within the globalized market place). Finally, future-oriented cultures value the philosophical notion of 'progress' (the belief that tomorrow will be better than today resulting from scientific and technical advances as well as significant improvements in material wealth (Usunier, 2000). Still, the depth of the future horizon differs among the industrialized countries, from the short-term in the United States (the fact of reporting every three months to predominantly short-term, profit-orientated share-holders obviously does not promote long-term thinking), to middle-term in Europe and long-term in Japan.

The marketing implications of the dominant collective temporal orientation are particularly pronounced in relation to product policy. Certain products imply taking an option on the future (financial products, for example) and marketing such products will involve some degree of adaptation to the local perceptions of the future. It is possible to spread the purchase of an apartment over several generations in Tokyo, while interest on a bank account is forbidden under Islamic law. In the same vein, innovation is often treated with suspicion in markedly past-oriented cultures, but references to the past will be positively valued; for example, in terms of the impor-tance accorded to the reputation of the firm and its products, or in the choice of topics used in films or in advertising. The growth of anti-ageing products is also character-istic of cultures dominated by an orientation to the future in which an obsession with what they will become takes precedence over the here and now.

Waiting time, as a core component of service quality, is also very much affected by cultural preferences. In Western cultures, and more generally in urbanized environ-ments, a lot of time is actually spent waiting, whereas for the Indian or the Bantu cultures, there is often neither expectation nor despair: people do not get impatient because they are not nervously dependent on an uncertain future time when this or that should happen. They do not 'wait' because, unconsciously or not, they are not eliminating the present (Usunier, 2000). At the other end of the scale, it will be very important to take into account the subjective perception of waiting time in modern societies; for example, in restaurants, leisure activities or transportation. Strategies for managing the reduction of the perceived waiting time can be used, such as announc-ing in advance how long one will have to wait (in a restaurant, on highways, in hotline services), or bringing to the table one-by-one all the components of a meal (e.g. the menu, then the water, then the bread, then the dish).

1.11   Conclusion

In this chapter we have outlined the importance of describing cultural value orienta-tions in order to better understand the psyche of people. Starting with the theoretical background of the value orientation model (Kluckhohn and Strodbeck, 1961) we focused on a few universal core dimensions of cultures that greatly impact on the success of cross-cultural marketing operations. The relationship to nature, others, power, rules, action, affect, space and time have been presented as universal domains of human experience, which are given meaning by social communities and which ultimately shape the behaviour of individuals and organizations. The profile of value orientations defines a conceptualization of reality and attendant most efficient ways (the so-called 'best ways') of doing things in different cultures in different situations. Examples in international marketing and international business have been used to show how one can learn to cope better (as far as that is possible) with ethnocentrism when designing and executing cross-cultural marketing programmes.

REVIEW QUESTIONS

1. Why is international marketing particularly sensitive to the impact of cultural diversity?
2. What is the risk of ethnocentrism in cross-cultural marketing activities? How can it be minimized?
3. Elaborate a definition of culture. Explain why understanding cultures requires a 'thick description' approach.
4. What is meant by 'cultural unity within diversity'?
5. What is a 'cultural universal'?
6. What is a 'value orientation'? How should this model be used?
7. What are the main value orientations that impact on marketing and international business situations?
8. Give examples of managerial implications regarding the relationship to nature, others, power, rules, action, affect, space and time.

Notes

1 There is a French saying that goes as follows: '*Seuls les imbéciles se font prendre*' (only stupid people get caught). By-passing the rules can be seen as a sign of intelligence, of being able to 'win' against the 'system' (often perceived as encumbering daily life).

2 From a linguistic point of view, Fromm notes that for the last two hundred years, more and more activities have been expressed in terms of having (i.e. using a noun instead of a verb), even if activities cannot be 'possessed' as such, but simply experienced. For example, in industrialized societies, at least in Western civilizations, this phenomenon has taken on enormous proportions: one 'has problems' (one *could* say that one is troubled), one 'has insomnia' (one *could* say that one cannot sleep), or one 'has children' (one *could* say that one is parent), etc. In this way, the subjective experience (the 'I') is replaced by possession (the 'it').

3 People do not live in the same temporal world and do not share the same cultural value of time. In fact, they do not even measure it the same way. Several calendars coexist in many non-Christian societies, including the Buddhist (as in Thailand) or the Islamic (as in Saudi Arabia) calendars which obviously do not locate the origin of history at the same point in time.

References

Adler, N. J. (1999) *International Dimensions of Organizational Behaviour*, 3rd edition, Kent Publishing Company.

Barnlund, D. C. (1989) *Communicative Styles of Japanese and Americans: Images and Realities*, Yarmouth, MA: Intercultural Press Inc.

Barsoux, J. L. and Lawrence P. (1997) *French Management: Elitism in Action*, London: Cassell.

Benedict, R. (1946) *The Chrysanthemum and the Sword*, Boston: Houghton Mifflin.

Blunt, P. and Jones, M. L. (1992) *Managing Organizations in South Africa*, Berlin: Walter de Gruyter.

Camilleri, J.-L. (1995) *La petite entreprise africaine*, Paris: L'Harmattan.

Crane, P. S. (1978) *Korean Patterns*, Seoul: Kwangyin Publishing Company.

De Mooij, M. (1998) *Global Marketing and Advertising: Understanding Cultural Paradoxes*, London: Sage Publications.

Doi, T. (1988) *Le jeu de l'indulgence*, Paris: Editions l'Asiathèque.

Dumont, L. (1970) *Homo Hierarchicus: The Caste System and its Implications*, Chicago, IL: Chicago University Press.

Eliade, M. (1968) *The Sacred and the Profane: The Nature of Religion*, Harvest Books.

Fromm, E. (1976) *To Have or to Be?* New York: Harper and Row Publishers.

Geertz, C. (1973) *The Interpretations of Cultures*, New York: Basic Books.

Graham, R. J. (1981) 'The role of perception of time in consumer research', *Journal of Consumer Research* 7 (March): 335–342.

Gurevitch, A. J. (1976) 'Time as a problem of cultural history', in L. Garder, A. J. Gurevitch, A. Kagame, C. Larre, G. E. R. Lloyd, A. Neher, R. Panikkar, G. Paharo and P. Ricoeur, *Cultures and Time: At the Crossroads of Cultures*, Paris: Unesco Presses.

Hall E. T. (1959) *The Silent Language*, Garden City, NY: Doubleday and Company.

Hall, E. T. (1976) *Beyond Culture*, Garden City, NY: Anchor Press.

Hall, E. T. (1983) *The Dance of Life*, Garden City, NY: Anchor Press/Doubleday.

Hall, E. T. and Hall, M. R. (1987) *Hidden Differences: Doing Business with the Japanese*, New York: Anchor Press.

Hall, E. T. and Hall, M. R. (1990) *Guide du comportement dans les affaires internationales, Allemagne, France, Etats-Unis*, Paris: Seuil.

Hallowell, I. (1955) *Culture and Experience*, Philadelphia, PA: University of Pennsylvania Press.

Hofstede, G. (1980) *Culture's Consequences*, London: Sage Publications.

Hofstede, G. (1999) 'Problems remain, but theories will change: the universal and the specific in the 21st-century global management', *Organizational Dynamics* (Summer): 34–43.

Hsu, F. L. K. (1981) *Americans and Chinese: Passage to Differences*, 3rd edition, Honolulu, Hawaii: University of Hawaii Press.

Inkeles, A. and Levinson, D. J. (1969) 'National character: the study of modal personality and sociocultural systems', in *The Handbook of Social Psychology* (eds. G. Lindsey and E. Aronson), 2nd edition, vol. 4, Reading, MA: Addison-Wesley.

Jackson, T. (1999) 'Managing people in South Africa: developing people and organizations', *The International Journal of Human Resource Management*, 10(2) (April): 306–326.

Jain, N. C. (1988) 'Some basic cultural patterns in India', in *Intercultural Communication: A Reader*, (eds. L. A. Samovar and R. E. Porter), 5th edition, Belmont, CA: Wadsworth Publishing Company. pp 104–109.

Kamdem, E. (1990) 'Temps et travail en Afrique', in *L'individu dans l'organisation, les dimensions oubliées*, (dir. J.-F. Chanlat), Les Presses de l'Université de Laval: Editions Eska. pp 231–255.

Khoza, R. (1994) 'The need for an Afrocentric management approach – A South African-based management approach', in *African Management* (eds. P. Christie, R. Lessem and L. Mbigi), Knowledge Resources. pp 117–124.

Kim, D.-K. (1989) 'The impact of traditional Korean values on Korean patterns of management', in *Management Behind Industrialization: Readings in Korean Business* (eds. D.-K. Kim and L. Kim), Seoul: Korea Press University. pp 133–160.

Kluckhohn, F. and Strodbeck, F. (1961) *Variation in Value Orientations*, Row Paterson.

Levin, R. (1997) *A Geography of Time*, New York: Basic Books.

McCall, J. B. and Warrington, M. B. (1984) *Marketing by Agreement: A Cross-cultural Approach to Business Negotiations*, New York: John Wiley and Sons.

Mermet, G. (1998) *Tendances*, Paris: Larousse.

Morris, D. (1995) *Bodytalk: The Meaning of Human Gestures*, Crown Publishers.

Mumford, L. (1963) *Technics and Civilization*, New York: Harcourt, Bruce & World.

Murdock, G. P. (1945) 'The common denominator of cultures', in R. Linton (ed.), *The Science of Man in the World Crisis*, New York: Columbia University Press.

Nydell, M. K. (1987) *Understanding Arabs: A Guide for Westerners*, Yarmouth, MA: Intercultural Press Inc.

Prime, N. (1994) *Culture, Temps et Négociation Commerciale Internationale*, Thèse de Doctorat, ESA, Grenoble: Université Pierre Mendès France.

Sinha, J. B. P. (1980) *The Nurturant-task Leader*, New Delhi: Concept.

Solomon, M. R., Bamossy, G. and Askegaard, S. (1999) *Consumer Behaviour: A European Perspective*, Prentice Hall Europe.

Spengler, O. (1991) *The Decline of the West*, Oxford: Oxford University Press.

Stewart, E. C. (1972) *American Cultural Patterns: A Cross-cultural Perspective*, Yarmouth, MA: Intercultural Press Inc.

Thompson, E. P. (1967) 'Time, work discipline, and industrial capitalism', *Past and Present* 38: 56–98.

Trompenaars, F. (1993) *Riding the Waves of Culture*, The Bath Press: The Economist Books.

Usunier, J.-C. (2000) *Marketing Across Cultures*, 3rd edition, Prentice Hall.

Zadi Kessy, M. (1998) *Culture africaine et gestion de l'entreprise moderne*, Abidjan: Editions CEDA.

Zeldin, T. (1996) *The French*, reprint edition, Kodansha International.

Zerubavel, E. (1981) *Hidden Rythms, Schedules and Calendars in Social Life*, Chicago, IL: University of Chicago Press.

CHAPTER 2

Multicultural marketing

Dawn Burton

LEARNING OBJECTIVES

At the end of this chapter readers will be able to:

▶ Understand the importance the ethnic minority market can have in different national contexts.
▶ Define the concepts of race, ethnicity and multiculturalism.
▶ Understand the differences between ethnic identity, acculturation and assimilation in a multicultural marketing context.
▶ Evaluate ways in which ethnicity can be incorporated into marketing strategy and management.

2.1 Introduction

This chapter is rather different from others in the collection. Although the material focuses on cross-cultural marketing, the discussion is at the level of the individual nation-state rather than marketing between countries. In multicultural societies the composition of the population can be highly culturally diverse, comprising many ethnic groups which necessitates a cross-cultural approach to marketing strategy and management. The focus of this chapter is to highlight the importance of ethnicity in marketing in multicultural societies, or as Wilkinson and Cheng (1999: 106) refer to it 'international marketing at home'. There are two aspects of ethnicity that are relevant to the discussion: these are intercultural and intracultural variations. Intercultural marketing focuses on variations between ethnic groups, for example differences between the shopping behaviour of Hispanic-Americans, Asian-Americans and African-Americans. The main concerns in intracultural research are within group comparisons, for example differences and similarities in shopping behaviour within the Hispanic-American ethnic group.

Ethnicity has not attracted a great deal of attention in marketing and much of the mainstream marketing literature is dominated by experiences in the USA. In most Anglo-Saxon countries the white middle classes have been perceived as the main target market and ethnic minorities have either been 'invisible' or perceived as a poor substitute. The potential of the ethnic market first began to be debated in the context of African-Americans and their portrayal in advertising in the US during the late 1960s. However, although multicultural marketing has been on the marketing agenda for over forty years, theory and practice has been slow to develop. During the 1990s ethnicity moved higher up the agenda of academics and practitioners as larger numbers of organizations in multicultural societies began to realize the potential of the ethnic market. Large companies including Kraft General Foods, Pepsi-Co, AT&T, Coca-Cola, Nabisco and Sear have set up multicultural marketing groups to specifically target the ethnic market (Clegg, 1998). Specialist advertising agencies and market research organizations have also been established to support this area of work.

It is within the context of these developments that the aim of this chapter is to assess in a little more detail the potential of incorporating ethnicity into marketing strategy and management. From the outset it should be recognized that since multicultural marketing management and strategy is still evolving, many pertinent issues have not been addressed or have only been partly discussed. The function of this chapter is therefore twofold: first, to provide an overview of the main issues in the debate; and second, to highlight where more research is required.

This chapter begins by getting to grips with the importance of the ethnic market within different national contexts. It is important to recognize from the outset that the ethnic market is more important in some countries than others. This issue is often overlooked in much of the multicultural marketing literature since most of it is highly dominated by experiences in the US where the ethnic market is very significant. The second section takes the form of a discussion of race, ethnicity and multiculturalism in order to clarify key concepts that form the basis of the subsequent material. Another set of issues that will be addressed concerns the relationship between ethnic identity, acculturation and assimilation. For a considerable number of years the predominant view was that ethnic minorities would eventually lose their ethnic identity and assimilate themselves into the host society. As a result, ethnic minorities would become little different from the indigenous population in relation to their behaviour and consumption patterns. This view is now being questioned as too simplistic and some of the most recent thinking on this issue is discussed. Having addressed some of the main conceptual features associated with multicultural marketing, the rest of the chapter will be devoted to marketing strategy management issues. Specific factors that will be included in the discussion are undertaking research with ethnic groups, marketing communications, the spatial distribution of ethnic populations, the product and services mix and relationship marketing.

2.2 The Importance of the Ethnic Market in Different National Contexts

Before addressing some of the main concepts that are relevant in multicultural marketing, it is important to recognize that there are significant divergences in the importance of the ethnic market between different countries. It is important that these variations are acknowledged since they have implications for the marketing resources that should be diverted towards ethnic minority consumers. The highest proportion of ethnic minorities per head of the population in advanced countries is in Australia where 40 per cent of the population are either migrants or the children of migrants. Pre-1970 most migrants came from Europe, especially the UK, whereas in more recent years there has been more migration from Asia (Wilkinson and Cheng, 1999). A similar proportion of minorities who are not of European extraction live in New Zealand where they comprise 40 percent of the population. Some of the largest groups are Maoris at 14.5 per cent, Pacific Islanders at 4.8 per cent and East Asians that contribute 3.2 per cent of the population (Light, 1997). The US is another highly multicultural society where ethnic groups comprise one third of the population. The African-American market is currently the largest ethnic market and is expected to reach 40 million by 2005. The growth of the Hispanic market is even more significant for marketers in the US and it will comprise the largest ethnic population by 2010. The highest rate of growth is occurring in the Asian-American market that is expected to increase its share of the population from 3 per cent in 1990 to 10 per cent by 2050 (Holland and Gentry, 1999). By 2050 ethnic minorities will comprise close to half the US population (Sandor and Larson, 1994). The situation in the UK is fundamentally different from that in the US, Australia and New Zealand. In Britain ethnic minorities only account for 5 per cent of the population. The profile of minorities in Britain is also dissimilar to that found in the USA, with Britain's minorities being concentrated in the Irish, Afro-Caribbean, Indian, Pakistani and Bangladeshi ethnic groups. The largest group of immigrants in Britain are the Irish, which tends to be forgotten as they are less 'visible' than other minority groups (Social Trends, 2000). The profile of minority groups in Canada is different from both the USA and the UK where the dominant group is Chinese.

One of the main reasons why ethnic minorities are attracting attention from marketers is because of their sheer numbers. Few organizations can afford to neglect such a large proportion of the population, as is clearly evident in Australia, New Zealand and the USA. Even in markets like Britain where ethnic minorities are a small minority of the total population, there are lucrative market segments that could be well worth targeting. Another important factor is the monetary value of the ethnic market. In Britain, the ethnic pound is estimated to be worth £12 billion a year, which is a considerable market in its own right (Golding, 1998). However, this figure pales to insignificance when compared to the spending power of the ethnic minority market in the USA. The figures for ethnic groups in the USA are considerably higher; for example, the African-American market is estimated at $280 billion and the Hispanic market at $134 billion a year (Holland and Gentry, 1999).

2.3   Race, Ethnicity and Multiculturalism

Having provided evidence that the ethnic market is significant in many societies there is a need to understand some of the key characteristics of the marketplace. This section begins to do this by defining the three main concepts of race, ethnicity and multiculturalism prior to assessing how they all interact. Race is a biological concept specifically focusing on physical characteristics that divide races. There is also an underlying assumption that these physical differences are heritable and reflect genetic differences between races. The view that biology separates races has been seriously questioned by scientists and social scientists alike over recent years. The scientific community who promulgated the biological view of race for a very significant period of time has rejected it. Among most biologists the current view is that race should be removed from the vocabulary of science because it is an artificial way to organize human beings (Root, 2001). Race is rarely used in contemporary marketing discourse and to a large extent has been replaced by the more wide-ranging, sociocultural concept of ethnicity.

Unlike race, ethnicity does not focus on biological attributes but instead stresses social and cultural features. However, there is some debate about the factors to be included and which should be given most prominence. At the centre of the debate is whether subjective or objective factors should be used. Subjective measures conceptualize ethnicity as a matter of personal belief and reflect an individual's psychological identity about their cultural attributes. By contrast, an objective view of ethnicity would include sociocultural features including country of birth, country of birth of mother, country of birth of father, religion, first language spoken or main language spoken at home and citizenship status amongst others (Skinner *et al.*, 1997).

In the USA, as in many other societies, there has been considerable discussion about the ways in which individuals are categorized, particularly in the Census, and this has implications for marketing academics and practitioners since these categories are extensively used. Powell (2000) notes that the US government defines a black person as an individual that has origins in any of the black racial groups of Africa. Yet conversely a white person is not defined by their relationship to the white groups in Europe, North Africa and the Middle East. By contrast Hispanics are not classified by race but by ethnic group as a person of Mexican, Puerto Rican, Cuban, Central or South American or other Spanish culture or origin. According to this definition Hispanics can be of any race. American Indians need to have origins in the original people of North America and must maintain cultural identification through tribal affiliations. The picture is complicated by the fact that definitions of individuals belonging in certain categories can change over time. For example, Lee (1993) has traced the ethnic and racial groups defined in the US Census over a century and highlights multiple changes (see Table 2.1). Different methods of categorization are also used in other large-scale government funded surveys that further blur the issue (Root, 2001; Bell, 1996).

Having identified that the concept of race is deficient and that ethnicity is a contested issue, attention is now turned to the concept of multiculturalism. Cashmore (1996: 244) defines multiculturalism as the 'harmonious co-existence of differing groups in a pluralist society'. Although there has been much discussion of the concept since the 1960s it is not new: multiculturalism has been a feature of the social sciences, from which the marketing discipline emerged, as far back as the eighteenth century (Robinson, 1994). The migration of human beings has also existed since time began and has played a pivotal role in the so called 'settler countries', including the United States of America, Canada, New Zealand and Australia. Despite migration existing for a considerable period of time and contributing to the intensification of multiculturalism in advanced societies, some academics believe we are currently witnessing something fundamentally different for two main reasons. The first important factor is the wide-ranging extent of migration that is affecting all regions and most countries simultaneously. Millions of people have multiple citizenship and live in more than one country, and millions of others do not live in their own country of citizenship. Globalization has increased the mobility of individuals across national borders, ensuring that populations become more heterogeneous and culturally diverse. The speed with which new ethnic minorities have emerged has confounded

Table 2.1 Changes in racial definitions in the US Census 1890–1990.

1890	1900	1910	1920	1930	1940	1950	1960	1970	1980	1990
White	White	White	White	White	White	White	White	White	White	White
Black	Black	Black	Black	Negro	Negro	Negro	Negro or Black	Negro or Black	Negro or Black	Negro or Black
Mulatto	Chinese	Mulatto	Mulatto	Mexican	Indian	American Indian	American Indian	Indian (Amer.)	Indian (Amer.)	Indian (Amer.)
Quadroon	Japanese	Chinese	Chinese	Indian	Chinese	Japanese	Japanese	Japanese	Japanese	Eskimo
Octoroon	Indian	Japanese	Japanese	Chinese	Japanese	Chinese	Chinese	Chinese	Chinese	Aleut
Chinese		Indian	Indian	Japanese	Filipino	Filipino	Filipino	Filipino	Filipino	Asian or Pacific Islander
Japanese		Other	Other	Filipino	Hindu	Other	Hawaiian	Hawaiian	Korean	Chinese
Indian				Hindu	Korean		Part Hawaiian	Korean	Vietnamese	Filipino
				Korean	Other		Aleut		Asian Indian	Hawaiian
				Other			Eskimo Other		Hawaiian	Korean
									Guamanian	Vietnamese
									Samoan	Japanese
									Eskimo	Asian Indian
									Aleut	Samoan
									Other	Guamanian
										Other

Source: Lee, 1993: 78.

policy-makers and has undermined laws and practices associated with integration and citizenship. The second feature relates to the characteristics of immigrants that are arriving from ever more distant parts of the world, not just in relation to kilometres but also cultural terms. Early immigrants often originated from former colonies or areas of military presence of receiving countries. For example, North and West Africans to France, Caribbeans, Indians, Pakistanis and Bangladeshis to Britain, and Mexicans, Filipinos, Koreans and Vietnamese in the case of the United States. More recent immigrants are being received from areas where economic and cultural linkages are more tenuous. For example, Arabs to the US, South East Asians to Japan and the Chinese to virtually all developed countries (Castles and Davidson, 2000). The net result is that advanced societies are becoming more multicultural and culturally diverse and marketing theory and practice needs to be developed to accommodate these changes.

2.4 The Ethnic Identity, Acculturation and Assimilation Debate

The discussion so far has demonstrated that in multicultural societies the ethnic market could be very lucrative. Within this context, the main issue that marketers have to address is whether ethnic minorities have different wants and needs from the majority population and thus whether special marketing strategies are required to effectively target them. If individuals from minority groups lose their ethnic identity

Figure 2.1
Assimilationist
model of ethnic
minority
acculturation.

Figure 2.1
Assimilationist
model of ethnic
minority
acculturation.

by adopting the behaviour of the indigenous population over time, a process of acculturation occurs. High levels of acculturation enable minorities to become assimilated whereby individuals become completely integrated into the host culture (see Figure 2.1). If ethnic minorities adopt the assimilationalist pattern of behaviour, marketers could safely assume that minority groups require no special targeting and that the same marketing strategies would work equally as well with minority populations as those designed for the indigenous population. In practice the situation is rarely this straightforward as ethnic minorities often have different levels of acceptance of the host culture and are therefore at various stages of acculturation. There is also a question mark over the very linear process that the assimilationist model predicts.

Whether or not minorities accept the culture of the host nation depends on a number of factors. Rex (1996) argues that an important feature is the attitude of the host nation towards ethnic minority groups. He notes that host nations can respond to ethnic minorities in one of three ways: assimilate minorities on equal terms; subordinate them as second class citizens; or recognize cultural diversity in the private, communal sphere while maintaining a shared, public, political culture. Depending on how they are treated, ethnic minorities adopt a behaviour similar to that of other consumers in the community. However, it does need to be acknowledged that it is easier for some ethnic groups to integrate into a given society than others. In the context of Britain, it is easier for other Europeans to integrate because their culture is not too dissimilar from that in Britain and because of their physical appearance they do not stand out as being very different from the indigenous population. Issues of ethnic identity, acculturation and assimilation are arguably easier for these groups than for those migrating from more distant countries with a very different cultural profile such as the immigration of Indians, Pakistanis and Bangladeshis to Britain.

From a different perspective Berry (1990) argues that another important set of factors that affect levels of acculturation are ethnic minority attitudes towards the host culture. He identifies four possible models of acculturation in ethnic populations. These include integration, whereby an individual adopts some of the host culture while simultaneously maintaining their own culture; separation, where consumers refuse to integrate into the host culture; assimilation, where consumers adopt the host culture and forget their original culture over time; and marginalization, where consumers feel rejected by the host culture but do not want to maintain their original culture.

In recent years there has been more research effort directed towards understanding the processes of acculturation and assimilation. The early literature was dominated by an assimilationist view of the world which argued that ultimately minorities would become fully integrated into society. This was one of the reasons why ethnic minorities were not given special treatment by marketers. However, more recently the simplistic view that in order to acculturate and assimilate, ethnic minorities would have to relinquish their 'old' culture has been questioned. For example, there is a greater appreciation of the effects of length of residence and social class on acculturation. In their research of White-Americans, African-Americans and Cuban-Americans Barlow *et al.* (2000) found that middle-class Cuban-Americans did not appear to want to adopt the American way of life as much as their lower-class counterparts did. While middle-class Cuban-Americans wished to protect their ethnic heritage and language those from the lower classes looked to fully integrate themselves into mainstream American life in the hope of furthering their prospects and those of their children. A similar point is made by Oswald (1999) in relation to Haitian middle-class immigrants in the US. She notes that Haitian immigrants straddle two cultures – they keep their own and adopt aspects of the indigenous US culture as necessary. Oswald argues that Haitian-Americans engage in a process of 'culture swapping' between the two cultures. A similar point is made by Pyong and Kim (2000) in their research with young Asian-American professionals. They argue that replacing ethnic culture with American culture is not a pre-requisite for social assimilation – straddling two cultures is entirely possible. This viewpoint is consistent with the concept of situational ethnicity, whereby social and cultural identity are affected by the social surroundings and the type of product and service being purchased (Zmud, 1992). The implications for marketers is that they must consider the complexity of ethnicity more closely and not presume that ethnic minorities will completely lose their ethnic identity and fully assimilate themselves into the host culture.

Most of the multicultural marketing literature focuses on immigrants; far less attention is directed towards second and subsequent generations of ethnic minorities. In instances of second and subsequent generations, the acculturation and assimilation issue is far more complex. For example, these groups of individuals may develop new loyalties and become more assimilated than first generation migrants. The greater assimilation of later generations has been known to prompt conflicts of identity, especially among young people. Intergenerational effects and ethnicity have not attracted a great deal of attention in the marketing literature and therefore how values, aspirations and practices are transmitted from one generation to the next are largely unknown. Psychologists that have addressed this issue have found that intergenerational effects can vary considerably within the same ethnic group in different national contexts, which suggests that national culture plays an important mediating factor in intergenerational acculturation (Phalet and Ute, 2001).

An additional complicating factor in the multicultural marketing debate relates to mixed race or biracial families. Interracial families are becoming increasingly common in many multicultural societies. In Britain during the mid-1990s only one per cent of all marriages were between individuals from different ethnic groups, but there are considerable variations between groups. For example, 20 per cent of marriages involving Caribbeans were mixed marriages compared with only one per cent in the Bangladeshi group (Berthoud and Beishon, 1997). The percentage of mixed marriages in the US is much higher, with some of the highest incidences among American-Asians where 50 per cent of American-Asians marry non-Asians. Furthermore, the proportion increases with each succeeding generation (Lee and Fernandez, 1998). These interracial unions are important for marketers to acknowledge, although in practice this rarely happens, since it has been argued that they can generate 'new ethnicities' that will have important implications for consumer behaviour (Luke and Luke, 1998).

Research in marketing has indicated that levels of acculturation are important indicators of consumer behaviour. For example, Laroche *et al.*'s (1997) work with French and English Canadians indicated that acculturation had a significant effect on consumer behaviour, whereas ethnicity did not. Ownby and Horridge (1997) develop this theme further by suggesting that acculturation levels could be used as a basis for market segmentation of ethnic immigrant populations. Marketing researchers have also demonstrated that an individual's strength of ethnic identification can have important implications for consumer behaviour in some goods and service categories.

2.5 Undertaking Inter- and Intracultural Market Research

The preceding discussion has demonstrated that effectively targeting the ethnic market is a highly complex undertaking and the ability to perform this activity successfully depends on the availability of good market research. While there is a very significant market research literature in existence, researching ethnicity is comparatively new and few marketing journal articles and books have been specifically written on this issue. It is possible that the cross-cultural methodology literature could be of some assistance in this regard, particularly with respect to recent immigrants, but issues of acculturation and assimilation complicate the issue. Another crucial factor is that cross-cultural scholars have acknowledged that the cross-cultural methodology literature is underdeveloped (Malhotra *et al.*, 1996). In reality inter- and intracultural market research is developing as a specialist area in its own right as the establishment of dedicated market research consultancies testifies. The aim of this section is to provide a brief overview of the issues that marketers need to give extra attention to when undertaking market research with minority groups.

The first issue that researchers need to address is how to select a sample. Experienced researchers have found that recruiting respondents can be difficult in some ethnic groups. Community and grassroots recruitment is generally more effective than door-to-door knocking and researchers have recruited participants from locations as diverse as local mosques, community centres, job centres and local businesses in addition to more conventional methods (Jamal and Chapman, 2000). Access difficulties have been discussed in detail by Sills and Desai (1996), with reference to their research with Asians in Britain. They note that recruiting Asians to take part in focus groups was particularly problematic and summarize the dilemma faced by members of some ethnic groups in the decision to participate in research: 'If respondents are approached in a language they do not fully understand by someone who knows little about their background and asked to attend a group in a location they would not normally go to with people whom they do not normally mix with, it is hardly surprising that they fail to attend or to contribute if they do arrive' (p. 258). However, a reluctance to participate in research projects is not a feature of all ethnic groups. Marin and Marin (1991) indicate that the opposite is true of Hispanic-Americans who are often very cooperative respondents.

Researchers have argued that the selection criteria for using conventional demographic variables need to be carefully considered before being applied to the ethnic minority community. Social class is a problematic concept among the white population, but even more so among the ethnic minority community, where discrimination in the labour market can often lead to individuals from ethnic minorities working in lower level occupations than might be predicted on the basis of their qualifications. Level of educational attainment may provide a better indicator than social class, but even in this instance within some minorities individuals have higher levels of education than the white population but are still more likely to be unemployed. Age may provide a rough indication of first generations and those born in the country of residence; however, this assumption is not totally reliable since young people are still actively migrating. Classifications such as sex are simple to identify, but gender needs further consideration with reference to household composition, paid and unpaid work and occupational status amongst others (Burton, 2000).

There is also a growing research literature that suggests matching the characteristics of researchers with respect to gender and ethnicity is also important. Webster's (1996) paper that assessed response quality and interviewer effects between Anglos and Hispanics in the US found that a higher response quality and more effective interviews were produced when the respondent's gender and ethnicity were matched. Respondents significantly biased their responses to items pertaining to the interviewer's culture. For example, Hispanic men assigned themselves to a higher socioeconomic status when interviewed by either Hispanic women or Anglo men. Women's response quality is relatively unaffected by the interviewer's sex, but men put more effort into a survey situation when there is a female interviewer. As they note: 'This is especially true for Hispanic men, who tend to have a traditional sex-role orientation and be particularly susceptible to the opposite-sex attraction factor' (p. 71).

Undertaking research with ethnic minorities at varying levels of acculturation and assimilation could also result in varying levels of expertise in the language of the host nation. In an ideal world, researchers would have the requisite language ability to converse with respondents in their mother tongue. Some researchers do have this ability (Bouchet, 1995; Penzola, 1994), but in reality many researchers resort to using translators or moderators. Edwards (1998) suggests that where it is essential to use interpreters they should be fully integrated into the market research process and be worked with as opposed to being used, since they can provide important insights. Mother tongue moderators from local communities are often more successful than translators. However, mother tongue translators with the desirable research expertise are sometimes difficult to find. Under certain circumstances it may be necessary to locate individuals with appropriate language skills and train them up as researchers (Sills and Desai, 1996).

2.6 Marketing Strategy and Management Issues

Incorporating Ethnicity into the Promotional Mix

Numerous decisions have to be addressed with respect to incorporating ethnicity into the promotional mix and some of the main issues are set out in Figure 2.2. Fifty years ago the first full-service African-American-owned advertising agencies were set up in the US. Advertisers were sold two main concepts: first, that there was an increasingly affluent African-American customer base waiting to be mined; and second, that it could be most effectively reached through the use of minority-owned advertising agencies and media (Ayres-Williams, 1999). Advertising and communication are areas of ethnic minority discourse that have attracted the most attention of any of the

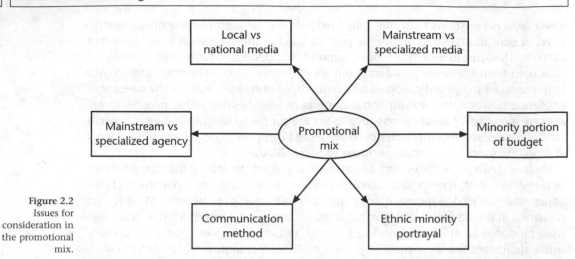

marketing specialisms. However, despite a significant amount of attention devoted to this issue, Seitz (1998) argues that marketers in the US have 'skimped' on marketing to some ethnic groups because they do not know how to communicate with them. Similar comments have been made in relation to advertising communications activities in Britain (Burton, 2000). Some of the largest corporations have recognized the value of reaching out to the ethnic markets. J. C. Penney, Proctor and Gamble, Coca Cola, Colgate Palmolive, Sears and Target are all committed to promoting themselves to the ethnic market and collectively these companies make up 90 per cent of the ethnic advertising billings (Ayres-Williams, 1998) (see Figure 2.2).

Cornwell (1994) argues that a proportion of advertising budgets should be directed towards ethnic media and this decision is as much a political decision of commitment and demonstrated support as a communications decision of reach and frequency. In recent years, many more ethnic media options have been available to marketers, ranging from dedicated ethnic TV channels, local radio stations, ethnic press including newspapers and magazines, dedicated websites, ethnic trading association literature and direct mail. In the US the growth in ethnic media has witnessed some massive increases. The circulation of Hispanic newspapers, of which 76 per cent are published exclusively in Spanish, has increased by 1225 per cent since 1970 (up from 420,000 to more than 24.1 million). Virtually all the major media companies own Spanish-language publications or TV programmes aimed at Hispanic consumers. Even cable television is developing multiple new programmes in Spanish (Nuiry, 1997). Given the highly spatially-concentrated nature of the ethnic population in many advanced societies, it has been suggested that local rather than national media could be a more appropriate and cost effective option. In Miami, San Antonio and Los Angeles, Spanish-language TV and radio stations consistently beat English stations in prime-time ratings.

Direct mail is also becoming a popular way to market to ethnic populations. Approaches can be targeted very specifically in terms of content and language. In the US, direct mail has been recognized as an important method of reaching African-Americans for some time (Direct Marketing, 1995). However, there is evidence that this practice could be usefully extended to other ethnic groups. For example, research has indicated that Hispanic-Americans are particularly responsive to direct mail. It has been estimated that 72 per cent of Hispanics always read their direct mail and 66 per cent respond. One reason for this positive predisposition is that they receive fewer pieces than the general market, only 10 pieces a year (Gunn, 1999). While the experience of targeting Hispanics and African-Americans via direct mail has been positive, this approach will not be suitable for all minorities in every national context. For example, Light (1997) argues that in the context of the Maori community in New Zealand direct marketing techniques are not appropriate for two main reasons. First, the existence of extended families often means that promotional materials placed in letterboxes are unlikely to reach decision-makers. Second, the Maori language is historically oral in tradition as opposed to having a written origin and the emphasis in communications should reflect this. Radio works far better within this cultural context.

Another wide-ranging debate has focused on a number of relevant issues with respect to media composition. One important factor is the way in which ethnic minorities are portrayed. There is considerable evidence that the portrayal of ethnic minorities in a very narrow range of images and roles can result in minorities being perceived in negative terms. For example, it has been noted that ethnic minorities are portrayed in more negative ways in France than they are in Britain (Hargreaves and Perotti, 1993). In Britain the extent of ethnic minority involvement in advertising is usually confined to Afro-Caribbean, high-profile sporting personalities, such as the campaign to reposition Lucozade from a medicinal drink for the frail and weak to a sports drink for the fit and active (Burton, 2000). Some of the most detailed analyses of ethnic minority portrayal in advertising have occurred in the US. For example, Taylor and Stern's (1997) research of commercials that included Asian-Americans found that they were presented in very stereotypical ways and were heavily skewed towards business settings and relations, whereas home settings, family and social relations were under-represented. There was also a gender bias with women rarely depicted in major roles.

It has already been noted that mixed race individuals are marginalized in the existing marketing discourse and therefore attempts to integrate them into the promotional mix as a segment in their own right are very limited. This said, some specialist advertising outlets have carved out a niche for themselves in this area of communications. There is a growing interracial media that is likely to significantly expand in the near future. One such example is the magazine *Interrace* based in Atlanta, USA that has 25,000 subscribers and is full of advertising for interracial consumers. Among the goods and services on offer are mixed race books, toys, dating and wedding services. The magazine also carries advertisements for counsellors who specialize in services for interracial couples.

2.7 Spatial Distribution of Ethnic Minority Populations and the Marketing Implications

One of the most important aspects of ethnic minority marketing is an acknowledgement of the highly spatially-concentrated nature of minority settlement patterns. In most countries, ethnic minorities live in communities with members of their ethnic group or other ethnic groups. For example, in Britain 30 per cent of the current population of London have either been born abroad or are the children of parents born abroad. In individual boroughs such as Hackney 144 different languages are spoken (Penn, 2000). Similar trends are evident in the US where in metropolitan areas like New York, Los Angeles, San Fransisco and Washington, DC ethnic groups including African-Americans, Asian-Americans and Hispanic-Americans easily comprise more than 50 per cent of the population, giving the white population the status of minorities. Forty per cent of the country's Asian population live in California (Gore, 1998). Frey (1998) notes that there are only 21 counties in the US that qualify as being truly racially diverse (the so-called melting pot metros). To qualify, the counties have to have at least two minority groups whose percentage of the county population is higher than the national average and where whites have a lower than average representation. This leads Frey to argue that the concept of true diversity in the US is little more than a myth. Similar concentrations of ethnic minorities are also evident in New Zealand where they comprise 53 per cent of the population of Auckland, the nation's capital (Light, 1997). In Canada, Vancouver is nicknamed 'Hongcouver' because of the dramatic increase of Hong Kong immigrants to the city (Lee and Tse, 1994).

The very high degree of geographical concentration of ethnic populations that is evident in many multicultural societies suggests that specific segments of the ethnic minority population should be fairly easy to target. For this reason community-based marketing strategies are thought to be the key to marketing to ethnic minorities. Developing links within the local community through the support and sponsorship of community activities and developing community relations to facilitate the relationship between consumers and organizations have all been used within this context. However, from a rather different perspective it is important to acknowledge that a feature of many multicultural societies is that ethnic minority consumers live in deprived circumstances and in ghettos. Virtually nothing is known about marketing in these circumstances and this issue was recognized by the American Marketing Association as far back as 1969 (Klein, 1969). Much of the existing multicultural marketing discourse has focused on marketing to middle-class consumers that are perceived to be a lucrative segment. However, this is a rather limited view of multicultural marketing. For example, only a little over 10 per cent of African-American consumers are classified as middle-class. If marketing as a discipline and professional activity is serious about targeting the ethnic market then the debate has to be extended from its current, fairly narrow base.

At one level the spatial concentration of ethnic minorities in particular localities is an important marketing issue, since it makes targeting segments of the population easier and can be cost effective. However, with the increasing use of diverse distribution channels that are spatially indifferent, space is not as an important factor as it perhaps once was. Mail order is a considerable enterprise worldwide, yet the ways in which retailers might usefully target the ethnic market are rarely addressed in the existing marketing literature. However, organizations that have integrated ethnicity into their mainstream marketing strategies have reported considerable success. One organization that has targeted ethnic minorities as a segment within its mainstream provision is the British-based Littlewoods mail order organization. The company recently offered a range of greeting cards to celebrate Diwali, the Hindu festival of light, and found that associating them with appropriate gift items increased sales by 24 per cent (Golding, 1998). In the US, research with Hispanics has demonstrated that the more assimilated the consumer the more likely they are to make direct purchases (Korgaonkar *et al.*, 2000).

Where information technology-based remote distribution and support channels are in operation, physical distribution channels become even less important. Because of the young profile of many ethnic minority populations, information distribution systems could become particularly important opportunities for reaching these consumers. In the case of telephone-based services, such as financial services providers, organizations in the US are developing multilingual call centres and placing bilingual administrators in key positions. Another relatively recent phenomenon is the development of Internet sites directed at the ethnic minority population. A significant and growing number of specialist ethnic dot com companies, including EthnicGrocer.com, AsianAvenue.com and BlackNet.com, are being developed to meet the needs of this specialist market. A further development for marketing professionals and researchers is the emergence of specialist providers of ethnic market intelligence and research, such as slinfo.com's Ethnic NewsWatch.

2.8 Goods and Services to Meet the Needs of Ethnic Minorities

A cornerstone of the marketing concept is delivering goods and services that consumers want or need. However, there are very few indications that organizations are taking this issue seriously in the context of ethnic minority consumers. In many instances the lack of sophisticated market research aimed at assessing ethnic minority preferences is lacking, and there is little awareness of whether or not minority consumers do in fact require the same goods and services as the indigenous population. In the absence of good market intelligence, myths and stereotypes that the indigenous population have about minority cultures can act as a barrier.

At the aggregate level there are differences in the consumption of consumer durables within different ethnic groups in the US (Thomas and Wetlaufer, 1997). There are also differences in household expenditure on food consumption. For example, Hispanics in the US spend $3370 a year on food consumed at home compared with only $2803 for white shoppers (Lewis, 1998). In Britain there are also variations in the ownership of consumer durables between ethnic groups (see Table 2.2). For example, Pakistani and Bangladeshi consumers have lower levels of ownership of freezers, tumble driers and CD players than other groups. By contrast, Indians and African-Asians have higher levels of ownership of particular technological items such as microwaves, video recorders and home computers.

One of the first retailers to market ethnic minorities was J. C. Penney in its targeting of black and Hispanic consumers. The national chain targeted 170 stores nationwide with black and Hispanic populations of at least 25,000 in the surrounding area. Goods on sale included women's, men's, juniors', and children's wear in addition to a home furnishing department that research indicated would have more appeal to minority shoppers. The strategy was developed as a result of nearly two years of studies, focus groups, merchandise selecting, and the success of a one-year-old catologue featuring a black company official. Food retailers are also adapting to the needs of ethnic minority consumers. One such example is Foodmart International in New Jersey, US which is a 138,000 square foot ethnic superstore that specializes in meeting the needs of Asians –

Table 2.2 Possession of consumer durables by ethnic group in Britain.

	White	All Ethnic	Caribbean	Indian	African Asian	Paki-stani	Bangla-deshi	Chinese
Fridge	98	99						
Colour TV	96	94						
Telephone	91	89				-10%		
Washing machine	90	85				-10%	-30%	
Freezer	82	74				-30%	-30%	
Video recorder	76	84		+10%	+10%			+10%
Car or van	70	67	-10%		+10%		-10%	
Microwave	65	67		+20%	+20%		-20%	
Tumble drier	50	36		-10%		-20%	-30%	
CD player	45	39				-20%	-30%	+10%
Home computer	26	34		+10%	+10%			+10%
Dishwasher	19	13	-10%			-10%	-10%	
Unweighted count	2952	3350	943	621	549	679	327	138

Source: Berthoud, 1997: 169.

Japanese, Chinese and Korean – and Hispanics from Puerto Rico, Mexico, Ecuador, Guatemala and the Dominican Republic. Instore signs segment the groceries according to ethnic group. Having appropriate goods in store is a starting point but how they are displayed is also important. Products should be integrated into the regular marketing mix, so for the Latin customer that would mean putting salsa alongside the ketchup and having tortillas in the bakery aisle. In this respect retailers are facilitating culture swapping where consumers keep some of their own culture and choose some of a new one when it suits them. The high incidence of cooking from scratch among Hispanic consumers means that stores wishing to target this group should focus on produce such as tomatoes, lemons, limes, cilantro, garlic and an assortment of dried chillies. Hispanics tend to be extremely brand loyal as do Asians, using many of the same ingredients in the US as they did before they migrated. There is a need for retailers to have in-depth knowledge about the cultural practices of their target market and problems can also arise with specialist suppliers. Retailers have also found the Hispanic market to be very price sensitive (Lewis, 1998).

The delivery of public sector services such as health and education also need to be included in the multicultural marketing debate and in some respects the public sector services literature is more developed than that which focuses on private sector services. Researchers with interests in health, social and medical services that are outside of the marketing discipline have been researching the effectiveness of marketing campaigns and service quality issues for years and they often have different priorities. Public sector service providers have had an agenda that has had the concept of equality at its core and therefore ethnic minorities have been openly integrated into marketing campaigns at a much earlier stage and more extensively than elsewhere. This said, social scientists in Britain have noted that social services departments do not always tailor their services to meet the cultural needs of Asians with respect to food provision (meals on wheels services) and personal hygiene (bath nurses) (Atkin *et al.*, 1989). There can also be communications difficulties with respect to health service provision. Communications can be particularly difficult in provision of complex information such as genetics or diagnosis across professional–lay cultures, Western and non-Western culture and through translation between English and other languages (Johnson, 1995). Lack of support services, such as inadequate or inflexible translators, merely add to the problem. Other barriers to ethnic minorities locating appropriate social services are the myths and stereotypes that the indigenous population may have about minority cultures. For example, one such myth in Britain is that Asians live in extended families and therefore have little need for various types of community services when this assumption is clearly untrue (Burton, 2000).

2.9 Service Quality Aspects of Multicultural Marketing

Although service quality is an area in services marketing that has attracted a huge amount of attention through the vehicles of SERQUAL and SERVPERF, there is little discussion of differences in intercultural and intracultural perceptions of service encounters. In its present state of development the multicultural marketing literature consists of largely conceptual papers and small-scale studies and as a consequence it is an area that is ripe for future development. Probably the most comprehensive account of the debate is the summary by Stauss and Mang (1999) who use a case study of airline passengers' accounts of critical incidents to explore multicultural service quality issues. Their starting position is that problems can occur as a result of the domestic service not meeting the expectations of the foreign consumer, which they refer to as the intercultural provider performance gap. The second gap, which they term the intercultural customer performance gap, is evident when the service cannot be fulfilled at the usual performance level due to foreign consumers not taking on the role behaviour expected by the domestic supplier. Intercultural provider gaps occur as a result of the physical environment, personnel, systems or as a result of co-consumers. Foreign consumers are very often aware of how a particular service should be delivered, but at the same time tolerate lower levels of service. It might also be argued that the greater the distance between the culture of the consumer and that of the host provider, the greater the likelihood that service gaps may occur since there is greater potential for misunderstandings.

When Stauss and Mang questioned airline passengers from Japan, the USA and Germany about their stay at airports in Tokyo, Frankfurt and Atlanta they found some surprising results. Their results indicated that there were more critical incidents of an intracultural nature than intercultural ones. Of the intercultural encounters two-thirds related to German–American interactions – cultures that have a closer cultural distance than those between German–Japanese and American–Japanese. The number of negative intracultural critical encounters also exceeded those of intercultural encounters when the reverse might have been expected.

In Canada research has also demonstrated that there are significant differences in service expectations of individuals from different ethnic groups with respect to the consumption of financial services. The important issue for marketers is to recognize the relative importance of service quality dimensions by market segment and then match those to company resources. The important service quality dimensions across all groups can be extensively resourced and those that ranked the lowest can be reduced. The greatest potential is in the middle range area where services can be tailored to meet the needs of various ethnic groups (Snow et al., 1996).

In some cultural contexts the ability to recognize consumers from different ethnic backgrounds and understand cultural differences can have important implications for the service delivery. In Singapore, where the tourist trade and shopping activities are very important to the national economy, research has been undertaken to assess customer recognition by ethnic group (the rationale behind the research being that if regular customers are recognized and feel welcome then that will enhance the service quality). The results indicated that recognition is higher for cultures with which we ourselves are familiar. For example, Asians who are more exposed to people of colour than to whites tend to recognize black faces better than white faces. These findings have implications in a range of service settings and suggest that face recognition should have a place in service employee training to counteract the other-race effect (Henderson *et al.*, 1999).

2.10 Relationship Marketing

Relationship marketing emerged as an important marketing strategy during the 1980s (Buttle, 1996). However, despite a significant amount of research literature on relationship marketing finding its way into quality journals, the ethnic aspects of this discourse have been marginalized. There is no established body of literature that assesses inter- and intracultural variations in relationship marketing from either the consumer or producer point of view. As already noted, ethnic minorities have not traditionally been considered a target market in their own right, with the preferred market being the white, middle classes in advanced Anglo-Saxon countries. Since ethnic minorities have been a neglected market, marketers' attempts at building relationships with them will not occur overnight, but will require sustained and genuine commitment over a long period of time. Positive initiatives including becoming involved in community affairs and working with community leaders will help, but in some instances these strategies will do little more than scratch the surface.

Other features that marketers who are seriously contemplating building relationships with ethnic minorities need to consider are racism and discrimination. Unfortunately, racism and discrimination are endemic features of most multicultural societies and it is against this backdrop that relationship marketing needs to be understood. For example, there has been a long history of conflict between financial institutions and ethnic minorities in Britain, with institutions being accused of discriminatory practices (Burton, 1995). Under these circumstances problems have to be recognized and dealt with, and a climate of trust has to be developed before relationship building can take place. In some countries, such as Canada for example, questions have been asked about whether the marketing industry is racist (*Marketing Magazine*, 1997). In Britain, one of the barriers to marketers building relationships with ethnic minorities is the misunderstanding that in some way the activity could be construed as racist (Clegg, 1998).

Another important relationship marketing issue that has emerged focuses on the ethics of target marketing ethnic populations. Much of the literature that exists on targeting the ethnic market is presented from a marketer perspective. What is rarely considered is how individuals from ethnic minorities feel about being targeted on the basis of their ethnicity. It may well be the case that some minorities do not want to enter into relationships with institutions on the basis of their ethnicity. Under these circumstances marketers may be alienating the very customers they are attempting to attract (Gentry and Holland, 1999). For example, the Penney initiative to target African-Americans and Hispanics cited earlier caused great resentment among these groups (*Marketing News*, 1993). There have also been issues about targeting ethnic minorities with potentially harmful products such as cigarettes and fast food. Such attempts at building 'relationships' with ethnic minorities have met with disapproval and consumer boycotts (Smith and Cooper-Martin, 1997). Relationship marketing will require a comprehensive review of marketing strategy and management. Starting from the top, organizations would do well to examine their mission statements to ensure that, whether in relation to their employees or consumers, everyone will be dealt with fairly, regardless of their ethnicity.

2.11 Conclusion

Cultural diversity within multicultural societies has not attracted nearly as much attention as it deserves in marketing discourse. Multicultural marketing is still in its infancy and is essentially an unfinished project. The material presented in this chapter has provided an insight into some of the important aspects of this specialized area of marketing and highlighted many more issues that require further consideration. Intercultural and intracultural research is destined to have a much higher profile in marketing given the value of the ethnic market and the disproportionate population growth in many ethnic groups. To date, much of the research on ethnicity has been conducted in the US, but this situation is changing as more interest is being generated from within the marketing community around the globe. Understanding the characteristics of highly diverse minorities from cultures very different from one's own can be a daunting task, but on the other hand it presents virtually unlimited possibilities for academics and marketers alike. Understanding the multicultural market is a complex issue, but hopefully the preceding discussion has gone some way to point readers in the right direction.

REVIEW QUESTIONS

1. What factors have led multiculturalism to become an important marketing issue in recent years?

2. What are the differences between the concepts of race and ethnicity?

3. Explain what you understand by the terms ethnic identity, acculturation and assimilation.

4. What additional factors need to be considered when undertaking market research with ethnic minorities?

5. In what ways can ethnicity be incorporated into the marketing mix?

6. What are some of the relationship management issues associated with inter- and intracultural marketing?

References

Atkin, K., Cameron, E., Badger, F. and Evers, H. (1989) 'Asian elders' knowledge and future use of community, social and health services', *New Community* 15(3): 439–445.

Ayres-Williams, R. (1999) 'Multicultural marketing at the millennium: are minorities being left on the bottom', *American Advertising* 15(2): 11–19.

Barlow, K. M., Taylor, D. M. and Lambert, W. E. (2000) 'Ethnicity in America and feeling "American" ', *Journal of Psychology Interdisciplinary and Applied* 134(6): 581–601.

Bell, C. S. (1996) 'Data on race, ethnicity and gender: caveats for the user', *International Labor Review* 135(5): 535–551.

Benson, S. (1981) *Ambiguous Ethnicity: Interracial Families in London*, Cambridge: Cambridge University Press.

Bernstel, J. B. (2000) 'Courting culturally diverse customers', *Bank Marketing* 31(10): 32–37.

Berry, J. W. (1990) 'Psychology of acculturation', in Berman, J. J. (ed.) *Cross-Cultural Perspectives: Proceedings of the Nebraska Symposium on Motivation*, 201–234.

Berthoud, R. and Beishon, S. (1997) 'People, families and households', in Modood, T. and Berthoud, R. (eds) *Ethnic Minorities in Britain*, London: Policy Studies Institute.

Bouchet, D. (1995) 'Marketing and the redefinition of ethnicity', in Costa, J. A. and Bamossy, G. J., *Marketing in a Multicultural World*, London: Sage, 68–104.

Burton, D. (1996) 'Ethnicity and consumer financial behaviour: a case study of British Asians in the pensions market', *International Journal of Bank Marketing*, 14(7): 21–31.

Burton, D. (2000) 'Ethnicity, identity and marketing: a critical review', *Journal of Marketing Management* 16: 853–877.

Buttle, F. (1996) *Relationship Marketing*, London: Sage.

Cashmore, E. (1996) *Dictionary of Race and Ethnic Relations*, London: Routledge.

Castles, S. and Davidson, A. (2000) *Citizenship and Migration*, London: Macmillan Press Ltd.

Clegg, A. (1998) 'Colour blind', *Marketing Week* 19(13): 38–41.

Cornwell, T. (1994) 'Advertising, ethnicity and attendance at the performing arts', *Journal of Professional Services Marketing* 10(2): 145–56.

Edwards, R. (1998) 'A critical examination of the use of interpreters in the qualitative research process', *Journal of Ethnic and Migration Studies* 24(1): 197–208.

Frey, W. H. (1998) 'The diversity myth', *American Demographics* 20(6): 38–43.

Golding, H. (1998) 'Racial integration', *Marketing Week*, July 16, 1–4.

Gore, J. P. (1998) 'Ethnic marketing may become the norm', *Bank Marketing* 30(9): 12–15.

Gunn, E. P. (1999) 'Direct and database marketing', *Advertising Age* 70(10): 1–3.

Hargreaves, A. G. and Perotti, A. (1993) 'The representation on French television of immigrants and ethnic minorities of Third World origin, *New Community* 19(2): 251–261.

Holland, J. and Gentry, J. W. (1999) 'Ethnic consumer reaction to targeted marketing: a theory of intercultural accomodation, *Journal of Advertising* 28(1): 65–78.

Henderson, G. R., Williams, J. D., Grantham, K. D., Lwin, M. (1999) 'The commodification of race in Singapore: the customer service impications of the other-race effect on tourism and retailing', *Asia Pacific Journal of Management*, 16: 213–227.

Jamal, A. and Chapman, M. (2000) 'Acculturation and inter-ethnic consumer perceptions: can you feel what we feel?', *Journal of Marketing Management* 16: 365–391.

Johnson, M. R. D. (1995) *Ethnic Minorities, Health and Communication: Research Review*, Warwick University: Centre for Research in Ethnic Relations.

Klein, T. A. (1969) 'Minority enterprise: the role of the American Marketing Association', in Morin, B. A. (ed.) *Marketing in a Changing World*, AMA Conference Proceedings, June.

Korgaonkar, P. K., Karson, E. J., Lund, D. (2000) 'Hispanics and Direct Marketing', *Advertising* 17(2): 1–16.

Laroche, M., Joy, A., Hui, M. and Kim, C. (1992) 'An examination of ethnicity measures: convergent validity and cross-cultural equivalence', *Advances in Consumer Research* 18: 150–157.

Lee, W.-N. and Tse, D. K. (1994) 'Changing media consumption in a new home: acculturation patterns among Hong Kong immigrants to Canada', *Journal of Advertising* 23(1): 57–71.

Lee, S. M. (1993) 'Racial classifications in the US Census: 1890–1990', *Ethnic and Racial Studies* 16(1): 75–94.

Lee, S. and Fernandez, M. (1998) 'Trends in Asian American racial/ethnic intermarriage: a comparison of 1980 and 1990 Census data', *Sociological Perspectives* 41(2): 323–42.

Lewis, L. (1998) 'Culture shock', *Progressive Grocer* 77(4): 22–30.

Light, Elizabeth (1997) 'Understanding ethnicity', *Marketing Magazine – Auckland* 16(6): 36–42.

Luke, C. and Luke, A. (1998) 'Interracial families: difference within difference', *Ethnic and Racial Studies* 21(4): 728–753.

Malhotra, N. K., Agarwall, J. and Peterson, M. (1996) 'Methodological issues in cross-cultural marketing research: a state-of-the-art review', *International Marketing Review* 13(5): 1–16.

Marin, G. and Marin, B. V. (1991) *Research with Hispanic Populations*, London: Sage.

Marketing Magazine (1997) 'Is Canada's marketing industry racist?', *Marketing Magazine* 102(8): 9–11.

Marketing News (1993) 'Minority leaders blast J. C. Penney plan to target blacks, Hispanics', *Marketing News* 27(21): 1–3.

Nevid, J. S. and Maria, N. L. (1999) 'Multicultural issues in qualitative research', *Psychology and Marketing* 16(4): 305–325.

Nuiry, O. E. (1997) 'Hispanics now a mass market in their own right', *Public Relations Quarterly* 42(3): 28–30.

Oswald, L. R. (1999) 'Culture swapping: consumption and the ethnogenesis of middle-class Haitian immigrants', *Journal of Consumer Research* 25 (March): 303–318.

Ownbey, S. F. and Horridge, P. E. (1997) 'Acculturation levels and shopping orientations of Asian-American consumers', *Psychology and Marketing* 14(1): 1–18.

Penn, R. (2000) 'British population and society in 2025: some conjectures', *Sociology* 34(1): 5–18.

Penzola, L. (1994) 'Atravesando froneras/border crossings: a critical ethnographic exploration of the consumer acculturation of Mexican immigrants', *Journal of Consumer Research* 21 (June): 32–42.

Phalet, K. and Schonpflug, U. (2001) 'Intergenerational transmission of collectivism and achievement values in two acculturation contexts', *Journal of Cross-Cultural Psychology* 32(2): 186–202.

Powell, J. A. (2000) 'The colorblind multiracial dilemma: racial categories reconsidered', in Torres, R. D., Miron, L. F. and Inda, J. X. (eds), *Race, Identity and Citizenship*, London: Blackwell, 141–157.

Pyong, G. M. and Kim, R. (2000) 'Formation of ethnic and racial identities: narratives by young Asian-American professionals', *Ethnic and Racial Studies* 23(4): 735–760.

Rex, J. (1996) 'National identity in the demographic multi-cultural state', *Sociological Research Online* 1(2) <http://www.socresoline/1/4/rex.html>

Robinson, C. J. (1994) 'Ota Benga's flight through Geronimo's Eyes: tales of science and multiculturalism', in Goldberg, D. T., *Multiculturalism: A Critical Reader*, Oxford: Blackwell.

Root, M. (2001) 'The problem of race in medicine', *Philosophy of the Social Sciences*, 31(1): 20–39.

Sandor, G. and Lason, J. (1994) 'The "Other" Americans', *American Demographics* 16(6): 36–42.

Seitz, V. (1998) 'Acculturation and direct purchasing behavior among ethnic groups in the US: implications for business practiconers', *Journal of Consumer Marketing* 15(1): 23–31.

Sills, A. and Desai, P. (1996) 'Qualitative research amongst ethnic minority communities in Britain', *Journal of the Market Research Society* 38(3): 247–265.

Skinner, T. J. and Hunter, D. (1997) 'Developing suitable designators for a multicultural society', *Statistical Journal of the UN Economic Commission for Europe* 14(3): 217–228.

Smith, N. C. and Cooper-Martin, E. (1997) 'Ethics and target marketing: the role of product harm and consumer variability', *Journal of Marketing*, 61 (July): 1–20.

Snow, K., Bartel, H. and Cullen, T. (1996) 'How ethnicity influences service expectations – a Canadian perspective', *Managing Service Quality* 6(6): 33–37.

Social Trends (2000) *Social Trends*, HMSO: London.

Stauss, B. and Mang, P. (1999) ' "Culture shocks" in inter-cultural service encounters', *Journal of Services Marketing* 13(4/5): 329–346.

Taylor, C. R. and Stern, B. B. (1997) 'Asian-Americans: television advertising and the "model minority" stereotype', *The Journal of Advertising* 26(2): 47–62.

Thomas, D. A. and Wetlaufer, S. (1997) 'A question of color: a debate on race in the US workplace', *Harvard Business Review*, Sept–Oct, 118–134.

Webster, Cynthia (1996) 'Hispanic and Anglo interviewer and respondent ethnicity and gender: the impact on survey response quality', *Journal of Marketing Research* 33(1): 62–72.

Wilkinson, I. F. and Cheng, C. (1999) 'Multicultural marketing in Australia: synergy and diversity', *Journal of International Marketing* 7(3): 106–124.

Zbar, J. D. (2000) 'Marketing to Hispanics', *Advertising Age* 71(39): 1–3.

Zmud, J. (1992) 'The ethnicity and consumption relationship', *Advances in Consumer Research* 19: 443–449.

Culture, Italian language and business: Links overlooked and underestimated

Laura Ancilli and Val Clulow

C1.1 Introduction

The issue of language in relation to the development of business relationships has been largely overlooked in research studies. Language is sometimes listed as an 'issue' for businesses looking to build new links abroad; however, little regard has been given to a more detailed analysis of contemporary business language in a global marketplace. The pilot study reported in this paper represents the beginnings of a more complex study of the language of the Italian business community, which has been modified in recent years by world events and the linking of business communities worldwide, through the proliferation of electronic communication technologies. Early analysis suggests that understanding the change from traditional Italian business language to the recent inclusion of neologisms is of importance to other nationals wanting to trade with Italy.

The internationalization of businesses has been a topic of extensive discussion in recent years (Harris, 1996; Simintiras and Thomas, 1998; Paliwoda, 1999) as organizations have tried to come to terms with the complexity of working across economic, legal, social and cultural boundaries. In addition, academics have for some time written papers concerned with the international marketing of products (Burton and Schlegelmilch, 1987) and more recently on the internationalization of services (Grönroos, 1999) concentrating on entry strategies. Whilst barriers to entry have been identified in many cases, (Zimmerman, 1999; Samiee, 1999) a plethora of directories, guides, books and websites offer businesses advice on matters such as how to export, culturally specific customs, political status, finance and logistics (Meredith, 2000). In the selective annotated bibliography to 'Doing business internationally' provided by Meredith, references to *language* are fleeting such as 'There are many factors to consider such as trade barriers, language, culture, customs, a government's attitude towards a certain country's business and the environment' (p. 224). Within entries too in this extensive bibliography, language appears to receive only a cursory mention. 'Jargon and baffling idioms' are mentioned by Axtell (1993) and country specific references in the 'Pocket Guide' series published by World Trade Press (<www.worldtradepress.com/pport/html>) where, for example, the 'Passport Italy' pocket guide offers chapters on 'Communication Styles' and 'Basic Italian Phrases', but does not provide a serious guide to Italian business language.

A search for cross-border business language research has to date identified only one detailed account of a serious study, which uses linguistic analysis in a business context to explain the issue of branding in China (Chan and Huang, 2001). The authors explain in some detail the differences between alphabet-based languages and the Chinese language and the implications for Westerners seeking to export their brands. The study exemplifies the value of such detailed analysis and although the background and foundational linguistic principles of the Chinese language are complex, the paper provides efficacious guidance for Western businesses. Apart from this example, it is largely under-researched to any depth, apart from language difference being generally identified as an obstacle to exporting activity (Grönroos, 1999).

The preliminary study reported here is the forerunner to more extensive research on Italian business language, in the context of changes to meaning in the past two decades and the need for foreign traders to be well informed of current usage.

C1.2   Background

Language is indeed a strong indicator of any historical, social and economic change, and Italian is no exception. In his book *Historical Linguistics of Unified Italy* Tullio De Mauro explains how industrialization and urbanization played an extremely important role in the shift from dialects to the Italian language of the twentieth century.

> [T]he industrialization had important consequences not only on the linguistic conditions of the country, but also on the peculiar characteristics of the language itself. Tullio De Mauro, *Storia linguistica dell'Italia unita*, p. 66 (translated from Italian by L. Ancilli).

The industrial revolution in Italy started in the first two decades of the twentieth century and the process of industrialization was only completed in the late fifties (Balcet, p. 25). Industrialization and urbanization are considered by many linguists to have been the big drive towards the unification of the Italian language. Until the fifties, the Italian language was not widely spoken: the majority of people would speak a regional dialect, or at least a regional variety of the Italian language, where a word related to an agricultural tool, for example, differed from region to region (De Mauro, p. 66).

Due to industrialization and the huge flux of migration from the south to the north, many new words, starting from those related to industrial machinery and tools, were incorporated as Italian words – therefore at a national level – into the many regional dialects. The result of a purely economic phenomenon contributed to a huge language shift, from a myriad of dialects to a national language.

In the years that followed many events have characterized the Italian language, leaving a permanent imprint of neologisms and structures that did not exist before. The so-called 'sinistrese' (literally 'the leftist') is a collection of words and expressions which resulted from the students' movement of the late sixties and seventies. More recently the biggest attempt to demolish Italian corruption, known as 'Mani Pulite' ('Clean Hands'), has left the Italian language with a heritage of a number of new words, of which probably the most well known outside Italy is 'Tangentopoli', which literally means 'Bribe-City'.

The present paper will analyze the impact that the spread of American capitalism had on the Italian language in the years following the fall of the Berlin Wall in 1989.

C1.3 Capitalism in Italy and Europe

Capitalism in Italy has been defined by many as 'capitalism without capital'. Italy is in fact well known for having an unusually high number of micro and small enterprises and very few multinationals (in April 2001 the Italian Bureau of Statistics counted only thirteen multinationals, compared to 26 in France).

The majority of Italian companies are family run – and that does not only apply to the small and micro companies, but also to larger ones like Fiat and Benetton. This peculiarity of the Italian economy accounts for the fact that only very small capital is involved and being a family business the company's presence on the share market would not be considered, preferring instead to keep the profits within the family.

In March 1947, American President Truman addressed his nation presenting an economic plan that became known as the Truman Doctrine. That day is considered as the official historic beginning of the Cold War, designed to oppose Soviet expansionism and fight communism in every corner of the Western world. In July 1947, with the introduction of the Marshall Plan, the USA established its economic and political leadership over Western Europe. At the same time, both on a political and social level, Italy was left divided and torn between the two great powers: Russia and communism on one side, and America and capitalism on the other.

In 1947, 40 per cent of the Italian population was still employed in the agricultural sector, and American financial aid was the spark from which Italian industrial development began. The Italian state was already heavily involved in the process of industrialization since the First World War and, having a small availability of capital, the new developing industries in the north became more and more dependent on banks and indirectly on the state, which was the owner of the banks.

A pivotal person in the history of Italian capitalism was Enrico Cuccia, founder in 1946 of a financial institution, the Banca di Credito Finanziario SpA, later known as Mediobanca. In postwar Italy, Mediobanca was responsible for ensuring the industrial development of the country. During the fifties, Mediobanca acquired major parts of all affiliated enterprises in such a way that private capital was almost non-existent. In 1989 this system came to an end and the major banks involved in Mediobanca decreased their share from 56.9 per cent to 25 per cent, in order to give more space to private capital. Incidentally, 1989 is also the year that saw the end of the Cold War, and the year in which the fall of the Berlin Wall signalled the end of the Russian power over Eastern Europe.

> The collapse of the Soviet experiment undermined support for communism, socialism, closed markets and state control of economies. It also signalled the apparent triumph . . . of market capitalism. R. C. Longworth, journalist for the *Chicago Tribune*.

When Enrico Cuccia died in June 2000, Guido Roberto Vitale – a partner in Mediobanca – said that '[Enrico Cuccia] maybe had not understood in time that with the fall of the Berlin Wall a certain way of seeing the [Italian] economy had also "fallen" with it.'

C1.4 The End of the Cold War and the Spread of the Internet

The internet system was developed by the US intelligence services in the early sixties. Its use was to allow communication through all Western countries, in case all other communication media like telephones or television would break down due to a Soviet attack. With the end of the Cold War, in the nineties, the Internet became widespread. It started to be more commonly used as a link between university researchers and later it became the indispensable medium that we use so extensively today. This study will not analyze the broader impact of Internet language on Italian, simply because it would deserve a study of its own given the vast number of sectors in our society that have been influenced by it, of which young people are probably the biggest group.

However, the Internet phenomenon has had a great impact on language used in the business sector due to the fact that 'new-technology' and 'e-commerce' are becoming more and more popular. Moreover, there are many other areas of business and the economy that use the Internet as one of the many channels for communication, even though they may not be using the Internet as the principal medium like 'e-commerce'. A few examples would be the job market, the shopping culture or the banking system. This paper aims to explore the impact that the Internet has had on the business-related Italian language.

C1.5 Methodology

In this pilot study, two sources of data were collected to explore the nature of recent changes to Italian business language. At this preliminary stage in the research, documentation analysis was considered an appropriate methodology. Heritage (1984), an ethnographer, suggested that 'an overwhelming proportion of the world's business is conducted through the medium of spoken interaction' (p. 239). This idea includes the telling of news, the reporting of business events and other social 'conversations'. To capture the language of these conversations in a business context, documentation analysis (Miles and Huberman, 1994) provided a means by which to unequivocally date the information collected, which allowed comparative discussion across time. In addition, the text of the daily press is regarded as a record of common usage of 'language of the day' which served the purpose of the pilot study. The text relating to usage of business language was collected from two document sources: *Il Sole 24 Ore*, a daily Italian newspaper (data source 1) and an article 'Il mercato delle merci' ('The commodities market'), from two editions of the same book entitled *Come si legge il Sole 24 Ore* (data source 2).

Data Source 1

The approach taken for collection of data from the newspaper was to select a paper at random (dated 5/2/01) and to undertake an analysis of articles related to 'business' to search for words or phrases from the English language adopted into the Italian news text. The importance of data source 1 was therefore to provide a snapshot of the presence of English terminology in the Italian business language at present.

Data Source 2

The second data source was an article taken from two editions of the same book, *Come si legge il Sole 24 Ore*, published in 1985 and later in 1997, therefore before and after the particular event believed to have triggered some changes. A particular article, 'Il mercato delle merci' ('The commodities market'),was used for the analysis. Most of the journalists involved in the contribution of both editions were the same ones, thus providing a sample of change in time.

C1.6   Analysis and Discussion

Data Source 1

The article published in *Il Sole 24 Ore*, the prominent national daily Italian newspaper on economy and business, entitled 'Impact of internet on the language', emphasizes the use of English abbreviations. They are apparently used even when writing in Italian and some examples are: 'u' instead of 'you', 'r' instead of 'are', '4' instead of 'for' and 'asap' instead of 'as soon as possible'.

On the same page of the paper, but in a different article, there is constant use of acronyms such as B2B (business to business), C2C (consumer to consumer), B2G (business to government) and all the other combinations possible. Only in the first paragraph are these acronyms spelled out and translated into Italian: in the remainder of the article only the acronyms are used.

In the same article the word 'business' appears in its English form a number of times. 'Business' has two different translations in Italian: 'commercio' has a broader and general meaning as in the sentence 'We do not do much business with them', whereas 'azienda' or 'impresa' would be used in a sentence such as 'He runs three different businesses'. In the above mentioned article the latter word (impresa) is used a couple of times in Italian, whereas in the case of the former one (commercio), the English word 'business' is constantly used as a substitute. This particular trend is also confirmed in other articles of the same newspaper where the word 'business' is always used in English when the broader meaning is implied.

In a different article by the title 'Soldi & Shopping' ('Money & Shopping') also related to the use of the Internet, the English language is used – once again – without giving the equivalent translation in Italian, even though appropriate words do exist in Italian. On page 5 of the supplement to *Il Sole 24 Ore* of 5/2/01 (Guida Famiglia, 2001) the author writes about the SET protocol and only gives the explanation of the acronym in English (secure electronic transaction). Only a couple of lines later the author uses the expression 'banche partner' (partner banks) where, instead of 'partner' she could have used 'affiliate' which is the Italian term for 'partner' in this particular meaning. The word 'shopping' is also used instead of the Italian equivalent 'acquisti'. Sometimes the English word seems to be used to avoid a repetition in the same sentence. This is the case of page 6 of the supplement to *Il Sole 24 Ore* of 5/2/01 (Guida Famiglia, 2001), where talking about bank cards the author of the article refers to 'carta' – which is the Italian term – and then to 'card' four words later in the same sentence.

The word 'online' is extensively used throughout the whole newspaper instead of its Italian equivalent 'in rete', as well as expressions such as 'e-commerce', 'm-commerce' (related to mobile phones) and 't-commerce' (conducted through the television). Mobile phones in Italian are called 'telefoni cellulari', and lately only the second word 'cellulari' is being used to refer to them. A paragraph on the same page 6 starts with the title, in bold, that says 'Pagamenti online, mobile e tv', where 'mobile' is clearly the English word to indicate a type of telephone that everywhere else in the article is called 'cellulari'. In this case, the choice of the English term instead of the Italian one aims to create a link in the reader's mind between 'm-commerce' and the type of business conducted via a mobile phone.

Data Source 2

The second part of this research, using an article from a book published before and again after the fall of the Berlin Wall, indicates changes in the Italian business language that have been triggered by the fall of the Berlin Wall and the consequent spread of so-called American capitalism in Europe and more specifically in Italy. For that purpose two different editions of the same book, published by Il Sole 24 Ore, were analyzed. The book is called *Come si legge il Sole 24 Ore* and contains a series of articles explaining the Italian economy. The two editions are from 1985 – therefore four years before the fall of the Berlin Wall – and from 1997, eight years after the fall. Most of the journalists and economists who contributed to the two editions of the book were the same.

One particular article, entitled 'Il mercato delle merci' ('The commodities market'), in both editions written by the same group of journalists, was closely studied. In the earlier edition, some English terms already appear, but they are introduced to the reader with an explanation of their Anglo-Saxon origin. For example, on pages 173–174 of the 1985 edition the text says 'consistono in operazioni di compravendita di merci mediante contratti a termine (chiamati in gergo commerciale anglosassone *futures*)' ['they consist in transactions of buying and selling of commodities through *contratti a termine* (called *futures* in the business English jargon)']. Further down on page 174, the authors of the article refer to 'manovre speculative (*corners* nel gergo anglosassone)' ['*manovre speculative* (*corners* in the Anglo-Saxon jargon)']. This way of using the correct Italian term and then using the English term in brackets points to the fact that the English word is still considered a 'foreign word' and that it is probably being used to allow the reader of the newspaper to be able to make a link between the 'manovre speculative' found in *Il Sole 24 Ore* and the 'corners' found in the 'Financial Review'. This system of linking the Italian term to the English equivalent is used many times within the article analyzed, but also in other articles of the same edition, indicating that it was a trend of the times rather than a peculiarity of the authors.

From page 176 onward the words 'materie prime' are frequently used in Italian only, without even mentioning in brackets the correspondent English term which would be 'commodities'. In the 1997 edition of the same article, written by the same group of authors, the words 'materie prime' have been completely substituted by the English term 'commodities', and overall there is a greater use of English words, in some cases with no attempt to translate them into Italian, as in the case of 'L'indice spot mostra quanto il pacchetto considerato sia rincarato' ['The spot index shows how much a certain package has increased in price']. In this particular case the word 'spot' is not even written in italics, as were the words 'commodities', 'settlement' and 'total return'. In one example only, on page 365 of the 1997 edition, the authors have used an Italian expression and then the English equivalent in brackets: 'i prezzi di chiusura del mercato (o *settlement price*, il valore al quale la cassa di compensazione)' ['the market closing prices (or *settlement price*, the value chosen for the cashing compensation)']. Further down the page the word '*settlement*' is used directly in English with no further mention to the Italian equivalent.

It is however quite important to note that when an English word was used in the 1985 edition, the authors would give the Italian version first and then in brackets they would specify the English equivalent mentioning the fact that it was 'English business jargon'. In other words, they made a clear distinction between language A (Italian) and language B (English). In the 1997 edition, however, the words in brackets were merely used to clarify the economic concept which was introduced.

C1.7   Conclusion

The preliminary research presented here serves to illustrate the potential for improved business communication of all sorts with the Italian business community through the acquisition of a point of reference for the current usage of modified business terms. For businesses looking to build international links with Italy, the competitive advantage of understanding words and terms that have developed through the impact of recent world events is evident. The cost to the Italian language is one of many associated with the drive for a global marketplace.

ACTIVITY

1. Why do you think that an understanding of language is an important cultural marketing concern?
2. What are some of the important language issues discussed in the case and what do you know about these issues?
3. How has industrialization influenced the Italian language?
4. Do you think that the continued diffusion of technologies such as the Internet will result in an homogenizing of language? Discuss.
5. Can you think of other cultures (and languages) that have been influenced in a similar way to that of the Italian situation?

References

Axtell, R. E. (ed.) (1993) *Dos and Taboos around the World*, New York: John Wiley and Sons.
Balcet, G. (1995) *L'economia italiana. Evoluzione, problemi e paradossi*, Milano: Elementi Feltrinelli.
Barca, F. (ed.) (1997) *Storia del capitalismo italiano dal dopoguerra ad oggi*: Roma, Donzelli Editore.

Burton, F. N. and Schlegelmilch, B. B. (1987) 'Profile analysis of non-exporters versus exporters grouped by export involvement', *Management International Review* 27(1): 38–49.

Canavesio, C. and Simone, G. L. (eds) (1985) *Come si legge 'Il Sole 24 Ore'*, Edizioni del Sole 24 Ore.

Chan, A. and Huang, Y.-Y. (2001) 'Chinese brand naming: a linguistic analysis of the brands of ten product categories', *Journal of Product and Brand Management* 10(2): 103–119.

Clyne, M. (1995) *The German Language in a Changing Europe*, Cambridge: Cambridge University Press.

Cortelazzo, M. and Cardinale, U. (1986) *Dizionario di parole nuove*, Torino: Loescher editore.

De Mauro, T. (1991) *Storia linguistica dell'Italia unita*, Bari: Editori Laterza.

Fromm, E. (1979) *To Have or to Be?* London: Abacus.

Galimberti, F., Sabbatini, R. and Simone, G. L. (eds) (1997) *Come si legge 'Il Sole 24 Ore'*, Edizioni del Sole 24 Ore.

Gensini, S. (1985) *Elementi di storia linguistica italiana*, Minerva Italiaca.

Ginsborg, P. (1990) *A History of Contemporary Italy: Society and Politics 1943–1988*, Harmondsworth, UK: Penguin Books.

Grönroos, C. (1999) 'Internationalization strategies for services', *Journal of Services Marketing* 13(4/5): 290–297.

Harris, G. (1996) 'Factors influencing the international advertising practices of multinational companies', *Management Decision* 34(6): 5–11.

Heritage, J. C. (1984) *Garfinkel and Ethnomethodology.* Cambridge: Polity.

Hudson, R. A. (1996) *Sociolinguistics*, New York: Cambridge University Press.

Magni, M. (1992) *Lingua italiana e giornali d'oggi*, Milano: Guido Miano Editore.

Meredith, M. (2000) 'Doing business internationally: an annotated bibliography', *Reference Services Review* 28(3): 223–239.

Miles, M. (1994) *Qualitative Data Analysis: An Expanded Source Book*, 2nd edition, London: Sage.

Paliwoda, S. (1999) 'International marketing: an assessment', *International Marketing Review* 16(1): 8–17.

Raffaelli, S. (1983) *Le parole proibite – Purismo di stato e regolamentazione della pubblicità in Italia (1812–1945)*, Bologna: Il Mulino.

Samiee, S. (1999) 'The internationalisation of services: trends, obstacles and issues', *Journal of Services Marketing* 13(4): 319–336.

Simintiras, A. and Thomas, A. (1998) 'Cross-cultural sales negotiations: a literature review and research propositions', *International Marketing Review* 15(1): 10–28.

Società di linguistica Italiana (ed.) (1983) *Linguistica ed antropologia*, Roma: Bulzoni.

Zimmerman, A. (1999) 'Impacts of services trade barriers: a study of the insurance industry', *The Journal of Business and Industrial Marketing* 14(3): 211–228.

Electronic References

<www.cooperweb.it/relazioni/> Chiocchi, A., Modelli di esclusione. Politicità dell'economia ed economicità della politica in Italia (1945–1980), 1998.

<www.cce.unifi.it/dse/spe/indici/numero35/macca.htm> Maccabelli, T., Linguaggio, definizioni e termini dell'economia politica: il contributo di Malthus, Whately e Senior.

Etics and emics: bridging a gap in international business culture

Anton Kriz and Jacqueline A. Flint

C2.1 Introduction

Managing relationships across borders is emerging as one of the most important challenges facing business in the new century. Part of managing those international relationships is developing an understanding of different cultures, how they compare and contrast, and how the differences and similarities can best be managed. This challenge is summed up in the globalization concept that suggests international managers should 'Think global, act local' (Fletcher and Brown, 1999; Trompenaars and Hampden-Turner, 1997). In other words, successful management of relationships across borders needs an understanding of issues that bridge cultures as well as issues within cultures.

Fang (1999: 9) suggests that 'there are two basic approaches to the study of cultures: emic and etic'. Emic studies take the perspective of 'insiders' or a within-culture view, whereas etic studies take a broad perspective that is cross-cultural. Two benchmark works in the area of etic studies are Hofstede's (1980) *Culture's Consequences* and Trompenaars and Hampden-Turner's (1997) *Riding the Waves of Culture*. Both of these studies develop classifications of cultures according to patterns of characteristics which are suggested to be present, to a greater or lesser degree, in most national cultures. Despite the widespread recognition of the value of these classifications and their contribution to the understanding of culture, these and other etic studies appear to have more surface than depth value.

An emic approach to understanding culture originated when Pike (1967) developed the 'emic' term and Berry (1980) subsequently elaborated a methodology for empirical investigation and comparison of cultures from an emic perspective. In essence, this suggests that the richer, more detailed layers below the surface of a culture able to be identified via 'bottom-up' emic studies can be compared usefully with similarly derived data from another culture in preference to generalized 'etic' perspectives. Since elaboration of Berry's (1980) methodology, however, there has been little application of it in business research, although discussion of the concept and its relevance has continued to evolve.

Given uncertainty regarding the value of etic studies and the emergent state of emic approaches to the study of culture, it seems reasonable to suggest that combining both approaches would be a useful way to gain a holistic, more convincing understanding of a given culture (Morris *et al.*, 1999). The aim of this case study, therefore, is to build on Morris *et al.* (1999) and to see whether a combination of both etic and emic approaches is to be preferred in the study of culture as part of improving the way that business is conducted across borders.

C2.2   Emic Investigation of Chinese Business

An empirical emic study of Chinese business people underpins this investigation. More specifically, the business culture of the Chinese is addressed through the construct of trust in business relationships. The construct of trust was chosen because this is cited (Fukuyama, 1995) as a key element in the social cum business interpersonal Chinese *guo qing* or character (Yan, 1994).

There is a valid reason for a study of trust in Chinese markets. The mainland or 'middle kingdom' (1.3 billion people), and its 57 million diaspora offer substantial opportunities. China represents a significant developing market with its recent inclusion into the World Trade Organization (WTO) and selection for hosting the 2008 Olympic Games. Such events come on top of its rapid development in the 1990s. The 50 million overseas Chinese living in Asia had a combined wealth of US$ 696 billion according to World Bank figures in 1997. This was just short of the US$ 745 billion of the 1.2 billion mainland Chinese (Lasserre and Schütte, 1999). According to the World Bank, if current trends continue, by the year 2020 the People's Republic of China will be the world's largest economy.

The author of the field study that this case study refers to recognized that Western empirical methodology bypassed the subtlety of Eastern cultures, especially Chinese (Redding, 1990). Opportunity has always been the lure of China, but there is a noted void between the West being able to turn opportunity into reality. The Economist Intelligence Unit noted, for example, that those companies failing in China should not worry, 'they are not alone' (*Business China*, June 1998, p. 1). Reporting on a survey by A. T. Kearney and *Business China*, the Economist Intelligence Unit identified that of seventy foreign multinationals with 229 projects, 34 per cent were unprofitable and 25 per cent were just breaking even. A review of the literature supports a view that business failures in Chinese markets, in part at least, seem to stem from an inability of foreigners to cope with the relational Chinese *inter-personal* versus *inter-organizational* orientation (Tung and Worm, 2000). How can we expect Westerners, for example, to acculturate to stratagem, *guanxi* (referred to here as connections), Confucianism and Taoism and the 'Rule of Man'? Westerners missed out when the Chinese dropped Han Fei's (280–233 BC) 'Rule of Law'.

The problem for a Western researcher is: how does one go about unmasking the layers and hidden face or '*mianzi*' of the Chinese when there is so much psychic distance? This is where emics come into play. It is important for Western researchers entering a foreign culture to accept, but also try to denude, what Berry (1980) sees as the imposed etic.

Effectively it is a case of finding empathy with your target. This study adopted a historical realist's perspective and endeavoured to demystify, layer by layer, what has become the 'black box' of Chinese culture. Building from Hofstede's 'Software of the Mind' metaphor, the study focused on the programming of the Chinese, but unlike some other studies it also acknowledged that Chinese have universals (Brown, 1991). By seeking the 'hard-wiring' and then going to the 'soft-wiring', the study was fundamentally unpacking layer upon layer to go inside the *guo qing*. This was all part of the acculturation process before even attempting to enter the field.

In effect, to understand culture the principal researcher had to 'think local' and that meant researching concepts like Sun Tzu's *Art of War*, the political and corporate programmes of the various Chinese markets, the moral philosophy and so on. As Sun Tzu described it in a military sense, 'Therefore measure in terms of five things, use these assessments to make comparisons, and thus find out what the conditions are. The five things are the way, the weather, the terrain, the leadership, and discipline' (Tzu, 1988). In modern terms one may describe it as an environmental and situational analysis.

C2.3   Methodology

Having studied the background the challenge now was to focus in on the target. The field sample included 43 Chinese business people operating in markets such as Shanghai, Xiamen, Beijing, Taipei, Hong Kong and Australia. All respondents were of Chinese ethnic origin and all were active in international business. The vast majority either lived in or had emigrated from the PRC.

A snowball sampling technique was adopted. This meant the researcher had to build a personal *guanxi* network. Such a network began with original Chinese contacts and referrals in Australia. In essence the researcher had developed what was metaphorically described as a '*guanxi* tree', an important element to a 'pre-understanding' and for 'accessing reality' (Gummesson, 1991). It was a case of 'when in China do what the Chinese do'. By building *guanxi*, the researcher was trying to avoid what Hofstede (1997) had described as the Chinese penchant for seeking 'harmony over truth'.

The Chinese focus on harmony also means other problems in terms of a particularly important factor for Western researchers called the scientific method (Redding, 1990). In historical terms, while the West was about to embark on its paradigm journey beginning with the Ancient Greeks, the Chinese were beginning their own paradigm journey from Confucianism to Neo-Confucianism. However, the later journey and worldview was humanistic and based on a highly mutating source open to misinterpretation called language. Looked at in this way it brings a new twist to the concept of 'Chinese whispers'.

Therefore, other techniques apart from *guanxi* also needed to be adapted for the purpose. As Jared Diamond (1997) suggested, science means knowledge from the Latin word 'scientia' and should be obtained by the most appropriate methods for that particular field. Data was collected using unstructured face-to-face interviews guided by a protocol and was analyzed using Nvivo and content analysis techniques. The researcher used a conversational style with vignettes to allow for the circular, high context, non-linearity of the culture; a lesson also based on etic contemporaries (Trompenaars and Hampden-Turner, 1997).

C2.4 **Results and Discussion**

The outcome from the analysis of the data suggests that 'trust', or *xinren* to the Chinese, has universal aspects, even though, as Blois (1999) points out, there is no accepted single definition of trust in the West so it is difficult to compare. At an etic level, it is recognized that trust is an important part of business relationships, the more so in Eastern cultures, and a challenge, therefore, for Westerners to manage across the West–East 'divide'. At the emic level of this study, however, it became clear that trust in cross-cultural business relationships is relatively trivial for the Chinese in contrast to that in social relationships developed with family and peers prior to entering the workforce. This deeper level of *xinren* is founded on emotional or *ganqing* ties. Further, the Chinese regularly use a strategy of imitating trust to secure a business relationship with Chinese and Western colleagues. This strategy is positive, based on mutual interest, but the display of trust is not at any full level that might suggest 'insider status' or being treated as what Fang (1999) has described as a 'Confucian gentleman'.

An important aspect to emerge in this research that relates specifically to the emic layer was the strong regional divide between Chinese business people. Chinese not within the in-group and outside of a region appear to be strategically at a significant disadvantage, more so in some cases than a Western not within. So what emerged was emics within emics or layers of subcultural business distinctions within layers. From a cross-cultural perspective, the aim was to go to culture, but what emerged were significant distinctions between subcultures. One respondent, for example, described the variation accordingly:

> Well I guess relationships are obviously important everywhere. It's a matter of extent. Certainly Hong Kong, China and Taiwan are quite different places, not only geographically but also culturally and so on. Within China, I think you have to divide China into different geographic regions to talk about how business is conducted there. In Hong Kong, I guess among the three, there is much less emphasis on relationship but still relationship is key, it opens doors, and it helps tremendously in building up trust and your track record.

The respondents built on such descriptions, making clear distinctions between the Shanghaiese more business-oriented approach to the Beijing more relationships-oriented approach. One of the important implications of such regional variations is the relational change, as mentioned, and in particular in notions such as *guanxi*. *Guanxi* appears to have various layers and coupled with these regional variations it appears to have led to some important theoretical misunderstandings. For example, not much has been written on *zou houmen* or the back door. Yet, according to respondents, this concept is embedded in the construct of *guanxi*. However, the use of *zou houmen* will vary in its use regionally. The mainland and Hong Kong vary, but there are also more subtle variations within China.

Another reason for the misunderstandings on *guanxi* is based on the emergence of this construct from Confucian and familial values. This view is somewhat removed from the business application of *guanxi* and what appears a complex self-organizing construct. The sociologists rightfully suggest that the two such views of *guanxi* are quite removed. It appears that researchers therefore have to be careful of using students as 'convenience' samples when the aim is business.

Some other important implications of the emic study refer to the changing face of Chinese research (Kriz and Fang, 2000). English is a language the Chinese are mastering for doing business and so communication is rapidly turning from the entropy of interpretation to one of simple translation. The use of predominantly bilinguals in the study offered the researchers insights into two 'faces': a face based on a strict Chinese orientation and a face based on experiential Western acculturation and with a more idiocentric perspective (Triandis, 1995). Accordingly, bilinguals have an interesting ability to compare and contrast. Another important benefit that has been overlooked for researchers looking at emic studies of Chinese markets is the Chinese pictographs and characters. The Chinese characters appear to offer a step up on constructs such as trust. Traditionally, in the West, these have been elusive emotional constructs, but for the Chinese they have more specific meaning. In the Chinese case a picture truly paints 'a thousand words'.

Finally, the study also confirms the view of Fang (1998) that simple binary distinctions (Brown, 1991) can be misleading when applied to 'unity of opposites' and the *yin* and *yang* of Chinese culture. All told, much can be learnt from traversing the inner depths of a culture.

C2.5 Conclusion

In conclusion, moving away from an etic understanding of trust in business relationships to one that is built from the bottom up via an emic study provides a richer, more detailed understanding of Western–Chinese business relationships. An etic understanding recognizes that the PRC is a relationship-oriented society and that trust is consequently important in business relationships. An emic understanding recognizes that the perceptions and relative importance of trust in Chinese business relationships varies. Appreciating this variation and the reasons behind it assists business people dealing across these borders to identify more reliably which relationships might put them 'on the inside' and which relationships are likely to leave them 'on the outside'. In short, combining both an emic and an etic perspective to the understanding of aspects of a business culture appears to be beneficial in unpacking layer after layer.

ACTIVITY

1. Why do you think that the Chinese are often treated as homogeneous?
2. What are some of the important Chinese programmes discussed in the case and what do you know about these programmes?
3. Can you think of a culture where similar subcultural emic implications appear to exist?
4. Will the Western pursuit of globalization make the search for emic understandings irrelevant?
5. Should researchers adapt to the cultural environment or should they stick to the scientific method and which do you think is more appropriate for business?

References

Berry, J. W. (1980) 'Introduction to methodology', in H. Triandis and J. Berry (eds), *Handbook of Cross-Cultural Psychology: Methodology – Volume 2*, Boston: Allyn & Bacon.

Blois, K. (1999) 'Trust in business to business markets: an evaluation of its status', *Journal of Management Studies* 36(2): 197–215.

Brown, D. (1991) *Human Universals*, McGraw-Hill, USA.

Diamond, J. (1997) *Guns, Germs and Steel*, Vintage, UK.

Fang, T. (1998) 'Reflection on Hofstede's fifth dimension: a critique of Confucian dynamism', *The Annual Academy of Management Conference*, San Diego, August 9–12.

Fang, T. (1999) *Chinese Business Negotiating Style*, Thousand Oaks: Sage.

Fletcher, R. and Brown, L. (1999) *International Marketing: An Asia-Pacific Perspective*, Prentice Hall, Australia.

Fukuyama, F. (1995) *Trust: The Social Virtues and the Creation of Prosperity*, Penguin, Australia.

Gummesson, E. (1991) *Qualitative Methods in Management Research*, Thousand Oaks: Sage.

Hofstede, G. (1997a) *Culture and Organisations: Software of the Mind*, McGraw-Hill, USA.

Hofstede, G. (1997b) *Culture's Consequences*, London: Sage.

Kriz, A. and Fang, T. (2000) *Reviewing Methodologies to Expose the Hidden 'Face' of Chinese Culture*, The 2nd Asia Academy of Management Conference, Singapore, 15–18 December.

Lasserre, P. and Schütte, H. (1999) *Strategies for Asia Pacific: Beyond the Crisis*, South Melbourne: Macmillan Education Australia Pty. Ltd.

Morris, M., Leung, K., Ames, D. and Lickel, B. (1999) 'Views from inside and outside: integrating emic and etic insights about culture and justice judgement', *The Academy of Management Review* 24(4): 781–796.

Pike, K. L. (1967) *Language in Relation to a Unified Theory of the Structure of Human Behavior*, The Hague: Mouton.

Redding, G. S. (1990) *The Spirit of Chinese Capitalism*, Berlin: De Gruyter & Co.

Triandis, H. (1995) *Individualism and Collectivism*, Boulder, CO: Westview Press.

Trompenaars, F. and Hampden-Turner, C. (1997) *Riding the Waves of Culture: Understanding Cultural Diversity in Business*, 2nd edn, London: Nicholas Brealey Publishing.

Tung, R. L. and Worm, V. (2000) 'Network capitalism: how Western firms are cracking the China market', *Organization Science*, (in press).

Tzu, S. (1988) *The Art of War*, trans. Thomas Cleary, Boston: Shambhala.

Yan, R. (1994) 'To reach China's consumers, adapt to *guo qing*', *Harvard Business Review*, Sept–Oct, pp. 66–74.

Developing a cross-cultural marketing strategy

The development of cross-cultural marketing strategies begins simultaneously at a macro level, with the understanding of the international marketing environment (covered in Part 1), and at the micro level with an understanding of consumer behaviour characteristics and response patterns across different cultures (covered in Part 2). Consistent with this view, Part 2 presents chapters in 7 key areas.

- cross-cultural marketing research;
- segmentation in cross-cultural settings;
- branding in cultural marketing;
- cross-cultural product issues;
- cross-cultural price strategies;
- cross-cultural distribution strategies;
- cross-cultural communication strategies.

Based on the knowledge gained at the macro level with the understanding of the international marketing environment, Chapter 3 begins by examining the role of marketing research in allowing for informed decision-making on the basis of the collation of relevant information from developed and emerging markets. Having tackled the issue of identifying the key factors influencing cross-cultural marketing research project designs, Chapter 4 turns our attention to how international markets can be segmented. The main argument presented here is predicated on the view that traditional segmentation theory is misused when applied to ethnic markets. It is suggested that as an increasing number of companies develop a global structure to their marketing strategies, new methodologies need to be identified for segmenting markets based on ethnic diversity. Marketing segmentation as applied to ethnic groups is then evaluated.

Chapter 5 discusses the issue of branding. An important point that is made here suggests that a brand that is familiar to a consumer carries a broad array of messages, and may communicate and establish long-term relationship and brand personality. Therefore, the development of marketing communications messages can often be directed by an association with the inner characteristics of the target market. The argument is essentially that these inner characteristics are determined by culture.

Chapters 6, 7, 8 and 9 present the tactical strategy elements, the '4ps', which comprise the marketing mix. Like most international marketing textbooks, these chapters follow the '4ps'. The marketing mix chapters explain how the '4ps' should be managed internationally and in different global villages with the view of generating the best possible outcomes and compromises between international ventures and local markets. Chapter 6 documents the strategic choices between adaptation and standardization of products across national and ethnic minority markets, and then proceeds to explain the role of the country of origin in the way products are perceived. The chapter also discusses consumer ethnocentrism and strategies for multiethnic markets.

Rather than treat price merely as the objective factor in the economics of international marketing, Chapter 7 examines the role of price as a central element of relational exchange, that is, as a signal conveying meaning between buyer and seller. This chapter explores price in the context of three areas: a) the tourist's ability to evaluate prices in foreign currencies; b) differences in cross-national tipping behaviour; and c) cultural attitudes towards price haggling.

Chapter 8 on 'place' is concerned directly with the role of distribution and environmental/cultural factors which give rise to different types or preferences for distributing products to consumers. Chapter 9 deals with various communication strategies as they apply to international and domestic settings and the underlying cultural relevance of selected strategies.

CHAPTER 3

Cross-cultural marketing research

Li-Wei Mai

LEARNING OBJECTIVES

At the end of this chapter readers will be able to:

▶ Understand the role of cross-cultural marketing research.
▶ Be able to apply the marketing research process in a cross-cultural context.
▶ Make adequate use of secondary and primary data.
▶ Select the most appropriate methods for dealing with marketing problems in a cross-cultural environment.
▶ Identify the key factors influencing a cross-cultural marketing research project design.

3.1 Introduction

Cross-cultural marketing research is marketing research activities conducted across nations or cultural groups. Accompanied by the process of globalization and international marketing, cross-cultural marketing research has become increasingly important. The nature of the research is becoming more diverse. *Marketing News* revealed that most of the marketing research in Europe is conducted in Germany, the UK, France, Italy and Spain, and with the globalization of markets the international characteristics of research are likely to continue (Malhotra *et al.*, 1996). A good understanding of the marketing environment is crucial for marketing products effectively. In the international context, marketing information is used to determine the attractiveness of the market, degrees of adaptation and competitive advantages. International marketing environments vary significantly from one nation to another. Marketing information provides decision-makers with indications of the extent to which products and strategies need to be adapted to a specific local market condition.

The essence of marketing research is to provide managers with information on the current market situations or predictions of future market trends, which managers use as a basis for making informed decisions, thereby avoiding or minimizing risk (Tull and Hawkins, 1990). There has been a shift of emphasis from descriptive studies of the marketing environment to a greater concern for managerial and strategy issues (Douglas and Craig, 1992). In order to resolve the managerial and strategy issues, the decision-maker must have the knowledge of the problem and marketing information or intelligence to resolve it. Marketing research is the common vehicle in marketing to gather the relevant information. Although the nature of marketing research is to help managers make informed decisions, the internal dissemination of information depends on the management style and the organizational structure (Deal and Kennedy, 1982; Hofstede, 1984; Schein, 1985). In contrast to external constraints, how to use information is viewed as an internal controllable managerial problem. The appropriateness of management styles and organizational structure affects the control and coordination of material acquisition, and the transformation and distribution activities of a firm's international operations (Narasimhan and Carter, 1990). Generally speaking, the managerial and strategic issues implied here cannot be separated from the cultural factors of corporate culture and national culture. Since corporate culture is an internal matter, the subsequent discussion will focus on broader cultural perspectives, particularly the local market with reference to the marketing information that can be obtained through research and which is required to enable management decision-making.

Even though most multinational companies (MNCs) with strong financial backing frequently commission marketing research projects from international or local marketing research companies, communication between them may not appear an easy task. Facing two organizations with different values and cultures, MNCs sometimes find it difficult to come to terms with the research proposal when the commissioned marketing research company subsequently draws up a marketing research plan. As a result, it is essential for managers involved in international marketing to acquire a clear cross-cultural marketing research concepts so that they are able to plan the research when it is needed or to evaluate the proposal when overseeing a research project when it is commissioned.

3.2 Marketing Research and Culture

As identified previously, 'cultural' factors strongly influence problem definition, choice of methods and research design in relation to the understanding of local environment. 'Cultural' issues are usually the first barriers confronted by MNCs operating in global markets. Marketing research has been systematically designed and intensively used only in the later stage of marketing philosophy, namely, consumer-driven and target marketing to utilize knowledge about the market. As companies realize that their success lies with satisfying customer needs and wants, it is important for a company or brand to occupy a distinct position in consumers' mind. Because 'culture' is embedded in the behaviour of target consumers, cross-cultural research is therefore employed to tackle the problem.

Marketing Research Process

In common with other types of research, cross-cultural marketing research requires a scientific approach in managing the data collection process. The marketing researcher ought to possess an unbiased attitude in designing the methodical approach concerned with gathering necessary information. More importantly, the researcher should have a clear view in order to distinguish what is fact as opposed to what is merely reported as fact, and the ability to synthesize relevant information into a logical and coherent report or presentation (Hamilton, 1990).

Needless to say, marketing research is initiated by the needs of certain information that should be translated into research problems or objectives. A tightly-defined research problem enables the researcher to obtain the information effectively. Before designing the research, the researcher must assess the financial support and resources required for the completion of the project. Cross-cultural research uses the same research process used in marketing research. The research process is often identified as follows (see Figure 3.1):

- problem definition;
- research design;
- execution of the research method(s);
- analysis of results;
- presentation of the findings and implications.

The first stage, problem definition, is very important for a marketing research project. As the scale and scope of cross-cultural marketing research is likely to be larger than other research, the effectiveness of research relies with the research problems. The problem definition not only specifies the information requirements, but also pinpoints exactly what will distinguish a unique piece of research from the mundane. The research problem should then be translated to the statement of research objectives. The clarification of the refined objectives is the determinant of successful marketing research. The research can be designed more effectively when the problem is tightly defined.

When comparing the marketing issues in two or more nations, comparability of the designs becomes essential. Most marketing research aims are concerned with identifying opportunities or solving problems. The 'identifying opportunity' type of research searches for possible factors to explain a company's growth, for example, market potential research and business trends. The 'solving problem' type of research needs to find a solution to a problem, such as segmentation and promotion research. Because of the complexity of the cross-cultural element in some research, it may involve two phases; firstly, problem identification, and then finding a solution to the problem. Preliminary research helps the researcher to delimit the base of research and make use of existing knowledge so the objectives can be acutely stated. The actual research framework involves appropriate use of research methods.

3.3 **Research Methods**

Marketing researchers have developed a body of scientific methods for undertaking marketing research activities over many years. The two main types of methods are

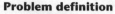

Problem definition
- International marketing environment
- Cross-cultural study
- Comparative/global market phenomenon

Research design
- Secondary data collection
- Selection of primary method(s)
- Questionnaire design
- Sampling design

Execution of research methods
- Relevant field work
- Interviewer/observer/experimenter's competence
- Evaluation of the field work

Analysis of results
- Data preparation
- Reliability test and estimation of errors
- Selection of analytical approach

Presentation of the findings and implications
- Interpretation of the findings
- Recommendations
- Report presentation and oral presentation

Figure 3.1
Cross-cultural
research process.

secondary and primary. When research involves data collected from existing sources, it is called secondary research. The advantage of using secondary research is that it saves time and cost. Nowadays, most of the published data can be gathered very quickly by looking through abstracts and indices using computer-aided search engines such as databases, CD-ROMs and the Internet. Although they may not provide up-to-date and sufficient information, secondary data are viewed as a prerequisite for any research since they may provide enough information for certain problems, such as provide the source of new ideas for the researcher, and/or a reference against which the researcher can evaluate the validity or accuracy of their own research. Researchers have to be critical in analyzing secondary data and consider the reliability of the information sources.

Secondary Research

In the cross-cultural context, most research begins with an intensive secondary research exercise concerned with collecting existing or published data, such as annual statistics, industry reports, newspapers and magazine articles. In most developed countries such as the USA, Canada, UK and Germany, many statistics are well recorded by the government office, trade organizations or independent agencies and secondary data are usually easily accessible. In some cases access to these data involves various ranges of subscription fees, for example, Mintel reports, Monitor, TGI data, ACNeilson consumer panel and media research.

As previously mentioned, the use of databases and CD-ROMs has facilitated the secondary data collection process. By typing keywords into a search engine, the researcher will either be able to have direct access to the data or be notified about the location of the data sources. A quick browse through titles and abstracts can help the researcher to determine the relevance of the data. Moreover, the 'information age' utilized by network sharing and the Internet has advanced secondary data collection a step further in recent years. Another important category of secondary data are directories which provide company and household lists that are a vital source of information for some secondary data analysis, and most primary research as a sampling frame. Not only that, many contemporary marketing research projects are mostly based on the secondary data in conjunction with the primary data.

However, in countries where information is not computerized or processed, for example some Eastern European countries, it will be a challenging task for the researcher to collect secondary data. The information can only be collected by browsing through published documents and sometimes a large amount of data ought to be transformed into spreadsheets for the purpose of analysis. Without computer-aided search engine or database storage, this proves extremely difficult and time consuming. Furthermore, in some parts of the world or industry, the secondary data may not be available or reliable. The government or society sometimes has different levels of openness about the secondary data. In countries such as Russia, the accuracy of the data is questionable. Very often, the figures shown in different reports do not add up or otherwise contradict each other. In Third World countries, most statistics related to consumers are non-existent and information relies principally on primary research.

Primary Research

In situations where secondary data is inaccessible or incomplete, the answer to the research problem then needs to be based on data collected through primary research. Primary research is used to collect data for specific needs and immediate questions at hand. Based on the problem definition or research objectives, the research goal usually falls into one of the following categories: (a) exploratory, (b) explanatory, (c) descriptive, or (d) predictive research. Exploratory research aims to probe issues related to certain problems of which marketing managers do not have sufficient understanding, such as consumers' perception of genetically modified ingredients in food products. The goal of explanatory research is to uncover the answers to certain questions, such as why people purchase life insurance products. Descriptive research unveils means of describing certain phenomena or consumer groups, such as the characteristics of Internet shoppers. Predictive research is designed to gather information that enables the researcher to predict what is likely to happen in the future, such as levels of satisfaction and likelihood of future purchases (Mai and Ness, 1999).

The goal of the research dictates the method(s) used in the research design. Qualitative research can normally satisfy exploratory and explanatory types of goals, while quantitative research can satisfy descriptive and predictive types of goals. In most marketing research textbooks, qualitative research refers to in-depth interviews, focus groups and projective techniques. In contrast, the survey is a common quantitative research technique, with results drawn from a large sample. Observations and experimentation are also frequently used in marketing research design, but they are difficult to categorize as either qualitative or quantitative methods since they both depend on the nature of the research design and the question of exploratory purpose or quantitative analysis of the results.

3.4 Qualitative Approach

There is a long existing debate about whether marketing research can ever be truly deductive with hypotheses being tested in a systematic way, or whether marketing research should remain a largely inductive process with observations reflecting patterns of market phenomena and concepts (Smith and Dexter, 1994). This debate highlights the differences between qualitative and quantitative approach in cross-cultural marketing research. Qualitative techniques, which include a variety of interview strategies such as individual in-depth interviews and focus groups, are the most frequently used in marketing research. Individual in-depth interviews are used when the researcher needs to gather information concerning details of an individual's behaviour, attitudes and private or emotional needs, or when investigating a highly complicated decision-making process, such as when interviewing a top management team. Furthermore, it always proves to be challenging to book an interview in a cross-cultural environment, not only because of the access to the target, but also the persuasiveness of the communication. Therefore, interviewers should undoubtedly learn how to establish contacts and acquire good communication skills, explaining clearly what the interview is about, why he/she is the person who should speak with you, and how useful the information will prove to the research.

When interviewing someone from an oriental country, the customary manner is to call the person with his or her job title. For example, when interviewing a Taiwanese manager whose surname is Lin, the interviewer needs to address the person as 'Manager Lin' rather than Mr Lin. It would be considered impolite or disrespectful to address the person by his first name, although in the UK it may be considered as being informal and friendly. Unlike the UK, students in Eastern societies, and some other countries such as Germany, never call teachers or lecturers by their first name but by their titles followed by their surname, because that would be considered offensive or inappropriate (which can be explained by the theory of 'power distance' (Hofstede, 1991).

Sometimes a face-to-face in-depth interview is also used when the research subject is associated with some socially unacceptable behaviour, requires confidentiality, or is of an emotional or embarrassing nature. For example, conducting research on people's choice of drinks in a culture where drinking is prohibited by religion, needs the information to be treated anonymously and confidentially since the decision-making process is relatively complex. Therefore, interviews will be the most suitable method for data collection. In comparison, in other countries where this type of behaviour is sociably acceptable, the information can be easily gathered and the decision-making process may not be considered 'complex'. In addition, the interviewer should be a good listener, listening to what the interviewee is saying and responding with both appropriate verbal and body languages. As a result, the interviewer needs to acquire competence in conducting an interview that generates rich and accurate information for analysis.

Not only an understanding of the culture, e.g. *free* versus *determinism*, *individualism* versus *collectivism*, *low context* versus *high context communication* (Kluckholm and Strodbeck, 1961; Hofstede, 1984; Hall, 1959), but also the interviewee's language and background become essential. It is important to speak the interviewee's 'language', both in a literal and non-literal sense. Mastering the interviewee's language is one of the important elements in determining the interviewer's competence. For instance, Americans have a different understanding when 'subject' and 'course' are mentioned compared with British students. For American students, the 'subject' indicates their specialization that is equivalent to a degree area in British terms, i.e. 'course'. On the other hand, a 'course' is likely to be an individual subject in the US, but refers to the name of a degree in the UK, i.e. module. Moreover, how a question is worded would also influence the response. When interviewing on consumers' attitudes towards foreign food, the questions should be addressed carefully, for example 'sushi' sounds exotic but 'raw fish' may not sound particularly appetizing. As a result, the interviewer's recruitment, selection and training procedures are undoubtedly highly technical and complex in the cross-cultural context.

Similarly, focus group discussions are used in exploring certain subjects or probing certain behaviours with a group of 10 to 12 participants. A relaxed meeting environment is very important for organizing the focus groups. People in different countries have different perceptions towards 'comfort', so the venue should be carefully selected. The moderator should follow the guidelines for establishing a rapport with the participants, implementing the agenda, and avoiding having an opinion leader in the group. There is a distinctive contrast when a moderator runs a focus group amongst a group of oriental students compared with a group of British students. Running a focus group among oriental students is more demanding compared with British students, since people from the oriental countries usually acquire a quiet and modest manner and are less eager to be the first to speak in a group. Evidently, the moderator needs to be observant and to acquire higher levels of interpersonal communication skills in order to commence the discussion with the former group of students.

In situations where the interviewer is unable to arrange a face-to-face interview with the interviewee, an alternative approach that has become increasingly popular is the use of suitable alternative communication media, such as the telephone, to generate immediate responses. It has been increasingly prevalent in some parts of the world such as the USA, UK, Germany and some south-east Asian countries to initiate interviews on the ICQ, generating immediate response, or entering a 'chat room' to run group discussions.

With respect to qualitative data analysis, conversations need to be recorded as a set of transcriptions, from which the key issues or factors can be derived. For all cross-cultural marketing research, qualitative data analysis requires special knowledge and understanding of the culture due to the complexity created by certain expressions, verbal cues, hidden texts, voice intonation or non-literal implications that may only be identified by someone who has the same cultural background. Analysis involves specialist knowledge and is highly time-consuming. Therefore, consultation with local experts can be invaluable. In addition, many researchers find it difficult to deal with the large volume and complexity of data. In recent years, researchers have used statistical software, such as NUDIST, to manage and quantify qualitative data. This approach attempts to describe and explain certain phenomena, producing conclusive results, although its effectiveness is debatable.

3.5 Quantitative Approach

Quantitative research involves systematic data collection by mail, personal interviews or other means from a sufficient volume of samples to allow statistical analysis. The most commonly used quantitative approach in marketing research is the survey. Many people confuse 'surveys' with 'questionnaires' and use questionnaires as a synonym for the quantitative method. Surveys are used to gather data for quantitative analysis whereas the questionnaire is merely a measuring instrument used to facilitate the process. Especially nowadays, questionnaires are more widely used than other methods, such as in-depth interviews and structured observations, to enhance the data recording process. Therefore, to avoid confusion, it is important to use 'surveys' to address the method, with 'questionnaires' being designed to standardize the format of the data, facilitating the data analysis process.

Survey

A survey is designed to describe certain phenomena or to predict future trends. It is usually used to generalize consumer behaviour or find a pattern in their attitudes, behaviour or decision-making process. The volume of data enables the researcher to interpret implications for marketing and strategic planning, such as segmenting the market and unveiling the central tendency of consumers' preferences and attitudes. Most surveys are conducted through personal, mail, telephone and computer interviews. A few years ago, computer-aided telephone interviews were very popular amongst marketing research companies. Due to the evolution of communication technologies, the Internet and e-mail have become alternative means for conducting surveys although the response rate is still relatively low (Mai *et al.*, 1999).

The criteria for the selection of the survey method mainly depend on the availability or accessibility of the medium in the target nations, the complexity of the questions, amount of data, desired accuracy, sample control, acceptable level of non-response rate and costs. Personal interviews are relatively expensive, but the interviewer will have an opportunity to explain questions that may be difficult for the respondent to answer, be able to choose the desired sample, and is likely to obtain a higher response rate compared to telephone and mail. For countries where the basic level of education or literacy is low, personal interviews may be the best option.

In addition to the criteria, the selection of methods may sometimes depend on the infrastructure of the countries. In West European, North American and Southeast Asian countries, as the postal system is well established and freepost license can be easily applied, postal surveys have been commonly used for large-scale surveys. Using incentives or prize draws can have a significant boost on the response rate. Again, the incentives or prize provided must be culturally adequate; for example, for the less developed countries, £200 would seem very attractive, but for countries like the UK, a holiday to southern France may sound more attractive than £200. For countries which have notoriously unreliable postal services, the mail survey is not recommended. On the other hand, in Third World countries and some countries where disparity of development between regions exists, such as Nigeria, China and South Africa, where telecommunications are still developing, telephone surveys may not be suitable.

Furthermore, for countries where company or household directories are not available, it is difficult to obtain sufficiently large samples from the sample frame, and personal interviews may be the only option. Sometimes other factors, such as seasonality, may need to be considered. In most Western countries, researchers should avoid conducting mail surveys over the Christmas period, unless the topic targets Christmas-related behaviour, because the response may be delayed by the holidays or the postal system. Similarly, delays occur as a result of the Chinese New Year celebrations in China, Hong Kong and Taiwan.

Sampling

Defining the population is always the first step in the sampling procedure. In the context of cross-cultural marketing research, the composition of the national population and cultural homogeneity become the main concerns in the sampling process. Very often, culture has served as a synonym for national culture without further conceptual grounding. In effect, considering the circumstance of a given culture being divided into several nations, as in African countries, the former Soviet Union, and some Eastern European states, several cultures exist in the same nation. In contrast, there are some nations, such as Bosnia, Macedonia, Indonesia, Singapore and Malaysia, where several cultures co-exist within a nation. Taking Malaysia as an example, it is comprised of Malay, Indian and Chinese subcultures. The diversity of the culture, therefore, must be addressed in order to select representative samples (McDonald, 2000).

Another issue to be considered in the sampling process is the identification of the sampling unit – should it be an individual, a household, a firm, or some other unit? It is very important for a cross-cultural study to emphasize the comparability of the sample because it may be a vital determinant of the reliability and validity of this study. In Western society, the composition of the social structure is likely to be different than in the Eastern ones. In the West, there is a greater number of single person households while in the East, where the family unit is stronger, bachelors tend to live with their parents until they are married. For example, in India and most African countries the family unit still tends to be an extended family. Therefore, factors associated with sociocultural factors should be considered in the sampling process – for example, subjects related to household food consumption – when designing a piece of cross-cultural research.

In line with the research objectives, cost and availability of the sampling frame (such as directories), the researcher will have to decide whether to use probability or non-probability sampling. Probability sampling, which includes simple random, systematic, stratified and cluster sampling, gives each population member an equal probability of being selected. The probability sampling methods can only be used in situations where the sampling frame can be identified. For countries where the industry or household directories are not available, probability sampling methods will not be applicable. In contrast, the non-probability approach, which includes convenience, judgment, referral, and quota sampling, is preferred when the sample frame is unavailable or the population is homogeneous (Aaker *et al.*, 1998). Sampling errors can be minimized if the researcher is able to recruit the most representative samples with an unbiased selection process. Access to and selection of the sample population is largely influenced by the geographical distribution, density or dwelling pattern of the city or rural population. For some countries where the population concentrates in a few cities – for example, Taiwan – or where the city population accounts for more than two-thirds of the total population, identification of the target cities becomes very important. Collecting statistics on the population profile and normal distribution of the target nation is one way to evaluate the sample validity.

Although many people still use a 'rule of thumb' in determining the sample size (Sudman, 1976: 87), statistical techniques can strengthen the reliability of the sample and minimize sampling errors. When a high level of accuracy is required in conducting a survey in countries as large as China, with diverse social groupings and disposable incomes, the statistically determined sample size will be more cost-effective compared with the large sample size derived by using a 'rule of thumb'.

Questionnaire Design

Questionnaires are often used as a research instrument in measuring consumers' behaviour, attitudes and perceptions in a survey. The advantages of using a questionnaire are: (a) obtaining accurate information; (b) structuring an interview; (c) standardizing the interview format; and (d) facilitating the data analysis process. On the other hand, because of the questionnaire, the respondents can provide the researcher with information required at ease and in a relatively short time.

The art of designing a questionnaire is very important for the collection of data. Researchers should be attuned to social and cultural backgrounds in order to better address global consumers' needs. Although survey is one of the most popular methods for measurement with culturally diverse populations, any flaw in the questionnaire design will lead to biased results. The questions must be structured to address the research problems and to obtain the information required. The researcher must ensure the instrument to be used for measuring is culturally applicable and appropriate. In other words, a literal translation of a questionnaire is not sufficient for conveying the equivalent of an instrument in cross-cultural research. A questionnaire that is not properly adapted can have serious ramifications for study conclusions (McGorry, 2000).

To target a sample population more effectively, filter questions are used to exclude those who do not belong to the research population. For example, suppose the population were identified as 'home owners', the filter question can be stated as 'are you a home owner?' The questionnaire thus effectively distinguishes the sample responses from the rest.

It is important to avoid social taboos in the questionnaire design, particularly when the personal interview is not used, because negative feelings will deter people from responding to the questionnaire; for example, sexuality and other private issues. To avoid people's unwillingness to answer the questions, researcher should be sensitive and diplomatic in phrasing the question. With respect to wording, some languages, such as German and Japanese, have different uses for formal and informal expressions, so it is important to state the questions with the appropriate utterance. When formulating the questionnaire, the researcher has to make sure the respondents have the ability to answer the questions.

Consequently, the structuring and wording or phrasing of a questionnaire determines the accuracy of the response. For example, sometimes there is a difference in using the same language; in terms of Chinese, in mainland China, people use simplified characters but in Taiwan they use traditional writing. Moreover, the meanings of some words and colloquialisms are different; for example, the Taiwanese expression of 'lover' means 'wife' in China. In contrast, in some countries where many languages are used in different regions, such as Belgium, Flanders in the North and Wallonia in the South, different language versions of questionnaires should be prepared to fulfil the needs. Also, as social changes are occurring continuously, society becomes more diverse. Researchers should phrase the question carefully and provide sufficient options to reflect various circumstances and social groupings; for example, 'single', 'living with a partner', 'separated', 'married', 'divorced' and 'widowed', can all reflect marital status.

The options or responses for the questions are recorded by measurement. There are four different types of measurement: (a) nominal; (b) ordinal; (c) interval; and (d) ratio measurement. Taking the previous example about marital status, the options indicate different categories of grouping of nominal measurements. Ordinal measurements indicate the ranking scales of certain preferences, behaviour or attitudes. Interval measurements are commonly designed as a five- or seven-point rating scale. Ratio measurements record the exact value, distance, length, width or time. Different measurements indicate different levels of precision in recording data. Ratio and interval measurements enable the researcher to record higher degrees of information and run more sophisticated statistical analyses compared with the other two.

Furthermore, the measurement method used in the questionnaire restricts the statistical analyses which can be employed. For example, in testing differences between groups, t-tests are used if there are metric data (interval and ratio data), while chi-squared analyses are used if there are non-metric data (nominal and ordinal). Although more precise data is always preferred, in reality respondents may not be able to remember or give certain information; for example, many of us may not remember the exact amount of money we spent on eating out. Therefore, the response should be moderated by considering the respondents' ability to answer. Pilot-testing the questionnaire among a small group of the target population is the best way to ensure the readability and suitability of the questionnaire design.

Statistical Analysis

After the survey has been completed, the next step is data analysis. Statistics has become one of the core modules of business studies and it is sometimes listed as the prerequisite for marketing research. Statistics transform the data into meaningful results. Univariate analyses, such as percentages, means, mediums and modes, can no longer satisfy marketing research needs, nor can bivariate analyses such as cross-tabulation. Although t-tests and ANOVA are often used to analyze the differences between sub-groups, overall similarities must be examined, using alternative statistics and comparing the significance of the results. Great progress has been made in marketing research, especially in the USA, in utilizing multivariate analyses to achieve the most comprehensive interpretation of the data.

For example, cluster analysis is able to draw sub-groups; a perceptual map is produced by using multi-dimensional analysis that plots the position of a product or company in the market in relation to its competitors. As a result, this helps the company with its positioning strategies. Much statistical software has been developed for processing large volumes of data, such as SPSS, Excel, SAS and Minitab. At present, SPSS (Statistical Package for the Social Sciences) is still the most popular software among marketing researchers, so it would be in the researchers' own interests to familiarize themselves with it.

3.6 Observations and Experimentation

The use of these two methods is unique. If they are applied in situations where the research aims to explore a defined problem area, then they are viewed as being a qualitative approach. However, if the researcher uses structured observations or the same experimentation repeatedly to collect a large set of data for analysis, then they are regarded as quantitative approaches.

Observational methods can study natural or contrived situations. An observational study of the buying behaviour of consumers in the wine section in UK supermarkets successfully identified that music influences the consumer's choice of wine. When Italian music is played in the display area, the wines with Italian origins are more likely to be chosen by the customers than wines with other origins. Similarly, the same is true with Spanish music and Spanish wine. Conversely, observational methods may not be suitable to be applied in some Chinese shops, where most people are only window-shoppers rather than genuine buyers. Frequently, marketing researchers use a contrived observation technique called 'mystery shopping' to evaluate the customer service aspect of a company's marketing. This type of technique is used in the mature market where intense competition and service quality may contribute to the competitiveness of firms, such as in department stores or supermarkets.

Experimentation is designed to examine the causal relationships between the independent and dependent variables. This type of design is borrowed from the framework of scientists' laboratory experiments. The process involves the manipulation of one or more variables by the experimenter in such a way that its effect on one or more other variables can be measured. The cultural factor should be closely controlled or monitored in the instrumentation, especially when experiments are conducted in groups subjecting to group reaction and interaction. Experiments can be conducted on the effectiveness of advertisements, such as the choice of products after the consumer saw the advertisement, or the memory of a brand name (McCracken and Macklin, 1998). However, since the experiment is frequently conducted as a blind procedure, some countries with a high awareness of consumerism and human rights may find 'experimenting on consumers' unethical.

3.7 Presentation of Findings and Implications

Apart from achieving the research objectives, the researcher must meet the deadline for the completion of the project. The final stage of the marketing research is to present the findings and implications. The format and structure of the marketing research report should conform to common practice and managerial expectations. The size of the report is adjusted in accordance with the industry or local customs. Before compiling the report, it may be a good idea for the researcher to obtain a few copies of marketing research reports which have been delivered before in a similar environment as a reference. Nevertheless, the demand for reading or listening to a simple, logical and clearly structured report or presentation is universal. Researchers have to make sure they follow the KISS law – keep it simple and stupid!

In addition to the basic elements of a report, namely, introduction, main body and conclusion, the first pages of the report need to contain the title, letter of transmittal or letter of authorization, executive summary and table of contents. It is important to identify the intended readers. A professional report adopts terminology when it is necessary and uses plain language in communication, avoiding unnecessary jargon. In the introduction, the research background, overview and methodology should be addressed, followed by the main body. The researcher should use tables and graphs as necessary to help illustrate the analyses and results. The conclusion needs to discuss the marketing implications from the findings and address the recommendations for strategic formulation. Ideally, the research should provide the managers with several possible alternatives for decision-making rather than only one option.

Likewise, for oral presentations, it is important to know the audience, and plan it to be as interesting as possible. If it is set in a multicultural environment, the presenter needs to consider the needs for every individual, pace themselves accordingly, use visual aids, and speak slowly and clearly. Many presenters do not realize that the layout of the meeting room is one of the factors determining the success of the presentation. The presenter should always confirm the venue of the presentation, taking into account the size of the room, and ask what facilities are available, particularly as facilities such as PowerPoint projectors are not widely used in some countries. Knowing the venue in advance definitely contributes to the success of the presentation.

VIGNETTE 3.1: Do Chinese prefer Western Dolls?

Marketed by Mattel Inc., Barbies, with their slender figures, blonde hair and blue eyes, are dominating the Chinese market for children's dolls. Western dolls are so much more popular than Chinese dolls with Chinese features such as black hair and brown eyes, that many department stores hardly stock any Chinese dolls. Stores that do carry them usually only have those modeled on China's ethnic minorities wearing unique costumes, mostly purchased by foreigners or Chinese who visit regions where minorities reside. Even these dolls are cast with blue eyes and Western facial features.

This phenomenon prompted Asian TV personality KAN Yue-sai, who is responsible for cosmetics products targeted at Asian women, to launch her own line of Chinese dolls wearing traditional Chinese dresses. It is unclear how well the new line of Chinese dolls will sell, as most young girls still prefer Barbies.

The preference for Western dolls reflects how the attitude that anything foreign is modern and trendy has become pervasive in Chinese society. Magazines published with Western faces on their front pages routinely outsell those without. However, consumers' preferences never stay static. Nobody knows if Barbies will sustain their market position in the next five years against other competitors like KAN.

Questions
1. How does an international company like Mattel decide the level of adaptation in a local market?
2. How does Mattel understand consumers' preferences and the reasons behind them?
3. How do Mattel's competitors determine other opportunities in the toy market targeted at girls?

Additional Exercises
Design a piece of cross-cultural marketing research for Mattel to solve the following marketing problems.
1. Why are Chinese parents buying Barbie dolls?
2. What segment(s) of the Chinese market should Mattel target? What marketing strategies will enable them to continue (or start) appealing to these segment(s)?

Source: M.A. Lin and Yin De An (2000), 11 November, *China News Digest*.

3.8 Conclusion

As the globalization process persists, the intense competition highlights the importance of cross-cultural marketing research. To help managers make informed decisions in the international context, an increasing amount of research is conducted across nations or designed by a foreign marketing researcher. Cross-cultural marketing research is a relatively new subject, although the research processes and methods themselves are the same as those commonly practiced in marketing research. However, the emphasis is placed on the differences in the marketing and research environment, particularly the cultural aspect in relation to conducting interviews or focus groups, interviewing methods and sample selections, as well as making adequate use of the local language.

In the past, critics of cross-cultural marketing research argued that all marketing research is essentially national, and the fact that a research may be carried out across different nations does not alter its national character (Kumar, 2000). Not until recent years has cross-cultural marketing research branched out as an individual subject by emphasizing the differences across nations associated with the culture, language, research process and infrastructure or facility and research capability.

Before preparing a proposal, researchers always have to ask themselves for whom they conduct the research, what the research problems are, where the research is to be conducted, when it needs to be done and how it is to be done. These questions give researchers a sense of the project requirements and scale as well as the choice of appropriate methods. Although there are unavoidable errors in the data collection process, such as response and non-response errors, and sampling errors, the researcher should ensure these errors are kept to a minimum. Errors like surrogate information errors, experimental errors, and methodological errors, can be eliminated by ensuring the data collected fulfils the research objectives, the variables and environments for experiments are tightly controlled and the methods selected are appropriate.

Since the late 1980s many multinational corporations have found the Chinese market very attractive. After entering the Chinese market, many Western firms have found that there are significant differences among consumers in terms of geo-demographical factors and preferences. For example, the differences in the preferences of ready-made meals or instant foods, with some preferring spicier, sweeter or saltier food than others in different regions. Despite the fact that many new Western entrants have high levels of resources, the market diversity and various sub-groups still took them by surprise.

On the other hand, McDonald's were able to enter the Chinese market successfully by retaining the international burger menus, augmented only by other sidelines which suited Chinese tastes. However, when McDonald's entered the Indian market, they had to create a new set of menus without any beef ingredients because cows and cattle are considered sacred in India. These expansions involved intensive new product development research. Different aspects of international strategic decisions are undoubtedly made based on high quality marketing information.

The increasing challenging task for the MNCs is the cultural diversity and the composition of consumers, even within the same nation. Cross-cultural marketing research is in the front line for international marketing to master market situations and competitive positions. It contributes to the understanding of the consumer. To satisfy the consumers, marketing research becomes the vehicle for accessing and assessing the marketing information related to customers' needs and wants. To increase the likelihood of success, the decisions made on marketing strategies – for example, marketing mix, segmentation, customer services and new product development – all depend on reliable marketing information. Therefore, it is important for the marketer to acquire the ability to design a marketing research project capable of solving a problem or identifying a marketing opportunity.

REVIEW QUESTIONS

1. If you were a marketing research director of a pets food and care manufacturer who is interested in entering the Japanese market, how and where would you source secondary data to establish a basic understanding of the Japanese pet food demand and market situation?

2. Compare and contrast the use of qualitative and quantitative research. Give examples.

3. Discuss the processes and practical issues to be taken into consideration in running focus groups successfully in cross-cultural marketing research.

4. If you were to conduct a survey examining consumer behaviours in purchasing luxury goods in India, how would you design the survey and what would be the key elements to be considered?

5. If you were commissioned by a fitness, leisure and sport operator to conduct a study aimed at investigating the market opportunities in China, how would you go about it?

References

Aaker, D. A., Kumar, V. and Day, G. S. (1998) *Marketing Research*, 6th edn., New York: John Wiley & Sons, Inc.

AMA (1987) 'New marketing research definition approved', *Marketing News* 21.

Burns, A. C. and Bush, R. F. (2000) *Marketing Research*, 3rd edn., Prentice Hall.

Deal, T. E., and Kennedy, A. A. (1982) *Corporate Cultures*, Reading, MA: Addison-Wesley.

Douglas, S. P. and Craig, C. S. (1992) 'Advances in international marketing', *International Journal of Research in Marketing* 9(4): 291–323.

Hall, E. T. (1959) *The Silent Language*, New York: Doubleday.

Hamilton, A. (1990) *Writing Dissertations*, London: RIBA Publications Ltd.

Hofstede, G. (1984) *Culture's Consequences: International differences in Work-related Values*, Thousand Oaks, CA: SAGE Publications, Inc.

Hofstede, G. (1991) *Cultures and Organizations: Software of the Mind*, London: McGraw-Hill.

Kluckholn, F. R. and Strodbeck, F. L. (1961) *Variations in Value Orientations*, Evanston, IL: Row, Peterson.

Kumar, V. (2000) *International Marketing Research*, Prentice-Hall.

Mai, L. W. and Ness (2000) 'Customers' satisfaction and future purchase of mail-order speciality food in the UK', *Journal of Food Products Marketing* 6(1): 1–10.

Mai, L. W., Chen, M. and Mai, L. C. (1999) 'The personality attributes and leisure activities of the Internet users: a Taiwanese case study', paper presented at the 1999 Academy of Business & Administrative Science (ABAS) International Conference, Electronic Proceedings <http://www.sba.muohio.edu/abas/>, 12–14 July, Barcelona.

Malhotra, N. K., Agarwal, J. and Peterson, M. (1996) 'Methodological issues in cross-cultural marketing research: a state-of-the-art review', *International Marketing Review* 13(5): 7–43.

McDonald, G. (2000) 'Cross-cultural methodological issues in ethical research', *Journal of Business Ethics* 27(2): 89–104.

McCracken, J. C. and Macklin, M. C. (1998) 'The role of brand name and visual cues in enhancing memory for consumer packaged goods', *Marketing Letters* 9(2): 209–226.

McGorry, S. Y. (2000) 'Measurement in a cross-cultural environment: survey translation issues', *Qualitative Market Research: An International Journal* 3(2): 74–81.

Narasimhan, R. and Carter, J. R. (1990) 'Organization, communication and co-ordination of international sourcing', *International Marketing Review* 7(2): 6–20.

Schein, E. H. (1985) *Organization Culture and Leadership*, San Francisco: Jossey-Bass Publishers.

Smith, D. and Dexter, A. (1994) 'Quality in market research: hard frameworks for soft problems', *Journal of the Market Research Society* 36(2): 115–132.

Sudman, S. (1976) *Applied Sampling*, New York: Academic Press, p. 87.

Tull, D. S. and Hawkins, D. I. (1990) *Marketing Research: Measurement and Methods*, 5th edn., New York: Macmillan Publishing Company.

CHAPTER 4

Segmentation in cross-cultural settings

Andrew Lindridge

LEARNING OBJECTIVES

At the end of this chapter readers will be able to:

▶ Gain an understanding of how traditional segmentation theory is misused within ethnic marketing.
▶ Appreciate ethnic diversity and its implications for marketing segmentation strategies.
▶ Evaluate methods of market segmentation applicable to ethnic groups.

4.1 Introduction

The concept of market segmentation is based upon the premise that separating a market into distinguishable differences will result in increased customer satisfaction and competitive advantage. Ultimately, the reward for the organization's endeavours will be increased profitability and/or market share. However, this traditional perspective of market segmentation has become increasingly difficult for organizations to implement. Globalization has led to unimaginable levels of international competition, often resulting in market saturation. The consumer, confused and dazed by the onslaught of competition, is increasingly resorting to purchasing products that they perceive directly address their self-image needs. Consequently, an organization's ability to maintain, let alone increase, its market share and profitability, is becoming increasingly difficult. Organizations need to identify new segments – one's which offer a high return on the financial investment required to develop them. Ultimately this need has led them to turn their attention to racial minorities.

The term 'race' describes a group of persons connected by a common descent. Yet such a description is problematic, since race is generally defined by an external source in terms of physical characteristics, such as skin colour (Betancourt and Lopez, 1993).

Often there are greater differences within rather than between racial groups, attributable to cultural and religious values, educational levels, family structure and geographical region of descent. For example, to define individuals of Afro-Caribbean origin as a market segment, on the basis of skin colour similarity, is an affront to their identity and ignores the very group differences that market segmentation aims to manipulate. Instead, the American Psychological Association (1994) recommends that any categorization and description of individuals should be by their ethnic group.

The term *ethnicity* derives from the Greek words 'ethnos' describing the *people of a nation or a tribe* and 'ethnikos', which stands for *national* (Betancourt and Lopez, 1993). These two Greek words form a recurring theme in defining ethnicity as a nation or group who share one or all of the following in common: culture, descent, language, nationality and religion (Betancourt and Lopez, 1993; Costa and Bamossy, 1995; Hirschman, 1983; Phinney, 1996; Venkatesh, 1995). Isajiw's (1974: 118, 120, author's additions in italics) definition of ethnicity presents a good basis for the marketing practitioner in approaching ethnic minority market segmentation:

> Group or category of persons who have common ancestral origin and the same cultural traits, who have a sense of peoplehood and Gemeinschaft type of relations . . . and have either minority or majority status within a larger society with membership of an ethnic group, an involuntarily group of people who share the same culture.

A chapter is too small an arena to present an in-depth discussion regarding the considerations and implications of segmenting multicultural markets. Instead, this chapter aims to increase the reader's understanding of humanity's differences and similarities, and how these can be incorporated into an effective marketing segmentation strategy. This chapter therefore consists of three themes: a discussion on traditional approaches to market segmentation, followed by ethnic minority market segment considerations, concluding with recommendations for segmenting multicultural markets.

4.2 Traditional Marketing Segmentation Theory

Market segmentation, as a concept, draws upon the premise that consumers within a market are heterogeneous in their needs and motivations, i.e. consumers have different needs. As a consequence of this heterogeneity, marketing practitioners are able to segment the market into identifiable and targetable segments. Consumers, within each segment, are subsequently viewed as a homogeneous group, united in their similarity of behaviours, values, and most importantly market needs. For each segment the organization develops a unique marketing strategy in the belief that such actions will ultimately be rewarded with higher levels of buyer loyalty and profitability. Such is this belief in the ability of the market to be segmented that notable marketing academics, such as Kotler (1994: 271) include race as a market segmentation variable. The pretence offered to the marketing practitioner that identification of a group of people, who share a similar racial category, constitute a market segment is at best naïve.

To understand the importance and role of market segmentation regarding ethnic minorities, the differences between ethnic marketing and multicultural marketing strategies needs to be understood. Multicultural marketing strategies, recognizing the ethnic diversity of modern societies, incorporate ethnic minority considerations within their marketing activities. For example, in Britain during the year 2000, Unilever's mainstream television commercials for Persil washing powder featured an Afro-Caribbean family. However, no attempt was made to specifically target and reach the Afro-Caribbean population per se. Although Unilever's television advertisement featured an Afro-Caribbean family, the visual imagery and setting replicated Caucasian values and social settings. In effect, the organization has made no attempt at segmenting the ethnic minority market and was relying on ethnic-product association to increase market awareness. An ethnic marketing strategy, however, actively uses ethnic categories and considerations to segment the market. This chapter is dedicated to those marketing professionals who strive to achieve the latter.

4.3 Considerations for Developing an Ethnic Marketing Segmentation Policy

This section discusses a variety of concepts that must be considered by the market practitioner in developing an ethnic minority market segmentation strategy. These concepts are not exhaustive, as each ethnic group will have a diverse range of issues that must be considered. However, the marketing considerations presented in this section provide a thorough appreciation for the marketing practitioner.

Religion

Engel, Blackwell and Miniard (1990) describe religion as a macro-level transmitter of a group's values. These values are based upon a set of requirements regarding how a person should behave so as to please a higher authority, i.e. God(s). Consequently, religious values inherently establish themselves in cultures and among ethnic groups through beliefs, general behaviour and the laws of a group. Hirschman's (1981) investigations into consumer behaviours by religious affiliation provide an interesting example of how religion can be used as a segmentation variable. The author identified significant behavioural differences between American respondents who identified themselves as either 'Jewish' or 'non-Jewish'. Within the parameters of the research conducted, 'Jewish' respondents were identified as being more innovative and likely to be opinion leaders. It was inferred that 'Jewishness' represented a viable variable for marketing segmentation.

Religious values present a particular problem to the segmentation of ethnic minorities. Individuals whose common behaviours lend them to being grouped as a market segment can fail because of religious specific behaviours. Nowhere is this better illustrated than by returning to our example of the Indian subcontinent. A characteristic of this area is the heterogeneity of its religious profiles, which include among them followers of Buddhism, Christianity, Judaism, Jainism, Hinduism and Islam. Since each of these religions has their own particular beliefs, rituals and values regarding a variety of behaviours, it becomes increasingly obvious that religion poses an important consideration to market segmentation of ethnic groups.

For example, supermarkets developing an ethnic minority market segmentation strategy targeted at South Asians will find religiosity a problematic issue. Where Muslims can consume beef instead of pork, any product containing beef or derivatives would be offensive and against the teachings of Hinduism. The supermarkets may find the process of satisfying religious values both an arduous one and potentially not commercially viable. Religion therefore becomes a topic which the marketing practitioner must approach with sensitivity.

Acculturation

The Social Science Research Council (1954: 974) describes the term *acculturation* as a 'Cultural change that is initiated by the conjunction of two or more autonomous cultural systems'. Acculturation therefore represents a negotiation between the two cultures in which the ethnic minority individuals exist. This negotiation process ultimately helps to determine both the individual's sense of identity and the culturally-determined behaviours they adhere to. Although *acculturation* represents a complex multi-dimensional aspect of behaviour, Berry's (1980) identification of *acculturation* as a bi-directional adjustment process is particularly relevant for market segmentation. Berry argues that individuals alternate between and accept both sets of cultural values as relevant to their lives. An ethnic minority individual therefore quite happily alternates between two sets of cultural values and their related behaviours. Acculturation and its identification of ethnic minority individual or group interaction with the host society and culture have important considerations for ethnic minority market segmentation.

Research suggests that ethnic minorities who identify with their country of origin may retain native cultural values and subsequently purchase products that carry inherent ethnic meanings (Maldonado and Tansuhaj, 1999; Wooten and Galvin, 1993). Alternatively, those ethnic individuals who wish to assimilate into the host culture may purchase goods that they believe reflect the host countries' cultural values. Wallendorf and Reilly (1983), for example, identified that those Hispanics who wanted to be recognized as American tended to display behaviour that over-identified with American culture. Those who did not wish to identify with American culture did more to retain their traditional Hispanic cultural traits. This example illustrates the difficulty facing the marketing practitioner when considering how to target an ethnic minority market segment.

The extent, therefore, to which an ethnic individual has acculturated to host/majority culture presents particular difficulties in market segmentation. For a marketer to assume that an ethnic minority group are also homogeneous regarding their level of acculturation is indicative of cultural naïvety. Instead, the ethnic minority group to be segmented may demonstrate differing levels of acculturation resulting in contrasting culturally-determined behaviours. Social scientists investigating acculturation have identified a variety of acculturation categories that are relevant to market segmentation – for example, Hutnik (1991). Hutnik identified four acculturation categories that are of interest to market segmentation:

- *Assimilation*: the individual identifies with the majority group and denies his or her ethnic roots.
- *Dissociation*: the individual identifies with the ethnic minority and not with the majority group.
- *Acculturation*: the individual identifies equally with both cultures.

- *Marginality*: the individual does not identify with either the ethnic minority or majority group. Instead, the individual identifies himself or herself on a social basis such as student, football player, etc.

An ethnic individual's behaviour can therefore be identified as belonging to one of four acculturation categories. Marketing strategists, in attempting to segment an ethnic minority, must now consider acculturation levels and any resulting differences in behaviour. In targeting an ethnic/racial group, the marketing practitioner may be confronted by a market segment which, although its members share cultural similarities, is fragmented in the extent to which they identify with their own ethnic culture. It is even possible that the sheer complexity of an ethnic minority group's cultural identity and values may prevent them from being treated as a homogeneous group. That is, the diversity of their needs may mean they are not a commercially viable market segment.

Consumer Socialization

Socialization describes the development and learning of socially relevant behaviours by an individual, allowing the individual to attach culturally-acceptable meanings to symbolic objects (Zigler and Child, 1969). Consumer socialization, an aspect of the socialization process, describes the role of the family as having a significant influence in teaching their children a rational approach to consumption (Moschis and Churchill, 1978). The previous section identified how acculturation affects ethnic minority individuals' negotiation of two sets of cultural values. Ultimately, socialization and subsequently consumer socialization is affected by the extent acculturation has occurred. Once again the marketing practitioner must accept and consider that an ethnic minority group is not necessarily a homogeneous one.

Consideration must therefore be given to whether consumer socialization between ethnic minority generations can be categorized by the acculturation categories used by Hutnik (1991). For example, would an ethnic minority individual whose societal behaviour was classified as 'assimilated', within the acculturation process, also demonstrate similar consumer socialization behaviours? If ethnic minorities' consumer socialization reflects their acculturation categories, then this would be expected to affect what they learn about brands and product uses. For example, a British Indian whose consumer socialization was classified as 'assimilated' would be expected to be socialized into British Caucasian consumer values. In contrast, a British Indian identified as 'dissociated' would be expected to be socialized into Asian Indian consumer values. The difficulty facing the marketing practitioner then is once again ethnic group heterogeneity.

National Identity

An individual's sense of national identity is based upon an emotional or rational identification with a specific country, such as 'I am an American' and so forth. However, with ethnic minorities the extent to which an individual adheres to or identifies with their host society may represent an ethnic minority marketing segment issue. Ultimately, national identity issues are related to acculturation (noted earlier) and should be considered with this issue as well.

Jun *et al.*'s (1993) study of national identity among Korean students in the United States provides a good indication of the problem facing the marketing practitioner. The authors noted that those Korean students who had applied for American citizenship identified themselves as Americans and demonstrated American behavioural traits. However, those Korean students who wished to return to Korea maintained their Korean behavioural traits and identity. The authors concluded that an individual's sense of national identity affected their culturally determined behaviours.

Jun *et al.*'s research suggests that ethnic minorities can be segmented on the basis of their sense of nationality and identification with the host society. However, this is not always possible. Ethnic minority individuals may demonstrate contrasting attitudes and behaviours regarding their national identity and subsequent behaviours. Hutnik (1991: 138) identified this trait among British Indians commenting that '[they] may see him/herself as British only and yet positively affirm many aspects of the culture or his/her origin'. Joy and Dholakia (1991) and Metha and Belk (1991) also noted this behaviour among Indian immigrants to North America.

The national identity of ethnic minorities therefore poses two problems to the marketing practitioner. First, if retention of an ethnic national identity is positively associated with native cultural values then this may result in heterogeneous behaviour within the ethnic minority group. Secondly, if ethnic minority individuals fail to identify a sense of nationality with their country of residence, then any product or marketing strategy that draws upon nationalistic traits may ultimately be rejected.

Geographical Distribution

A key tenet of segmentation theory and practice is the desire and need for a 'large' number of consumers to segment. Large segments offer the population size and/or wealth to justify a separate marketing strategy. Yet, the size and consequently the appeal of an ethnic minority market segment may be limited by geographical distribution.

In multicultural countries, like the USA, ethnic minorities have grown so fast as to represent a significant percentage of a state's population. For example, in 2001 the state of California became the first American state not to have a Caucasian majority. Furthermore, in countries like the USA, ethnic minorities have tended to concentrate in those states that are near to their countries of origin. For example, South American Hispanics are concentrated in those states with either strong historical connections to South America or which adjoin the American–Mexican border. With this situation, and considering the considerable number of ethnic groups, specific American states can be identified for ethnic marketing segmentation.

However, the experiences of the USA are not necessarily relevant to Western Europe, mainly because of the diverse range of ethnic minorities and the small numbers that constitute these minorities. This problem is further exacerbated by the geographical dispersion of these ethnic minorities. For example, this can be illustrated by the geographical dispersion of ethnic minorities within Britain (see Table 4.1).

If we accept the earlier argument that there are greater differences within racial groups rather than between them, then geographical distribution becomes a formidable obstacle to market segmentation. For example, Afro-Caribbeans and 'Black others' represent a potential market segment of 1.1 million people. Yet their geographical

Table 4.1 Estimate of British ethnic minority population for 1999 (000's)

Region	Total	Black-Caribbean	Black-African	Black-other	Indian	Paki-stani	Bangla-deshi	Chinese	Other Asian	Other
North East	43	1	2	2	5	13	7	4	4	5
North West	258	19	13	19	55	89	18	15	9	22
Greater Manchester	175	13	9	12	26	74	14	8	5	14
Yorkshire and Humberside	290	22	8	17	39	145	11	5	8	34
West Yorkshire	225	16	5	8	33	128	10	1	5	19
East Midlands	216	26	8	16	113	27	1	4	7	14
West Midlands	518	76	6	28	170	154	43	16	4	20
Eastern	198	19	10	19	69	24	16	8	9	23
London	1812	283	303	165	390	123	115	44	135	214
South East	263	25	15	20	66	43	7	16	21	51
South West	75	13	4	10	8	7	7	3	5	18
England	3872	484	368	296	916	625	264	155	202	401
Wales	53	3	3	8	5	5	2	8	4	16
Scotland	80	3	5	4	9	33	2	14	3	7
Britain	4005	490	376	308	930	663	268	177	209	424

Source: Labour Force Survey (1997), Office for National Statistics.

distribution is predominately concentrated in London rather than any other geographical area. The marketing practitioners must then ask themselves whether an ethnic marketing strategy should be based upon such a widely geographically distributed area or whether their efforts should be focused on the majority ethnic population within a small geographic area. In other words, does their geographical distribution preclude them from representing a viable and profitable market segment?

The issue of geographical distribution is an important one since the ethnic minority exists within a dominant host society whose cultural values are often different. Ultimately, this may affect their sense of identity and consequently behaviours. Nemeth (1986) argues that the majority group rather than minority groups exert greater influence over an individual's behaviour, since the individual seeks their approval. If this argument is accepted, then it can be argued that ethnic minorities will ultimately conform to the majority around them, such as in behaviours and values, and therefore preclude themselves from representing a viable and profitable market segment.

Gender Issues

Gender and related social roles represent a further consideration within the development of an ethnic minority market segmentation. Cultural values regarding gender and social roles differ, ranging from equality to highly patriarchal systems. Ultimately, these values are affected by those acculturation and socialization considerations noted earlier. Once again, the marketing practitioner is faced with another cultural consideration that requires careful consideration and negotiation in the development of an ethnic minority market segmentation strategy.

Dosanjh and Ghuman (1997) provide a good example of how gender roles affect behaviours. The authors, investigating British Indians, noted that the reliance of some British Indian families on traditional Asian Indian patriarchal values resulted in allocation of household chores to girls. As a result, British Indian girls were discouraged from furthering their education and employment. British Indian males were, in contrast, encouraged to socialize to British Caucasian cultural values (*Ibid*.). Such findings, which might be replicated among similar ethnic minorities, illustrate the difficulties in categorizing ethnic minority behaviour for market segmentation.

The importance of gender roles ultimately impacts upon decision-making roles within the family unit. This is evident among Hispanics living in the USA. Webster (1994) investigated the role relationship between Hispanic cultural identity and patriarchal roles in purchasing decisions. The argument that Hispanic culture tends to be patriarchal and would subsequently result in the husband making the principal decisions was confirmed. Those Hispanics sampled, who adapted to American culture, were more likely to actively involve their wife in purchasing decisions.

An assumption that gender and related roles is a non-ethnic marketing segmentation issue among Caucasians would be misleading. Kim, Laroche and Zhou (1993) investigated the financial task-sharing behaviours among married English- and French-speaking Canadians. Although the authors found few significant differences between the two ethnic groups, those males who had a French-speaking wife demonstrated a more egalitarian approach to financial task sharing. What is important to note is that even in those societies that appear to be homogeneous by racial categories, subtle but important differences still exist – differences that depending upon their importance need to be considered within an ethnic minority market segmentation strategy.

Overall then, gender roles may differ significantly among ethnic groups and, when considered with related issues identified in this section, indicate the difficulty and complexity facing the marketing practitioner. The marketing practitioner must carefully consider the role of gender and related roles when developing an ethnic minority marketing strategy.

Education Levels

Education provides ethnic minorities with a greater appreciation and understanding of their host's cultural values, thereby allowing them to adapt accordingly. However, educational achievement is not consistent among any ethnic group and this poses a further obstacle to segmentation.

Research conducted into educational levels and adaptation to the host culture suggests the two are inter-linked. In Europe, Bhopal's (1997) investigation of British Indian women suggested that those with an education level beyond the age of eighteen were more likely to consult with friends and interact with the British Caucasian community. Considered within the context of acculturation, noted earlier, this would suggest that those ethnic minorities with a higher level of education would demonstrate greater identification with the host society and its values.

This then presents an important consideration for the marketing practitioner. Increasing educational levels among an ethnic minority group may result in heterogeneity as highly-educated ethnic minority individuals acculturate to their host culture's behaviours and values. The marketing practitioner may then be confronted with an ethnic minority market segment, whose diverse range of educational achievement and resulting levels of acculturation and behaviours precludes them from representing a viable market segment.

Product Usage

Product usage is a generic term simply describing how an individual perceives and uses a product. However, certain ethnic groups may purchase and use a product for reasons that are not recognized by the marketing practitioner. This section will review three product usage considerations when segmenting an ethnic minority market: acculturation, ethnic specific uses and self-reputation.

Acculturation has already been discussed throughout this chapter and does not require further discussion here. However, certain ethnic minorities may purchase products as an indicator of their ability and/or willingness to adapt to the host society. Wallendorf and Reilly (1983), in a pioneering study, identified that those Hispanics who wanted to be identified as American tended to purchase goods that they believed reflected the host's cultural values. In effect, these Hispanics were over-identifying with American cultural values. However, Maldonado and Tansuhaj (1999), investigating Haitian immigrants to America, noted that although American goods were purchased this was not tantamount to adapting an American identity. The Haitians still retained a sense of pride in their ethnic origins. Regardless of whether product consumption is linked to a specific identity, the marketing practitioner must be aware and consider how ethnic minority consumers interact with a product from a national identity perspective.

An interesting area of product usage relates to alternative product uses. Marketing practitioners may be unaware that ethnic minority consumers may use the very products they market for alternative purposes. This behaviour is evident among two British ethnic minority groups: British Indians and British Afro-Caribbeans. Almond oil, sold as cooking oil, is used by British Indians as a hair conditioner and added to warm milk to form a drink. British Afro-Caribbeans use condensed milk in soft drinks and Nivea hand lotion as an overall body lotion (Sambrook, 1990). In both instances, manufacturers were unaware of how ethnic minorities were using their products. The point should be evident here. The marketing practitioner must be aware and consider that the very products they market may have alternative uses by ethnic minority consumers and consequently present themselves as a marketing opportunity.

Self-reputation describes how people use products to project a desired image: an image often determined by the cultural values adhered to. Certain countries and cultures, typically Asia-Pacific, tend to place greater emphasis on group belonging than Western cultures that emphasize individual autonomy. Anthropologists and other researchers have termed this group-orientated behaviour as 'collectivism'. One consequence of collectivism is the need for group belonging that results in a collective identity, i.e. the individual and the group they belong to are perceived as one and the same. Triandis (1990: 96) identified this as 'homogeneity of affect . . . pride is then taken in the group's successes and achievements rather than any one individual's contribution'. Consequently, products are purchased not necessarily for their utilitarian purposes, but for their ability to project an image of group success. For example, Mehta and Belk (1991: 408) noted among Asian Indian immigrants 'that even seemingly identity-relevant status objects such as televisions and photographs documenting personal achievement are thought to bring *prestige to the family* more than to the individual'. Consequently, any marketing strategy that did not emphasize product association with group success may fail to reach certain ethnic minority market segments.

Language Usage

The language an individual chooses to speak represents a marketing segmentation issue. Farb (1974) indicated that language choice reflected cultural values and consequently an individual's cognitive patterns, i.e. language was a determinant of behaviour. Research into language and behaviour/identity suggests retention of the native language is positively associated with retention of native behaviours and identity. For example, Krishnan and Berry (1992) identified that Asian Indian immigrants to the United States had a greater retention of their Indian identity where Indian language usage was predominant.

If an ethnic minority predominately speaks with its native tongue, then an ethnic minority marketing segmentation opportunity presents itself. Any marketing activity aimed at a particular ethnic market segment, using their native language, will potentially achieve a positive response from the ethnic minority. However, language choice represents a difficult issue for marketing. If the individuals that constitute an ethnic minority market segment identify with either their native or host country's language then once again this suggests ethnic group heterogeneity. This implies that any attempt to communicate with a particular ethnic minority market segment may unintentionally marginalize a section of the very ethnic population being targeted. Consequently, the potential viability of that market segment may be seriously undermined.

Summary of Problems

The purpose of this section was to identify the fundamental problems in segmenting ethnic minority markets. Acculturation, representing a process of cultural adaptation, indicated the difficulties in segmenting any ethnic minority group. When acculturation is considered with the other marketing considerations, the financial and marketing attractiveness of ethnic minority market segments may rapidly diminish. Ultimately, the biggest problem facing the marketing practitioner is ethnic group heterogeneity. Quite simply, ethnic markets may be too diverse, small and potentially too culturally dissimilar to be profitable.

However, the reader should not be dissuaded from tackling this difficult issue. Instead, with the use of planning, a number of active steps can be taken to create a viable ethnic marketing segmentation strategy.

4.4 Towards an Approach of Ethnic Market Segmentation

This section presents a number of viable solutions to the problems of ethnic minority marketing segmentation. As such, these solutions do not propose to be all-inclusive. Indeed, the reader is actively encouraged to question the viability of these solutions and develop them further. This section therefore covers three areas: imposed homogeneity, development of ethnic profiles and social identity characteristics.

Imposed Homogeneity

A key argument against ethnic minority market segmentation is ethnic heterogeneity. However, this should not detract the marketing practitioner. Instead, segmentation can be performed by the imposition of group homogeneity. The marketing practitioner must identify a certain number of characteristics that are common to the ethnic minorities under consideration. Such an approach is appropriate where certain cultural issues between ethnic groups are minimalized. For example, a diverse number of ethnic groups may share a similar cultural value, such as religion. Religion may then become the basis for segmenting that group.

Although this approach may be less than ideal, since it ignores a potentially diverse number of other culturally sensitive considerations, it does provide a means of segmentation. More importantly, it indicates to the relevant segment that some recognition of their behavioural differences is being actively recognized and supported.

Development of Ethnic and Racial Profiles

Although market segmentation by racial characteristics was criticized earlier for assuming racial homogeneity, it does provide some basis for market segmentation. In some instances a common underlying theme may be identified among racial groups.

For example, North America or Britain's Afro-Caribbean population can be categorized into two loosely-based groups: those who voluntarily migrated directly from Africa and those directly descended from Africans forced into slavery. Although it may be argued, quite rightly, that these groups are uniquely different due to historical circumstances, their common ancestral origins provide a means of segmentation. The last twenty years have witnessed the growth of personal identification with Africa – a recognition and pride in their ancestral origins. Consequently, it is entirely feasible that a large section of the Afro-Caribbean community can be segmented on their sense of historical–moral identification with Africa.

Identification of Shared Cultural and Social Identity Characteristics

An alternative method of segmenting ethnic minority markets is through shared social identity characteristics. The term social identity, in this context, refers to how an individual constructs their sense of self, that is, how they see themselves. Social identity is determined by a number of inter-related areas, most notably including culture. It is how the individual's cultural values help them construct their social identity that is of interest here. Although each ethnic group can rightly claim to have its own unique culture, there will exist a number of similar cultural values that lend themselves to market segmentation.

For example, the use of products to enhance group status, derived from a group's cultural values, has already been identified as an ethnic minority market segmentation consideration. Market segmentation may then be conducted on the basis of underlying cultural values that can be identified with certain ethnic groups, such as the use of products to enhance group status. British Bangladeshis, Indians and Pakistanis can, to a certain extent, be identified with the collectivist cultural values of strong family allegiance. Consequently, the marketing practitioner can group three distinct ethnic groups into one segment on the basis of a common cultural value and sense of social identity.

Community Allegiance

Although the term 'community' is often vaguely used within society, it represents an important socioeconomic support mechanism for ethnic minorities. Community, from an ethnic minority perspective, represents a group of people or an area that share similar cultural or national identities. As such it represents an embodiment and continuation of their beliefs and value systems, often, in some situations, against a hostile dominant society.

Community allegiance may often transcend ethnic group boundaries and arise from a common racial identification. Examples of these exist throughout the world. For example, Southall in London, Britain, is home to people who identify themselves as 'South Asian'. However, an ethnographic profile of these people indicates that this group consists of people from: Afghanistan, Bangladesh, India, Kenya, Pakistan, South Africa and Uganda. Their group identification is based upon either a shared religion or common ancestral origin from the Indian subcontinent. Although such diversity may represent complex issues in segmenting, noted earlier, it does provide a means of market segmentation by perceived sense of community. The marketing practitioner may then choose to segment an ethnic market on this basis.

4.5 Conclusion

The market segmentation approaches suggested to overcome ethnic group heterogeneity do not claim to provide an ideal solution. Instead, they represent an approach to the difficult problem of segmenting a heterogeneous group of people who share some common characteristic. In attempting to segment any culturally derived or sensitive group of people, marketing practitioners must consider the implications of their actions. It would be easy to segment ethnic minorities on some identifiable common feature, while ignoring other cultural or related factors. Although this approach may produce some justifiable result, it may also have broader implications regarding ethical considerations and racism.

Ultimately, in segmenting people, the marketing practitioner must consider the broader context that the identified group of people exist within. Both native and host cultural interactions must be considered along with personal and group histories. Failure to consider these additional factors may render, quite rightly, the marketing practitioner vulnerable to accusations of ignorance and potentially racism. The creation of ethnic marketing segments is difficult for the marketing practitioner, but is also highly rewarding.

REVIEW QUESTIONS

1. Considering the financial implications of any marketing activity, what criteria would you use to justify an ethnic minority market segmentation strategy? Particular thought should be paid to the costs of developing and implementing such a strategy compared to the financial returns in the short and long term.

2. Critics of ethnic marketing segmentation might argue that such a strategy not only perpetuates racism from categorizing people into groups but also indicates the desperation of marketers to push the boundaries of profit maximization. To what extent is such an opinion valid?

3. Patriarchal values and gender roles have been identified as varying among ethnic minorities. To what extent would an ethnic minority market segmentation strategy be justified in perpetuating these values in order to penetrate an ethnic market segment?

4. Ethnic minorities have, to varying degrees, been shown to exist outside a nation's majority culture. Should an ethnic minority marketing segmentation strategy then aim to assist ethnic minorities in their assimilation into a nation's majority culture?

5. Postmodernists would argue that the concept of classifying people by ethnic group, religion, community allegiance, etc. is both an irrelevance and naïve. Yet these criteria underpin the arguments for an ethnic minority segmentation strategy. Evaluate the arguments for and against using such a criteria to categorize ethnic minorities.

References

Berry, J. W. (1980) 'Introduction to methodology', in H. C. Triandis and J. W. Berry (eds) *The Handbook of Cross-Cultural Psychology*, Volume 2, Boston: Allyn and Bacon, pp. 1–29.

Betancourt, H. and Lopez, S. R. (1993) 'The study of culture, ethnicity and race in American psychology', *American Psychologist* 48(6): 629–637.

Bhopal, K. (1997) *Gender, Race and Patriarchy: A Study of South Asian Women*, Aldershot, UK: Ashgate.

Costa, J. A. and Bamossy, G. J. (1995) 'Perspectives on ethnicity, nationalism and cultural identity', in J. A. Costa and G. J. Bamossy (eds) *Marketing in a Multi-cultural World: Ethnicity, Nationalism and Cultural Identity*, Beverly Hills, USA: Sage, pp. 3–25.

Dasgupta, S. S. (1989) *On the Trail of an Uncertain Dream: Indian Immigrant Experience in America*, New York: AMS.

Dosanjh, J. S. and Ghuman, P. A. S. (1997) 'Punjabi child-rearing in Britain: development of identity, religion and bilingualism, *Childhood: A Global Journal of Child Research* 4: 285–303.

Engel, J. F., Blackwell, R. D. and Miniard, P. (1990) *Consumer Behaviour*, 6th edn, Hinsdale, USA: The Dryden Press.

Farb, P. (1974) *Word Play: What Happens When People Talk*, New York: Bantam.

Hirschman, E. C. (1981) 'American Jewish ethnicity: its relationship to some selected aspects of consumer behaviour', *Journal of Marketing* 45: 102–110.

Hirschman, E. C. (1983) 'Cognitive structure across consumer ethnic subcultures: a comparative analysis', *Advances in Consumer Research* 10: 197–202.

Hogg, M. A., Abrams, D. and Patel, Y. (1987) 'Ethnic identity, self-esteem and occupational aspirations of Indian and Anglo-Saxon British adolescents', *Genetic, Social and General Psychology Monographs* 133(2): 487–508.

Hutnik, N. (1991) *Ethnic Minority Identity in Britain: A Social Psychological Perspective*, Oxford: Clarendon Press.

Isajiw, W. W. (1974) 'Definitions of ethnicity', *Ethnicity* 1: 111–124.

Joy, A. and Dholakia, R. R. (1991) 'Remembrance of things past: the meaning of home and possessions of Indian professionals in Canada', *Journal of Social Behaviour and Personality* 6(6): 385–402.

Jun, S., Ball, D. A. and Gentry, J. W. (1993) 'Modes of consumer acculturation', *Advances in Consumer Research* 20: 76–82.

Kim, C., Laroche, M. and Zhou, L. (1993) 'An investigation of ethnicity and sex-role attitude as factors influencing household financial task sharing behaviour', *Advances in Consumer Research* 20: 52–58.

Kotler, P. (1991) *Marketing Management Analysis: Planning, Implementation and Control*, Englewood Cliffs, NJ: Prentice Hall.

Krishnan, A. and Berry, J. W. (1992) 'Acculturative stress and acculturation among Indian immigrants to the United States', *Psychology and Developing Societies* 4(2): 187–212.

Maldonado, R. and Tansuhaj, P. (1999) 'Transition challenges in consumer acculturation: role destabilisation and changes in symbolic consumption', *Advances in Consumer Research* 26: 135–140.

Mehta, R. and Belk, R. W. (1991) 'Artefacts, identity and transition: favourite possessions of Indians and Indian immigrants to the United States', *Journal of Consumer Research* 17 (March): 398–411.

Moschis, G. P. and Churchill, G. A. (1978) 'Consumer socialisation: a theoretical and empirical analysis', *Journal of Marketing Research* XV (November): 599–609.

Nemeth, C. J. (1986) 'Differential contributions of majority and minority influence', *Psychological Review* 93(1): 23–32.

Phinney, J. S. (1996) 'When we talk about American ethnic groups, what do we mean?', *American Psychologist* 51(9): 918–927.

Sambrook, C. (1990) 'Shopping for answers in the black market: rewards await marketers who discover the black Britain. All it takes is a clear focus-targeting', *Marketing Weekly*, 20th September.

Social Science Research Council (1954) 'Acculturation: an exploratory formulation', *American Anthropologist* 56(6): 973–1002.

Triandis, H. C. (1990) 'Cross-cultural studies of individualism–collectivism', *Nebraska Symposium on Motivation* 35, Lincoln, USA: University of Nebraska Press, pp. 33–41.

Venkatesh, A. (1995) 'Ethnoconsumerism: a new paradigm to study cultural and cross-cultural consumer behaviour', in *Marketing in a Multicultural World: Ethnicity, Nationalism and Cultural Identity*, Beverley Hills, USA: Sage, pp. 68–104.

Wallendorf, M. and Reilly, M. D. (1983) 'Ethnic migration, assimilation and consumption', *Journal of Consumer Research* 10: 292–302.

Webster, C. (1994) 'Effects of Hispanic ethnic identification on marital roles in the purchase decision process', *Journal of Consumer Research* 21: 319–331.

Wooten, D. B. and Galvin, T. (1993) 'A preliminary examination of the effects of context induced felt ethnicity on advertising effectiveness', *Advances in Consumer Research* 20: 253–256.

Zigler, E. and Child, I. L. (1969) 'Socialisation', in G. Lindzey and E. Aronson (eds) *The Handbook of Social Psychology: The Individual in a Social Context*, Volume 3, Reading, MA: Addison-Wesley, pp. 450–489.

CHAPTER 5

Branding in cross-cultural marketing

Frances Ekwulugo

LEARNING OBJECTIVES

At the end of this chapter readers will be able to:

▶ Gain a broad understanding of the concept of branding.
▶ Evaluate the role of branding in cross-cultural marketing communications.
▶ Identify the cross-cultural factors that influence branding.
▶ Examine the future of cross-cultural branding.

5.1 Introduction

Companies enter into dialogue with their consumers through marketing communications. To do this effectively they are expected to evaluate a range of factors, in order to establish the groups that are to be reached and with what mode of communication. One way of communicating with target groups is through the concept of branding. A brand that is familiar to a consumer carriers a broad array of messages and may communicate and establish long-term relationship and brand personality. Development of marketing communications messages can often be directed by an association with the inner characteristics of the target market, and essentially these inner characteristics are determined by culture.

Culture is a society's distinctive and learned mode of living, interacting and responding to environmental stimuli. This mode is shared and transmitted between members of a particular culture. Product attributes could mean different things to different cultures. The use of product attributes in marketing communications is long established. Hence branding and brand management have become centrally important in creating the bases for sustainable international competitiveness. It is now recognized that branding is an integral part of marketing management that must revolve around the basic nature of the consumer and the sort of appeal that a firm wishes to communicate.

For example, a brand name may communicate the reputation, image and quality of a product and the manufacturer. Brand generates relationship and association with customers. Indeed, studies have shown that brands complement advertising and that brands are rarely created by advertising. Doyle (1995) argues that advertising is not the basis of a brand development, rather it communicates and positions it. This chapter examines the issues of cross-cultural branding as a marketing communications tool.

5.2 The Concept of Branding

A brand is a name, term, sign, symbol or design, or a combination of them, which is intended to identify goods or services of one seller or group of sellers, and to differentiate them from those of competitors (Kotler *et al.*, 1996). A brand name represents totality of product image, company image and corporate identity (Dowling, 1993; Doyle, 1995; Levitt, 1983). Branding enables consumers to recall memories, thereby facilitating the initial buying process or perhaps more frequent buying. This adds to customers' loyalty. Therefore branding creates association with consumers' culture, characteristics and the environment where they operate. It enhances the effectiveness of advertising because of the built-in advantage of product recognition and appeal. Doyle argues that successful branding could only be achieved through advertising because of the exposure of the product to strong media coverage. Of course, Doyle's position raises some concerns when related to some practical contexts. Marks & Spencer (a famous UK store) in the past have succeeded in establishing their brand using only small-scale advertising. Although Marks & Spencer was previously able to succeed without advertising, currently the brand no longer communicates quality, value and credibility. Even with the increased advertising strategy that has recently been adopted, the sales of Marks & Spencer products (especially fashion and accessories) are at their lowest.

Together with a product's physical element, brand is a very important component of product development strategy. Motorola, facing strong competition from Japanese companies, concentrated on quality to establish a brand image, which made them leaders in the cellular telephone market. Motorola achieved this success by dedicated quality control and manufacturing improvement. Furthermore, Motorola also extenuated its quality control to its suppliers, knowing that a product is only as good as the components it is made of. They gained credibility from one product area of the business, which they extended to the other products. Today, Motorola is known for its brand image, though with increasing competition in this market Motorola is no longer performing as well as before.

Many customers are quite knowledgeable in terms of what they expect from products or services, and expectation varies from individual to individual, country to country and culture to culture. Sophistication and the affluent society have played a great part in shaping the expectations of customers. Thus, a basic product can be made more complex, hence, firms carry various product ranges and many product portfolios and are continuously trying to establish what customers could easily spend their money on to meet their needs and wants. Theodore Levitt (1983) explains in his 'total product concept' that the expectation of customers has gone beyond the basic satisfaction of core benefit – that a product is more than a physical entity. He then identifies other factors that play a part in whether a consumer would lift a product off the shelf or not. He describes the physical product as features, styling, quality brand name, and packaging. He states that firms now compete on augmented products, taking into account such factors as installation, after sales service, warranty and delivery credit terms. These factors could be environmental and situation specific. It can be concluded that a product is a web of benefits and attributes that may be compiled in different ways to meet the different customers' needs across cultures.

As the brand name is a part of a product, the name given to a product could mean different things to people with different cultures and backgrounds. Branding creates powerful images. This knowledge has often led firms to spend large sums of money trying to create brand images to bolster their established reputation and credibility. Reputation is an offshoot of quality, and is delivered from experience built over a long period of time, which can be shared by different cultures. When a product is bought and it has served its purpose satisfactorily, the customer will perceive the product to be of good quality. To achieve credibility for high quality, a company must first develop a reputation for producing and delivering quality products (Bell, 1984; Fitzgerald, 1988). Milewicz and Herbig stated that: 'Credibility is the believability of the current intention; reputation is a historical notion based on the sum of the past behaviours of the entity. Both credibility and reputation are dynamic in nature – both are prone to change over time and are a function of time.' To maintain credibility and reputation firms must embark on developing mechanisms for brand management. The extent to which a company is able to satisfy customers and maintain brand loyalty depends on the company's capabilities in terms of finance, management and quality of employees. These are, to an extent, controllable factors, but there are also wider issues such as the macro environment that plays a major part in international branding.

A brand can be said to represent the totality of a product, including the company's image. The brand of a product is related to the image of the company or the country of origin. Many writers have contributed to the concept of 'made in'. Country of origin effect manifests itself in various ways and could conjure a negative or positive image of a product. For example, in the 1950s and 1960s products made in Taiwan and Japan conjured a poor image and suggested inferior quality. Today, Japanese products are synonymous with superior quality; however, the concept of 'image' could be said to be in the eyes of the beholder. If 'beauty' varies from person to person, culture to culture and nation to nation, there is obviously bound to be stereotyping of products depending on the country of origin. As to the case with Japan, the country worked continuously to have the world's strongest economy through quality production. Now other countries are striving to emulate the Japanese. The Taiwanese make many world-market clothes and electronics, but these are not sold under Taiwanese brand names. Many of the products are produced for internationally famous brand names and sold all over the world. Therefore, it could be concluded that consumers are loyal to the brand, not to the producers. Powerful brand names command consumers' loyalty.

5.3 Consumer Behaviour and Branding

The way marketing communications persuade consumers is largely explained through the 'black box' – a process that is susceptible to multiple interpretations. In the hierarchy of effect models, the consumer is assumed to go through a hierarchical process of cognitive, affective and behavioural responses to communications stimuli.

Depending on the type of product and buying situation, this hierarchy may differ. Many researchers have worked on cultural dimensions in analyzing the similarities and dissimilarities amongst cultures. Harris and Moran identify a number of social cultural dimensions, which were selected on the basis of their relevance. These consist of communication and language, beliefs and attitudes, values and norms, sense of self and space, relationship, time and time consciousness, mental process and learning, reward and recognition, dress and appearance, food and eating habits. These dimensions interrelate with each other and need to be taken into consideration whilst developing a branding strategy in cross-cultural contexts.

Concern for language is equally important. Language is the primary means of communication and it is the medium that is used to convey meaning, thoughts and feelings. Language is not restricted to spoken and written words, but also includes symbolic communication through spatial proximity, gestures, facial expressions and body movements. In branding, as a communication tool, the marketer is involved in the explicit and implicit elements of the language (important non-verbal elements are gestures, grimaces, posture, colour and distance and are typically conditioned by culture). Here are some examples of language that went wrong globally. The Pepsi slogan 'Come alive you are in the Pepsi generation' was translated into German as 'Come alive out of the grave'; GM's brand Chevy Nova was translated in Spanish as 'doesn't go'; 'Hertz put you in the driving seat' became 'let Hertz make you a chauffeur'.

Colours are also important issues and do have different meanings in different cultures. Not knowing the different meanings might lead to brand failure, for example, the wrong package colour. In many countries white means death (Japan, Hong Kong and India); however, in Mexico and Taiwan yellow signifies death and in Western Europe and Brazil the colours are respectively black and purple. The brand name is part of a product and these factors need to be addressed in order to get the total product right, especially those products intended to appeal to consumers across cultures (see Vignette 5.1).

5.4 Branding and Channels of Distribution

International business has dominated a great proportion of the world's business (Johnston *et al.*, 1994; Czinkota *et al.*, 1995). Export sales with their long established trend are growing at more than seven per cent per year (Still *et al.*, 1988). It has also been established that international business is growing faster than domestic business (Johnston *et al.*, 1994). Most of these international sales are done through personal contacts, hence international companies avail in personal selling and sales negotiations which cross cultures and national boarders. The international personal selling process requires cultural adjustment and adaptation on the part of the salespeople and any other personnel that make contact with the host company. Sappien (1993) refers to adjustment as accepting the host culture and the differences between it and the home culture. Mendenjall and Oddou (1988) refer to adaptation as understanding developed through interactions of why foreigners behave the way they do. Good relations could increase the rate of success in international markets.

The stereotyping of brands does not stop only with individuals or countries, but also with the channels of distribution. Branded products are easily acceptable by channels

---

VIGNETTE 5.1:   Persil case

RJB Marketing became involved in the launch of Persil into the Middle East. Unimaginatively packaged without marketing support and expensive, Persil was launched into a mature laundry detergents sector, traditionally dominated by established international brands, and had thus far failed to build any market presence. This is a market where new products are slow to be adopted and it is important to have a simple approach. In addition, consumer demographics present their own problems. Arab consumers are discerning shoppers for whom quality, value and product understanding are fundamental. The traditionally large family tends to buy larger packs in bulk, so trial of a new product is more risky. Henkel formed a joint venture with the Arabian Company for Detergents (DAC) to improve distribution prospects and launch Persil into the Middle Eastern market. The product was soft launched last year in the GCC territories of Kuwait, Qataar, Bahrain, Oman and the UAE. The hard launch ran with promotional activity developed to maximize trial and repeat purchase of what was virtually an unknown brand. Small size tubs of a leading local hand cream brand (owned by DAC) were inserted in packs of Persil in order to overcome the lack of brand recognition versus the other, better-known detergents. Sampling, display support and TV ads were produced to promote the offer. This is a success story.

Source: Adapted from *Marketing Week*, September (1999), pp.10–11.

---

of distribution because a branded product will tend to sell itself, and it is easier for customers to find and select. For branded goods price differentials are not of considerable significance. It is an uphill task to gain the acceptance of an unbranded product in most retail outlets. In Britain Virgin had considerable problems getting its brand of Cola to the outlets. A brand name not only identifies a company but, at the same time, brings to mind certain attributes. Thus Mercedes suggests expensive, well-built, well-engineered, durable, high prestige, high resale value. Attributes need to be translated into benefits. A brand is more than attributes: customers buy benefits not attributes. Branding is about valuing something that the producers value along with consumers. It is about norms and values. Brand communicates culture. It projects personality. International distribution channels are influenced by cultural differences that in turn affect the international company's entry and channel management decisions.

5.5   Cross-cultural Branding as a Segmentation Strategy

Segmentation is the act of grouping customers into similar characteristics in order to meet their needs. In cross-cultural segmentation, there needs to be a somewhat similar culture shared across countries. Several multinationals have used this strategy to serve many markets. Sami and Hill (1998) describe two categories of criteria for segmenting international markets. The first category is macro-level and includes objectively-based variables, such as language, religion, geography, economic block or economic development. The second level is micro-level and includes subjectively-based variables, such as behaviour, lifestyles and attitudes. Branding cuts across both categories and is the key to segmentation. For example, umbrella brands could be formed with layers of segments; Nike and Reebok serve mainly male and sports segments. A brand name increases the value of the product in the eyes of the customer. Consumers associate with the name, symbol, device or packaging and some other factors of value, which are beyond the core product. A brand conveys something about the buyers' values – Mercedes buyers value high performance, safety and prestige across cultures. Cadburys as an organization have deliberately developed a strong image for the Cadbury corporate name to act as an umbrella for their entire product range; hence their products benefit both from the affection that consumers hold for the corporate name and from the individual character developed by, for example, Cadbury's Flake, Cadbury's Dairy Milk, Cadbury's Drinking Chocolate and all their other products. In the car market, Ford similarly use their corporate name in conjunction with individual identities for their models (Ford Escort, Ford Fiesta, Ford Mondeo, etc.), whereas both Volvo and Peugeot rely more on the company name and so do not try to build character through model names. Thus Volvo have produced the Volvo 440 series, while Peugeot also label their individual models by numbers, such as 106, 309, 405. These brand names represent many things to the consumer and many cultures, and, as Kotler pointed out, the best brands often stand for quality, value and product satisfaction. Organizations develop brands as a way to attract and keep customers by promoting value, image, prestige, lifestyle and culture.

5.6 Social Issues and Branding

The social standards of customers differ from culture to culture; one man's meat is another man's poison. The ethical values of an organization determine its corporate image and, ultimately, its brand identity. For example, the company's history, style and dynamism are often the determining factors in the creation of a brand image (Serraf, 1964). A company's image encompasses a broader set of factors that contribute to its formation and diffusion (e.g., retailers, shareholders, employees, trade unions) and thus expands the range of rational and emotional elements that are part of the brand image (Cohen and Gachwind, 1971). Companies with high brand equity have more leverage in bargaining power.

In some markets customers have strong bargaining powers and these influence the way companies offer their products. The saying that the consumer is king still prevails; therefore, if manufacturers do not cater for consumers' complex sets of needs and expectations, they will lose business. O'Malley (1991) goes a step further by suggesting that what is underneath the label should be in line with the personal values of today's consumer and firms should reposition their brands to reflect those values. By and large, values are driven by cultures.

Brands are not static and need to change with the environment (Berry, 1993). The recent thrust for companies has not been towards new brands, but towards strengthening and expanding those which already exist. Consumers are continually evaluating goods and services, not just on the basis of how they will satisfy their immediate material needs, but also on how they will satisfy their deeper moral needs. Drucker (1973) wrote of consumerism as the 'shame of marketing'. Not only are customers' wants inadequately considered, but also there is much reason for fearing that goods and services of many organizations are against the long-term interests of customers and society as a whole (e.g. harmful food and drugs).

Marketing should aim to maximize customer satisfaction, but within the constraints that all firms have a responsibility to society and to the environment as a whole. For instance, Body Shop gained fame through ecological friendliness. Indeed, a customer may purchase a brand of goods not because of its quality, but because the manufacturer supports a good cause which the consumer approves of. Co-operative Bank do not invest money in areas that do not support environmental causes. In the 1970s and 1980s, Barclays Bank was boycotted by many customers and countries because the bank's policies supported apartheid in South Africa. In Europe, Barclays Bank is a number one bank, but in most African countries it represented apartheid, the face of the despicable system. It was therefore no surprise that the bank changed its brand in many African countries during the 1980s; for example, it changed its brand to Union bank in Nigeria so that the local operations might be distinguished from the international operations.

It is difficult to reconcile the needs of internal stakeholders across cultures with marketing needs. Satisfying the needs of internal stakeholders could boost the marketing effort, as enlightened work policies may secure greater commitment and loyalty from workers, and therefore better output and improved image. Communication of a company's values are a key part of internal marketing. Being a good employer, a profitable company and a caring company (especially for the environment where the company operates) count considerably in the eyes of the customers, and how this can be achieved varies from culture to culture. 'The best brand customers are your employees. The real cost of replacing key staff is at least 150% of their salary' (Evans, 2001). Oil companies have met customer requirements for a range of energy products; however, there has been a cost in terms of environmental damage even to those societies who have not directly benefited from the cheap, accessible energy sources. This created a bad reputation that is transferable to the brand image. A clearer example of the effort of this was the well-orchestrated case of Shell in Africa.

Societal marketing has an endowment effect. The benefit derived could be cumulative and matures late in the process. In the past, marketing has to some extent disregarded the wider needs of the society. These needs could be communicated through branding. The wider needs of customers vary greatly owing to culture, nationality and the environment where the company operates. Marketing may bring together suppliers and customers whose needs are both met, but at the expense of other members of society.

5.7 Cross-cultural Market Orientation/Cross-cultural Global Branding

Market orientation is a culture that has great influence on how organizations and employees think. Jaworski and Kohli (1993: 54) define market orientation as 'the organization's wide generation of market intelligence pertaining to current and future needs of the customers, dissemination of intelligence horizontally and vertically within the organization and organization-wide action or responsiveness to it'. Desphhandi, Farley and Webster (1993) explained that the basic components of an organization's belief is that it should put the customer's interest first. Many researchers (e.g. Shaphire (1998), Naver and Slater (1990) and Naver, Park and Slater (1992)), have generally described it as the coordination and integration of the firm's resources, human and others, directed toward the creation of superior customer value. Organizations that market across culture must create superior value for their customers.

Since Levitt's (1983) article on globalization of markets, academics and practitioners were in confusion as to whether international markets are becoming homogeneous, and if the international marketing paradigm is now going to change from highlighting national differences to exploring international similarities (Ghoshal, 1987; Walters, 1986; Wind, 1986). Supporters of global marketing argue that market needs are becoming homogeneous and that country differences are less relevant to international marketing planning (Samie and Roth, 1992; YIP, 1989), whilst others argue that the existence of global markets is a myth. Quelch and Hoff (1986) and Douglas and Wind (1987) point out many contradictory trends around the world, suggesting differences in national marketing based on individual country differences. National differences sometimes means cultural differences. In the past, many companies went international with national products. These products were exported to countries where there were demands for them, hence brand owners had the opportunity to take advantage of the world markets. When extending a brand beyond its national borders, companies can choose from a number of branding strategies. They may want to standardize all aspects of the marketing mix, standardize the name or the product only, or they may vary both the name and the product to fit local needs. It is difficult to classify a totally globalized product with any form of adaptation, in terms of packaging, language, colour, etc.

When a firm uses the same name for essentially the same product worldwide, it is said to have a global branding strategy. A global brand is more than a single name for an identical or similar product. It also has the basic personality, strategy and positioning in world markets. Coca-Cola, Levi-Strauss, Mercedes-Benz and Sony are examples of brands that have made the transition from national to global brand. Many global brands adapt the product or positioning strategy in such a way as to meet local market needs. For example, Avon carries different types of skin products based on the various skin types of women around the world. Likewise, *Time Magazine* publishes 257 weekly editions around the world. McDonald's adapted its products in India and has made changes to its menu to cater to local tastes elsewhere in the world. In 1996 McDonald's launched its first restaurants in India and to respect local custom the menu there did not include beef. Instead, there was a novel item – the Maharaja Mac, made with mutton but served in the McDonald's sesame-seed bun.

There is strong evidence in favour of the continued internationalization of brands. But the international brand, with similar market positioning and communication strategies in different markets, has been limited to selective product categories, such as soft drinks, jeans and perfumes. The question is, can the concept be applied more generally? Does the ill-defined concept of 'globalization', when applied to the international marketing of standard brands (Levitt, 1983), inevitably lead to, at the extreme, a bland appeal that would then open up areas for exploitation by international companies? It has, however, been argued that a truly global brand does not exist and is unlikely to. As Clark wrote, 'Consumers do not see them [global brands], do not expect or want them and so do not respond to them in any meaningful way' (1987: 36). The author suggests that the focus on global brands is supply-driven, affected by the manner in which businesses view the world. Brands could be adopted differently in different geographical areas and economic environments. Value, perception and usage could vary widely. Heineken beer, for example, is viewed as high quality beer in the United States and France, a grocery beer in the United Kingdom and cheap beer in Belgium.

It is also evident that even well quoted examples of so-called global brands have been adapted in some way to take account of local conditions (Mead, 1993). Indeed, Bradley (1991) notes that it may be an essential requirement to acknowledge cultural dissimilarities and adjust marketing strategies to suit specific requirements. Generally, those who question the feasibility of a global standardized branding strategy argue that the dissimilarities from language alone far outweigh any similarities, and that adaptability and variation in marketing strategies across geographical markets are likely to be the norm.

When the same product has different brand names in different countries, it is a world product. World products are quite common, evolving naturally in companies that have been multinational in orientation. The multinational firm focuses on adapting to local conditions, and typically finds a good reason to choose a local 'invented here' name for a product sold worldwide. Almost every company that has operated as a multinational has world products. Lever Brothers, for example, manufacture the same formula of detergent in several European countries. It is sold under different brand names like Viss or Cif. Many companies are re-evaluating their world-product policies and converting to global brands. Mars, until recently a USA candy company, marketed the Snickers candy bar as a world product with a different name in every major market. For example, it was called Marathon in Britain because it was felt that 'Snickers' was too close to the word 'knickers', a British term for a woman's undergarment. In response to the rapidly emerging single market in Europe, however, Mars recently decided to switch from a world product strategy to a global brand strategy for their candy bar, to take advantage of the efficiency and leverage of a single block of a global brand. It now uses a single, common name. Now Marathon is known as Snickers worldwide. To create a global brand, a firm will also have to work towards creating the same personality, image and positioning for the brand in all world markets.

Different language, different customs and different marketing tactics in different nations may complicate the implementation of a global brand strategy. For example, Vauxhall thought it would be simple to extent its Nova as a global product. Unfortunately, the words 'no va' in Spanish mean 'does not go'. Clearly, in this context, Nova is a wrong brand name. The word 'diet' also poses problems, even when correctly translated. In the United States, the term has come to mean 'low-calorie', but in some foreign countries, diet connotes a medicinal or therapeutic product that must conform to local laws for pharmaceuticals.

Another challenge facing marketers as they try to create global brands is the development of a global brand personality. If a personality is based on a single country or culture, it may or may not be extendable. The jolly Green Giant, for example, may be seen as intimidating in some nations. Despite the many difficulties of developing global brands, the rewards of achieving such branding can make the effort very worthwhile.

Companies could, by skilful branding, build, develop and sustain an advantage over their competitors, and thereby maintain or increase their sales or market share. The development of competitive advantage is particularly crucial in mature, low-tech markets. Turning to specific instances, it is difficult to develop competitive advantage in the food and drink market because companies can easily imitate product developments or packaging improvements, using different brand name labels, packaging and advertising.

5.8 Brand Equity

Universally, branding has become a central issue in product management strategy because companies with high brand equity have more bargaining power in the market place. Firms are desperate to increase their market share and attain economies of scale, especially where the market is very competitive. Many multinationals have turned to the newly-growing market economies of Central and Eastern Europe, mainly as a way of increasing their market share but partly as a way of escaping from the highly competitive market in which they operate. Developing a brand in a country like Russia has proved to be difficult. In the confectionery market, Mars went to Russia first, followed by Cadbury, Nestlé, etc., but they have all suffered economic setbacks, such as devaluation of the rouble and high duties and taxes. Another major problem is the lack of marketing infrastructure and market information that are fundamental to brand management. Brands depend on mass distribution, but Russia's retail industry is still in a state of transition. There is no means of measuring targeted TV audiences, and alternative means of promotion and evaluation are not feasible (Teather, 1995).

To develop a brand the firm needs to define the benefits to the consumer and the attributes of the product. These benefits and attributes go a long way to meet the consumer's needs and wants and must be communicated by the products. In branding services, augmentation plays a major part. McKenna (1991) states that brands could succeed if marketers get close to their customers and identify the services they appreciate. In buying financial services, augmented elements could be the quality of the cashier serving customers and the quality of advice received; hence brands take the image and the corporate culture of the company.

The criterion of brand image is sometimes totally out of the control of the producers or company. Marion and Michael (1986) undertook a study of how to understand the concept of brand image. A representative example is branding in the hotel industry, where branding is of increasing importance globally. The major companies in the hotel industry see it as the most important tool in building sales and developing trade, particularly in the corporate sector. International hotel companies are experiencing an enormous increase in clients demanding discounts and incentive packages in order to use a single hotel chain worldwide, especially in the Business-to-Business markets. In the fashion sector, Gucci began selling leather goods in 1923. By the 1950s its expensive bags, shoes, belts, scarves, ties and watches had established a quality image around the world. Today the firm's value on the stock market is more buoyant than it has ever been.

International branding development facilitates the adaptation process and acceptance of new products, because users assume that new products have the same quality level as existing ones. The firm will incur a minimal cost because they are already established. Also, name research will not be needed, nor will extensive advertising for brand name awareness and preference be necessary; user response will tend to be faster, thereby reducing the introduction stage in the product cycle and, in turn, creating early profits recovery. In addition, another advantage is greater ease in gaining distribution (particularly shelf-space) due to a familiar name. The reputation of the established brand name can facilitate the introduction of a new product. Any problems with the new product can, conversely, affect the saleability of all items bearing the same name. If consistency in new product quality is not maintained, user dissatisfaction may result and may carry over to older successful brands in the line. Family branding, therefore, places high demands on quality control because every single item is considered representative of the entire line. A lower quality item may hurt sales of the better quality product. This may result in credibility gaps among potential buyers.

5.9 Cross-Cultural Brand Positioning

Brand positioning is one of the techniques which is critical in developing a brand. This is done through a series of activities in which the key elements of product perception are examined and subsequently tested in relation to key ideas, which may be used in the brand communication strategy. It is essential that the brand should have a distinct position in the eyes of the customer. Each brand needs to have a unique niche independent of the similarity of the substance of the product with which it competes. Discovering a niche in the market can be the first step in developing an effective brand.

This niche could also include an international market. There might be a need to reposition an established brand in the market for many reasons. Perhaps a competitor has launched a rival brand next to the company brand and cut into its market share. Customers' needs and wants may have changed, creating less demand in the market; in this case repositioning may require changing the image and adapting the product. For example, Kentucky Fried Chicken changed its menu, adding lower fat skinless chicken and non-fried items such as broiled chicken and chicken salad sandwiches to reposition itself toward more health-conscious fast food consumers, just as the culture changed. It also changed its name to KFC. Cross-cultural marketing encourages repositioning in different markets.

5.10 Brand Extension

Brand extension is when a company introduces a product under a new category or under the same brand name. Honda uses its company name for all its products. Reckitt and Colman established the Dettol brand name in 1933 and have since used the name for all its products very successfully. Reasons for brand extension are: to utilize excess manufacturing capacity, meet new consumer needs, match a competitor's new offering or gain more shelf space. It gives new products instant recognition and enables the company to enter new product categories more easily. For instance, Sony puts its name on all its electrical products. New products are easily recognized and accepted. Brand extension reduces advertising to establish awareness. However, brand extension has its limitations; it may lead to loss of meaning, especially where the subsequent lines are not as good as the original or where the cultural acceptance is weak. It could also cause confusion, especially where the original brand product is too strong in the market.

5.11 Cross-cultural Branding and Advertising

Marketing communication is the process of both informing and educating users and dealers about the company and its objectives, and of influencing attitudes. It has been established that firms communicate through personal and non-personal means, and branding is one of the very powerful ways of communicating the characteristics of the product. The brand name is sometimes the name of the product: i.e. the 'language' is taken as meaning the product itself and whoever makes it. A good example of this is the classic case of the name 'Hoover', the name of the American company manufacturing vacuum cleaners. Many people refer to all vacuum cleaners as 'Hoover' when they actually mean a vacuum cleaner, and when the vacuum cleaner is used people say they are 'hoovering'. There are many products which have given rise to the use of a generic name (examples include Bic and Coke).

Careful brand management is necessary in order to generate successful brands. The generation of successful brands involves the building up of image, instilling distinctiveness into customers' minds. 'After spending resources on naming a product, it is imperative to support it through advertising and communication' (Berry *et al.*, 1988). Gregory (1993) says that the first job of advertising is to build brand awareness and corporate brand approval. He suggests that there is a correlation between the level of advertising investment and the level of brand awareness achieved. For many decades the famous brand names were: Hovis bread, Kelloggs corn flakes, Cadbury's chocolate, Schweppes mineral water, Brooke Bond tea, Colgate toothpaste, Kodak film, Heinz beans, Mars bars. It is worthwhile to evaluate these brands as to where they are now. Are they still brand leaders in their various markets? The success of these brands is a result of continually maintaining the quality of output and the relevance to consumers over a long period. Success has resulted from putting through the right communication message to the customers. For example, Coca-Cola has continuously used this approach. Furthermore the strength of advertising depends on affordability. For instance, a small business with limited finance might find it extremely difficult to communicate its message through advertising; therefore, it could be difficult to build a brand image by using this promotional tool.

In Liesse's (1990) article, John S. Bowen, chairman emeritus of D'Arcy Mesius, Benton and Bowles says, 'Brands that offer consumers a consistent advertising message and regularly updated product will lead their industries' (p. 5). He goes on to say that companies that believe in outstanding advertising are those which will build leadership brands. The commitment to the brand's success is encompassed in its advertising. Advertising enhances branding. In the increasingly competitive marketplace, advertising and promotion may be the only things that differentiate extremely similar products (Coonan, 1993). Set against this view, as mentioned earlier, Marks and Spencer built up its brand image without intensive advertising. They relied on High Street presence and customer experience. Recently, though, Marks and Spencer is lagging behind because it did not respond quickly to the change in organizational environment and people culture. This resulted in Marks and Spencer closing many of their branches worldwide. Anita Roddick, who believes that advertising is wasteful, has made her alternative brand-building methods the basis of her company's strategy. However, advertising positions the product through creative messages communicating brand values that meet the requirements of the targeted audience. In order to achieve this, national cultures must be studied and taken into consideration.

5.12   Branding and E-commerce

Customer perception of a product is always the same whether the customer bought online or from the conventional shop. With many offers made online each time a customer browses the web most brands are under scrutiny for the simple reason that the websites provide information for making easy choices which is not readily available on a normal shopping floor. In a traditional shop, where there is an array of similar products, it is sometimes difficult to examine all the products and assimilate the necessary information required, especially when the sales assistant is looking over your shoulder. Online shopping provides the opportunity to browse at home. Competition generated by online shopping is having an impact on every sector, and the only escape route is to expand into other markets. Many businesses are building up international corporate branding rather than individual branding. Corporate branding facilitates recognition and enhances global branding. For instance, IBM, Kodak and Nescafé have gained from corporate branding. For companies to survive in the digital economy and new communications environment, they need to reach other markets. Recently, in the UK, supermarkets are incorporating banks and Post Offices, and are opening branches abroad.

According to research carried out by Global Sight Corp., eighty per cent of European multinationals now consider web globalization an integral component of their online business objectives. The company studied 26 European multinationals including British Airways, Saab and Credit Suisse. It was established that two-thirds already have a corporate web globalization initiative underway, but stated some difficulties in setting up structures due to organizational challenges, such as meeting the different international marketing environments in terms of culture regulations, economic and political issues.

5.13   Barriers to Cross-cultural Branding

For effective cross-cultural branding, companies need to examine the environmental context in which they wish to operate. It is vital for companies to understand the macro influence on branding. Country of origin effect is one of the factors influencing the acceptability of a product in a given country. Products from Israel are not acceptable in many Middle Eastern countries, whereas products from England, Britain and Japan are more widely acceptable and are usually seen as good quality. In some cases, there could be political boycott as a result of stressed relationships between countries. Political economic policies geared towards rectifying economic imbalances could exclude top brands, as they are seen as luxuries and could contribute to foreign exchange problems, especially among developing countries. Countries with problems of imbalance of trade, especially with trade deficits, could embark on different economic policies to reduce this state of affairs.

Technological issues cannot be ignored. Countries are taking a number of steps in an effort to preserve their cultural integrity and protect their economies and societies from being invaded by other cultures. In 1998, Canada called together 19 other governments to discuss ways to ensure that their cultural independence is maintained from the United States.

For some years, the American way of life has influenced many European countries. Restaurants such as McDonald's and Pizza Hut, brands such as Nike and Disney, and American-made motion pictures and TV soaps have penetrated many countries of the world. Many countries are worried that the American way of life will rob them of their country's way of life. Recently, many consumers have shown negative reactions towards American-made products, not because the products are functioning poorly, but as a form of protest against perceived American culture. The developing countries have their own specific boundaries: for example, African concepts of democracy affect global competitiveness. Many African countries practice democracy towards market economy, but constantly the governments intervene – disrupting the market. The role of decision-makers, and decision-making systems at family levels, as well as the role of economic, political, legal and social factors are considered to be barriers to cross-cultural branding.

5.14   The Future of Cross-cultural Branding

In the retail sector, own brands, whether local or national, do not cross cultures easily. Many consumers are realizing the virtue of own brands and are now looking for the value for money that many global brands do not offer. Highly successful brands are very expensive, and are internationally over-priced. Customers' consideration for value and the ability to pay differ from culture to culture, country to country. Many countries are now producing their own brands, thereby competing with international brands. In a subsistence economy, national brands will thrive.

Major brand manufacturers have recognized the opportunities offered by own-label manufacturers. Companies like Body Shop, Benetton and Marks and Spencer carry their own brands. In the UK, one of the largest supermarkets, Sainsbury, carries 50 per cent of its own brands. This is due to aggressive competition in the sector and also to over-capacity at the manufacturing plant. For example, Heinz produces own brands for UK supermarkets and is now looking out for customers in Europe. Some brand owners have refused to supply products for retailers' own label items in order to avoid misconception on the side of the consumer. Companies like Kelloggs advertise the fact that they do not make goods for anyone else, making it clear that its brand is not duplicated. Despite this, many own brands are thriving in the market and challenging the popular brands. When manufacturers produce for other companies, they may be in danger of sending the wrong signals to consumers. Consumers believe that if a major brand manufacturer produces an own brand for another company, the own brand is as good as the popular brand. Gordon (1994) states that retailers have invested in their own brands to the extent that their quality levels are often on a par with leading brands. In Europe, the European partners have established legislation on intellectual property and law has been made to prevent own label brands from imitating the 'distinctive signs' of brands. The group wanted to strengthen this to 'overall appearance' and to have 'look alikes' treated as unfair competition, as they are in other countries. This step by the European partners is an encouragement to cross-cultural branding. Own label brands tend to be localized, and this tendency has grown from 34 per cent to almost 40 per cent of supermarket sales in the UK in just three years. The trend is spreading across Europe. The threat of own labels should not be ignored. Mars has moved into own-label manufacture of 'wet cooking sauces' (for example, Dolmio bolognese sauce in a jar) after 60 years of resistance to such supply. The reason for such a move is the existence of aggressive competition in the sector.

Indeed, it is suggested that retailer brands are increasingly perceived as equal to or superior to traditional brands (de Jonquieres, 1993) and customers may increasingly question whether or not manufacturers' brands possess additional values which qualify them for premium prices. Retailers are themselves more actively engaged in internationalization and their established domestic brands will in most cases accompany them. In addition, their own brands could be globalized. Many multinationals are currently involved in strategic alliances, thereby having easy access to many markets.

5.15　Conclusion

It emerges clearly from the above that cross-cultural branding is a complex matter. This is so for several reasons. Firstly, at risk of stating the obvious, people are different; for example, we have seen that words can and do mean very different things to members of different cultures. Secondly, among different cultures we have seen that there is a very wide range of different attitudes, values and behaviours. Thirdly, a product that meets the needs of large numbers of people in one culture may fail badly in another culture because customers have very different needs. Fourthly, cross-cultural distribution requires both organizational and individual adaptation to the culture of the host country. Finally, new technology provides an array of information for customer choice.

It is abundantly plain that companies wishing to market their products globally must do extensive research in relation to the market they intend to target. Looking to the future, it would seem that more and more companies are likely to market own-brand products. This tendency seems likely to be reinforced by an increasing nationalistic outlook on the part of customers, and it appeals as customers increasingly believe that own-brand products offer good value. As a result, any companies wishing to adopt a cross-cultural global strategy will have to compete more aggressively, especially with regard to price. One thing is certain, whether own brands are being promoted or whether companies are adopting a global outlook, branding itself would be of crucial and ever-increasing importance in the successful promotion of products.

REVIEW QUESTIONS

1. What are the major differences between cross-cultural branding and global branding?

2. Discuss the factors which could impact cross-cultural branding strategies.

3. 'Macro-economic factors are of no significance to cross-cultural branding.' Discuss this statement, using appropriate examples to illustrate your answer.

References

Bell, C. (1994) 'Building a reputation for training effectiveness', *Training and Development Journal of Marketing Research* 28 (February): 16–28.

Berry, J. (1993) 'Brand value isn't about stocks, it's sales and profits', *Brandweek*, 34:14.

Berry, L., Lefkowith, E. and Clark, T. (1988) 'In services, what's in a name', *Harvard Business Review* 66: 28–30.

Bradley, F. (1991) *International Marketing Strategy*, London: Prentice Hall, pp. 1–23.

Clark, H. (1987) 'Consumer and corporate values: yet another view on global marketing', *International Journal of Advertising* 6(1): 29–42.

Chung, K. K. (1995) 'Brand popularity and country image in global competition: managerial implications', *Journal of Product and Brand Management* 4(5): 21–33.

Cohen, J. and Gachwind, K. (1973) 'Behavioural science foundations of consumer behaviour', *Journal of Marketing* 3 (April), 116–135.

Coonan, C. (1993) 'Coke battles Pepsi', *Business and Finance* 30: 30.

Czinkota, M. R., Ronkainen, I. A., Moffett, M. H. and Moyniham, E. O. (1995) *International Marketing*. New York: The Dryden Press.

Daniels, J. D. and Radebaugh, L. H. (1995) *International Business: Environments and Operations*, 7th edn., Boston: Addison Wesley World Student Series.

Deshpande, R., Farley, J. U. and Webster, Jr., F. (1993) 'Corporate culture, customer orientation, and innovativeness in Japanese firms: a quadrad analysis', *Journal of Marketing* 53 (January): 3–15.

De Chernatony, L. (1992) 'Brand pricing in a recession', *European Journal of Marketing* 26(3): 14.

de Chernatony, L. (1993) 'Categorising brands: evolutionary processes underpinned by two key dimensions', *Journal of Marketing Management*, 173–188.

de Jonquieres, G. (1993) 'Not just a question of price', *Financial Times*, 9 September, p 8.

Dowling, G.R. (1993) 'Developing your image into a corporate asset', *Long Range Planning* 26(2): 101–109.

Douglas, S.P. and Wind, Y. (1987) 'The myth of globalisation', *Columbia Journal of World Business* (Winter): 19–29.

Doyle, P. and Baker, M. (1995) *The Marketing Book*, 3rd edn., London: Butterworth-Heinemann.

Drucker, P. (1973) *Management: Tasks, Responsibilities & Practices*. London: Heinemann.

Dubois, B. (1993) 'The market for luxury goods: income versus culture', *European Journal of Marketing* 27(1): 36–44.

Evans, P. (2001) 'The demanding consumer', *The News Letter of the British Brands* (Spring) 13: 7.

Fitzerald, T. J. (1988) 'Understanding the differences and similarities between services and products to exploit your competitive advantage', *Journal of Services Marketing* 2 (Winter): 25–30.

Fishban, E. (1993) 'What's in a label?' *World Trade* 6 (June): 10.

Ghoshal, S. (1987) 'Global strategy: an organising framework', *Colombia Journal of World Business* (Winter): 19–29.

Gordan, R. (1994) 'Cognitive style of consumer initiators', *Technovation* 15(5) (June): 269–88.

Gregory, J. R. (1993) 'Strong brands stick out in a crowd', *Business Marketing* pp. 39, 78.

Herbig, P. and Milewicz, J. (1993) 'The relationship of reputation and credibility to brand success', *Journal of Consumer Marketing* 10(3).

Irvin, C. (1999) 'Eastern promise', *Marketing Business* Sept., 10–11

Johnston, E. M., Kurtzz, D. L. and Scheuing, E. E. (1994) *Sales Management: Concepts, Practices and Cases*, 2nd edn., New York: McGraw-Hill International Editions.

Jaworski, B. J. and Kohli, A. K. (1993) 'Market orientation: antecedents and consequences', *Journal of Marketing* 57 (July): 53–70.

Kotler, P., Armstrong, G., Saunders, J. and Wong, V. (1996) *Principles of Marketing*, London: Prentice Hall Europe.

Levitt, T. (1983) 'The globalisation of markets', *Harvard Business Review* 61 (May–June): 92–102.

Levitt, T. (1993) *The Marketing Imagination*, New York: Collier Macmillian.

Marion, W. and Michael, T. (1986) 'Effects of brand equality on B2B', Proceedings of the annual conference of the Academy of Marketing Science, Bal Harbour Florida, May 26–9.

Mead, G. (1993) 'A universal message', *Financial Times* 27 May, p. 20.

Mendenhall, M. and Oddou, G. (1988) 'The overseas assignment: a practical outlook', *Business Horizons*, September/October: 78–84.

McKenna, R. (1991) 'Marketing is everything, everything is marketing', *Harvard Business Review*, Jan-Feb, 65–69.

Narver, J. C., Park, S. Y. and Slater, S. F. (1992) 'Market orientation information and marketing strategies'. Paper presented at the 1992 American Marketing Association Summer Educators Conference.

O'Malley, D. (1991) 'Brand means business', *The Economist* 107: 107–108.

Pringle, D. (1994) *Packaging Week* 10(26): 12.

Quelch, J. and Hoff, E. (1986) 'Customising global marketing', *Harvard Business Review* 64 (May–June): 59–68.

Samie, S. and Roth, K. (1992) 'The influence of global marketing standardisation on performance', *Journal of Marketing* 56: 1–17.

Sappien, J. (1993) 'Expatriate adjustment on foreign assignment', *European Business Review* 93(5): 3–11.

Saurudin, A. (1993) 'Cross-national evaluation of mae-in concept using multiple cues', *European Journal of Marketing* 27(7): 39–52.

Serraf, G. (1964) 'Propositions pour définir un véritable marketing des problèmes sociaux'. *Revue française du marketing*, 60: 46–83.

Still, R. R., Cundiff, E. W. and Coconi, N. A. P. (1988) *Sales Management Decisions: Strategies and Cases*, 5th edn., New York: McGraw-Hill Company.

Thakor, M. V. and Katsanis, L. P. (1997) 'A model of brand and country effects on quality dimensions: issues and implications', *Journal of International Consumer Marketing* 9(3): 100.

Teather, D. (1995) 'Out of the Gold', *Marketing*, 2 Nov: 26–9.

Walters, P. G. (1986) 'International marketing policy: a discussion of the standardization construct and its relevance for corporate policy', *Journal of International Business Studies* 7 (Summer): 55–69.

Wind, Y. (1986) 'The myth of globalisation', *Journal of Consumer Marketing* 3 (Spring): 23–6.

Yip, G. S. (1989) 'Global strategy in a world of nations?', *Sloan Management Review* 31 (Fall): 29–41.

CHAPTER 6

Cross-cultural product strategy

Greg Elliott and Chandrama Acharya

LEARNING OBJECTIVES

After reading this chapter, readers will able to:

▶ Understand the specific issues that relate to product strategy in global villages, whether they be domestic multi-ethnic markets or international markets.
▶ Appreciate the potential pitfalls for companies who assume that the product mix does not require modification or adaptation from the 'domestic' market to reflect the differences and demands of the 'differing local or foreign' market.
▶ Manage the meaning of products as a consequence of the effects of 'country of origin' and 'ethnocentrism', and the implications for manufacturers operating in both domestic and international markets.
▶ Be conscious of the possible existence of the 'home country bias'.
▶ Recognize the potential interrelationships between the 'country of origin' effects and the existence and potential importance of 'global brands' in international markets.

6.1 Introduction

It is widely accepted that the first element of the marketing mix 'product' is the most critical of the '4Ps', as it defines the business in which a company is involved and therefore dictates the nature of pricing, promotion and distribution strategies to be applied in selling it in the relevant domestic or international marketing environment.

The purpose of this chapter, therefore, is principally to consider how product strategy applies to the cross-cultural marketing context. This chapter discusses the issues of adaptation and standardization to demonstrate from the offset that a product must be modified in order to be sold to a foreign market. The chapter begins by acknowledging that the extent of the modifications, whether physical or psychological, will be dictated by the marketplace. The chapter then discusses the importance of managing the meaning of products as a consequence of the effects of 'country of origin' and 'ethnocentrism', and the implications for manufacturers operating in both domestic and international markets.

The chapter concludes by discussing the implications for a 'product strategy' based on an objective understanding of the additional complexity of issues involved in marketing a firm's products in foreign countries. The discussions also recognize the existence and potential importance of 'global brands' in international markets.

6.2 Adaptation or Standardization of Product Attributes?

A central issue in product strategy where 'different' markets are involved is the decision of whether to adapt products on the basis of known consumers, national or foreign market idiosyncrasies or to standardize the product based on experience and economic considerations. According to Ursunier (2000), the real issue is not a dichotomous choice, whether to adapt or to standardize completely. Ursunier argues that the performance of products has been found to be a combination of both adaptation and standardization strategies, as well as the influence of a large number of factors related to the four components of the marketing mix.

6.3 Product Strategy in a Cross-cultural Context

The topic of product strategy in a cross-cultural context is very wide-ranging as it potentially embraces all the usual product dimensions. These range from the physical attributes (e.g. product design and development, and features such as size, weight, packaging and colour, etc.), the point at which any standardization policy would apply.

Secondly there are the service attributes such as maintenance, spare part availability, warranties, installation, after-sales service etc. Third are the symbolic attributes, which usually represent the interpretative elements of the physical attributes such as quality, branding, styling, colour, etc. For instance, colour is simultaneously a chemical formula and also the symbolic meaning conveyed by the material. Clearly, symbolic attributes affect the choice between adaptation and standardization in a fairly ambiguous manner.

Product strategy is concerned with the issue of how, or if, the 'domestic' product needs to be in any way modified to reflect the peculiarities and exigencies of the many foreign markets. In many cases, however, consumers may be torn between a preference for domestic products based on their nationalistic instincts and a fascination for a foreign product based on its durability, quality and image of the foreign producer/country.

Clearly, the decision to adapt or standardize symbolic attributes which convey specific meanings will be based on the requirements for nationalistic attributes and symbols of exoticism. As for many important marketing issues, the question in practice should be resolved after reference to the important contingent factors – most notably, those reflecting the key characteristics of the foreign market and those surrounding the product. In practice, and as implied earlier, it is frequently the joint effect of these considerations. A simple example would be the Subaru Legacy, as it is known internationally and in Japan, which was renamed Liberty in Australia to avoid confusion and potentially offending Australians who continue to suffer losses as a result of World War II ('Legacy' is the name of the national charity for war widows and their children).

In seeking to resolve the issues introduced above, cross-cultural marketers will need to concern themselves with a wide array of issues. However, a central concern will be the influence of the 'country of origin' of the foreign product on the product evaluations and subsequent purchase behaviour of buyers and consumers in the range of foreign markets. This central concern will be reflected in the degree of 'consumer ethnocentrism' among the foreign market target consumers.

To marketers operating in a cross-cultural environment, these issues add new dimensions to the already-complex issue of product strategy. Thus, as an initial generalization, it is dangerous to presume that a product which is a proven success in the domestic market will achieve the same response in foreign markets. The long history of published research in this field demonstrates that the development of appropriate product strategies should be based upon a detailed examination and understanding of the attitudes of consumers/end users in the target country, and that the recommended approach might require modification and adaptation in each foreign market. For instance, the international marketing textbooks are replete with quaint and amusing anecdotes concerning the culturally inappropriate naming of products in markets in the local native language. The choice by Mitsubishi of the name 'Pajero' for its rugged and otherwise excellent four-wheel drive vehicles which, reportedly, in Spanish, translates as an unspeakable insult to masculine machismo is, perhaps, proof of the failure of modern managers to adequately consult the textbooks.

6.4 Managing Product Meanings

For some time now there has been much discussion and general agreement in the international marketing literature that products are evaluated not only on their attributes, but also on the basis of perceptions in the consumer's eyes of their country of origin (i.e. of manufacture) of that product (the 'country of origin' effect). Numerous studies have pointed to a systematic bias in favour of the products of particular countries, based on a number of contingent variables. One such variable is the level of economic development of the country, with consumers showing a consistent bias in favour of countries with higher levels of economic development (e.g. Western Europe, North America, Japan, Australasia) over products from countries with lower levels of economic development. The general conclusion is that the link with perceived product quality is generally the most important mediator in this relationship.

Beyond the evidence of a generalized country of origin effect, the most notable finding is the identification of a systematic bias of consumers in favour of domestically-made products at the expense of comparable foreign-made products (i.e. the so-called 'home country bias'). It is clear that consumers evaluate domestic products more favourably than foreign products, when the products are identical in all other respects. A range of explanations have been advanced for this 'home country bias', such as the effects on consumer perceptions of the economic, or technological development of the producing country, quality reputation, cultural similarity, geographical or cultural proximity, or political status.

An underlying theme of the discussion is that such preferences are simple expressions of a more pervasive and generalized concept of 'consumer ethnocentrism'. A consumer, for instance, may feel strongly that the quality offered by French wine is superior to that of domestic brands, and yet refuse to purchase the foreign wine because of the moral and/or economic implications. A number of plausible explanations could be advanced for this refusal. One explanation of such behaviour is that the consumers are ethnocentric in their choice behaviour. Alternatively, of course, the concept of ethnocentrism may be independent of the country of origin bias. Further, it may happen that ethnocentrism's effects on buying behaviour may vary depending on the characteristics of the product's country of origin. It may also happen that the consumers value highly the quality of wine and purchase it just because it is French (the 'country of origin' effect). It is an objective of this paper to explore these complex interdependencies between consumer ethnocentrism, the 'country of origin' effect and the 'home country bias'.

6.5   Consumer Ethnocentrism

The term 'consumer ethnocentrism' was coined to 'represent the belief held by American consumers about the appropriateness, indeed morality, of purchasing foreign products'. To ethnocentric consumers, the products from other countries (i.e. 'outgroups') are objects of contempt or rejection, whereas locally-made products are preferred as either an object of national pride or duty.

Variables like socioeconomic, demographic and regional economic factors have been found to act as moderator variables in the study of consumer ethnocentric tendencies. Research shows that consumer ethnocentric tendencies play a more influential role under two circumstances: firstly, when products are perceived as relatively unnecessary, and secondly, when consumers perceive themselves and/or the domestic economy to be threatened by the import of a particular product. It has also been shown that animosity towards a foreign country could have a strong effect on the product choice by the consumer.

However, the generalized concept of ethnocentric tendencies among consumers to explain consumers' rejection of foreign-made products has been refuted. More recent findings show that country of assembly and country of design both generally affect beliefs about products and attitudes towards buying them; however, the nature and directionality of these effects depend on the levels of consumer ethnocentric tendencies. Also, significant country effects for high and low ethnocentric consumers have been noted; however, no effects were found among moderately ethnocentric consumers.

The situation which applies for domestic firms and marketers when contemplating exporting their products (either 'goods' or 'services') to foreign countries, obviously, also applies for international companies contemplating entry into the 'domestic' market. In the discussion that follows, these issues will be tested in the context of foreign companies contemplating entry into a multicultural market such as Australia. More specifically, what is the likely response of consumers to their products? Further, to what extent should their products (or their production) be modified to reflect the attitudes, demands and perceptions of multi-ethnic consumers? As with many similar and familiar questions in marketing, the answer is likely to begin: 'It all depends . . .'

The remainder of this chapter will seek to 'flesh out' this conclusion and also to explore its implications for marketers.

6.6 International and Global Brands

According to McCarthy and Perreault (1987), branding started during the middle ages – when craft guilds (similar to labour unions) and merchant guilds formed to control the quantity and quality of production. Each producer had to mark his goods so that output could be cut back when necessary. This also meant that poor quality – which might reflect unfavourably on other guild products and discourage future trade – could be traced back to their producer. Brands also served as important competitive strategies.

Today, brands still have a similar role – that is, to establish an awareness, recognition and identity, and with it goodwill that results in repeat purchase and loyalty. According to Usunier (2000), international brands share at least one common trait, that of long-term orientation. Companies like Procter and Gamble have retained brands for over a century, and, importantly, have equally taken time to build this recognition and recall capacity.

According to Shalofsky (1987) an important factor amongst international brands is that many of them have a *basic credibility* or reputation based on their countries of origin image. When one hears of names like Coca-Cola or Marlboro, one immediately associates these names with Americans, Paco Raban *pour hommes* and Chanel No. 5 are associated with the French, just as Toyota and Sony are associated with Japanese technological superiority.

When marketing one's products cross-culturally, the issue of 'what's in a name' takes on a completely new significance. For instance, when translated quite literally, brand names like Coca-Cola have had quite negative connotations in the Chinese language. Similarly, motor car names such as 'Nova' literally translated meaning 'No go' in Spanish were not surprisingly responsible for poor sales in the Latin American markets. Quite clearly in each society consumers repaint each supposed international brand image with their own local image (Clark, 1987).

Usurnier (2000) correctly points out that the interplay between brands and national images is a game of complex meanings, and that one needs to be cautious before assuming that a brand is universal.

According to Kotler and Dubois (1994), a primary pre-requisite for a brand to belong to the very small and exclusive club of global brands, is to have built brand equity over a number of years. This would have been achieved through extensive advertising spending on consistent advertising themes. The value of brands like Marlboro is estimated at $31 billion, Coca-Cola at $24 billion, and that of Kodak at $13 billion (Usunier, 2000).

Although some authors such as Peebles (1989) have advocated the concept and notion of global brands, others such as Usunier (2000) argue that the concept is somewhat blurred and could be deceptive (*Ibid.*, p. 340). The latter argues that global brands may in fact be portfolios comprised of localized marketing assets. Essentially, the argument is that the capital outlay and legal complications of managing global brands remain high. Therefore, when a company considers starting such an exercise from scratch, particularly with different cultures in mind, the company should prepare itself for a long tenure of tough marketing and other related activity, i.e. a long-term orientation.

6.7 Implications for Cross-cultural Product Strategy

There are several implications for cross-cultural strategy presented in this chapter. The implications are discussed in the context of global villages. First, is the importance of understanding and appreciating the inherent differences and demands of differing markets. In particular, the important potential pitfalls which face companies that assume that the product mix does not require modification or adaptation from the 'domestic' market to reflect the differences and demands of the 'differing local or foreign' market.

Second, the chapter has considered the importance of managing the meaning of products as a consequence of the effects of 'country of origin' and 'ethnocentrism', and the implications for manufacturers operating in both domestic and international markets. In this context, a number of writers argue that a strong relationship exists between ethnocentrism and preference for domestic products. Whilst acknowledging this view, we also present an alternative view which suggests that an apparently weak relation between ethnocentrism and preference for domestic products exists. According to Elliott and Cameron (1994), this situation has important implications for 'Australian made' and other similar campaigns. For example, Elliott and Cameron (1994) have found that Australian consumers would generally prefer the Australian-made product.

However, where its quality and price are comparable to the imported competition, in the current circumstances, the objectives of the campaign to buy Australian-produced goods seem to be thwarted. Elliot and Cameron's study (1994) found that though moderately ethnocentric, consumers do not necessarily prefer to buy domestically assembled and designed products. Australian consumers appear to prefer to buy cars from Japan and jeans assembled and designed in the US. Only in the case of tinned pineapple was the domestic product the first choice. However, this choice might not simply be because the consumers are ethnocentric. It might be because the Australian people trust Australian foods more than food from another country (Rawlings, 1993) – a very plausible explanation.

Third, it appears that consumer ethnocentrism might not strongly influence purchasing decisions, especially for high-involvement products. In addition, a further interesting result is that the correlation between consumer ethnocentrism and the quality perception of domestically designed products is much lower than that between ethnocentrism and the domestically assembled product. This shows that the ethnocentric consumers rate domestic assembly of products as more important than the domestic design. This suggests that ethnocentric consumers might draw a stronger link between local manufacture and economic welfare (for example, in manufacturing employment), than the link with local design (and possibly foreign manufacture). Among ethnocentric consumers, any switch from domestic design and manufacture to merely domestic design could be expected to have adverse sales consequences.

Fourth, the chapter has presented the argument that in order to be successful, one has to be conscious of the possible existence of the 'home country bias'. This argument is based on the consistent thrust of past research on consumer ethnocentrism (Shimp and Sharma, 1987; Netemeyer *et al.*, 1991) that highly ethnocentric consumers will discard products from foreign countries. This finding however, is not conclusive.

Finally, the chapter has considered product implications, relating to the potential interrelationships between the 'country of origin' effects and the existence and potential importance of 'global brands' in international markets. Although some authors have advocated the notion, the concept remains somewhat blurred as to what constitutes global brands. Since the investment in global brands is so high, a company considering starting such an exercise from scratch, particularly with different cultures in mind, should adopt a long-term orientation.

REVIEW QUESTIONS

1. What does the term 'country of origin' effect mean? What are its implications for both importers and local manufacturers?

2. Similarly, what is implied in the 'home country bias' for both importers and local manufacturers?

3. What do you feel are the implications of the existence of strong consumer ethnocentrism (among certain consumer segments) for governments wishing to promote local manufacturing through 'Buy Local' advertising campaigns?

4. How would you explain the market dominance of some globally-branded products in markets where there is also a significant degree of 'consumer ethnocentrism'?

5. Similarly, what are the implications for international companies who market strong global brands when entering local markets where there is strong consumer ethnocentrism among some market segments?

6. In Australia, the fact that a product is produced by a company which is 'Australian-owned' is being increasingly used as a competitive claim against products which are 'Australian-made' but by companies which are foreign-owned. As the marketing manager for the 'foreign owned' company, how would you react to such claims?

7. In international marketing, an inevitable clash arises from the pursuit of efficiencies through 'economies of scale' in production and distribution against the imperative to modify the product to suit the preferences of the consumers in the local market. As the importer and marketer of foreign-made products, how would you resolve this issue in practice?

References

Acharya, C. and Elliott, G. (2000) 'Consumer ethnocentrism, perceived product quality and choice – an empirical investigation', *International Marketing Review*.

Ahmed, S. A. and d'Astous, A. (1996) 'Country-of-origin and brand effects: a multi-dimensional and multi-attribute study', *Journal of International Consumer Marketing* 9(2): 93–115.

Bagozzi, R. P., Rosa, J. A., Celly, K. S. and Coronel, F. (1998) *Marketing Management*, Upper Saddle River, NJ: Prentice Hall.

Bilkey, W. J. and Nes, E. (1982) 'Country-of-origin effects on product evaluations', *Journal of International Business Studies* 13 (Spring/Summer): 89–99.

Boddewyn, J. J., Soehl, R. and Picard, J. (1986) 'Standardization in international marketing: is Ted Levitt in fact right?' *Business Horizons* 29(6): 69–75.

Brodowsky, G. H. (1998) 'The effects of country of design and country of assembly on evaluative beliefs about automobiles and attitudes toward buying them: a comparison between low and high ethnocentric consumers', *Journal of International Consumer Marketing* 10(3): 85–113.

Cateora, P. R. (1996) *International Marketing*, 9th edn., Chicago: Richard D. Irwin.

Cateora, P. R. and Keaveney, S. (1987) *Marketing: An International Perspective*, Homewood, IL: Richard D. Irwin, Inc.

Daniels, J. D., Radebaugh, L. H. and Sullivan, D. P. (2002) *Globalization and Business*, Upper Saddle River, NJ: Prentice Hall.

Elliott, G. R. and Cameron, R. S. (1994) 'Consumer perception of product quality and the country-of-origin effect', *Journal of International Marketing* 2(2): 49–62.

Evans, J. R. and Berman, B. (1997) *Marketing*, Upper Saddle River, NJ: Prentice Hall.

Ferraro, G. (2002) *The Cultural Dimensions of International Business*, Upper Saddle River, NJ: Prentice-Hall.

Fishman, A. (1990) 'International mail order guide', *Direct Marketing* (October).

Griffin, T. (1993) *International Marketing Communications*, Oxford: Butterworth-Heinemann Ltd.

Gronroos, C. (1991) 'The marketing strategy continuum: towards a marketing concept for the 1990s', *Management Decision*, 29(1): 7–14.

Hall, E. T. (1960) 'The silent language in overseas business', *Harvard Business Review* (May–June): 87–96.

Hall, E. T. (1976) 'How cultures collide', *Psychology Today* (July): 66–97.

Hawkins, D. I.,. Best, R. J. and Coney, K. A. (2001) *Consumer Behavior: Building Marketing Strategy*, New York: McGraw-Hill.

Han, M. C. and Terpstra, V. (1988) 'Country-of-origin effects for uni-national and bi-national products', *Journal of International Business Studies* (Summer): 235–254.

Herche, J. (1990) 'The measurement of consumer ethnocentrism: revising the CETSCALE', in B. J. Dunlap and N. C. Cullowhee (eds.) *Developments in Marketing Science*, Academy of Marketing Science, XIII, 371–375.

Hofstede, G. H. (1984) *Culture's Consequences: International Differences in Work-Related Values*, Beverly Hills, CA: Sage Publications.

Hofstede, G. (1991) *Cultures and Organizations: Software of the Mind*, London: McGraw Hill.

Hofstede, G. H. (1983) 'National cultures in four dimensions: a research-based theory of cultural differences among nations', *International Studies of Management and Organizations* 13(1–2): 46–74.

Hollensen, S. (1998) *Global Marketing: A Market-Responsive Approach*, New York: Prentice Hall.

Ishikawa, M. (1987) 'Latest trends in Japanese advertising', Paper presented at the Fifteenth World Industrial Advertising Congress, Brussels.

Iyer, G. R. and Kalita, J. K. (1997) 'The impact of country-of-origin and country-of-manufacture clues on consumer perceptions of quality and value', *Journal of Global Marketing* 11(1): 7–28.

Keegan, W. J. and Green, M. S. (2000) *Global Marketing*, New York: Prentice Hall.

Klein, J. G., Ettenson, R. and Morris, M. D. (1998) 'The animosity model of foreign product purchase: an empirical test in the People's Republic of China', *Journal of Marketing* 62(1): 89–112.

Klenosky, D. B., Benet, S. B. and Chadraba, P. (1996) 'Assessing Czech consumers' reactions to Western marketing practices – a conjoint approach', *Journal of Business Research* 36: 189–198.

Kluckhohn, F. R. and Strodtbeck, F. L. (1961) *Variations in Value Orientations*, New York: Harper & Row.

Kotler, P. (2001) *Marketing Management*, Upper Saddle River, NJ: Prentice Hall.

Kramer, H. E. and Herbig, P. A. (1993) 'The Suq model of haggling: who, what, when, why?', *Journal of International Consumer Marketing* 5(2): 55–69.

Levitt, T. (1983) 'Globalization of markets', *Harvard Business Review* 61(3): 69–81.

Liefeld, J. P., Heslop, L. A., Papadopoulos, N. and Wall, M. (1996) 'Dutch consumer use of intrinsic, country-of-origin, and price cues in product evaluation and choice', *Journal of International Consumer Marketing* 9(1): 57–81.

Louviere, J. L. (1988) *Analyzing Decision Making*, Newbury Park, CA: Sage Publications.

Lynn, M., Zinkhan, G. M. and Harris, J. (1993) 'Consumer tipping: a cross-country study', *Journal of Consumer Research* 20(3): 478–488.

McCarthy, E. J. (1960) *Basic Marketing: A Managerial Approach*, 1st edn. Homewood, IL: Irwin.

Maheswaran, D. (1994) 'Country-of-origin as a stereotype: effects of consumer expertise and attribute strength on product evaluations', *Journal of Consumer Research* 21(2): 354–365.

Monroe, K. B. and Lee, A. Y. (1999) 'Remembering versus knowing: issues in buyers' processing of price information', *Journal of the Academy of Marketing Science* 27: 207–225.

Montgomery, D. B. (1991) 'Understanding the Japanese as customers, competitors and collaborators', *Japan and the World Economy* 3(1): 61–91.

Nes, E. and Bilkey, W. J. (1993) ' A Multi-cue test of country-of-origin theory', in N. Papadopoulos and L. A. Heslop (eds), *Product Country Images: Impact and Role in International Marketing*, New York: International Business Press. pp. 179–196.

Netemeyer, R. G., Durvasula, S. and Lichtenstein, D. R. (1991) 'A cross-national assessment of the reliability and validity of the CETSCALE', *Journal of Marketing Research* XXVII (August): 320–327.

Okechuku, C. (1994) 'The importance of product country of origin: a conjoint analysis of the United States, Canada, Germany, and the Netherlands', *European Journal of Marketing* 18(4): 5–19.

de Mooij, M. (1998) *Global Marketing and Advertising: Understanding Cultural Paradoxes*, Thousand Oaks, CA: Sage Publications Inc.

Murphy, J. H. and Cunningham, I. C. M. (1993) *Advertising and Marketing Communication*, New York: The Dryden Press.

Papadopoulos, N., Heslop, L. A. and Bamossy, G. J. (1989) 'International competitiveness of American and Japanese products', in N. Papadopoulos (ed.), *Dimensions of International Business*, volume 2, Ottawa, Canada: International Business Study Group, Carlton University.

Papadopoulos, N., Heslop, L. A. and Bamossy, G. J. (1990) 'A comparative analysis of domestic versus imported products', *International Journal of Research in Marketing* 7(4).

Parente, D. (2000) Advertising Campaign Strategy: A Guide to Marketing Communications Plans, New York: The Dryden Press.

Pereira, P. (1999) 'E-business washes into Latin America', *Computer Reseller News* 873 (December 13): 5.

Ricks, D. A. (1993) *Blunders in International Business*, Cambridge, MA: Blackwell Publishers.

Schultz, D. E., Tannenbaum, S. and Lauterborn, R. F. (1993) *Integrated Marketing Communications: Pulling It All Together and Making It Work*, Lincolnwood, IL: NTC Business Books.

Sharma, S., Shimp, T. A. and Shin, J. (1995) 'Consumer ethnocentrism: a test of antecedents and moderators', *Journal of the Academy of Marketing Science* 23(1): 26–37.

Shimp, T. A. and Sharma, S. (1987) 'Consumer ethnocentrism: construction and validation of the CETSCALE', *Journal of Marketing Research* XXIV (August): 280–289.

Tellis, G. (1998) *Advertising and Sales Promotion Strategy*, New York: Addison-Wesley.

Terpstra, V. (1988) *International Dimensions of Marketing*, 2nd edn., Boston: PWS-Kent Publishing Company.

Toyne, B. and Walters, P. G. P. (1993) *Global Marketing Management: A Strategic Perspective*, Boston: Allyn and Bacon.

Thakor, M. V. and Katsanis, L. P. (1997) 'A model of brand and country effects on quality dimensions: issues and implications', *Journal of International Consumer Marketing* 9(3): 79–100.

Wall, M. and Heslop, L. A. (1986) 'Consumer attitudes toward Canadian-made versus imported products', *Journal of Academy of Marketing Science* 14(2): 27–36.

Usunier, J.-C. (2000) *Marketing Across Cultures*, London: Prentice Hall Europe.

CHAPTER 7

Cross-cultural pricing issues

Michael Callow and Dawn Lerman

LEARNING OBJECTIVES

At the end of this chapter readers will be able to:

▶ Gain an overview of existing research in the area of cross-cultural pricing as it relates to business practices and consumer purchasing behaviour.

▶ Understand recent developments around the world that are likely to have a significant impact on cross-cultural pricing strategies and consumer purchasing habits in the future, namely, the launch of the Euro, international tourism and global e-commerce.

7.1 Introduction

Pricing can be one of the more powerful weapons in a firm's competitive arsenal, since it is directly linked to corporate sales and profits. Developing an appropriate international pricing strategy is therefore a vital – yet invariably highly complex – managerial decision. Indeed, managers judge international pricing to be among the most crucial decisions in their business practice (Gaul and Lutz, 1994; Myers, 1997). Academic research in international pricing has focused on four main areas (Stottinger, 2001): (i) microeconomic issues (e.g. price elasticities of demand); (ii) export pricing issues (e.g. price escalation); (iii) internal pricing issues (e.g. transfer pricing); and (iv) consumer-oriented issues (e.g. consumer reference prices). Of the various internal and external elements that shape a company's pricing strategy, culture has received perhaps the least attention. There is a tendency to assume that pricing is primarily an economic issue that, in conjunction with quality, helps create value, and therefore culture is not a major determinant of pricing strategies. Quite to the contrary, current research in cross-cultural pricing suggests that the relative importance of culture on pricing is largely under-appreciated and that cultural differences can have a significant effect on not only the types of pricing strategies that corporations select, but also on the consumer's response to these pricing strategies.

7.2   Streams of Research in Cross-cultural Pricing

Price has achieved relatively little attention by cross-cultural researchers in comparison to the other elements of the marketing mix. Of the research that has been conducted in this area, the focus has been on comparing: (i) consumer shopping and purchasing experiences; (ii) consumer biases towards the value of foreign-made products and foreign-based brands; and (iii) the various pricing strategies used by companies from different countries.

Consumer Shopping and Purchasing Experiences

Cross-cultural research in retailing suggests that shopping is a social event shaped by culture that goes far beyond a simple economic transaction (Miller *et al.*, 1998). Researchers have used Hofstede's individualism and collectivism dimension of culture to help explain potential cross-cultural differences in the purchase of products used for private and public consumption.

Products that are purchased for private consumption are generally considered of less importance among consumers from collectivist cultures than among consumers from individualist cultures. The Chinese consumer, in particular, is viewed as a price-conscious and pragmatic shopper who places less emphasis on material possessions than consumers from more individualist-oriented cultures (Li and Gallup, 1995; Ackerman and Tellis, 2001). This increased price sensitivity among collectivists may help explain why price haggling is so widely accepted in retail stores in places like Hong Kong, Taiwan and Singapore (Fang, 1999). Furthermore, a recent study by Ackerman and Tellis (2001) found that Chinese-American consumers tended to take more time shopping around and on average examined more items per product purchased than mainstream American shoppers. Their study also revealed that supermarkets catering towards the Chinese-American market had consistently lower prices than the mainstream supermarkets in order to accommodate the increased price sensitivity and comparison shopping behaviour of their market segment.

Cross-national price perception research also suggests that people from collectivist cultures are more inclined than those from individualist cultures to take into account face considerations (Zhou and Nakamoto, 2001). Face consideration refers to a person's desire to enhance, maintain and avoid losing face in social activities. This cultural factor helps explain why in countries such as China there are strong social needs that make consumers pay more attention to public considerations as opposed to private considerations when purchasing a product (Belk, 1988; Zhou and Nakamoto, 2001). In more individualistic cultures, on the other hand, purchasing decisions are encouraged to be made individually, with less consideration to others, and are more likely to reflect the private will of the consumer.

Products that are purchased for public consumption (for example, gifts) are of considerable importance in collectivist cultures (Ahuvia and Wong, 1998). In this instance, social recognition is more important in collectivist cultures than in individualist cultures, and high prices are strongly associated with the high status of a product or brand. Similar results have been found among Japanese consumers, suggesting that the Japanese will purchase more expensive items and brands when shopping for guests rather than themselves in order to look good in the eyes of the guests (McGowan and Sternquist, 1998).

There is some research suggesting that the use of price as an indicator of quality or value is a marketing universal that occurs across various cultures and that the standardization of pricing strategies across markets is therefore a viable and desirable strategic option. The work by McGowan and Sternquist (1998) points to a universal relationship between price and quality as well as value consciousness. They found that a segment of consumers from Japan and the United States associated higher prices with better product quality and/or brand prestige. At the same time, they found evidence of a segment of consumers in both countries that exhibited more negative perceptions of price relating to value consciousness (the higher the price, the lower the chance that the consumer will purchase the product). This would imply that global marketers could employ standardized pricing and positioning strategies that targeted either the positive or the negative perceptions of price among consumers. However, one could also argue that the relative importance of these two segments within a country may vary based on the predominant cultural value system. Indeed, a study by Maxwell (2001a) found significant differences in the importance and meaning of brands and prices among consumers from India and America. When compared to Americans, Indian consumers are more value conscious, which may be explained by the fact that they feel a certain degree of guilt about consumption.

In another study, Agarwal and Teas (2001) found evidence suggesting that the importance of price as a signal of quality varies from culture to culture. They found that Belgian respondents were more inclined to use price primarily as an indicator of the quality of wristwatches, whereas American and Swedish respondents would look at brand and store name as well as price to attribute quality. Their research does indicate support for the existence of marketing universals across cultures in terms of the way that consumers process information. For instance, they found positive relationships between perceived quality, perceived value, and willingness to buy, and a negative relationship between perceived sacrifice and perceived value across the three cultures. However, their results suggest that the types of signals used to impute perceived value differ in importance from one culture to another.

There is some research suggesting that culture may also play a role in a consumer's attribution for higher than expected prices (Maxwell, 2001b). In individualist-oriented countries, consumers are prone to placing blame on the retailer for this negative outcome. In collectivist-oriented countries, on the other hand, the consumer is less likely to blame the retailer. Furthermore, the consumer in the collectivist-oriented country is more likely than the consumer from the individualist-oriented country to purchase an item that has a higher than expected price.

Another cultural factor that influences how consumers perceive pricing strategies is Hall's (1989) high versus low context framework. In high-context cultures (e.g. China), people tend to read into what is not being said as much as what is being said. In low-context cultures (e.g. America), people rely on explicit cues to derive information. Consumers from high-context countries, therefore, are more likely to question sales and coupon promotions, wondering for instance whether the product on sale is defective or of inferior quality. Consumers from low-context societies, on the other hand, will view these types of promotions as a simple reduction in price that makes the purchase more of a bargain. This may explain why sale and coupon promotions are highly successful in America and less so in China (Zhou and Nakamoto, 2001).

Finally, there is some initial research suggesting that the visual appeal of pricing numbers may differ cross-culturally. Suri, Anderson and Kotlov (2001) found that the highly popular strategy of using 9-ending prices (e.g. $29.99) in the United States is not well received in Polish markets. This finding highlights the importance of considering every aspect of the pricing strategy to determine what can be standardized and what should be customized when operating in a cross-national environment.

Country-of-origin Biases

Consumers across the world often do hold positive or negative biases towards a product's country-of-origin, which may determine a foreign product's pricing strategy (Keegan, 2002). Multinational corporations often charge premium prices for their products in countries where consumers have a preference for foreign products. For example, Budweiser is positioned as a superpremium import beer in Britain, whereas it is positioned as a value domestic brand in the United States. British consumers therefore pay more than double the price for a six-pack of Bud compared to their American counterparts.

The country of manufacture can also play an important role in determining the consumer's perceived risk of purchase and how much he or she is therefore willing to pay. A study by Witt and Rao (1992) found that American consumers perceived greater risk in purchasing Mexican-made jeans and microwave ovens compared to American-made ones, even though the products made in Mexico were American brands. This would imply that the Mexican-made jeans or microwaves would have to be significantly lower priced than the American-made jeans in order to overcome the consumer's uncertainty regarding the quality of Mexican-made products. At the same time, it suggests that manufacturers should consider country-of-origin effects when outsourcing or relocating factory facilities abroad. It is also important to remember that the image of a particular country may vary around the world, and will likely depend on the product category (Keegan, 2002).

Cultural Comparison of Pricing Strategies

The few studies that have made cross-cultural comparisons of pricing strategies do indicate differences in how businesses from different countries set prices. For instance, Li and Noble (1999) compared industrial pricing strategies used by Singaporean firms relative to US firms in terms of the conditions facing the companies at the time decisions were made. Additionally, in Islamic countries the religious notion of legitimacy that encourages fair dealings and reasonable levels of profits in business means that companies often operate under a profit-satisficing pricing strategy instead of a profit-maximizing pricing strategy (Jeannet and Hennessey, 1998). Finally, Japanese multinational corporations have traditionally employed a price penetration strategy for entering markets, whereas American firms have conventionally employed a price skimming strategy. The price penetration strategy reflects the Japanese emphasis on long-term goals measured by market share. The price skimming strategy reflects the American emphasis on short-term results measured by the corporation's stock value. However, nowadays corporations from both countries often use a combination of price penetration and price skimming strategies depending on market conditions.

Overall, current research on cross-cultural issues in pricing has been scarce. The above sections highlight the main research that has been conducted in this area. These studies suggest that culture does have an effect on price in terms of how it is perceived by the consumer and how it is set by the company. However, a lot more research into this area is needed to further our knowledge on the cross-cultural effect on pricing issues.

7.3   Recent Developments in Cross-cultural Pricing

International marketing textbooks will invariably discuss the growing internationalization or globalization process facing corporations. It is important to remember, however, that the *consumer* is also being affected by this internationalization process through exposure to foreign products and brands at home and abroad and through increasing regionalization of international markets. Some argue that this increased exposure to international brands, products and media has made consumers from all around the world more homogeneous (see, for example, Levitt, 1983). The degree to which a firm should therefore standardize – as opposed to customize – the marketing mix continues to spark lively debate among practitioners and academics (see, for instance, Levitt's article proposing standardization or the article by Boddewyn *et al*. (1986) proposing customization). There is general consensus that true homogenization of cultures will not take place in the foreseeable future. Cultural issues are therefore of paramount importance to the marketer in most aspects of the marketing mix, including pricing. It is also important to remember that cultures change over time, each in their own way.

Managers must understand how to adapt their pricing strategies to reflect this change in the international marketplace. It could be argued, however, that the main cross-cultural issue affecting price is the currency itself. It is important to remember that a nation's currency is part of the culture's symbolic system and that consumer purchasing decisions are indeed affected by the shopper's culture. How else can we explain the recent debate over the Euro and whether its implementation signifies the end of each member state's national identity? Countries use an established currency that consumers take for granted when determining the worth of transactions. A major cross-cultural issue of late is the consumer's exposure to new currencies in the local and international shopping environment. Three current international pricing issues addressed in this chapter that relate to the consumer's exposure to a new currency are: (i) the adoption of the Euro in the retail environment; (ii) pricing dilemmas facing the tourist abroad; and (iii) making purchases from foreign corporations across the internet.

International Tourism: Dealing with Unfamiliar Pricing Environments

The number of consumers making purchases in foreign markets whilst travelling abroad is on the rise. Of fundamental importance to this cross-cultural shopping exchange is the tourist's general lack of familiarity with the shopping environment.

Three issues of particular concern are: (1) the tourist's ability to evaluate prices in foreign currencies; (2) differences in cross-national tipping behaviour; and (3) cultural attitudes towards price haggling.

Consumer Unfamiliarity with Foreign Currencies

Cross-cultural differences in the currency's denomination have an impact on the consumer's evaluation of the host country's pricing strategies. The spot rate for the Turkish lira to the US dollar in July 2001 was approximately 1,300,000 lira. This means that something costing $15 would be priced at 19,500,000 lira. Turkey's currency therefore reflects a high denomination currency, whereas the US currency would be considered a low denomination currency (see Figure 7.1).

According to the information-processing model, consumers develop acceptable price ranges for products based on a subjective or psychological judgment scale that is influenced – amongst other things – by previous pricing experience (Monroe and Lee, 1999). It is likely, therefore, that consumers will rely on previous experiences with their own currency when evaluating prices in the foreign currency. Indeed, tourists often convert prices from the foreign currency into their own currency, in order to evaluate the value of the offer relative to internal reference prices that were developed in the home market. Current exchange rates therefore play a vital role in determining whether products abroad are seen as inexpensive or expensive. Indeed, American tourists prefer to travel to Europe when the dollar is strong relative to European currencies, since their money will go a lot further than where the dollar is weak. It should be noted that the actual prices in Europe are not changing and are generally a lot more expensive than in America, but the American tourists perceive the prices to be lower given a favourable exchange rate.

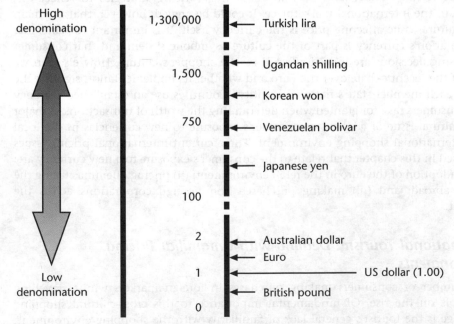

Figure 7.1 Countries with high versus low denomination currencies (based on July 2001 spot rates).

A study by Callow and Lerman (2001) examined the relationship between the consumer's home country currency denomination and the foreign country's currency denomination when evaluating price discounts abroad. Their study investigated whether significant discrepancies between the home country and the host country's currency denomination would lead to different types of evaluations regarding price discounts. The authors proposed that consumers familiar with a low denomination currency (for example, Americans) travelling abroad are more likely to be swayed by price discounts in countries with high denomination currencies (for example, Turkey), than by price discounts in countries with a similarly low denomination currencies (for example, Australia). In other words, a price discount of 13,000,000 lira looks and sounds a lot more impressive than a $10 discount! The researchers found that American respondents who were shown price discounts in a high denomination currency exhibited greater perceptions of price fairness, lower perceptions of product expensiveness and a higher purchase intention than American respondents who were shown percentage equivalent price discounts in a low denomination currency. These differences were obtained even thought the respondents were given exact exchange rate information for both the high and the low denomination currencies and could therefore have converted the price discounts into US dollars.

Callow and Lerman (2001) also hypothesize that consumers from high denomination currencies such as Turkey and South Korea, who are unaccustomed to low denomination currencies, would have much higher pricing differential thresholds and would therefore be less susceptible to price variations abroad, and may therefore perceive the price of competitive brands to be similar when in fact they vary considerably.

The research by Callow and Lerman suggests that the international tourist may be at a disadvantage compared to local shoppers when evaluating and comparing prices displayed in foreign currencies. The advent of the credit card has hardly made matters any easier. An English friend of one of the co-authors recently purchased a painting in South Africa for 6990 rand, or what he imagined to be approximately £60. Unfortunately, his currency conversion calculations were off by one decimal place (£1 was at that time worth approximately 11.8 rand), a fact that he learned upon arrival of his credit card bill a month later in London. In fact, the true price of the painting was close to £600! The potential for confusion is therefore an important issue confronting consumer advocacy groups and retailers catering for the international tourism market in terms of the type of pricing information that can and should be made available to potential customers in order for them to process the information as they would in their home market.

Cross-cultural Differences in Consumer Tipping Behaviour

Another transaction issue that often varies from one culture to another, and is therefore likely to confuse the consumer when travelling abroad, is the tradition of tipping. A tip, or gratuity, is a gift or sum of money tendered for a service performed or anticipated. The word 'tip' is an acronym for 'to insure promptness', although in some cultures tipping is viewed as an integral part of a person's wages. For instance, tipping is a widespread phenomenon in the USA, and consumers often pay that little bit extra for services rendered from waiters, porters, taxi drivers, mailmen, paper couriers, etc. In other cultures, tipping is not a part of the transaction process or is assumed to be already included in the price. In Britain, Japan and France, a standard service charge is usually included in restaurant or hotel bills. Research by Lynn, Zinkhan and Harris (1993) suggests that cross-country differences in the prevalence of tipping reflect cross-country differences in values (Lynn, Zinkhan and Harris, 1993). The amount to tip also varies from one culture to another. In America, tips at a restaurant usually range between 15–20 per cent, whereas in Italy it is 10 per cent (data from *The Original Tipping Page* at <www.tipping.org>). The type of tip given for a service may also differ from one country to another. In Britain, for instance, customers at a pub may purchase an additional drink for the bartender (to be consumed after-hours!), whereas in the United States customers will often leave their spare change at the bar.

Cross-cultural Attitudes towards Price Haggling

Haggling is generally an economic process with the goal of seeking a common solution acceptable to all sides through bargaining (Kramer and Herbig, 1993). As with tipping, the propensity to haggle varies from culture to culture. In many Latin American countries, for instance, cultural attitudes favour price haggling (Pereira, 1999). In Europe and the USA, on the other hand, haggling is not as common. This means that they are less accustomed to the haggling experience and on average end up paying more than necessary for products in countries where haggling is an important part of the shopping experience.

The types of products that a consumer can haggle for will also vary from one country to another. The American consumer is conditioned to bargain at used car dealerships and flea markets. Consumers in the Middle East, on the other hand, expect to haggle for a wide variety of products at the market bazaar. The bargaining process itself may also vary from one culture to another. Research on this issue by Kramer and Herbig (1993) suggests that the *suq* model of haggling employed in the Middle East differs markedly from the traditional haggling seen in Western cultures. In the West, haggling is seen as a means for achieving the best deal, whereas in the Middle East it is seen as a social process for pursuing and establishing personal relationships. Western tourists visiting the Middle East, therefore, will be at a cultural disadvantage since they are likely to be unfamiliar with the complexities of this type of price haggling.

Pricing on the Internet

The final pricing issue that this chapter addresses relating to the consumer's exposure to a new currency is the emergence of international e-business. The Internet has meant increased global exposure for businesses and consumers alike. Domestic companies expand internationally simply by going on-line and investing in e-business. At the same time, consumers can expand their shopping horizons by using the Internet to search for the best deals and expose themselves to e-tailers from around the world. There is still a certain degree of cultural resistance to shopping online, especially among those cultures that favour price haggling and face-to-face transactions (Pereira, 1999). However, the multicultural nature of the Internet is becoming more and more apparent as consumers from around the world gain access to the worldwide web. American e-tailers can no longer assume that their audience is the American consumer; consumers from places such as England, Canada, Australia, Germany and

Hong Kong can also access their websites. E-tailers are therefore being forced to consider not only whether international purchases should be permitted, but also how culture-friendly their website content should be.

The interactive nature of the Internet allows web designers to tailor web page content depending on the consumer's nationality. A good example of a global web page is Nike's website at <www.nike.com>. The company's global website lets the consumer choose between four different geographic regions: North America, Europe, Asia Pacific and Latin America. The product content and information is tailored for each region. In Europe, the content is tailored towards soccer merchandise, whereas in North America it is tailored towards merchandise from the NBA, the NFL, the PGA and other major American professional sporting events. Nike's website also allows you to select a particular language (you can select Spanish, German, French, English or Italian in the European region). Online purchases can be made through the North American, Asian Pacific and European regions, but currently not on the Latin American website. In the European online store, shoppers are asked to identify their country before entering the store for delivery, price and tax reasons. A *Fútbol Club Barcelona* soccer shirt, for instance, would cost an English shopper £40 online, whereas it would cost a Spanish shopper Ptas. 9,995. Using the current exchange rate of Ptas. 267.93/£1, this means that the British consumer is paying £3.70 more than the Spanish consumer. There is little – if any – overlap of merchandise available for sale between the three geographic regions; the Barcelona soccer shirt is not available for purchase online in North America or Asia Pacific.

It seems, then, that companies with a presence on the Internet have imposed restrictions on where purchases can be made from, the types of products that can be purchased, and at what price. In other words, the Internet is similar to the physical environment when it comes to international marketing. Surprisingly, the Internet appears to be more restrictive on international consumers than in the real world. It is possible for British tourists to purchase a Nike sports shirt at a lower price when holidaying in Spain, yet they can only make the purchase online at the Spanish price if it is to be delivered to a Spanish postal address.

7.4 Conclusion

This chapter has addressed various cross-cultural aspects affecting price. Unfortunately, very little research has been conducted in this area. Previous studies on cross-cultural pricing have compared consumer shopping and purchasing experiences, consumer biases towards foreign-owned brands and foreign-produced products, and corporate pricing strategies across various countries. Their findings highlight culture's impact on corporations and consumers alike. The chapter has also looked at currency as the consumer's cultural frame of reference for determining worth and discussed the cultural shock of the Euro, international tourism and global e-commerce on the consumer.

REVIEW QUESTIONS

1. How do you think that your own cultural identity influences your shopping experience? How would your shopping experience differ if you were shopping for a birthday gift for: (a) a close relative (brother, sister, father, etc.); (b) a friend; and (c) yourself. What would you purchase, where, how long would it take to shop, how brand conscious would you be, what would be your price range? Would you care if people found out how much the gift cost you? Which shopping characteristics do you feel are culturally determined, and why? If possible, compare your answers with someone from another country.

2. Select a product category in which both imported and domestic brands compete in your country (for example, cars, wine, cheese, etc.). Compare prices between the imported and domestic brands and evaluate their positioning strategies. Are there any country-of-origin biases towards the imported and domestic brands? Are these biases reflected in the pricing strategies adopted by the various imports and domestic brands?

3. The introduction of the Euro has renewed interest in the creation of a single currency for the United States and Europe. The so-called 'eurodollar' would replace existing national currencies. Do you think that this is a viable proposal given today's economic, political and cultural climate? Develop a list of advantages and disadvantages for creating a single currency for Europe and the United States.

4. In 1993, the US consumer electronics retailer giant Circuit City opened its first CarMax superstore. As of June 2001 it operated 40 used-car and new-car superstores and was currently the largest car retailer in the United States. Circuit City credits its success to consumer preference for the company's no-haggle pricing policy and friendly shopping environment. Would you as a consumer prefer to shop for a car at a dealership that is willing to negotiate pricing terms, or would you prefer to purchase your car at a place where the price is fixed? Explain your preference. If possible, compare your answer with someone from another country.

5. Visit various national and global brand websites and determine whether they have a domestic, multinational or global orientation. Select three websites that sell their merchandise online and determine how many countries they cater to. How much overlap is there between the selection of merchandise sold in each country? Using current exchange rates, compare prices between countries for various overlapping merchandise.

References

Ackerman, D. and Tellis, G. (2001) 'Can culture affect prices? A cross-cultural study of shopping and retail prices', *Journal of Retailing* 77(1): 57–82.

Agarwal, S. and Teas, R. K. (2001) 'Quality cues and perceptions of quality, sacrifice, value, and willingness-to-buy: an examination of cross-national applicability', *Iowa State University Working Paper* 37-1b.

Ahuvia, A. and Wong, N. (1998) 'The effect of cultural orientation in luxury consumption', *Advances in Consumer Research*, edited by Eric J. Arnould and Linda M. Scott, 25, Ann Arbor, MI: Association for Consumer Research, pp. 29–32.

Antweiler, W. (2001) 'The EURO: Europe's new currency', PACIFIC Exchange Rate Service, <http://pacific.commerce.ubc.ca/xr/euro/menu.html>.

BBC News Online (2001) 'Euro and the consumer', Business Section, Thursday, 31 May.

Beirne, C., Fitzpatrick, M., Lengvel, Z. and Richards, M. 'The estimated total one-off costs to the UK private and public sectors, should the UK join the Euro', Report prepared for Business for Sterling by Chantrey Vellacot DFK.

Belk, R. W. (1988) 'Third World consumer culture', *Marketing and Developments*, edited by Wrdogan Kumcu and A. Fuat Firat, Greenwich, CT: JAI, pp. 103–127.

Boddewyn, J. J., Soehl, R. and Picard, J. (1986) 'Standardization in international marketing: is Ted Levitt in fact right?', *Business Horizons* 29(6): 69–75.

Cateora, P. R. and Graham, J. L. (1999) *International Marketing*, 10th edn., New York: Irwin/ McGraw-Hill.

Cooper, H. and Sesit, M. R. (1998) 'International news: devaluation fails to fuel export boom – absence of thriving markets appears partly to blame', *Wall Street Journal*, New York; October 8, Eastern edition, page 1.

Fang, T. (1999) *Chinese Business Negotiating Style*, Thousand Oaks, CA: Sage Publications Inc.

Gaul, W. and Lutz, U. (1994) 'Pricing in international marketing and Western European economic integration', *Management International Review* 34(2): 101–124.

Hall, E. T. (1989) *Beyond Culture*, New York: Anchor Books.

Hofstede, G. (1991) *Culture and Organizations: Software of the Mind*, New York: McGraw-Hill.

Jeannet, J.-P. and Hennessey, H. D. (1998) *Global Marketing Strategies*, 4th edn., Boston: Houghton Mifflin Company.

Keegan, W. J. (2002) *Global Marketing Management*, 7th edn., Upper Saddle River, NJ: Prentice Hall.

Knox, A. (1999) 'Pricing in Euroland', *World Trade* 12(1): 52–56.

Kramer, H. E. and Herbig, P. A. (1993) 'The *suq* model of haggling: who, what, when, why?, *Journal of International Consumer Marketing* 5(2): 55–69.

Laffer, A. B. (2001) 'Europe must reverse the Euro's slide', *Wall Street Journal*, New York; July 19, Eastern Edition, page A22.

Levitt, T. (1983) 'Globalization of markets', *Harvard Business Review* 61(3): 69–81.

Li, D. and Gallup ,A. M. (1995) 'In Search of the Chinese consumer', *Chinese Business Review* 22 (September/October): 19–23.

Li, J. C. A. and Noble, P. M. (1999) 'Pricing strategies for industrial goods in Singapore and the US: same or different?', *The Asia Pacific Journal of Management* 16 (August): 293–303.

Littlechild, M. and Gunde, L. (1999) 'The cost of price transparency', *Accountancy* 123(1265): 40.

Lynn, M., Zinkhan, G. M. and Harris, J. (1993) 'Consumer tipping: a cross-country study', *Journal Of Consumer Research* 20(3): 478–488.

Maehr, M. L. (1976) 'Sociocultural origins of achievement', in *Basic Concepts in Educational Psychology Series*, series editor L. R. Goulet, Monterey, CA: Brooks/Cole.

Maxwell, S. (2001a) 'An expanded price/brand effect model: a demonstration of heterogeneity in global consumption', forthcoming in *International Marketing Review*, Special Edition edited by Naresh Malhotra.

Maxwell, S. (2001b) 'Biased Attributions of a Higher than Expected Price: A Cross-Cultural Analysis', EMAC 2001 Conference.

McGowan, K. M. and Sternquist, B. J. (1998) 'Dimensions of price as a marketing universal: a comparison of Japanese and US consumers', *Journal of International Marketing* 6(4): 49–65.

Miller, D., Jackson, P., Thrift, N., Holbrook, B. and Rowlands, M. (1998) *Shopping, Place and Identity*, New York: Routledge.

Monroe, K. B. and Lee, A. Y. (1999) 'Remembering versus knowing: issues in buyers' processing of price information', *Journal of the Academy of Marketing Science* 27: 207–225.

Mundell, R. A. (1961) 'A theory of optimum currency area', *American Economic Review* 51.

Myers, M. B. (1997) 'The pricing of export products: why aren't managers satisfied with the results?', *Journal of World Business* 32(3): 277–289.

Pereira, P. (1999) 'E-business washes into Latin America', *Computer Reseller News* 873 (December 13): 5.

Ricci, L. A. (1997) 'A model of an optimum currency area', working paper of the International Monetary Fund, June, WP/97/76.

Schiffman, L. G. and Kanuk, L. L. (2000) *Consumer Behavior*, 7th edn., Upper Saddle River, NJ: Prentice Hall.

Stottinger, B. (2001) 'Strategic export pricing: a long and winding road', *Journal of International Marketing* 9(1): 40–63.

Suri, R., Anderson, R. E. and Kotlov, V. (2001) 'Comparison of the popularity of 9-ending prices in the US and Poland', *Advances in Consumer Research* 28, edited by Mary C. Gilly and Joan Meyers-Levy, Valdosta, GA: Association for Consumer Research, p. 141.

Taylor, B. (1998) 'The Eurodollar', *Global Financial Data*, <http://www.globalfindata.com/articles/euro.htm>.

Wentz, L. and Mussey, D. (1999) 'European marketers await pricing effect of the Euro', *Advertising Age* 70(2): 6.

Witt, J. and Rao, C. P. (1992) 'The impact of global sourcing on consumers: country-of-origin effects on perceived risk', *Journal of Global Marketing* 6(3): 105–128.

Zhou, Z. and Nakamoto, K. (2001) 'Price perceptions: a cross-national study between American and Chinese young consumers', *Advances in Consumer Research* 28, edited by Mary C. Gilly and Joan Meyers-Levy, Valdosta, GA: Association for Consumer Research, pp. 161–168.

CHAPTER 8

Cross-cultural marketing channels

Robert Rugimbana and Byron Keating

LEARNING OBJECTIVES

At the end of this chapter readers will be able to:

▶ Appreciate the catalytic role of marketing channels in a cross-cultural environment.
▶ Appreciate the existence of various distribution systems.
▶ Pinpoint the effective cross-cultural distribution mechanisms.
▶ Understand the specific issues that relate to distribution in global villages and multi-ethnic countries.

Consider the following Parable

Many years ago, there was an old man who lived in a remote village in the heart of Africa. This old man had three sons and was a donkey breeder by occupation. Breeding and selling donkeys was and is an important means of meeting subsistence transport needs in many parts of Africa. One day the old man told his three sons that in the event of his passing away, they would inherit his wealth of donkeys. He willed his first son, half (1/2) his wealth, his second son one third (1/3) and his third son one ninth (1/9). By and by the old man passed on. Immediately, the three sons set about dividing up the herd of donkeys according to their father's will. Their father had left them seventeen (17) donkeys. It was not long before the three sons realized that the task of dividing the odd number of donkeys was near impossible without having to slaughter some. Since none of the men wanted to slaughter the donkeys, heated arguments ensued in regards to how best to distribute their wealth. Since they could not reach a compromise they sought advice from a well-known wise old man who happened to be passing by on his own donkey.

The wise old man listened to the three sons carefully. After they had explained their dilemma he offered them his own donkey to be added to the seventeen (17), thus increasing the total to be divided up to eighteen (18) donkeys. The astonished men were then asked to proceed with the division of their extended wealth. The first son was asked to take half his allotted wealth, which now amounted to nine (9). Then the second son was asked to take his share, which amounted to six (6) donkeys and the third son two donkeys (2). In all, the sons had allotted themselves a total of 17 donkeys. The wise old man then took back the remaining donkey, which was his, and proceeded on his travels having resolved a major distribution problem.

(Anonymous)

8.1   Introduction

The above parable essentially outlines what the role of an effective marketing channel is. A marketing channel's main role is to catalyze the process of distributing goods and services as epitomized by the wise old man. The difficulty in coordinating the distribution function has seen it become a major source of competition when marketing overseas (Fletcher and Brown, 1999). This is because it is often time-consuming and expensive to establish effective distribution networks, and the relationships that support such networks. In many cases, the complexity of negotiating such arrangements can act as a barrier to the conduct of cross-cultural business, particularly in the case of smaller firms with limited financial and physical resources.

A marketing channel can be viewed as a large arterial network through which products, their ownership, communication, financing and payments flow. Various catalysts dictate this flow. These catalysts include: (1) various channel members; (2) sales promotion efforts; and (3) the sales force. These catalysts allow for the smooth flow of oftentimes complicated distribution processes, involving careful negotiations, buying and selling of products, and assisting in the change of ownership between buyers and sellers in the course of moving products from producers/suppliers to the end users.

Whereas the role and influence of intermediaries or catalysts such as sales promotion and the sales force are well explained and generally understood, albeit in a generic sense, the cultural perspective is less clearly understood. This chapter addresses the cultural perspective in an eclectic sense, since an exhaustive analysis is not possible. In the process, the chapter focuses from a cross-cultural perspective on two alternative distribution systems. The first, known as the informal distribution system, is more commonly associated with developing societies. The second is the more semi-formal distribution system found in Japan known as *Keiretsu*. The chapter discusses these systems with the view of illuminating the weaknesses of focusing too narrowly on the traditional frameworks for strategic positioning. These traditional approaches have been criticized for being too narrowly focused on *transactions* at the expense of the influence of customer characteristics and their cultures. This is particularly relevant where efforts to market to *global villages* are concerned. For instance, Gronroos (1991) contends that the future of marketing, particularly in the highly globalized marketplace, will require a relational focus that is premised largely on meeting the long-term needs and *orientations* of customers. The purpose of this chapter, therefore, is to consider how this element of the marketing mix applies to the cross-cultural marketing context. A discussion follows of the main strategic issues that need to be considered when applying distribution systems within and across different countries.

8.2 Alternative Types of Distribution Systems

Traditional international marketing textbooks will invariably discuss the growing internationalization or globalization process facing corporations in the context of distribution mechanisms typically utilized in Western (international) settings. The international settings, however, are far more complicated, with distribution systems that vary widely from the informal to the more complicated semi-formal systems such as those that exist in Japan. Since formal distribution settings are well-known, this chapter will focus more strongly and in an eclectic manner on the alternative systems proposed above, which often coexist side-by-side with the traditional distribution channel systems.

Informal distribution systems defined

Despite the number of studies on the informal distribution sectors in many different countries, there is still a lack of consensus on what the concept represents (Kulindwa, 1996; Omari, 1995). It is for this reason, perhaps, that there are various terminologies used to describe this sector, resulting in a multiplicity of meanings. Sethuraman (1976) argues that the controversial nature of the sector may partly explain its ambiguity and the lack of a clear-cut agreeable meaning of the concept.

Despite this lacuna, there appear to be at least two views in existence in regard to the sector. The first view, typically found in developed societies, describes this sector in somewhat negative connotations; that is, a grey market which represents a system of parallel importers, and therefore which threatens the viability of multinational firms and their channel partners.

Fletcher and Brown (1999: 366) refer to them as the practice of circumventing authorized distribution channels by 'buying a firm's products in low-price countries and selling them in high-price countries at prices lower than those offered by authorized members of the distribution channel'. Fletcher and Brown (1999: 366) argue that while the practice is no longer considered illegal, particularly in many developing society governments, it has two significant consequences for those international firms wishing to operate in environments with such systems. Firstly, it can dilute the value of a product by artificially creating a surplus of supply; and secondly, it can damage the quality of channel partner relationships.

Tan *et al.* (1997) point out that, ironically, the process of product/packaging standardization has attributed to the practice of grey marketing, as it is virtually impossible for consumers and suppliers to distinguish between 'grey' products and legitimate products. For these and other such writers, informal systems abound as fragmented markets in many developing as well as developed societies.

The alternative view, which perceives these types of distribution systems in a more positive light, is one that exists in many developing countries where the formal structures for the distribution of goods and services are virtually non-existent. Some writers view these distribution sectors as the mainstay of many market economies. According to Arellano (1994) the informal sector in many developing societies employs up to 90 per cent of the adult working population and has been recognized as a 'legitimate' form of doing business in such societies.

The informal distribution system, in many parts of Africa for instance, is seen as playing a very vital role at the level of the household by ensuring that practically every remote village household that is not serviced by formal channels can gain access to important products, thus enabling the survival of these households. Omari (1996) supports this view through his research, which shows that this type of distribution system contributes substantially to the household budget in Africa and that without it households would suffer great economic hardship.

The Workings of Informal Distribution Systems

Whilst informal distribution systems in Western societies are referred to as grey markets, in other societies they are seen as panaceas to survival. In developed societies they are viewed as systems that circumvent legal or authorized channel member activities and erode the formal system. On the contrary, in many developing societies, where most products let alone those from the West are seen as scarce, and in high demand, the existence of these systems is considered critical by those consumers.

Informal distributors are comprised of individuals who usually operate as informal channel members distributing goods from authorized wholesalers and retailers to consumers and households that may be situated in places where the local infrastructure presents obstacles to the performance of formal transactions. This has led to the rise of highly mobile, efficient and cost-effective distributors who come up with very sophisticated physical distribution and sales promotional strategies that are congruent with the cultural norms of the societies they reside in.

Informal distributors such as the Machingas in Tanzania and the Spåza retailers in South Africa utilize all the characteristics of formal channel agents, and in addition exercise extreme flexibility and marketing tactics in the way they conduct their business. In many ways, their survival and effectiveness resides in their strong relational norms, which are usually based on collectivistic cultural goodwill and their adaptability to both Western and local environment requirements.

Strategies Utilized by Informal Distributors

Since informal distributors rely very much on the relational norms, they engage in activities that are based on relation-building typical of collectivistic cultures. Flexibility in pricing, mobility to ensure that customers are reached in a timely and convenient manner, as well as direct selling are used to a great extent. To achieve this end, these distributors rarely have fixed physical localities and utilize bargaining as a means of effecting a sale. Bargaining, sometimes referred to as haggling, is generally an economic process with the goal of seeking a common solution acceptable to all sides through bargaining (Kramer and Herbig, 1993). As with tipping, the propensity to bargain varies from culture to culture. In many Latin American countries, for instance, cultural attitudes based on collectivistic virtues favour haggling (Pereira, 1999). In Europe and the USA, on the other hand, bargaining is not as common. This means that Americans are less accustomed to this experience and on average end up paying more than necessary for products in countries where haggling is an important part of the shopping experience.

The types of products that a consumer can haggle for will also vary from one country to another. The American consumer is conditioned to bargain at used car dealerships and flea markets. Consumers in the Middle East, on the other hand, expect to haggle for a wide variety of products at the market bazaar. The bargaining process

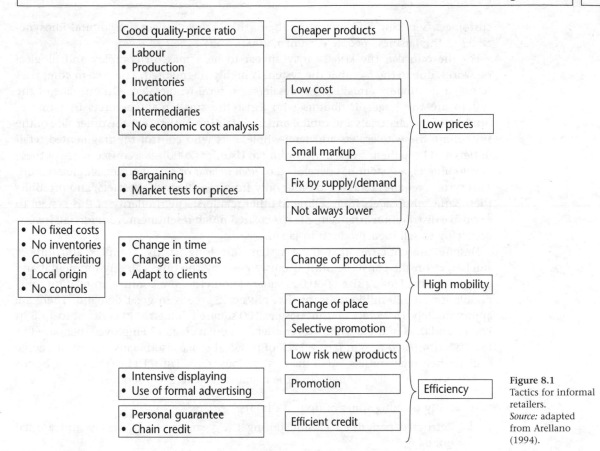

Figure 8.1
Tactics for informal
retailers.
Source: adapted
from Arellano
(1994).

itself may also vary from one culture to another. Research on this issue by Kramer and Herbig (1993) suggests that the model of haggling employed in the Middle East differs markedly from the traditional haggling seen in Western cultures. In the West, haggling is seen as a means for achieving the best deal, whereas in the Middle East it is seen as a social process for pursuing and establishing personal relationships. A summary of the marketing tactics and practices utilized by the informal distributors is demonstrated in Figure 8.1.

The Keiretsu Distribution System

The Japanese distribution system has evolved not only due to the constraints of the physical infrastructural needs of that society but also in concert with the cultural norms of Japan. A key feature of the distribution system is the very strong relationships of service and loyalty in both directions along the entire distribution system, which includes the customers. Essentially, the distribution process is based on systems of vertical control between producers, wholesalers and retailers, referred to as *keiretsus* – 'distribution channel arrangements' or 'integrated marketing networks' (Czinkota and Woronoff, 1991: 57). Since channels involve direct relationships with final customers, servicing and informing them, they deeply reflect the cultural idiosyncracies of the Japanese people (Ursunier, 2000).

For the outsider, the *keiretsu* may appear to be a mass of complex and illogical networks, due to the fact that the system is highly fragmented. The system comprises of major distributors, retailers, wholesalers and semi-wholesalers. On one side of the system are the huge distributors who assist the small manufacturers in terms of funding of raw materials and capital and in obtaining outlets. On the other side of the system are the wholesalers and semi-wholesalers who control the fragmented retail outlets and keep them stocked. According to Usunier (2000), as a consequence of these developments, a system has developed of *itten itchoai* or single outlet, single account. This system requires retailers to order only from specified wholsesalers, and prohibits these same wholesalers from selling to other retailers. The similarity of this system to exclusive distribution arrangements has created much resentment from foreign investors trying to sell their products in Japan.

Despite the criticisms that these systems are long, costly, complex and impose surcharges on the consumer, this is outweighed by the physical, environmental and cultural reality. Japan's size of 60,000 square kilometres as a country, in relation to its population of 120 million, means that physical space is in great demand. There are approximately 18.95 retail businesses per 100 square kilometres in contrast to 1.68 in France and 0.28 in the USA. However, there are on average 12 employees per outlet in the USA compared to 4 in Japan. Lack of physical space also means that most people walk to their retail outlets rather than risk serious traffic jams. Hence the strong bonds between outlets and customers and the demand for extensive services:

1. Daily opening times of up to 12 hours.
2. Restricted periods of closure during the year, for both weekly and annual holidays.
3. Availability of free high-frequency home deliveries.
4. Easy acceptance of returned goods, even though the goods may not be defective.
5. Credit payment periods of up to 120 days and discounts.

The cultural realities also show that the Japanese are very hierachichal, with power distance (PD) indices (Hofstede, 1988). Since the notion of social status is central to Japanese culture, the notion of a vertical structure is an essential part of their *mental programming* or culture. Foreign companies that have succeeded in Japan are those that have adopted selling methods congruent with Japanese ways such as door-to-door selling (Cateora, 1996) and catalogue sales (Montgomery, 1991).

8.3 Effective Cross-cultural Distribution Methods

Direct Marketing Globally

From the examples cited above, it appears the most effective cross-cultural distribution mechanism is direct marketing. It is an interactive system of marketing that typically utilizes one or more channels or advertising media to effect measurable response in the form of an order, an inquiry or a visit to a store or other place of business for the purchase of a specific product. Direct marketing can generate inquiries, build loyalty, create awareness, build store traffic and generate or qualify leads. Examples of direct marketing tools are direct selling, direct mail, telemarketing, catalogue marketing, permission e-mail and e-direct mail. The company determines the objectives of such an endeavour, defines the target market, develops a database to reach the target, determines appropriate direct marketing strategies to employ to effect the desired outcome and evaluates the effectiveness of the efforts. In evaluating the effectiveness of a direct marketing tool, one could consider the cost per thousand, number of inquiries, number of inquiries converted to sales, per cent of repeat purchases, number of orders, promotion efficiency (i.e. profits divided by promotion costs) and costs per order.

Whereas direct selling appears to be very effective from a cross-cultural perspective, direct mail has the potential to become problematic generally and in particular in developing societies. In countries such as Chile, where the mail recipient may be expected to pay up to half of the mailing cost, direct mail could have the opposite of the intended effect. When considering cross-national mailing initiatives, factors to consider are: limited availability of mailing lists; higher costs of and wide variance in postal rates; stricter advertising and promotion claim regulations; lower credit card penetration rates for payments; and differences in merchandise return policies (Fishman, 1990: 48–58).

Direct mail is becoming a popular way to market to ethnic populations. Approaches can be targeted very specifically in terms of content and language. In the US, direct mail has been recognized as an important method of reaching African-Americans for some time (Usunier, 2000). However, there is evidence that this practice could be usefully extended to other ethnic groups. For example, research has indicated that Hispanic-Americans are particularly responsive to direct mail. It has been estimated that 72 per cent of Hispanics always read their direct mail.

In societies where the infrastructure is poor, most of these mechanisms are either difficult to implement or simply not possible. In such societies, direct selling becomes the most critical area of interaction particularly because of its powerful cultural relevance.

Distribution on the Internet

Whereas the role of the Internet is discussed more extensively in Chapter 14 of this text, this chapter examines the distribution utility of this media. As a means of distributing information and products the Internet has meant increased global exposure for businesses and consumers alike. Domestic companies expand internationally simply by going online and investing in e-business. At the same time, consumers can expand their shopping horizons by using the Internet to search for the best deals and expose themselves to e-tailers from around the world. There is still a certain degree of cultural resistance to shopping online, especially among those cultures that favour face-to-face transactions and the social aspect of bargaining (Pereira, 1999). However, the multicultural nature of the Internet is becoming more and more apparent as consumers from around the world gain access to the worldwide web.

American e-tailers are finding that they can no longer assume that their audience is the American consumer alone; consumers from countries such as England, Canada, Australia, Germany and Hong Kong can also access their websites. E-tailers are therefore being forced to consider not only whether international purchases should be permitted, but also how culture-friendly their website content should be.

The interactive nature of the Internet allows web designers to tailor web page content depending on the consumer's nationality. A good example of a global web page is Nike's website at <www.nike.com>. The company's global website lets the consumer choose between four different geographic regions: North America, Europe, the Asia Pacific and Latin America. The product content and information is tailored for each region. In Europe, there is a tendency for content to be tailored to the most popular cultural pastime such as the sport of soccer. Hence soccer merchandise is utilized extensively. In North America, sport is also an important cultural pastime, and content is tailored towards merchandise from the NBA, the NFL, the PGA and other major American professional sporting events.

Nike's website allows potential customers to select a particular language (one can select Spanish, German, French, English or Italian in the European region). Online purchases can be made through the North American, Asian Pacific and European regions, but currently not yet on the Latin American or African websites. In the European Nike online store, shoppers are asked to identify their country before entering the store for delivery, price and tax reasons. A *Fútbol Club Barcelona* soccer shirt, for instance, would cost an English shopper £40 online, whereas it would cost a Spanish shopper Ptas. 9,995. Using the current exchange rate of Ptas. 267.93/£1, this means that the British consumer is paying £3.70 more than the Spanish consumer. There is little – if any – overlap of merchandise available for sale between the three geographic regions; the Barcelona soccer shirt, for instance, is not available for purchase online in North America or the Asia Pacific.

It appears that companies with a presence on the Internet have imposed restrictions on where purchases can be made from, the types of products that can be purchased, and at what price, in order to avoid the distribution problems of parallel importing. In many ways, the Internet is similar to the physical environment when it comes to international marketing as practiced in most developed societies. For instance, it is possible for British tourists to purchase a Nike sports shirt at a lower price when holidaying in Spain, yet they can only make the purchase online at the Spanish price if it is to be delivered to a Spanish postal address.

8.4 Physical Considerations for Global Distribution

This section discusses some of the main physical considerations that impact on the process of distribution in global markets.

Customer service. The tyranny of distance can often impact negatively on a firm's ability to service their customers, creating an impression of apathy and feelings of disenfranchisement. For example, it is quite common for foreign companies to offer only a single contact point in countries where access to even the most basic telecommunications and transport is extremely difficult.

Packaging and protection. When designing packaging, cross-cultural marketers need to give consideration to the method of transport, variations in weather conditions and accessibility of storage. For instance, common packaging dimensions in Australia may be unsuitable for transport and storage in another country. Also, firms need to ensure that packaging is secure against theft, or otherwise open themselves to claims for loss.

Transportation. This is an area of major concern when considering cross-cultural marketing. Firms need to give attention to how products are moved from their home country to the foreign country, as well as the complications associated with receiving and then forwarding the product to the end consumer in the destination country. While the urgency of the order will often decide the methods used for infrequent transactions, consideration also needs to be given to whether the physical infrastructure exists to support more regular distribution. For instance, it is quite common for multinational firms to be burdened with infrastructural investment costs when expanding overseas (particularly in developing countries).

Documentation. The red-tape associated with exporting and importing into different countries is an area that could absorb an entire chapter by itself. The use of intermediaries such as brokers and freight forwarders can often reduce a lot of the worries, but nevertheless the process of doing business across borders is complicated by the need to provide the necessary paperwork to support distribution. Furthermore, consideration also needs to be given to the language of host countries to ensure that those involved in the distribution process can adequately assess the accuracy of the information provided.

Main Strategic Issues for Distribution to Global Villages

Although the standardization/customization debate is discussed with reference to the other marketing mix elements, it deserves special consideration here in the context of global distribution. This is because standardization can occur as either process standardization, or as a more holistic standardization of the entire marketing mix. Firms that are new to the domain of cross-cultural marketing tend to view all international markets in a homogeneous way, with simplistic distribution that tends to be coordinated from a central location and has an emphasis on the use of minimal intermediaries. However, as firms develop a better understanding of the nuances of international marketing, they can begin to dig deeper into the emic segments of individual countries (Kriz *et al.*, 2001). Successful global marketers often develop specific distribution strategies that reflect the individual characteristics of the target market and are supported by strategic relationships with channel partners such as host governments, financiers, wholesalers and retailers. Pioneers into new and developing markets can often use such relationships to restrict access for competitors, in effect creating virtual trade barriers that are often more effective than financial tariffs.

8.5 Conclusion

This chapter has addressed various aspects affecting the distribution of products and services from both a cross-cultural and multicultural context. In particular, consideration has been given to the main strategic issues confronting a firm when operating in a formal or informal sector and in diverse domestic and/or global villages.

REVIEW QUESTIONS

1. What are the distinguishing features of the informal distribution system that typically occur in developing societies ?

2. Discuss the distinguishing features of the Japanese distribution system.

3. To what extent do cultural differences explain differences in outlet operational behaviours in different societies, e.g. business hours.

4. Discuss how store size can be related to culture.

5. How important are cultural values in regard to positive perceptions of types of services, e.g. self-service and automated.

References

Arellano, R. (1994) 'Informal underground retailers in less developed countries: an explanatory research from a marketing point of view', *Journal of Macromarketing* Fall: 21–23.

Acharya, C. and Elliott, G. (2000) 'Consumer ethnocentrism, perceived product quality and choice – an empirical investigation', *International Marketing Review* (in press).

Ahmed, S.A. and d'Astous, A. (1996) 'Country-of-origin and brand effects: a multi-dimensional and multi-attribute study', *Journal of International Consumer Marketing* 9(2): 93–115.

Bagozzi, R. P., Rosa, J. A., Celly, K. S. and Coronel, F. (1998) *Marketing Management*, Upper Saddle River, NJ: Prentice Hall.

Bilkey, W. J. and Nes, E. (1982) 'Country-of-origin effects on product evaluations', *Journal of International Business Studies* 13 (Spring/Summer): 89–99.

Boddewyn, J. J., Soehl, R. and Picard, J. (1986) 'Standardization in international marketing: is Ted Levitt in fact right?', *Business Horizons* 29(6): 69–75.

Brodowsky, G. H. (1998) 'The effects of country of design and country of assembly on evaluative beliefs about automobiles and attitudes toward buying them: a comparison between low and high ethnocentric consumers', *Journal of International Consumer Marketing* 10(3): 85–113.

Cateora, P. R. (1996) *International Marketing*, 9th edn., Chicago: Richard D. Irwin.

Cateora, P. R. and Keaveney, S. (1987) *Marketing: An International Perspective*, Homewood, IL: Richard D. Irwin.

Czinkota, M. R. and Woronoff, J. (1991) *Unlocking Japan's Market*. Chicago: Probus Publishers.

Daniels, J. D., Radebaugh, L. H. and Sullivan, D. P. (2002) *Globalization and Business*, Upper Saddle River, NJ: Prentice Hall.

Elliott, G. R. and Cameron, R. S. (1994) 'Consumer perception of product quality and the country-of-origin effect', *Journal of International Marketing* 2(2): 49–62.

Evans, J. R. and Berman, B. (1997) *Marketing*, Upper Saddle River, NJ: Prentice Hall.

Ferraro, G. (2002) *The Cultural Dimensions of International Business*, Upper Saddle River, NJ: Prentice-Hall.

Fishman, A. (1990) 'International mail order guide', *Direct Marketing* October.

Fletcher, R. and Brown, L. (1999) *International Marketing: An Asia Pacific Perspective*. Prentice Hall Australia pty.

Griffin, T. (1993) *International Marketing Communications*, Oxford: Butterworth- Heinemann Ltd.

Gronroos (1991) *Service Management and Marketing*. Ontario: Lexington Books.

Hall, E. T. (1960) 'The silent language in overseas business,' *Harvard Business Review* (May–June): 87–96.

Hall, E. T. (1976) 'How cultures collide,' *Psychology Today* (July): 66–97.

Han, M. C. and Terpstra, V. (1988) 'Country-of-origin effects for uni-national and bi-national products', *Journal of International Business Studies* (Summer): 235–254.

Hawkins, D. I., Best, R. J. and Coney, K. A. (2001) *Consumer Behavior: Building Marketing Strategy*, New York: McGraw-Hill.

Herche, J. (1990) 'The measurement of consumer ethnocentrism: revising the CETSCALE', in B. J. Dunlap and N. C. Cullowhee (eds), *Developments in Marketing Science*, Academy of Marketing Science XIII, pp. 371–375.

Hofstede, G. H. (1983) 'National cultures in four dimensions: a research-based theory of cultural differences among nations', *International Studies of Management and Organizations* 13(1–2): 46–74.

Hofstede, G. H. (1984) *Culture's Consequences: International Differences in Work-Related Values*, Beverly Hills, CA: Sage Publications.

Hofstede, G. (1991) *Cultures and Organizations: Software of the Mind*, London: McGraw-Hill.

Hollensen, S. (1998) *Global Marketing: A Market-Responsive Approach*, New York: Prentice Hall.

Ishikawa, M. (1987) 'Latest trends in Japanese advertising', paper presented at the Fifteenth World Industrial Advertising Congress, Brussels.

Iyer, G. R. and Kalita, J. K. (1997) 'The impact of country-of-origin and country-of-manufacture clues on consumer perceptions of quality and value', *Journal of Global Marketing* 11(1): 7–28.

Keegan, W. J. and Green, M. S. (2000) *Global Marketing*, New York: Prentice Hall.

Klein, J. G., Ettenson, R. and Morris, M. D. (1998) 'The animosity model of foreign product purchase: an empirical test in the People's Republic of China', *Journal of Marketing* 62(1): 89–112.

Klenosky, D. B., Benet, S. B. and Chadraba, P. (1996) 'Assessing Czech consumers' reactions to Western marketing practices: a conjoint approach', *Journal of Business Research* 36: 189–198.

Kluckhohn, F. R. and Strodtbeck, F. L. (1961) *Variations in Value Orientations*, New York: Harper & Row.

Kotler, P. (2001) *Marketing Management*, Upper Saddle River, NJ: Prentice Hall.

Kramer, H. E. and Herbig, P. A. (1993) 'The *suq* model of haggling: who, what, when, why?', *Journal of International Consumer Marketing* 5(2): 55–69.

Kriz, A. and Flint, J. (2001) 'Ethics and emics: Bridging a gap in international business culture', presented in the Doing Business Across Borders Conference, Newcastle NSW, Australia.

Kulindwa, K. A. (1996) 'The informal sector: present and future prospects', paper presented at workshop on Education and Training Encouraging Understanding and Collaboration, British Council, Dar-es-salaam, 30–31 July.

Levitt, T. (1983) 'Globalization of markets', *Harvard Business Review* 61(3): 69–81.

Liefeld, J. P., Heslop, L. A., Papadopoulos, N. and Wall, M. (1996) ' Dutch consumer use of intrinsic, country-of-origin, and price cues in product evaluation and choice', *Journal of International Consumer Marketing* 9(1): 57–81.

Louviere, J. L. (1988) *Analyzing Decision Making*, Newbury Park, CA: Sage Publications.

Lynn, M., Zinkhan, G. M. and Harris, J. (1993) 'Consumer tipping: a cross-country study', *Journal Of Consumer Research* 20(3): 478–488.

McCarthy (1960)

Maheswaran, D. (1994) 'Country-of-origin as a stereotype: effects of consumer expertise and attribute strength on product evaluations', *Journal of Consumer Research* 21(2): 354–365.

Monroe, K. B. and Lee, A. Y. (1999) 'Remembering versus knowing: issues in buyers' processing of price information', *Journal of the Academy of Marketing Science* 27: 207–225.

Montgomery, D. B (1991) 'Understanding the Japanese as customers, competitors and collaborators', *Japan and the World Economy* 3(1): 61–91.

Nes, E. and Bilkey, W. J. (1993) ' A multi-cue test of country-of-origin theory', in N. Papadopoulos and L. A. Heslop (eds), *Product Country Images: Impact and Role in International Marketing*, New York: International Business Press, pp. 179–196.

Netemeyer, R. G., Durvasula, S. and Lichtenstein, D. R. (1991) 'A cross-national assessment of the reliability and validity of the CETSCALE', *Journal of Marketing Research* XXVII (August): 320–327.

Okechuku, C. (1994) 'The importance of product country of origin: a conjoint analysis of the United States, Canada, Germany, and the Netherlands', *European Journal of Marketing* 18(4): 5–19.

Omari, C. (1995) 'The informal sector: the missing link in entrepreneurship research', in L. Rutashobya and D. Olomi (eds), *African Entrepreneurship and Small Business Development*.

de Mooij, M. (1998) *Global Marketing and Advertising: Understanding Cultural Paradoxes*, Thousand Oaks, CA: Sage Publications.

Murphy, J. H. and Cunningham, I. C. M. (1993) *Advertising and Marketing Communication*, New York: The Dryden Press.

Papadopoulos, N., Heslop, L. A. and Bamossy, G .J. (1989) 'International competitiveness of American and Japanese products', in N. Papadopoulos (ed.), *Dimensions of International Business*, volume 2, Ottawa, Canada: International Business Study Group, Carlton University.

Papadopoulos, N., Heslop, L. A. and Bamossy, G .J. (1990) 'A comparative analysis of domestic versus imported products', *International Journal of Research in Marketing* 7(4).

Parente, D. (2000) *Advertising Campaign Strategy: A Guide to Marketing Communications Plans*, New York: The Dryden Press.

Pereira, P. (1999) 'E-business washes into Latin America', *Computer Reseller News* 873 (December 13): 5.

Ricks, D. A. (1993) *Blunders in International Business*, Cambridge, MA: Blackwell Publishers.

Schultz, D. E., Tannenbaum, S. and Lauterborn, R. F. (1993) *Integrated Marketing Communications: Pulling It All Together and Making It Work*, Lincolnwood, IL: NTC Business Books.

Selthuraman, S. V. (1975) 'Urbanisation and employment: a case study of Djarkata', *International Labour Review* 112(2–3): 191–201.

Sharma, S., Shimp, T. A. and Shin, J. (1995) 'Consumer ethnocentrism: a test of antecedents and moderators', *Journal of the Academy of Marketing Science* 23(1): 26–37.

Shimp, T. A. and Sharma, S. (1987) 'Consumer ethnocentrism: construction and validation of the CETSCALE', *Journal of Marketing Research* XXIV (August): 280–289.

Tan, S. J., Lim, G. H. and Lee, K. S. (1997) 'Strategic responses to parallel importing', *Journal of Global Marketing* 10(4): 45–66.

Tellis, G. (1998) *Advertising and Sales Promotion Strategy*, New York: Addison-Wesley.

Terpstra, V. (1988) *International Dimensions of Marketing*, 2nd edn., Boston: PWS-KENT Publishing Company.

Thakor, M. V. and Katsanis, L. P. (1997) 'A model of brand and country effects on quality dimensions: issues and implications', *Journal of International Consumer Marketing* 9(3): 79–100.

Toyne, B. and Walters, P. G. P. (1993) *Global Marketing Management: A Strategic Perspective*, Boston: Allyn and Bacon.

Usunier, J.-C. (2000) *Marketing Across Cultures*, pp. 397–399. London: Prentice Hall Europe.

Wall, M. and Heslop, L. A. (1986) 'Consumer attitudes toward Canadian-made versus imported products', *Journal of Academy of Marketing Science* 14(2): 27–36.

CHAPTER 9

Cross-cultural communications and promotion

William Darley and Denise Luethge

LEARNING OBJECTIVES

At the end of this chapter readers will be able to answer the following questions:

▶ How may cultures be different or similar?
▶ How does the communication process work?
▶ How does one go about developing an integrated marketing communications programme?
▶ What are the major elements in an integrated marketing communications programme?
▶ How is multicultural marketing communications different?
▶ What are the major factors to be considered when developing a multicultural marketing communications plan?

9.1 Introduction

The focus of this chapter is on multicultural marketing communications. To provide a backdrop, we start with a discussion of how cultures may differ and the implications of such differences for communication in general, and marketing communications in particular. We then look at how communication works. This is followed by a discussion of the steps in developing a marketing communications programme. We also include a discussion of the major factors to be considered when developing a multicultural marketing communications plan.

9.2 Contrasting Cultural Values

Culture is a distinctly fuzzy concept. It is broad and extremely complex. Hollensen (1998) defines culture as the learned ways in which a society understands, decides and communicates. It is the sum total of learned beliefs, values and customs that are shared by a society. Cultural differences are not necessarily visible and can be quite subtle. The visible aspects (e.g. body language, clothing, lifestyle, eating habits) are the manifestation of the invisible aspects comprising underlying values and social norms (e.g. family values, sex roles and friendship patterns) and basic cultural assumptions (e.g. national identity, ethnic culture and religion) shared by a group of people (Hollensen, 1998).

The implementation of the marketing programme across countries and cultures requires an understanding of cultural underpinnings. In particular, appreciating such differences is vital in advertising, direct marketing and interpersonal interactions (e.g. personal selling and negotiations) (Bagozzi, Rosa, Celly and Coronel, 1998). Thus, our interest is in determining whether cultural differences exist, the extent to which such differences exist and their potential influences on marketing communications.

In this section, we look at various aspects of culture and present three ways to approach the analysis of cultural influences and differences. We examine cultures (a) by means of a high/low context analysis (Hall, 1960); (b) along Kluckhohn–Strodtbeck's (1961) framework for studying cultural differences on dimensions such as focus on past or future events and beliefs in individual or group responsibility for personal well-being; and (c) along Hofstede's (1983, 1984, 1991) framework for studying cultural differences on dimensions such as individualism/collectivism and power distance. Throughout the discussion, implications arising among various cultures are discussed.

High and Low Context Analysis. Edward T. Hall suggested the concept of high and low context to help us understand different cultural orientations. In low context cultures, messages are explicit and the words carry most of the information. By contrast, in high context cultures, less information is contained in the verbal part of the message; hence the meaning of a message cannot be understood without its context. The context is critical to receiving the complete message (Keegan and Green, 2000; Hall, 1976).

It is said that non-verbal messages communicate up to 90 per cent of the meaning in high context cultures (Hall, 1960). Thus, particular attention ought to be paid to non-verbal communication in high context cultures. For example, a sales presentation that details a large number of facts about a product may be quite effective with a customer in a low context culture, while it may be quite ineffective with a customer in a high context culture, where he or she wonders why the presenter is giving all this information that either is not relevant or is already known through their personal networks (Mooij, 1998).

Contextual Orientation. Cultures vary in how explicit message content is. Messages may be explicit, verbal and contained in words, or depend on implicit, non-verbal cues. Kluckhohn and Strodtbeck (1961) identified five value orientations common to all human groups: human nature orientation, man and nature orientation, time orientation, activity orientation and relational orientation. Orientations vary by culture, and the type of orientation in a particular culture impacts not only how an individual sees the world, but also how they communicate. For example, an advertisement that focuses on pleasing only an individual may not work well in cultures where pleasing the group rather than the individual has higher priority.

- *Human Nature Orientation.* This addresses the character of innate human nature (i.e. the innate goodness or badness of human nature). Human nature can be conceived as innately good, innately bad, or a combination of the two.
- *Man and Nature Orientation.* This dwells on the relation of man to nature or supernature. Potential options include mastery over nature, subjugation to nature, or harmony with nature.
- *Time Orientation.* This covers the temporal focus of human life (past, present and future), and whether time is directed at the past, present or future.
- *Activity Orientation.* This focuses on the modality of the human activity (i.e. the nature of man's mode of self-expression) and covers whether people value an individual's accomplishments or his/her innate personal traits.
- *Relational Orientation.* This refers to the modality of man's relationship to other men and deals with the extent to which individualism is more highly valued than commitments and obligations to the wider group such as family, neighbourhood or society (Kluckhohn and Strodtbeck, 1961: 10–20).

Hofstede's Framework. Dutch psychologist Geert Hofstede also developed five dimensions for examining cultures (Hofstede, 1984; 1991). The model was based on over 30 years' of data and was originally developed to explain differences in work-related values, although it has also been used to describe consumption-related values and motives as well, especially with regard to marketing and advertising (Mooij, 1998).

- *Individualism versus Collectivism.* This focuses on emphasizing the goals, needs and views of the in-group over those of the individual or subjugating the individual's goals, needs and views to the group.
- *Power Distance.* This refers to the acceptance of inequality in power and authority between individuals in a society.
- *Uncertainty Avoidance.* This captures the degree to which individuals in a culture feel threatened by ambiguous, uncertain or new situations.
- *Masculinity versus Femininity.* This examines the degree to which cultures prioritize performance, achievement and winning (masculine), versus consensus, sympathy and quality of life (feminine).
- *Long-term Orientation.* This focuses on pursuit of peace of mind versus pursuit of happiness.

Taken together, these three approaches provide a way of looking at culture. Table 9.1 presents nine questions for the cultural analysis (see Table 9.1). Based on responses to these questions, a given culture can be studied to determine whether it should be approached differently in terms of marketing communications. Note that Hofstede's (1984, 1991) individualism/collectivism dimension captures the same essence as the Kluckhohn and Strodtbeck's (1961) relational orientation. For example, an individualistic society where communication is fairly explicit, power distance is high and uncertainty avoidance is weak could be placed into one segment, whereas a collectivist society where communication is implicit, power distance is high and uncertainty

	Cultural clusters		
Cultural questions	*Segment 1*	*Segment 2*	*Segment K*
1. To what extent does the culture rely on spoken and written language for meaning or interpret more of the elements surrounding the message?[a]			
2. Do people believe that their environment controls them or that they control the environment or that they are part of nature?[b]			
3. Do people focus on past events, on the present, or on future implications of their actions?[b]			
4. Are people easily controlled and not to be trusted, or can they be trusted to act freely and responsibly?[b]			
5. Do people desire accomplishments in life, carefree lives, or spiritual and contemplative lives?[b]			
6. Do people believe that individuals or groups are responsible for each person's welfare?[b]			
7. Does society value equality or inequality in interpersonal interactions?[c]			
8. What is the attitude towards risk in society?[c]			
9. Do people define success of high status material accumulations or good working relationships and spiritual growth?[d]			

Table 9.1 Classifying cultures along twelve dimensions.

Notes: [a] Hall (1960); [b] Kluckholm and Strodbeck (1961); [c] Hofstede (1984, 1991); [d] Ferraro (2002).

avoidance is strong could be placed in another cultural segment (Usunier, 1996). Also, an advertisement where a younger person shows an older person how to do something differently would be much more effective in a low power distance country, while an advertisement where an older person shows a younger person the importance of keeping with tradition would be more effective in a high power distance case. Trying to approach communication with both of these audiences in exactly the same way is likely to be ineffectual.

What is appropriate or acceptable, what is important and what is desirable are determined by cultural values and attitudes and expressed differently by different cultures. Thus, values and attitudes have to be monitored. Also, aesthetic factors such as product, package design, colour, brand name and symbols, to the extent that they reflect on or affect marketing communications, need to be evaluated and taken into account. In addition, religion can provide the basis of transcultural similarities under shared beliefs and may affect the global marketing communications strategy directly or indirectly.

9.3 The Communication Process: How Does it Work?

In today's business world, companies need to communicate with their customers and stakeholders about their products and services. 'What to say', 'how to say it', 'when to say it', 'where to say it' and 'how often to say it' are all critical. Thus, to better understand the marketing communications process, one has to understand the communication process.

Communication is the process of influencing the behaviour of others by sharing ideas, information or feelings with others. Communication starts with a source or sender, which can be an organization or a person. This source creates a message or encodes a message in words, symbols and signs intended for the receiver. When crossing cultures, it is essential that the source of the communication think of the product in terms of the culture to which the communication will be directed rather than the home culture (Cateora and Keaveney, 1987). To the extent that products are viewed or used differently, the source of the communication must be aware of those variations.

Encoding is a process of putting a message into words, symbols and signs to convey the sender's intended meaning. Since the message encompasses both words and other types of cues, the context of the communication is vital. Any differences in contextual communication between the sender and the receiver must be acknowledged, so that the intended and actual messages are the same. For example, an advertisement that focuses on an individual showing off his new car to a neighbour might work in the United States, but it would be inappropriate in the Netherlands where such behaviour is considered to be in bad taste.

This intended message is sent via a channel, which can be direct, person-to-person or telephone, or indirect, using a traditional medium (e.g. advertising) or non-traditional medium (e.g. sky writing). Although most media are available globally, the limitations of those media vary widely. For instance, newspapers in many countries have distinct political leanings and advertising one's product in a particular newspaper may impact perceptions of not only the product, but the company that produces the product as well.

Decoding is a process of translating or interpreting the words, symbols and signs of the sender's intended meaning. For effective communication, however, the intended or encoded message must match the perceived or decoded message.

The receiver can be an individual or members of a target market. The receiver's interpretation of the message as he or she deciphers words, symbols and signs is critical to effective communication. Thus, the intended or encoded message and the perceived or decoded message may be the same or different, depending upon the impact of cultural differences on either encoding or decoding.

The following points are also noteworthy. All planning begins with the consumer or the target market. The source, message and media decisions cannot be made unless the promotional planner has some insight into how the target market will respond. The more knowledgeable the sender is of the receiver and his or her needs, the more likely the sender can tailor his or her message to the receiver. There must be a common ground or thinking between the sender and the receiver. That is, the fields of experience must overlap. The sender or source must use words, symbols and signs that have the same meaning to the sender and the receiver. Also, if the source is a company, the message must be presented in terms of the consumer's needs, interests and problems. To the extent that the sender and receiver are from very different cultures, this can be a difficult, though not insurmountable task. One way to ensure that the intended and actual communications convey the same message is to involve

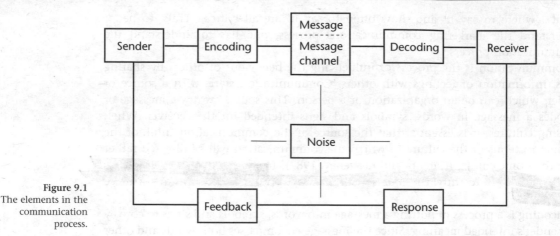

Figure 9.1
The elements in the
communication
process.

local nationals from the receiver's country in the development of the communication.

Feedback is an essential component of the communication model. It is through the feedback control mechanism that senders are able to determine whether or not there may be possible disconnects between the intended message and the interpreted message. It is essential that firms engaging in communications across borders monitor feedback (e.g. attitude change, sales impact).

Figure 9.1 presents a typical communication model. A brief description of the nine elements found in the communication model is presented in Table 9.2. The reader is cautioned, however, that cultural differences may act as a 'noise' factor that can disrupt virtually any part of the communication.

Language is a key dimension of culture and it is through communication, especially spoken or written language and silent language, that cultural contact occurs. Non-verbal issues such as colour association, sense of appropriate distance, symbols, time and status cues, gestures and body language make up the unspoken or silent part of

Sender	The party sending the message (also called source)
Encoding	The process of putting thought into symbolic form
Message	The set of symbols that the sender transmits
Media	The communication channels through which the message moves from sender to receiver
Decoding	The process by which the receiver assigns meaning to the symbols transmitted by the sender
Receiver	The party receiving the message (also called audience)
Response	The set of reactions from the receiver after being exposed to the message
Feedback	The part of the receiver's response that the receiver communicates back to the sender
Noise	The occurrence of unplanned static or distortion during the process resulting in the receiver receiving a different message than the sender sent

Table 9.2
Communication
process elements.

language. These cues impact the marketing communications process, and they must be factored into marketing communications decisions (Daniels, Radebaugh and Sullivan, 2002: 94–96). For example, United Airlines initially offered white carnations to passengers when they began service in Hong Kong. It was only after they had made this mistake that they realized white carnations meant death and bad luck to many Asians (Ricks, 1993). In addition, the entire approach to communication may vary by culture. Japanese advertisements tend to be very emotional and designed to entertain rather than providing rational reasons for purchase (Ishikawa, 1987).

However, regardless of the culture, the basic tenets of the communication process remain the same. The marketer's message must be encoded, conveyed via the appropriate channel and decoded by the customer. Communication only takes place when there is sharing and when meaning is transferred (Keegan and Green, 2000). As a result, the more culturally different the source or marketer is from the receiver, the more likely difficulties will be encountered somewhere in the communication process.

9.4   Developing a Marketing Communications Programme

Integrated marketing communications requires that all communications with consumers be coordinated, that the consumer be the focal point of the communications, that one-on-one communications with consumers be fostered and that two-way communications between the firm and its consumers be engendered (Schultz, Tannenbaum and Lauterborn, 1993). The overall goal in integrated marketing communications, from a manager's perspective, is to integrate and coordinate the timing, budgeting and content of all promotion to produce a positive and consistent message that enhances brand equity.

There are six steps in developing an effective marketing communications programme. The marketing communicator must: (1) identify the target market; (2) determine the objectives to be accomplished; (3) establish a budget; (4) develop a media plan; (5) design the message; and (6) assess the effectiveness of the marketing communications effort. Different cultures influence these six steps in different ways. However, regardless of the culture, the basic tenets of the marketing communications process remain the same.

1. Identifying the Target Market

The target market is an important component of the marketing communications programme because it influences decisions regarding what to say, how to say it, when to say it and where to say it. Thus, it is also important to know whom you are trying to reach and how the target market members feel and think about your product, keeping in mind that these groups' feelings and thoughts will vary by culture. For example, Nestlé very successfully markets coffee in a number of countries, but the flavour varieties and coffee usage patterns vary dramatically from one country to the next.

To communicate effectively with the target market, it is also important for the marketing communicator to have some understanding of the factors that influence individual purchase behaviour, the process by which purchase decisions are made, the goals and motivations individuals seek to achieve, the process by which consumers acquire, use and integrate information to choose among alternatives, the ways consumers relate to products, how consumers form attitudes, and how consumers can be persuaded. Since factors, processes and the ways consumers act and interact with products may vary by culture, it is important to gain as much information as possible about each of the cultures a firm intends to target.

In defining the target market, marketing managers use four key dimensions: geographic, demographic, psychographic and strategic. For more details of these dimensions see Table 9.3. The marketer should ask whether the geographic area is homogeneous or heterogeneous with respect to culture, or if the geographic boundaries coincide with cultural boundaries. Can the product fill the proposed need in the culture (Hawkins, Best and Coney, 2001)? It is also noteworthy that marketing communications campaigns must be developed for cultural groups, not just countries (Hawkins, Best and Coney, 2001: 68–70).

Thus, aside from looking at the geographic, demographic, psychographic and strategic dimensions, one has to examine the cultural similarities and differences in the target market formulation. Hence, a fifth dimension is cultural. This dimension includes elements such as values associated with the product, consumer habits,

---

Who are we trying to reach? This question can be addressed along five dimensions:

Geographic
- ▶ Region (Middle-East, Central Asia, Sub-Saharan Africa, etc.)
- ▶ Density (urban, suburban, rural)
- ▶ Climate (northern, southern, tropical, etc.)

Demographic
- ▶ Age
- ▶ Income (disposable, discretionary)
- ▶ Household size
- ▶ Education
- ▶ Etc.

Psychographics
- ▶ Lifestyle patterns
- ▶ Personality traits

Behavioural/strategic
- ▶ Benefits sought (quality, service, economy, etc.)
- ▶ User status (non-potential, first-time, regular user, etc.)
- ▶ Loyalty status (none, medium, strong, absolute)
- ▶ Usage rate (light, medium, heavy user)
- ▶ Readiness stage (unaware, aware, informed, interested, desirous, intending to buy)
- ▶ Attitude towards the product (enthusiastic, positive, indifferent, negative, hostile, etc.)

Cultural elements
- ▶ How product is used
- ▶ Values associated with product and its use
- ▶ Verbal and non-verbal communication system
- ▶ Consumer habits
- ▶ Cultural values and attitudes
- ▶ Religion

Table 9.3
Defining the target market.

cultural values and attitudes, and religion. To the extent that differences exist in cultures in terms of perceptions, preferences, language (verbal and non-verbal), manners and customs, values and attributes, and aesthetics and religion, the marketing communicator has to factor these differences in the decision-making process.

2. Determining the Objectives

Clearly stated objectives serve two key functions. They provide: (a) a useful guide for decisions regarding budgeting, media, and creative; and (b) serve as a benchmark against which success or failure can be judged. Good objectives, generally: (a) have singularity of purpose; (b) are measurable and quantitative; (c) are time bound; and (d) are specific and realistic. Although objectives within different cultures may vary, the need for setting objectives is universal.

There are two basic approaches to setting objectives. One way of setting an objective is to express it in terms of sales (e.g. increase sales by five per cent) or market share (e.g. increase market share by two per cent). A second way is to set objectives in communication terms or as non-sales objectives (e.g. increase awareness of a product's attribute by 10 per cent, or increase by 10 per cent the number of target members who have some knowledge of the product's benefits).

If a communication-based objective is employed, the marketing communicator must decide on the desired response sought. Basically, the marketing communicator wants members of the targeted group to think or feel or act in a certain way as a result of the marketing communications effort. One has to keep in mind that different cultures may react to the same communication in different ways. For example, Proctor & Gamble reused an advertisement for Camay soap in Japan that had been successful in Europe. The advertisement showed a woman's husband entering the bathroom while she was bathing. It was considered to be inappropriate in the Japanese market and Proctor & Gamble had to withdraw it (Ricks, 1993).

Since the primary role of marketing communications is to communicate, the plan or programme should seek a response that is: (a) cognitive (e.g. increase knowledge of something, increase awareness of something); (b) affective (e.g. increase interest in a product, change feelings toward something, change an attitude, change image of something); and/or (c) conative or behavioural (e.g. get the consumer to act in a certain way). Advocates of this approach, which include many academics worldwide, use some form of hierarchy of effects models or response process models found in Figure 9.2. The reader is cautioned that the hierarchy of effects models were developed using the assumption that perceptions are formed using a logical, sequential process. This is very much a Western concept. There are many different forms of logic and this type of sequential process is not necessarily the only type of process used (Mooij, 1998).

3. Establishing a Budget

Deciding on how much to spend is always a difficult task. In this section, we discuss six common approaches: affordable method; incremental or historical method; media multiplier method; competitive parity method; objective–task method; and percentage of sales method.

1. AIDA model:
   Attention → Interest → Desire → Action

2. Hierarchy of effects model:
   Awareness → Knowledge → Liking → Preference → Conviction → Purchase

3. Innovation adoption model:
   Awareness → Interest → Evaluation → Trial → Adoption

Figure 9.2
Models of the
response process.

4. Information process model:
   Presentation → Attention → Comprehension → Yielding → Retention behaviour

The *affordable method* sets the budget based on what a company thinks it can afford. This approach completely ignores the impact of promotion on sales, leads to an uncertain annual promotion budget and makes long-range planning difficult.

The *incremental or historical method* sets the budget based on last year's budget with an increase for inflation. For example, we could add five per cent to last year's budget to come up with this year's budget. In any event, this approach can lead to under- or overspending.

The *media multiplier method* is similar to the incremental method. It recognizes that media costs tend to go up. Thus, the media multiplier rule requires that the previous year's budget be increased by the same rate that media costs have gone up.

The *competitive parity method* is called share of voice budgeting. In this method, the company spends approximately the same rate as its competition. Matching the percentage of advertising to sales ratio sets budgets. The competitive parity method relates the amount invested in advertising to the share of the market. It assumes that sales determine the level of promotion and argues falsely that competitors' total expenditures reflect the collective wisdom of the industry. However, the collective wisdom may not be very wise, especially since it does not take strategy or promotional objectives into account.

The *objective–task method* is probably the most logical method for determining the budget level and the only approach that takes into account the objectives of the marketing communications effort. It identifies the specific objectives and the activities or tasks required to accomplish each objective. It then determines the cost of accomplishing each task and the various costs are added to arrive at a budget. The objective–task method is appropriate for situations where: (a) a company is introducing a new marketing programme or changing a marketing programme; and (b) the competitive strategy changes.

For the *percentage of sales approach* the budget is determined as a percentage of sales revenue. The percentage sales figure may be based on a percentage of projected future sales or industry standard percentage. For example, to determine the advertising budget using the percentage of sales approach, we will follow these two steps: step 1 – (past advertising dollars/past sales) × 100 = % of sales; step 2 – % of sales × next year's projected sales = new advertising budget.

The percentage of sales approach is simple to use. However, it is not appropriate if the firm has made significant changes to its marketing programme, if the competitive situation has been altered or if a new product is being introduced. Also, advertising is viewed as a result rather than as a cause of sales. For a firm selling in many countries, this method appears to guarantee equality among markets (Hollensen, 1998) that may or may not be appropriate.

Although companies may choose to use the same or different methods in various countries, the need to apply a logical, consistent method and evaluate it regularly is important. For a reality check, it is important to cross-check the method employed against at least another method.

4. Developing the Media Plan

The basic purpose of media is to deliver the message efficiently and effectively. *Efficiency* is concerned with delivering the message to the target market at a relatively low cost. Thus, a medium that costs less to reach a thousand people within the target market will be seen as more cost efficient. *Effectiveness* is concerned with delivering the message effectively by selecting media that both influence and enhance the message.

To do this, media planners incorporate reach and frequency figures in their media objectives. *Reach* is the number of different people or households exposed to a media schedule within a given period of time. This is usually expressed as a percentage. *Frequency* is the number of times a person or household is exposed to a media schedule within a given period of time. Three exposures within a purchase cycle are regarded as optimal. In general, the more frequency one has in a schedule, the fewer people one reaches, because in practice it is difficult for your message to get to most of your target market a greater number of times. Hence, the marketer has to balance reach and frequency figures and also link them to campaign objectives. Setting objectives in terms of reach and frequency is helpful for new product launches and for campaigns that are undergoing major strategic shifts (Parente, 2000).

Timing or scheduling issues also need to be addressed. The primary objective of scheduling is to coincide the highest potential buying times with the promotional efforts. Such decisions are about when advertisements appear and how they are scheduled over a period of time. How and when to schedule or advertise depends on the media objectives, buying cycles, budget, seasonality or product type and competitive presence. The three common scheduling methods used by media planners are continuity, flighting and pulsing. *Continuity* refers to a continuous pattern of advertising. A regular pattern is developed, with no gaps in the advertising periods. Products such as food items and laundry detergents that are consumed on an ongoing basis and are not affected by seasonality are good candidates for such advertising scheduling. *Flighting* has periods of no advertising (i.e. hiatus) and periods of advertising. Some time periods will have heavy promotional expenditures and at other times there will be none. Seasonal products such as snow skis are advertised heavily between October and April, not at all in June and July, and less in May, August and September. Banks also normally advertise during most parts of the year but have no summer advertising. Finally, *pulsing* combines continuity and flighting. It maintains continuity, but at certain times the promotional effort is increased. In the United States, automobile dealers advertise year round, but they increase their advertising for the Presidential Day holiday, April (for the tax refund) and September (for the new car models).

The media schedule usually takes into account the costs of the media buy. A measure called *cost per thousand* is traditionally used. The cost per thousand is obtained by multiplying the cost of placing the advertisement by 1000 and dividing by the size of the audience, i.e. (cost × 1000)/size of the audience. However, when different national markets or cultures are the target, the cost per thousand measure is adjusted by a number of quantitative and qualitative factors such as target market weight, vehicle exposure weight, perception weight and cumulative frequency weight (Toyne and Walters, 1993).

Table 9.4 presents qualities and characteristics of the traditional media. The media mix selection depends heavily on the objectives and intended outcomes. For example, if you want to build awareness for your product, want to use peripheral cues (e.g. using popular music or celebrity to attract attention) or demonstrate the capabilities of a product, television is probably the most preferable – although television saturation in some countries is very low, allowing only the upper income population to be reached. Also, television allows you to show, at a glance, what your product does and how. However, television is relatively language dependent, so it may be expensive in terms of production costs when a targeted country has multiple languages.

When you want to stimulate impulse buying, want to advertise offerings that change frequently, or the purpose involves a highly personal and intimate presentation of a product, what better medium to use than radio. Radio also has the capability to stage a 'theatre of the mind' and allows the listener to become part of the action or scene.

For products that demand an aura of quality, when you want to build a long lasting image or when you want image editorial content to transfer to a product, magazines readily come to mind. Magazines also create a bond of creativity and quality that cannot be developed as well in any other medium. *Reader's Digest* is published in 38 editions in 15 languages reaching 100 million readers (Griffin, 1993). A number of other United States originating magazines, such as *Cosmopolitan* and *Harper's Bazaar*, publish in languages other than English. However, lead times are very long internationally, and for smaller regional magazines in developing countries the paper quality may not be of the highest standards.

In contrast, if you are interested in targeting specific geographic markets, if you need information to be distributed quickly, or if you want to provide news about a product or relate the story behind the events, newspapers can be used. Unfortunately, circulation in many countries is limited, so in order to reach a large number of people in any one market advertisers must be in several or perhaps many newspapers. Also, a number of newspapers abroad have political positions, and advertisers may need to position their product in more than one newspaper in order to cover various political groups. Finally, newspapers are also literacy and language dependent, which may be a problem in some markets.

If you want to build awareness within a community, if you want to reach a mass community audience, if you want to convey a message 'bigger than life', or if you are interested in package identification, outdoor advertising (e.g. bill boards, inflatables, rolling boards and skywriting) may be optimal. This may be a particularly good medium for those countries with language and literacy limitations, since this medium typically carries a limited written message and may be more appropriate for signs or symbols.

In addition to the traditional media (i.e. magazines, newspapers, radio, television and outdoor), there are several non-traditional media or support media that should be considered. The support media include out-of-home media (e.g. transit), speciality

Advertising	Any paid form of non-personal communication about an organization, product, service or idea by an identified sponsor
Sales promotion	Marketing activities that provide extra value or incentive to consumers or middlemen for purchasing the product or to salespersons for selling the product
Personal selling	Direct person-to-person communication whereby a seller attempts to persuade prospective buyers to buy a company's product, service or to act on an idea
Publicity	Non-personal communications about an organization, product, service or idea that are not directly paid for nor run under identified sponsorship
Direct marketing	An interactive system of marketing, which uses one or more advertising media to effect a measurable response and/or transaction at any location.

Table 9.4
Marketing
communications
mix.

advertising or promotional products, yellow pages or telephone directories, and others such as the Internet. Table 9.5 provides additional information on the support media.

It is also worth noting that there is no one right media plan. It depends on the company's philosophy, the competition, the budget, the marketing communications tasks to be accomplished and the interaction with other marketing mix elements (i.e. pricing, distribution and product). However, there are some common elements to consider when evaluating a media plan. Is it focused toward the target audience? Does it take into account the audience delivery versus goals? Does it use the appropriate mix of media vehicles? Is the scheduling appropriate? Does the plan match competitive activity? Does the plan complement other marketing elements?

Thus, a good media plan has the following features. First, it covers the 'media objectives'. The media objectives, in addition to presenting the goals, address the target audience, geographic concentration and timing issues. Second, the 'media strategy' spells out in broad terms how the objectives will be met and discusses the total media mix to be used and the allocation by media. The third element is 'tactical plan and rationale'. This provides the detailed schedules, budgets for each medium and rationale and flow charts. Fourth, the 'support data' provides plan documentation. To ensure that the media selected reflect cultural realities of the region and its people, some adaptations may be necessary. Media availability and effectiveness vary

	Advertising	Public relations	Sales promotion	Direct marketing	Personal selling
▶ Ability to deliver a personal message	————————	Low	————————		High
▶ Ability to reach a large audience	————————	Low	————————		Low
▶ Level of interaction	————————	Low	————————		High
▶ Cost per contact	————————	Low	————————		High
▶ Wastage	————————	Low	————————		Low

Table 9.5
A summary of the
key characteristics
of the tools of
marketing
communication.

across countries and most likely across cultures; the use of media may, thus, require adaptation (Kotler, 2001).

5. Creating the Message

The message must be crafted in a way that is consistent with the objectives of the campaign and it must match the target audience's needs. Copy writers, artists and creative directors involved in the creative process take ideas and transform them into advertisements.

There are also several other situations that suggest the appropriateness of standardized or adaptive strategies within and across cultures. In situations where: (a) the product is utilitarian and the message is informational; (b) the reasons for buying and product usage are rational or less likely to vary in different cultures (e.g. batteries and gasoline); and (c) a brand's identity and desirability are integrally linked to a specific national character (e.g. McDonald's and Coca-Cola are American products and Chanel is a French product), standardized strategies would seem most appropriate and effective (Evans and Berman, 1997: 169).

However, in situations where: (a) product usage varies according to the culture (e.g. most foods and beverages such as coffee and tea); (b) the product benefits are more psychological than tangible, requiring an understanding of the psychologies of different cultures (e.g. snacks and clothing are products with intangible benefits); and (c) the appeal is emotional and a recognition of the vast differences in emotional expression is called for, it would be generally more appropriate and effective to adapt or modify strategies and campaigns to local customs and cultures (Evans and Berman, 1997: 169).

Usually, the creative process involves a creative strategy or *copy platform*. The copy platform has five basic elements. The first element is the objective (i.e. what the advertising should do, think or feel as a result of the campaign). Next, the target audience is identified and described. Basically, you want to know who is your customer. Third is the key consumer benefit (i.e. why should the consumer buy your product), something that also may be different for different countries. Fourth is the 'support'. This addresses whether there is a reason to believe in this benefit? Finally, the 'tone and manner' is important. This is a statement of the product's 'personality'. It asks, 'if the product were a person, what kind of person would the product be' and it reflects the image you want to portray with the product.

6. Measuring Effectiveness of the Marketing Communications Effort

One needs to assess effectiveness of the marketing communications effort to avoid costly mistakes, to evaluate alternative strategies and to determine the effectiveness of the entire programme. The assessment must be relevant to the objectives and must be based on a model of human response to communications. The marketer could assess: (a) what people think or feel about the company's marketing communications message; (b) reactions to the message and content; (c) whether subjects comprehend or remember essential parts of the message content; (d) general awareness of the company's product attributes; (e) beliefs and evaluations of the perceptions of salient product attributes; and (f) overall feelings toward the advertised brand. Such assessment can take place before a full-scale marketing communications campaign is started

Television	Magazines	Newspapers	Radio	Outdoor
Demonstration	Elegance	Information	Imagination	Package identification
Intrusion	Features	News	Personal	Bigger than life
Excitement	Quality	Price	Intimacy	
Entertainment	Beauty			
One-on-one	Sex appeal			
Product-in-use	Sub appeal			
Humour	Recipe			
Leadership	Tradition			
Event	Authority			
	Prestige			

Table 9.6
Qualities of media that give it vitality (life).

by pre-testing various aspects of the message style, form and content, or can be performed after the major campaign has been initiated to see if changes need to be made. In either case, the assessment procedures must match the stated objectives of the marketing communications effort.

In assessing effectiveness, the research conducted must take into account cultural differences. Issues such as who should be interviewed, how individuals are selected, how they are interviewed, when the respondents should be interviewed and who should do the interviewing all require attention.

9.5   The Promotion Plan

To communicate with customers, a marketer chooses from one or more of the five promotion mix elements. The promotion mix includes: advertising, sales promotion, personal selling. publicity/public relations and direct marketing (see Table 6). As a marketing communicator, you want to combine the promotion mix elements to provide clarity of purpose, consistency and maximum impact. This section elaborates on each element and highlights some common problems that marketers must consider when crossing borders (see Table 7).

Advertising

This is any paid form of non-personal communications about a company and its products by an identified sponsor. It uses one of the media (e.g. television, radio, newspapers, magazines and outdoor) and the sponsor must be identified. Advertising's role in the purchase process is generally to create awareness, positioning, consideration and preference. It is best suited for situations where a company wants to build a long-term image, communicate product features and benefits and gain consumer awareness and acceptance of offerings. In short, it is intended to create awareness and favourable attitudes.

The importance of advertising and its cultural role in a society varies dramatically (Terpstra, 1988). In addition, government regulations can affect the content, language, target audience (such as no advertising towards children) and format of advertising. Some countries, such as Germany, allow no comparative advertisements, while other countries may limit the frequency of advertisements, such as Italy which allows no more than 10 showings per year, none closer together than 10 days (Cateora, 1996).

1. *Out of home media*
(a) Transit
(b) Others
   ▶ Trash cans
   ▶ Parking meters
   ▶ Ski chair poles
   ▶ Sides of trucks

2. *Speciality advertising/promotional products*
   ▶ Advertising specialities (e.g., pens, coffee mugs, desk caddies)
   ▶ Premiums

3. *Yellow Pages/telephone directories*

4. *Others*
   ▶ Cereal packaging
   ▶ Advertising in movie theatres
   ▶ Advertising on videotapes
   ▶ Product placement in movies
   ▶ In-flight advertising
   ▶ Internet

Table 9.7
Support media.

Sales promotion

This communication method involves short-term activities that provide extra value or incentive to consumers, retailers and wholesalers for buying or carrying the product and to a company's sales force for selling the product. Tellis (1998: 212) defines a sales promotion as 'any time-bound program of a seller that tries to make an offer more attractive to buyers and requires their participation in the form of an immediate purchase or some other action'. Sales promotion's role is at final stages of the purchase process and is intended to stimulate shopping and actual purchase. It may be directed at consumers (e.g. coupons, rebates, premiums, sweepstakes, contests and price-off), at retailers and wholesalers (e.g. discounts, sales contests, free goods, price deals and promotional allowance) or at the company's sales force (e.g. bonuses, contests and sales rallies).

Forms of sales promotion include the following examples: point-of-purchase or point-of-sale advertising, premiums, speciality advertising, coupons, sampling, deals, sweepstakes, cooperative advertising, trade incentives and event marketing. Sales promotion is best suited for situations when or where a company wants short-term product movement, encourages customers to buy new products and gains awareness and acceptance by retailers and wholesalers. In short, it is intended to encourage immediate action or purchase and to encourage product trial.

As with many forms of promotions, regulations of sales promotions vary greatly by country. For example, both France and Austria do not allow sales premiums where a particular good may be sold below cost. In fact, some countries such as Finland make the use of the word 'free', as in 'buy one get one free', illegal (Cateora and Keaveney, 1987).

Personal Selling

This involves a seller in a person-to-person communication with a buyer or buying team, whereby there is an attempt to persuade the buyer, buying team, or buying centre to buy a company's product. The objectives are to find prospects, convert prospects to customers and to get the buyer to buy a company's product.

The selling process has six steps. The first involves prospecting and qualifying. A possible customer must be identified and a determination must be made as to whether the prospect is a potential customer. Next is the presale preparation. Information about potential customers can be obtained from secondary data sources and referrals. Third is the presentation and demonstration. Here a memorized sales talk may be used to ensure uniform coverage of selling points, or a flexible presentation adaptable to each customer and focused on customer needs may be used. Fourth, objections raised must be resolved and questions answered adequately before the sale can be made. Fifth is the closing. Closing involves getting the customer to agree to buy and, finally, salespeople should follow-up after the sale of major purchases to ensure that the customer is satisfied. Also, if the sale is not made, a follow-up may be necessary to understand why the sale did not occur.

It is worth noting that the selling process will vary across cultures. In some Eastern cultures, the concept of saving face would not allow the sales person to ask directly for a sale. To do so would cause both the seller and the potential buyer to 'lose face'. In addition, it would be considered inappropriate to disagree with or say 'no' to anyone. In Latin American cultures, such a sales process may be very long and drawn out over several weeks or even months. It would never be appropriate to discuss a sales presentation on the first or second meeting, and the actual contract may very well be predicated upon the establishment of a strong, trusting relationship built over time.

Publicity and Public Relations

Publicity is non-personal communication about a company that is run in the media for free and is not directly paid by the company. A company could employ any of the following to gain positive publicity: press releases, event sponsorship, feature articles, exclusive interviews, community involvement, press kits and press conferences.

Public relations attempts to present the whole organization in a positive light and often operates through non-paid media. A company shows its public responsibility and concerns for the public good through its public relations. It communicates with its internal publics (i.e. employees, stakeholders and board of trustees) to maintain their support and provide them with the necessary information for meaningful interaction with the external publics. Through internal memos, company events and company magazines, newsletters and newspapers, the public relations function with respect to the internal publics can be carried out. It also communicates with its external publics (i.e. customers, suppliers, the government, the press, consumer advocates and financial institutions) to maintain a positive image and gain needed support for its functions. The influence of the firm's external publics cannot be ignored. Thus, a firm must continuously communicate with these external stakeholders through all available channels to maintain a positive image (Murphy and Cunningham, 1993).

It is essential that companies communicate effectively with international publics (see external publics above). A firm's reputation should be consistent from country to country, and a consistent, coordinated, global public relations campaign is essential for that to happen. Good public relations programmes will ensure that companies are perceived as good corporate citizens, as environmentally responsible and as contributing to the good of society.

Direct Marketing

This is as an interactive system of marketing that uses one or more advertising media to effect a measurable response in the form of an order, an inquiry or a visit to a store or other place of business for the purchase of a specific product. It can generate inquiries, build loyalty, create awareness, build store traffic and generate or qualify leads. Examples of direct marketing tools are direct mail, telemarketing, catalogue marketing, permission e-mail and e-direct mail. The company determines the objectives of such an endeavour, defines the target market, develops a database to reach the target, determines appropriate direct marketing strategies to employ to effect the desired outcome and evaluates the effectiveness of the efforts. In evaluating the effectiveness, one could consider the cost per thousand, number of inquiries, number of inquiries converted to sales, percentage of repeat purchases, number of orders, promotion efficiency (i.e. profits divided by promotion costs) and costs per order.

Direct mail is not without problems internationally. In countries such as Chile, where the mail recipient may be expected to pay up to half of the mailing cost, direct mail could have the opposite of the intended effect. When comparing United States and European mailing systems, European factors to consider are: limited availability of mailing lists; higher costs of and wide variance in postal rates; stricter advertising and promotion claim regulations; lower credit card penetration rates for payments; and differences in merchandise return policies (Fishman, 1990: 48–58).

9.6 Conclusion

The basic tenets of the marketing communications process are the same regardless of the cultural context. However, marketing communications in different cultures requires an understanding of the differences in the cultures and how such differences might impact on the marketing communications process.

This chapter has discussed six steps in developing an effective marketing communications programme. The marketing communicator must: (1) identify the target market; (2) determine the objectives to be accomplished; (3) establish a budget; (4) develop a media plan; (5) design the message or develop a creative strategy; and (6) assess the effectiveness of the marketing communications effort. Also discussed were the target market, objectives, creativity strategy, media strategy and effectiveness. The different types of promotions (advertising, direct marketing, sales promotion, publicity/public relations and personal selling) will be discussed in the marketing mix chapter to follow.

In developing a multicultural marketing communication process, the marketer must manage these elements to produce a unified, positive and consistent message across cultures. Decisions must be made regarding budget. Promotion costs vary tremendously across cultures, as does receptivity. Also, decisions must be made with respect to what channels to use, how the programme will be executed and how results will be measured. Thinking globally but acting locally would suggest taking into account the differences in the firm's marketing objectives and media effectiveness across cultures. Cultural differences should also be taken into account in crafting the message form, style, content and theme. Coordinating the timing, budgeting and content decisions is necessary if one wants to have maximum impact and to build brand equity.

REVIEW QUESTIONS

1. Assume you have to allocate your company's budget – identify and discuss problems associated across three cultures, namely, Brazil, the Netherlands and Japan.

2. Develop a marketing communication campaign for a global restaurant chain.

3. As a marketing manager for a United States-based French book publisher that is entering French-speaking West Africa for the first time, devise a promotion budget relying on the objective–task method.

4. Discuss the multicultural marketing communications process. How would differences in culture affect this process?

5. Identify and discuss potential problems likely to be encountered in a multicultural marketing communications assessment of effectiveness.

6. Explain how personal selling may differ in a culture different from your own.

References

Bagozzi, R. P., Rosa, J. A., Celly, K. S. and Coronel, F. (1998) *Marketing Management*, Upper Saddle River, NJ: Prentice Hall.

Cateora, P. R. (1996) *International Marketing*, 9th edn., Chicago: Richard D. Irwin.

Cateora, P. R. and Keaveney, S. (1987) *Marketing: An International Perspective*, Homewood, IL: Richard D. Irwin.

Daniels, J. D., Radebaugh, L. H. and Sullivan, D. P. (2002) *Globalization and Business*, Upper Saddle River, NJ: Prentice Hall.

Evans, J. R. and Berman, B. (1997) *Marketing*, Upper Saddle River, NJ: Prentice Hall.

Ferraro, G. (2002) *The Cultural Dimensions of International Business*, Upper Saddle River, NJ: Prentice-Hall.

Fishman, A. (1990) 'International mail order guide', *Direct Marketing*, October.

Griffin, T. (1993) *International Marketing Communications*, Oxford: Butterworth-Heinemann.

Hall, E. T. (1960) 'The silent language in overseas business', *Harvard Business Review* (May–June): 87–96.

Hall, E. T. (1976) 'How cultures collide', *Psychology Today* (July): 66–97.

Hawkins, D. I. , Best, R. J. and Coney, K. A. (2001) *Consumer Behavior: Building Marketing Strategy*, New York: McGraw-Hill.

Hofstede, G. H. (1983) 'National cultures in four dimensions: a research-based theory of cultural differences among nations', *International Studies of Management and Organizations* 13(1–2): 46–74.

Hofstede, G. H. (1984) *Culture's Consequences: International Differences in Work-related Values*, Beverly Hills, CA: Sage Publications.

Hofstede, G. (1991) *Cultures and Organizations: Software of the Mind*, London: McGraw-Hill.

Hollensen, S. (1998) *Global Marketing: A Market-Responsive Approach*, New York: Prentice Hall.

Ishikawa, M. (1987) 'Latest trends in Japanese advertising', paper presented at the Fifteenth World Industrial Advertising Congress, Brussels.

Keegan, W. J. and Green, M. S. (2000) *Global Marketing*, New York: Prentice Hall.

Kluckhohn, F. R. and Strodbeck, F. L. (1961) *Variations in Value Orientations*, New York: Harper & Row.

Kotler, P. (2001) *Marketing Management*, Upper Saddle River, NJ: Prentice Hall.

de Mooij, M. (1998) *Global Marketing and Advertising: Understanding Cultural Paradoxes*, Thousand Oaks, CA: Sage Publications.

Murphy, J. H. and Cunningham, I. C. M. (1993) *Advertising and Marketing Communication*, New York: The Dryden Press.

Parente, D. (2000) *Advertising Campaign Strategy: A Guide to Marketing Communications Plans*, New York: The Dryden Press.

Ricks, D. A. (1993) *Blunders in International Business*, Cambridge, MA: Blackwell Publishers.

Schultz, D. E., Tannenbaum, S. and Lauterborn, R. F. (1993) *Integrated Marketing Communications: Pulling It All Together and Making It Work*, Lincolnwood, IL: NTC Business Books.

Tellis, G. (1998) *Advertising and Sales Promotion Strategy*, New York: Addison-Wesley.

Terpstra, V. (1988) *International Dimensions of Marketing*, 2nd edn., Boston: PWS-KENT Publishing Company.

Toyne, B. and Walters, P. G. P. (1993) *Global Marketing Management: A Strategic Perspective*, Boston: Allyn and Bacon.

Usunier, J.-C. (1996) *Marketing Across Cultures*, London: Prentice Hall Europe.

Exploring the impact of consumer ethnocentrism, country of origin and branding on consumer choice

Greg Elliott and Chandrama Acharya

C3.1 Introduction

The objectives of this study were, broadly, to examine the relationships between consumer ethnocentrism and home country bias, perceptions of quality and expressed choice for products assembled and designed domestically[1] or in foreign countries.

The scale used for measuring consumer ethnocentrism is the original CETSCALE as developed by Shimp and Sharma (1987). CETSCALE uses 17 items to measure the ethnocentric tendencies of the consumer using a 7-point bi-polar scale. Psychometric properties such as reliability, validity and dimensionality were tested.

The effects of 'Country of Assembly' (COA) , 'Country of Design' (COD) and the existence (or otherwise) of a home country bias were measured using 'full-profile conjoint analysis' with $3 \times 3 \times 3 \times 3$ factorial design. The procedure is similar to that of an experimental design with repeated measures (Louviere, 1988). A set of product profiles (short product descriptions) is constructed by combining the attributes in a factorial manner. The subjects were asked to rate the quality of product according to a seven-point Likert scale ('extremely good'/'extremely poor'). Purchase intentions were measured using a five-point Likert scale ('definitely buy'/'definitely not buy').

Finally, the study also explored the statistical correlation between consumer ethnocentrism and perceptions of product quality and expressed product choices.

Table C3.1 displays the study design. Three product categories were considered according to their presumed level of involvement, viz. car (high involvement), jeans

Attributes	Product category		
	Car	Jeans	Tinned pineapple
Country of assembly	Australia	Australia	Australia
	South Korea	South Korea	Philippines
	Japan	The USA	Japan
Country of design	Japan	The USA	Australia
	Australia	Australia	Philippines
	South Korea	South Korea	Japan
Brand	Ford Festiva	Levi's	Del Monte
	Toyota Starlet	Giordano	SPC
	Hyundai Excel	Jag	Kara
Price	$12,000	£85	$1.60
	$15,000	£70	$2.00
	$18,000	£55	$2.40

Table C3.1
Study design for
conjoint analysis.

(medium) and tinned pineapples (low). This study used four attributes, each with three levels. In the case of the car, three brands with similar features were chosen; Toyota Starlet, Ford Festiva and Hyundai Excel. For jeans, the three brands chosen were Levi's, Jag and Giordano. In the case of tinned pineapple, Del Monte, SPC and Kara were the three brands. Three countries of assembly and three countries of design were chosen, namely, Japan, Australia and South Korea for cars; the USA, Australia and South Korea for jeans; and Japan, Australia and the Philippines for pineapple.[2] Three price levels have been incorporated in the conjoint model: the regular price of the product and two other price levels – 20 per cent less and 20 per cent more than the regular price. For all the three products, Australia has been chosen both as a country of assembly and country of design. To make the study more realistic, all the brand names, countries of origin and countries of design and price levels were chosen according to the particular market conditions that prevailed in Australia at the time of designing the research.

The survey was administered through mail questionnaires to a sample of one thousand randomly selected students at the Graduate School of Management, Macquarie University in Australia, between November 1997 and March 1998. In total, 275 completed questionnaires were received, of which 248 were considered as useable – an effective response rate of approximately 25 per cent. Of the 248 respondents, 59.7 per cent were male and the mean age of the sample was 36.7 years. The average personal income was $34,765.82. This accords with the known distribution of students at the school (allowing for full-time students). The obvious income, age and sex bias of the sample is acknowledged and replication within the broader population is advocated for future research.

C3.2 Results of the Study

Objective I. To examine whether CETSCALE is a reliable, consistent and unidimensional scale when tested on Australian consumers and adequate to measure consumer ethnocentric tendencies in Australia.

Reliability of CETSCALE was assessed using Cronbach's α (Fornell and Larcker, 1981). For the sample of Australian consumers, Cronbach's α for the CETSCALE is 0.9449. This indicates that the scale is highly reliable. In this study the *standardized item* α value is

0.9458, which is close to α value of 0.9449. This reinforces the conclusion that the CETSCALE is a reliable measure of consumer ethnocentric tendencies in Australia. The result obtained above is closely comparable with those reported in previous studies. According to the study by Shimp and Sharma (1987) on the US sample the alpha value ranged from 0.94 to 0.96. Similarly, Herche (1990) reported Cronbach's α of 0.929 and 0.946 for the original and modified version of the CETSCALE in the US. In a cross-national study, Netemeyer *et al.* (1991) recorded an alpha of 0.91 for the Japanese sample, 0.95 for the US sample, 0.92 for the French sample and 0.94 for the West German sample.

The unidimensionality of CETSCALE was explored using factor analysis. Based on the *eigenvalue*-greater-than-one rule and the *scree* plot, the exploratory factor analysis yielded a two-factor solution for the CETSCALE. The first factor accounted for 54.8 per cent of the variation and the second factor accounted for 7.5 per cent of the variation. It appears that the first factor is the main factor and could explain the construct of ethnocentrism acceptably. The presence of second factor explain only a small proportion of the total variance. From the confirmatory factor solution, the standardized correlation between the two factors is 0.824. This correlation is so high that it could be argued that the two factors represent the same construct of ethnocentrism. Therefore, it can be taken that the scale is somewhat unidimensional, although the results are not as 'pure' as anticipated, nor does the scale capture the high level of variance which might be expected.

Total score on the 17-point CETSCALE might vary between 17 and 119, due to the use of a 7-point Likert scale. The mean scale value is the predictor of the intensity of ethnocentrism (Shimp and Sharma, 1987). A higher mean scale value indicates higher consumer ethnocentrism. The mean value of the scale is found to be 56.31 for Australian consumers. This result is also comparable to those from Shimp and Sharma's study in the USA, where the value ranges from 56.62 to 68.58 (Shimp and Sharma, 1987). The total

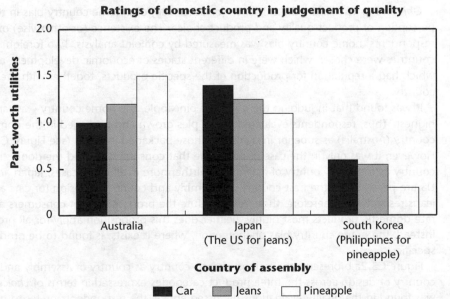

Ratings of domestic country in judgement of quality

Figure C3.1a
Country of
assembly and
perceived quality.

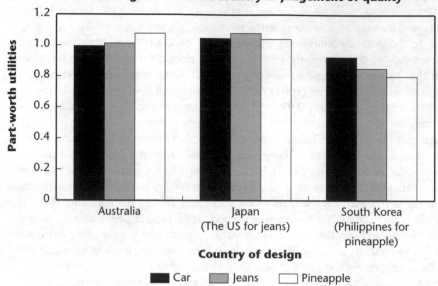

Ratings of domestic country in judgement of quality

Figure C3.1b
Country of design
and perceived
quality.

mean of the scale is 3.31 with a standard deviation of 2.47, and there is very little variation in the individual item means.

From the above results it is evident that Australian consumers display similar levels of consumer ethnocentrism to similar groups in foreign countries, and that CETSCALE's high internal consistency and validity were reconfirmed. However, there is evidence that the scale is not unidimensional, suggesting that consumer ethnocentrism may be a more complex phenomenon. The modest variance explained by the two-factor solution is also a noteworthy finding.

Objective II. To identify the existence (or otherwise) of a home country bias in the perception of product quality and product choice. The existence (or otherwise) of the respondents' home country bias was measured by conjoint analysis. Two foreign countries were chosen which were in different stages of economic development and which had a reputation for production of the specific products, together with the home country.

It was found that in judging the *quality* of pineapple, the home country was ranked highest. Thus, respondents evaluated pineapples grown and packaged in the domestic country (Australia) as superior in quality to those packaged in Japan (see Figure C3.1a,b). However, it was only in the case of pineapple that consumers judged the domestic country as the best 'country of assembly'. Furthermore in all other cases, Japan and the US are perceived as the best country of assembly and country of design for cars and jeans respectively. Therefore, these results refute the proposition that consumers always rate domestic products most highly; neither does this proposition apply for all products. Instead, the home country bias phenomenon, where it exists, is found to be product-specific.

Figure C3.2a,b presents the ratings of each country as country of assembly and country of design across the three product categories expressed in terms of *choice*. As was found in the quality evaluations discussed above, the respondents prefer to buy

Ratings of domestic country on choice

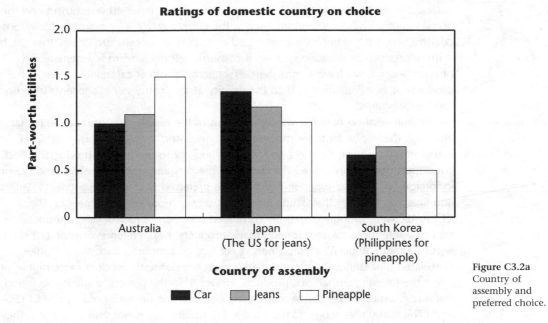

Country of assembly

■ Car ▨ Jeans □ Pineapple

Figure C3.2a
Country of
assembly and
preferred choice.

domestically assembled and designed pineapple. In the case of cars and jeans, the consumers prefer to buy products assembled and/or developed in Japan and the US respectively, instead of the domestic equivalent. Thus, the existence of a universal preference for domestic products is refuted. Presumably, Australia is ranked as superior to Japan and the Philippines in the case of tinned pineapple because of the high domestic and international reputation of the Australian food industry.

Ratings of domestic country on choice

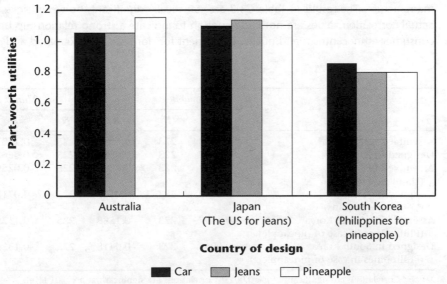

Country of design

■ Car ▨ Jeans □ Pineapple

Figure C3.2b
Country of design
and preferred
choice.

Objective III. To identify the relationship between consumer ethnocentrism and the home country bias. An important issue in the current study is to examine if the home country bias is a function of a generalized consumer ethnocentrism or whether the bias is more product- or situation-specific. If consumer ethnocentrism is a generalized phenomenon, it will have a consistent effect across product categories. If it is more product- or situation-specific, then the validity of the 'consumer ethnocentrism' concept can be questioned.

One immediate conclusion which arises out of the results discussed above is that although the respondents are moderately ethnocentric as measured by CETSCALE, in an actual product choice situation, they were found *not* to prefer local products. In fact, consumers not only evaluated the quality of the cars and jeans assembled and designed in foreign countries as superior, but they also preferred to buy those products. Shimp and Sharma (1987) in their study on US consumers reported that scores on the CETSCALE were strongly negatively correlated with consumers' beliefs, attitudes and purchase intentions towards foreign-made products. Also, Netemeyer *et al.* (1991) reported that ethnocentric consumers reject foreign products. Both these studies postulated that ethnocentric consumers regard the domestic product more highly, and reject the foreign competitors' products. However, in the present study it was found that the Australian consumers were moderately ethnocentric (as measured by the CETSCALE), and exhibited similar scores as reported in US studies, yet it was also found that they evaluated foreign products highly and were likely to buy such products.

The relationship between consumer ethnocentrism (as measured by the CETSCALE) and expressed choice and quality perception (as measured by the conjoint analysis) is further examined in the following table. Table C3.3 presents the Spearman correlation coefficients between consumer ethnocentric tendencies and consumers' judgement of quality of products assembled or designed domestically versus their foreign counterparts.

Table C3.2 examines how Australian consumers assess their own country's product (i.e. assembled and designed in Australia), relative to other countries' competing products. Theoretically (Shimp and Sharma, 1987; Herche 1990, 1992; Netemeyer *et al.*, 1991), the ethnocentric consumer will always regard their own country as the best country of manufacture. The results in Table C3.3 are statistically significant, however, since the actual correlation values are not large enough to indicate a strong relationship between consumer ethnocentrism and quality judgement for domestically assembled and

	Automobiles		Jeans		Tinned pineapple	
	R	N	R	N	R	N
Assembled in Australia[a]	0.1863	223	0.1887	225	0.1623	228
Designed in Australia[b]	0.0592	223	0.0561	225	0.0662	228
Assembled in Japan (US in case of jeans)[b]	0.0311	223	0.0269	225	−0.0259	228
Designed in Japan (US in case of jeans)[b]	0.0642	223	−0.0109	225	−0.0718	228
Assembled in South Korea[b] (Philippines in case of pineapple)	−0.1497	223	−0.1588	225	−0.1175	228
Designed in South Korea (Philippines in case of pineapple)	−0.0057	223	−0.0418	225	−0.1329	228

Table C3.2 The correlation between CETSCALE scores and the evaluation of quality of products.

Notes: [a] Correlations are significant at $p < 0.001$. [b] Correlations are significant at $p < 0.01$ level.

	Automobiles		Jeans		Tinned pineapple	
	R	N	R	N	R	N
Assembled in Australia[a]	0.3274	205	0.2879	235	0.2373	238
Designed in Australia[a]	0.2483	205	0.1411	235	0.0601	238
Assembled in Japan (US in case of jeans)[b]	–0.1030	205	–0.0733	235	–0.1527	238
Designed in Japan (US in case of jeans)[b]	–0.1860	205	–0.1169	235	–0.1206	238
Assembled in South Korea[b] (Philippines in case of pineapple)	–0.1949	205	–0.2131	235	–0.1302	238
Designed in South Korea (Philippines in case of pineapple)	–0.0840	205	–0.0177	235	–0.1675	238

Table C3.3
The correlation between CETSCALE scores and the choice of products.

Notes: [a] Correlations are significant at $p < 0.001$. [b] Correlations are significant at $p < 0.01$ level.

designed products. In other words, this study finds that there is not a strong relationship between ethnocentrism and quality evaluations of the locally designed or assembled product. Nonetheless, the relations between these two are positive, i.e. the higher the ethnocentrism, the higher will be the evaluation of quality. In the case of products assembled and designed in South Korea (and the Philippines for tinned pineapple), the ethnocentric consumers evaluated the quality as inferior which is depicted by the clear negative correlation between the CETSCALE score and the perception of quality values. Hence, it can be said that the higher the consumer ethnocentrism, the lower would be the quality perception of the products assembled or designed in a foreign country. However, the absolute value of r is not high enough to represent a strong negative relation. Note also that consumers, in the case of products like car and jeans, evaluated these foreign products as good in quality (Figure C3.1a,b). This is contrary to the concept of consumer ethnocentrism which suggests that ethnocentric consumers will be antagonistic towards foreign products and will reject them.

Similarly, the correlations between consumer ethnocentrism and product choice for domestically assembled and designed products are presented in Table C3.3. All the values are positive and statistically significant, although they are not high in absolute terms.

The results shown in Table C3.3 are consistent with the proposition that Australian ethnocentric consumers prefer to purchase a product assembled and designed in the domestic country and discard the products assembled and designed overseas. The findings of this study support the existing theoretical framework. However, the low values of the correlation coefficient suggest that ethnocentric consumers would not always buy domestically-made products. The results of this study thus support the existence of a positive relation, but question the strength of relationship.

C3.3 The Impact of Branding

The results of this study also provide an examination of the impact of 'branding' on consumer preferences, relative to the other product attributes studied, notably, 'country of design', 'country of assembly' and 'price' across the three product categories. From the perspective of the foreign manufacturer, at a simple level, it provides evidence of the

Perceived quality	Automotive		Jeans		Pineapple	
	(%)	(Rank)	(%)	(Rank)	(%)	(Rank)
Country of assembly	38.8	(1)	36.1	(1)	45.3	(1)
Country of design	24.6	(2)	22.6	(3)	19.4	(3)
Brand	17.6	(4)	24.9	(2)	20.1	(2)
Price	19.0	(3)	16.4	(4)	15.2	(4)

Table C3.4 Relative importance of attributes in quality judgements.

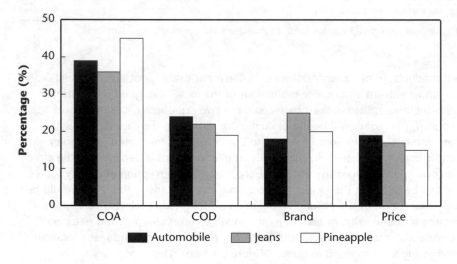

Figure C3.3a Relative importance of attributes in judgements of quality.

importance of branding and whether the foreign-branded imported product will be preferred over the locally-made brand. It also suggests whether or not the foreign brand should be locally-designed and/or manufactured in preference to foreign-designed and imported.

As Table C3.4 and Figure C3.3a show, in judgements of quality, 'country of assembly' is by far the most important attribute of those studied across all three product categories. Arguably, country of assembly is used as a 'surrogate' indicator by consumers where they are unable to evaluate or judge quality prior to purchase. Brand is last in importance in relation to cars and second in relation to jeans and pineapple respectively. This finding suggests that branding may play a more important role in consumers' judgements of quality in low- and medium-level involvement products. In the case of high-involvement products, with the higher attendant risks, consumers seem to look beyond the brand name.

Table C3.5 and Figure C3.3b show the relative importance of the four product attributes on expressed product choice. Again, the importance of country of assembly is evident as the most important attribute across the three product categories studied. Branding is second for both jeans and pineapple (medium- and low-involvement products respectively), and fourth in importance in the case of cars (high-involvement). In the case of the latter, price becomes the second most important criterion, presumably

Perceived quality	Automotive		Jeans		Pineapple	
	(%)	(Rank)	(%)	(Rank)	(%)	(Rank)
Country of assembly	35.2	(1)	31.2	(1)	39.6	(1)
Country of design	21.2	(3)	21.7	(3)	20.0	(3)
Brand	19.2	(4)	27.5	(2)	22.6	(2)
Price	24.4	(2)	19.6	(4)	17.6	(4)

Table C3.5
Relative importance of attributes in choice.

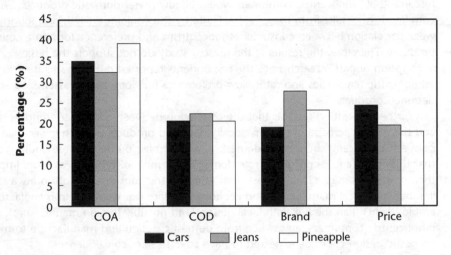

Figure C3.3b
Relative importance of attributes on choice.

as a reflection of the absolute level of consumer risk associated with high-priced product categories.

Collectively, these results indicate that branding is important in consumers' judgements of quality and in their expressed product choices. When combined with local country of assembly, strong international brands would appear to have an almost unassailable position in the minds of consumers. However, on the basis of the above results, companies which market imported international brands need to be particularly aware of the power of locally assembled products, especially those which are strong brands.

C3.4 Discussion and Implications

This study has found an apparently weak relation between ethnocentrism and preference for domestic products. This has important implications for 'Australian Made' and other similar campaigns. Whilst Elliott and Cameron (1994) have found that Australian consumers would generally prefer the Australian-made product, where its quality and price were comparable to the imported competition, in the current circumstances, the objectives of the campaign to buy Australian–produced goods seem to be being thwarted. This study shows that consumers, though moderately ethnocentric, do not necessarily prefer to buy domestically assembled and designed products. It was noted that consumers appear to prefer to buy cars from Japan and jeans assembled and designed in the USA. Only in the case of tinned pineapple was the domestic product the first choice. However, this choice might not simply be because the consumers are ethnocentric. It might be because the Australian people trust Australian foods more than food from another country (Rawlings, 1993) – a very plausible explanation. It appears, moreover, that consumer ethnocentrism might not strongly influence purchasing decisions, especially for high-involvement products.

These findings also have important implications for the usefulness, or otherwise, of the 'consumer ethnocentrism' concept. This study has tested the basic assumption of past research that ethnocentric consumers would blindly prefer domestic products. This study correlated the results from the CETSCALE and by the conjoint analysis and found only a weak correlation between consumer ethnocentrism and preference for home country products. Therefore, the results of the present study do not support the basic assumption of past research since the respondents reported rather moderate ethnocentric tendencies and rather low preferences for domestically assembled and designed products.

A further interesting result is that the correlation between consumer ethnocentrism and the quality perception of domestically designed products is much lower than that between ethnocentrism and the domestically assembled product. These findings show that the ethnocentric consumers rate domestic assembly of products as more important than domestic design. This suggests that ethnocentric consumers might draw a stronger link between local manufacture and economic welfare (for example, in manufacturing employment) than the link with local design (and possibly foreign manufacture). Among ethnocentric consumers, any switch from domestic design and manufacture to merely domestic design could be expected to have adverse sales consequences.

Of more immediate concern for Australian manufacturers is the finding that, even though consumers are moderately ethnocentric, products such as cars and jeans which are Australian designed and/or Australian assembled do not seem to be regarded as high in quality, nor are they the preferred choice. The exception appears to be Australian-made food.

A consistent thrust of past research on consumer ethnocentrism (Shimp and Sharma, 1987; Netemeyer *et al.*, 1991) is that highly ethnocentric consumers will discard products from foreign countries. The results from the present study, however, only partially support these past findings. It would seem likely that the reputations of Japan and the USA for excellence in designing and manufacturing overpower the effect of ethnocentrism in terms of quality judgements at the average levels of ethnocentrism recorded in this study.

Therefore, an important conclusion of this study is that, at the level of ethnocentrism measured in the current study, consumers will not always evaluate domestic products highly and foreign products negatively. Given that the levels of ethnocentrism measured in this study are very similar to those measured in Shimp and Sharma's (1987) comparable US study, the question arises as to the 'threshold' level of consumer ethnocentrism, at which it makes a material impact on consumers' choice behaviour.

Thus, a more fundamental question about the usefulness of CETSCALE is raised by this study. Can CETSCALE measure the choice behaviour of consumers or it is similar to other scales such as IQ and GMAT, with their debatable low predictive validity? The issue is whether it is a scale just to measure consumer ethnocentrism, *per se*, or whether it can predict and explain choice behaviour. On the basis of the present studies, and the moderate levels of consumer ethnocentrism observed, the link to choice behaviour is tenuous.

C3.5 Conclusion

It was found that Australian consumers are moderately ethnocentric and that the scale is reliable. However, the correlation between the CETSCALE score and the actual purchase intention for domestic products was found to be low. Therefore, for moderately ethnocentric consumers there is no guarantee that they will purchase domestic products. More commonly, a range of other factors such as brand, price and product type will be more important moderators. An important question arises at this point – at what level would the score of the CETSCALE be a reliable predictor of consumers' choice behaviour? Future examinations of ethnocentrism should address this issue if the scale is to have significance beyond its narrow psychometric application.

Notes

1. This study followed Han and Terpstra (1988) and Chao (1993) in drawing the distinction between 'country of design' and 'country of manufacture' rather than the more common 'country of origin' to better reflect the growing trend towards transnational design and manufacturing arrangements. A contemporary example would be the 'Ford Courier' one-tonne truck sold in Australia which is, in reality, designed by Mazda in Japan and manufactured by Mazda in Thailand. The implications of this distinction are discussed in detail elsewhere (Acharya and Elliott, 2000).
2. In the case of pineapples the term 'country of design' is thought to be inappropriate or misleading. To make the variable meaningful and realistic, the term actually used in the questionnaire was 'country where design or idea was first developed'.

ACTIVITY

1. What does the term 'country of origin' effect mean? What are its implications for both importers and local manufacturers?

2. Similarly, what is implied in the 'home country bias' for both importers and local manufacturers?

3. What is the relationship between the 'country of origin' effect and 'consumer ethnocentrism'? Under what conditions would these terms be 'positively' and 'negatively' correlated? Can you suggest examples of products in your country which display positive and/or negative correlation?

4. What do you feel are the implications of the existence of strong consumer ethnocentrism (among certain consumer segments) for governments wishing to promote local manufacturing through 'Buy Local' advertising campaigns?

5. How would you explain the market dominance of some globally-branded products in markets where there is also a significant degree of 'consumer ethnocentrism'?

6. Similarly, what are the implications for international companies who market strong global brands when entering local markets where there is strong consumer ethnocentrism among some market segments? *continued* ☞

ACTIVITY cont.

7. In Australia, the fact that a product is produced by a company which is 'Australian Owned' is being increasingly used as a competitive claim against products which are 'Australian Made', but by companies which are foreign-owned. As the marketing manager for the 'foreign owned' company, how would you react to such claims?

8. In international marketing, an inevitable clash arises from the pursuit of efficiencies through 'economies of scale' in production and distribution, against the imperative to modify the product to suit the preferences of the consumers in the local market. As the importer and marketer of foreign-made products, how would you resolve this issue in practice?

References

Acharya, C. and Elliott, G. (2001) 'An examination of the effects of "country of design" and "country of assembly" on quality perceptions and purchase intentions', *Australasian Marketing Journal*.

Chao, P. (1993) 'Partitioning country of origin effects: consumer evaluation of a hybrid product', *Journal of International Business Studies*, Second quarter, 291–306.

Elliott, G. R. and Cameron, R. S. (1994) 'Consumer perception of product quality and the country-of-origin effect', *Journal of International Marketing,* 2(2), 49–62.

Han, M. C. and Terpstra, V. (1988) 'Country-of-origin effects for uni-national and bi-national products', *Journal of International Business Studies*, (Summer), 235–54.

Herche, J. (1990) 'The measurement of consumer ethnocentrism: revising the CETSCALE', in B. J. Dunlap and N. C. Cullowhee (eds), *Developments in Marketing Science*, Academy of Marketing Science, XIII, 371–75.

Louviere, J. L. (1988) *Analyzing Decision Making*, Newbury Park: CA: Sage Publications.

Netemeyer, R. G., Durvasula, S. and Lichtenstein, D. R. (1991) 'A cross-national assessment of the reliability and validity of the CETSCALE', *Journal of Marketing Research*, XXVII (August), 320–27.

Rawlings, S. (1993) 'Patriot games', *B & T*, March 5, 12–13.

Shimp, T. A. and Sharma, S. (1987) 'Consumer ethnocentrism: construction and validation of the CETSCALE', *Journal of Marketing Research*, XXIV (August), 280–89.

The Euro: a cultural shock to shopping

Michael Callow and Dawn Lerman

C4.1 Introduction

One of the more significant pricing issues in the cross-national arena is the circulation of Euro notes and coins in Europe. The Euro was officially launched at the beginning of 1999 as an electronic currency to be used mainly by banks and companies operating in the Eurozone. As of 1 January 2002, more than 300 million consumers in the twelve participating countries have come face to face with a brand new shopping experience upon the much anticipated arrival of Euro bills and notes. Those countries that are participating include Germany, France, Italy, Spain, the Netherlands, Belgium, Austria, Portugal, Finland, Ireland, Luxembourg and Greece. The three remaining members of the European Parliament – Britain, Sweden and Denmark – have opted not to participate in the Euro. During a two-month transition period, consumers in participating countries were able to purchase products using their local currency, but received change in Euros and cents. After the transition period, the Euro has replaced national currencies and the Euroconsumer has made purchases in the new currency.

The success or failure of the single European currency will be measured in terms of its effect on the economic, political, social and cultural environments. It is noteworthy that not all of the 15 member states are participating in the single currency experiment. The main arguments for and against a single European currency are as follows (Antweiler, 2001).

C4.2 Arguments for the Euro

1. *Reduction of transaction costs.* A fundamental benefit of dealing with a single currency means that businesses and consumers alike will not need to incur any currency conversion costs when purchasing or selling among member nations.
2. *Elimination of exchange rate uncertainty.* A constant source of headaches in international business is the fluctuation of exchange rates and their effect on international pricing strategies. The introduction of a single currency eliminates this

potential problem and provides greater strategic control on pricing policies within the twelve nations. From a consumer perspective, the ability to pay in Euros for products when travelling to neighbouring countries allows for a more direct comparison of prices between the host country and the home country.

3. *Price transparency and increased competition.* The fact that products and services across the 12 nations will be priced in the same currency provides an opportunity for businesses and consumers to shop around for the best deal. This price transparency is likely to increase competition beyond the domestic market. Additionally, businesses will be pressed to justify the practice of variable national pricing policies within Europe. This should in theory lead to some degree of price convergence among the member nations (Littlechild and Gunde, 1999).

4. *A strong currency in the global marketplace.* It is expected that the Euro will rival the US dollar and the Japanese yen as one of the leading global currencies. To date, the Euro has fared poorly relative to the dollar (Laffer, 2001). However, proponents of the Euro argue that over time the Euro will become the second most important reserve currency after the dollar (Antweiler, 2001).

5. *Elimination of competitive devaluations among member nations.* In order to jump-start a sluggish local economy, individual nation governments have in the past reverted to devaluating their currency to gain a trade advantage over other countries (Taylor, 1998). The idea behind this is that a weaker currency will increase the country's exports while at the same time making imports more expensive (Cooper and Sesit, 1998). This can therefore be viewed as a trade barrier by the country's main trading partners, since it artificially increases the price of imported goods and services and provides a competitive price advantage for the country's exports. The introduction of a single currency would eliminate this type of competitive devaluation by individual nations.

C4.3 Arguments against the Euro

1. *Cost of introduction.* Once the Euro began circulation in 2002, consumers and businesses alike needed to exchange their bills and coins for new ones. In addition, all prices and wages have been converted into Euros. This changeover generated substantial costs, since banks and businesses needed to update IT software for accounting and payroll purposes, and businesses were required to to update price lists, train staff and inform consumers about the changes (Antweiler, 2001). Opponents fear that the financial costs of introducing the Euro far outweigh any potential savings derived from single currency transactions. Indeed, chartered accountants Chantrey Vellacot DFK estimate that it would cost Britain roughly £36 billion to join the Euro (Beirne *et al.*, 2001).

2. *Non-synchronicity of business cycles.* An 'optimum currency area' is created when the benefits of adopting a single currency (discussed in the preceding section) far outweigh the costs of relinquishing national exchange rates and fiscal autonomy (Mundell, 1961; Ricci, 1997). Opponents of the Euro argue that member nations do not have similar business cycles and, therefore, national exchange rates and fiscal autonomy are needed as internal instruments of adjustment. A one-size-fits-all monetary and fiscal policy would necessitate a commonality of economic and social needs between member nations. Let's consider the following futuristic scenario:

Germany would benefit from higher interest rates to curb growing inflation, whereas Italy would benefit from lower interest rates to help support its sagging economy. The European Central Bank (headquartered in Frankfurt, Germany) increases interest rates, which has a short-term effect of strengthening the Euro relative to the dollar. This makes Italian exports even pricier in the US market, further hindering the Italian economy and leading to higher unemployment in the country. Whereas, in theory, the Italian worker could seek work elsewhere in the European Union, labour mobility is generally much lower than in the USA (Ricci, 1997).

3. *A loss of cultural identity.* Opponents of the Euro argue that it is the first step towards greater integration in the form of a federalist union similar to the United States of America. In Britain in particular, several anti-Euro campaigns have emerged in an attempt to keep the pound as Britain's currency (visit <www.keepthepound. org.uk/> and <www.no-euro.com/>). These campaigns argue that monetary union and political union are deeply intertwined, and that national sovereignty would be imperiled by joining the Euro. They deplore the notion of a federalist Europe that would lead to greater monetary, fiscal, political and cultural harmonization.

The main arguments for implementing the Euro are essentially driven by economic considerations. Arguments against the Euro, whilst incorporating economic issues, also address the sociocultural ramifications of a single European currency. We now look at some of the cultural aspects that are likely to be affected by the introduction of the Euro.

The dissolution of national currencies in favour of a single European currency among the participating member states has important ramifications for the consumer from a cultural perspective. Culture is, after all, the sharing of a symbolic system among members of a society (Hofstede, 1991). This symbolic system allows an individual to make sense of his or her external environment, allowing the person to perceive, explain, make choices and act (Maehr, 1976). It enables a person to structure experiences in the form of a cultural schema, thus providing him or her with the necessary tools to assimilate new information. A nation's currency constitutes part of the symbolic system that is used in the market place to communicate the value of goods and services. The shopping experience itself is rooted in culture. Across Europe, laws abound that protect the small family stores from larger, more innovative retail outlets in order to preserve a certain way of life (Cateora and Graham, 1999). Thus, the introduction of the Euro is likely to encounter some cultural resistance by parts of the consumer base.

C4.4 Consumer Reference Prices

In 2002, millions of Euroconsumers will essentially be re-learning how to shop in their current environments. Instead of purchasing their groceries from their local store in pesetas, francs, marks, drachmas, and so on, they will be faced with a new pricing system that complicates their current reference prices. A reference price is any price that a consumer uses as a basis for comparison in judging another price (Schiffman and Kanuk, 2000). An internal reference price is one that is retrieved by the consumer from memory, whereas an external reference price is one that is present at the time of shopping (for instance, another brand's price, or an advertising claim comparing the store's price to higher prices in rival outlets). It is generally thought that consumers rely more on internal reference prices when evaluating the value and believability of price deals.

Euroconsumers will have to convert their reference price points from their existing local currency to the Euro. This can be done by directly translating the Euro price into the local currency (just as a tourist would do when travelling abroad), or by converting the internal reference prices into Euros. Over time, it is expected that the Euroconsumer will be able to create a new set of internal reference prices in terms of the single Euro currency and will not have to convert back to the national currency for making purchasing decisions. This transitional period requires significant effort on the part of the Euroconsumer. Indeed, governments and businesses have been actively preparing the Euroconsumer for the changeover. Businesses were encouraged to use a dual pricing policy in the run-up to Euro-Day. Dual prices essentially show the price of a product in both the local currency and in Euros in order to familiarize the consumer with the new currency and help create a smooth transition in 2002. According to Le Bureau Européen des Unions de Consommateurs (BEUC), only 30–40 per cent of the industry has adopted the dual pricing display, which is essentially a voluntary policy at the European level (BBC News Online, 2001). A more recent agreement on good practices, signed in April 2001, encouraged retailers to start fixing and displaying Euros more visibly than national currencies as of September 2001, and to maintain a dual pricing practice throughout the transition period. It was hoped that this would prepare Euro consumers for 1 January 2002, when they would come face to face with the new currency for the first time.

C4.5   Price Transparency: Fact or Fiction?

The introduction of the Euro brings a certain degree of price transparency to the Eurozone. Consumers from Italy can, in theory, compare local prices to prices in Germany, France, and so on. With the advent of direct marketing, it becomes more feasible to shop around the Eurozone for the best price. This increased sense of cross-border price competition, together with the elimination of exchange rate uncertainty, is expected to lead to greater harmonization of prices across member states (Littlechild and Gunde, 1999). Significant price differentials between countries can only be sustainable if they represent true differences in production and exporting costs. Even if these price differences do reflect legitimate price escalation in terms of transportation costs, longer channels of distributions, taxes, etc., this does not preclude the possibility of the consumer deciding to purchase the product abroad. For instance, the Playstation 2 game console was recently priced on a French retailer's website at 2790 francs and on a Spanish retailer's website at 69,900 pesetas (both prices included taxes and delivery). The French price is equivalent to 425.33 Euros, whereas the Spanish price converts into 420.10 Euros. Purchasing the game console from the Spanish retailer would therefore save the consumer 5.23 Euros, the equivalent of 34 francs or 870 pesetas. This is not to say that consumers buy on the basis of price alone, or that the information is readily at hand in order to make an informed purchasing decision. It may be that the French consumer still prefers to purchase from the French retailer for a variety of non-price reasons. Or that the French consumer is unable to take advantage of this supposed price transparency due to language constraints (the Spanish website is exclusively in Spanish) and/or technological difficulties (the Internet search engine is country-specific).

C4.6 Pricing in the Euro Market

The introduction of the Euro should bring new challenges to firms pricing within the Eurozone. The main cultural issue facing marketing managers is the consumer's lack of familiarity with the value of the new currency. The main economic benefit of the Euro area for the consumer is the promise of price transparency. Yet cultural resistance to the new Euro, together with pricing conversion issues, put into question the real extent to which price transparency will prevail within the Euro market.

Theoretically, the price transparency of the single currency is expected to increase competition and lower prices within the Eurozone. This of course depends on the price elasticity of demand of the product or service in question. It is unlikely that the Euro will have much of an effect on price-inelastic goods that are not highly transportable. Consumers are not going to stray too far for their daily newspaper or morning cup of coffee. At the same time, highly transportable and more costly items such as personal computers, televisions and cars are more likely to receive greater consumer scrutiny vis-à-vis price discrepancies between countries. The potential for European distributors to engage in grey marketing activities (products sold at lower prices in one country are bought in volume and resold in another country where the prices are higher) also means that price harmonization within the participating member states may become a necessity (Wentz and Mussey, 1999). The increase in competition is expected to drive prices for these types of products down, in essence creating a single European market similar to that of the United States of America. American companies may have an advantage over European firms, given their experience in their home market, and in the fact that most of them already treat Europe as a single market, unlike their European competitors (Knox, 1999).

How easy is it going to be for companies to eliminate price differentials between countries? Pure standardization of prices would negate the likely impact of national differences in transportation costs, taxes, wages and other market conditions on profit margins. It may be easier for companies to alter other elements of the marketing mix (offering different product configurations, add-ons, packaging, distribution, etc.) in order to justify price differentials between countries.

Another pricing issue that corporations must consider is the actual price to use in Euros. Consider our example of 69,900 pesetas in Spain for the Playstation 2 console. The true equivalent in Euros would be 420.107 Euros. The Spanish retailer would most likely select one of four potential prices (assuming it wishes to pursue an equivalent pricing strategy); 420, 421, 420.10 or 420.11 Euros. Spanish consumers are not accustomed to fractions in their prices, and prices are generally rounded (e.g. ptas. 1990 or ptas. 39,900) to create pricing sweet spots that are embedded in the customers' brains (Knox, 1999). This would make the last two options perhaps too confusing for the Spanish consumer. If the retailer were to choose 420 Euros they would lose out on 18 pesetas per purchase. At the same time, if they were to price at 421 Euros, they would have essentially increased the price by 148 pesetas. According to consumer advocacy groups such as the *Le Bureau Européen des Unions de Consommateurs*, many consumers fear that companies will take advantage of the consumer's low awareness of the new currency and use the currency conversion period as an opportunity to raise prices (BBC News Online, 2001).

C4.7 Conclusion

In conclusion, the Euro poses significant challenges and uncertainties to consumers and companies operating in the twelve participating countries. Is it the first step towards a greater European identity, or will national identities prevail? Will a single currency lead to greater competition and harmonization of prices, or will price differentials between countries still exist? One thing is certain: during the transition period, the Euro will be a considerable culture shock to most Eurozone consumers and will require marketers to re-evaluate their existing pricing strategies.

ACTIVITY

1. The introduction of the Euro has renewed interest in the creation of a single currency for the United States and Europe. The so-called 'Eurodollar' would replace existing national currencies. Do you think that this is a viable proposal given today's economic, political and cultural climate?

2. Develop a list of advantages and disadvantages for creating a single currency for Europe and the United States.

References

Ackerman, D. and Tellis, G. (2001) 'Can culture affect prices? A cross-cultural study of shopping and retail prices', *Journal of Retailing*, 77(1), Spring, 57–82.

Agarwal, S. and Teas, R. K. (2001) 'Quality cues and perceptions of quality, sacrifice, value, and willingness-to-buy: an examination of cross-national applicability', *Iowa State University Working Paper*, No. 37-1b.

Ahuvia, A. and Wong, N. (1998) 'The effect of cultural orientation in luxury consumption', *Advances in Consumer Research*, E. J. Arnould and L. M. Scott (eds), 25, Ann Arbor, MI: Association for Consumer Research, 29–32.

Antweiler, Werner (2001), 'The EURO: Europe's new currency', *PACIFIC Exchange Rate Service*, <http://pacific.commerce.ubc.ca/xr/euro/menu.html>

BBC News Online (2001) 'Euro and the consumer', *Business Section*, Thursday, 31 May.

Beirne, C., Fitzpatrick, M., Lengvel,Z. and Richards, M. 'The estimated total one-off costs to the UK private and public sectors, should the UK join the Euro'. Report prepared for *Business for Sterling*, Chantrey Vellacot DFK.

Belk, R. W. (1988) 'Third world consumer culture', *Marketing and Developments*, W. Kumcu and A. F. Firat (eds), Greenwich, CT: JAI, 103–27.

Boddewyn, J. J., Soehl, R. and Picard, J. (1986) 'Standardization in international marketing: is Ted Levitt in fact right?' *Business Horizons*, 29(6), 69–75.

Cateora, P. R. and Graham, J. L. (1999) *International Marketing*, 10th edn, New York: Irwin/McGraw-Hill.

Cooper, H. and Sesit, M R. (1998) 'International news: devaluation fails to fuel export boom – absence of thriving markets appears partly to blame', *Wall Street Journal*, New York, NY; October 8, Eastern edn, p. 1.

Fang, T. (1999), *Chinese Business Negotiating Style*, Thousand Oaks, CA: Sage Publications.

Gaul, W. and Lutz, U. (1994) 'Pricing in international marketing and western European economic integration', *Management International Review*, 34(2), 101–24.

Hall, E. T. (1989) *Beyond Culture*, Anchor Books: New York.

Hofstede, G. (1991) *Culture and Organizations: Software of the Mind*, New York: McGraw-Hill.

Jeannet, J-P. and Hennessey, H. D. (1998) *Global Marketing Strategies*, 4th edn, Boston: Houghton Mifflin Company.

Keegan, W. J. (2002), *Global Marketing Management*, 7th edn, Upper Saddle River, NJ.: Prentice Hall.

Knox, A. (1999) 'Pricing in Euroland', *World Trade*, 12(1), January, 52–6.

Kramer, H. E. and Herbig, P. A. (1993) 'The *suq* model of haggling: who, what, when, why?', *Journal of International Consumer Marketing*, 5(2), 55–69.

Laffer, A. B. (2001) 'Europe must reverse the Euro's slide', *Wall Street Journal*, New York, NY; July 19, Eastern edn, p. A22.

Levitt, T. (1983) 'Globalization of markets', *Harvard Business Review*, 61(3), 69–81.

Li, D. and Gallup, A. M. (1995) 'In search of the Chinese consumer', *Chinese Business Review*, 22, September/October, 19–23.

Li, J. C. A., and Noble, P. M. (1999) 'Pricing strategies for industrial goods in Singapore and the US: same or different?' *The Asia Pacific Journal of Management*, 16, August, 293–303.

Littlechild, M. and Gunde, L. (1999) 'The cost of price transparency', *Accountancy*, 123(1265), January, p. 40.

Lynn, M., Zinkhan, G. M. and Harris, J. (1993) 'Consumer tipping: a cross-country study', *Journal of Consumer Research*, 20(3), 478–88.

Maehr, M. L. (1976) 'Sociocultural origins of achievement', in *Basic Concepts in Educational Psychology Series*, L. R. Goulet (series ed.), Monterey, CA: Brooks/Cole.

Maxwell, S. (2001a) 'An expanded price/brand effect model: a demonstration of heterogeneity in global consumption', in *International Marketing Review*, Special edn, N. Malhotra (ed.), forthcoming.

Maxwell, S. (2001b) 'Biased attributions of a higher than expected price: a cross-cultural analysis', *EMAC 2001 Conference*.

McGowan, K. M. and Sternquist, B. J. (1998) 'Dimensions of price as a marketing universal: a comparison of Japanese and US consumers', *Journal of International Marketing*, 6(4), 49–65.

Miller, D., Jackson, P., Thrift, N., Holbrook, B. and Rowlands, M. (1998) *Shopping, Place and Identity*, New York: Routledge.

Monroe, K. B. and Lee, A. Y. (1999) 'Remembering versus knowing: issues in buyers' processing of price information', *Journal of the Academy of Marketing Science*, 27, 207–25.

Mundell, R. A. (1961) 'A theory of optimum currency area', *American Economic Review*, 51.

Myers, M. B. (1997) 'The pricing of export products: why aren't managers satisfied with the results?' *Journal of World Business*, 32(3), 277–89.

Pereira, P. (1999) 'E-business washes into Latin America', *Computer Reseller News*, 873, December 13, 5.

Ricci, L. A. (1997) 'A model of an optimum currency area', *Working Paper of the International Monetary Fund*, June, WP/97/76.

Schiffman, L. G. and Kanuk, L. L. (2000), *Consumer Behavior*, 7th edn, Upper Saddle River, NJ: Prentice Hall.

Stottinger, B. (2001) 'Strategic export pricing: a long and winding road', *Journal of International Marketing*, 9(1), 40–63.

Suri, R., Anderson, R. E. and Kotlov, V. (2001) 'Comparison of the popularity of 9-ending prices in the US and Poland', *Advances in Consumer Research*, M. C. Gilly and J. Meyers-Levy (eds), Valdosta, GA: Association for Consumer Research, 28, p. 141.

Taylor, Bryan (1998), 'The Eurodollar', *Global Financial Data*, <http://www.globalfindata.com/articles/euro.htm>

Wentz, L. and Mussey, D. (1999) 'European marketers await pricing effect of the Euro', *Advertising Age*, 70(2), January 11, p. 6.

Witt, J. and Rao, C. P. (1992) 'The Impact of global sourcing on consumers: country-of-origin effects on perceived risk', *Journal of Global Marketing*, 6(3), 105–128.

Zhou, Z. and Nakamoto, K. (2001) 'Price perceptions: a cross-national study between American and Chinese young consumers', *Advances in Consumer Research*, M. C. Gilly and J. Meyers-Levy (eds), Valdosta, GA: Association for Consumer Research, 28, 161–168.

Implementing a cross-cultural marketing strategy

The previous two Parts have examined the development of cross-cultural marketing strategy within an increasingly changing environment. In Part 3 the text addresses the implementation issues by focusing the question of how marketers can make the strategy work on an international level. Readings in this Part indicate that whilst in theory implementation may appear deceptively easy, in reality the success of the implementation stage of cross-cultural marketing is determined by the marketer's ability to develop appropriate delivery mechanisms across culturally diverse markets and contexts.

Chapter 10 addresses the issue of how, compared to predominantly tangible products, highly intangible products or services are likely to pose unique challenges for non-mainstream consumers. The chapter also examines service provision across goods and services and across mainstream and non-mainstream consumers. Chapter 11 assesses the importance of relationship marketing in cross-cultural contexts from a networks perspective. This chapter also presents interesting insights into how different conceptions of culture impact on cross-cultural relationship marketing research. Finally, the chapter presents a process of model building and its attendant parameters for analyzing aspects of cross-cultural relationship marketing management and the managerial implications arising therefrom.

Chapter 12 addresses corporate social responsibility issues and concerns, particularly in light of their growing relevance to developing country contexts as large-scale companies globalize. Chapter 13 discusses the question of internal marketing in the context of the complexity and diversity of cultures, employing six metaphoric 'mental images'. The chapter concludes by challenging readers not only to understand the impacts of these mental images or culture types, but also their impact on the thrusts of relationship marketing management.

PART 3

Implementing a cross-cultural marketing strategy

CHAPTER 10

Marketing services across cultures

Guilherme Pires and John Stanton

LEARNING OBJECTIVES

At the end of this chapter readers will be able to:

▶ Understand that there is a link between ethnic affiliation and consumer behaviour, hence minority ethnic groups are potential important targets for marketers.

▶ Understand the potential limitations for businesses that assume that the markets of developed culturally-diverse countries are ethnically homogeneous and represented by mainstream consumers.

▶ Understand the potential usefulness of using specific non-mainstream media (information sources) for reaching specific non-mainstream consumer groups.

▶ Understand the limitations of the traditional model of linear acculturation and the implications thereby ensuing for market segmentation and the estimation of market size.

▶ Understand that compared with predominantly tangible products, highly intangible products are likely to pose unique challenges for non-mainstream consumers.

▶ Recognize the need to adapt cognitive models of the process of selection of service providers across goods and services and across mainstream and non-mainstream consumers.

▶ Understand the role of perceived risk, availability of and accessibility to information sources and consumers' communication skills in the process of service provider selection.

▶ Recognize that marketing synergies are likely to exist between non-mainstream consumer groups and their members.

▶ Understand that access to non-mainstream consumers is through their group of affiliation.

10.1 Introduction

In advanced economies, household expenditure on services grows in relative budgetary importance as household incomes rise, providing strongly growing and potentially profitable markets for providers of those services. To benefit from this growing market, a provider of services needs to identify and target selected market segments (homogeneous consumer groups) better than competitors. In this process, service providers seeking to market their services to ethnic minority consumers (EMCs) in advanced economies need to address whether and how they can market their services to resident EMCs. Service providers need to develop targeting strategies that address problems EMCs may face in selecting providers of services. This is necessary because many advanced economies in Europe and North America, as well as Australia, are today more culturally diverse than they were 50 years ago. Inward migration and differences in birth rates largely explain the existence of minority ethnic groups (MEGs) with which EMCs identify. Marketing services to EMCs requires careful consideration of:

- Whether mainstream marketing strategies will effectively reach members of MEGs.
- Whether various MEGs can be combined to create larger, more attractive markets.

For providers of services to address these issues requires consideration of the problems associated with consumer selection of service providers, and how these problems may be heightened if a consumer does not identify with the mainstream or dominant culture. Services are performances that lead to experiences. Services have no shape, colour, weight or smell. As experiences, they cannot be owned, stored or indeed dropped on one's foot. Services cover a spectrum of a continuum ranging from service-products with a highly intangible element to service-products with a very high tangible element (see Figure 10.1).

Whether a service-product is primarily tangible or intangible is sometimes difficult to decide, because few services are without tangible elements and few goods are

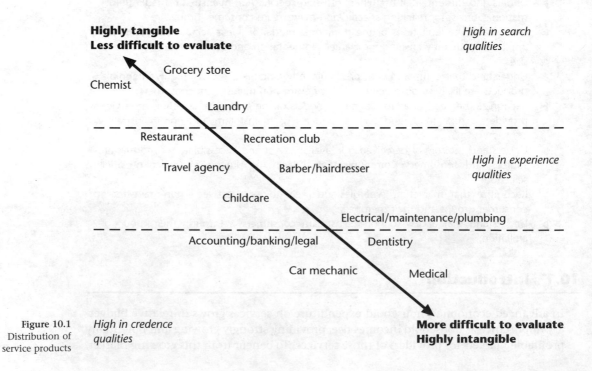

Figure 10.1
Distribution of
service products

without a service component (Lovelock, 1996). Visualize a bounded line: one end denotes a pure good (a physical object), at the other end a pure service – implying respectively no intangible or non-tangible elements are present. Services containing a highly tangible component may be perceived as high in search qualities associated with some characteristic (such as size, shape, colour or smell) that can be pre-determined, examined and evaluated before purchasing takes place.

Service-products high in tangibility may be easier to search for compared with those high in intangibility. Selecting a service provider is increasingly difficult where services are high in intangibility and experience or credence based. In the case of EMCs, the information sources used and the criteria that lead to the selection of a particular service provider may involve strong reliance on the networks that exist within their MEG of affiliation and the use of providers preferred by the MEG.

Ensuing from a brief discussion of the rationale for targeting MEGs, this chapter proceeds to discuss a cognitive model of the decision-making process that integrates relevant models of selection of providers of services applicable to consumers in general. A model of the decision-making process is developed that commences from the 'traditional' flow chart decision process diagrams for 'products', and is extended to cover the evaluation process for services. It is argued that the process depicted in this model does not provide sufficient detail to allow prediction of choice, an issue further discussed in association with a model of social choice relative to service provider selection. An important conclusion is that the characteristics of services may lead to evaluation processes dissimilar to those for goods; hence, the chapter proceeds to outline the grounds for that dissimilarity, concluding that the model offers a general description of the selection process but lacks a focus. As this focus changes from goods to services, different steps in the process of selection by consumers in general become more or less important. This sets the scene for enquiring whether the model requires adaptation when applied to decision-making by EMCs.

Decision-making is difficult for EMCs essentially because of market inexperience, limited access to perceived risk-reducing sources of information, communication difficulties and challenging characteristics of services. These issues are discussed in the context of a model of the process of selection by EMCs of preferred service providers, an adaptation of the integrated model discussed earlier. EMCs exchange information and experiences with other EMCs in their MEG of affiliation, and group consumer behaviour is a reference for their own. It is argued that this leads to the maintenance of relationships between EMCs and service providers preferred by the group.

The chapter concludes that if marketers recognize the diversity of ethnic groups that exist within advanced economies and tailor their services marketing strategies to the needs of individual groups, this has the potential to create loyalty by EMCs to their service providers. The implications for marketing practice are elaborated.

10.2 Why Target Minority Ethnic Groups (MEGs)?

There is growing recognition in the marketing literature that many national markets are not homogeneous. In many nations of Western Europe, in North America and Australia, there is growing cultural diversity. Cultural diversity is used here to describe the coexistence of a variety of ethnic groups within the one national market. These groups are important to marketers because, if there are differences between groups in the information sources and the criteria they use to select service providers, then a marketing strategy targeted to a group's specific needs may provide a provider with a competitive advantage over its competitors, provided general criteria for effective segmentation are met. A model that describes the process of how EMCs select service providers provides a basis for explaining why and how marketers of services can tailor marketing strategies to better meet the needs of MEGs.

10.3   The Process of Service Provider Selection

Figure 10.2 depicts a cognitive process model of the consumer decision-making process.[1] The process is depicted as a flow chart linking various steps involved. The buyer passes through five stages (need recognition, information search, evaluation of alternatives, purchase decision, post-purchase behaviour) to reach a buying decision. Such a model does not distinguish choices for goods, services, brands, retail and service outlets or service providers (Hawkins *et al.*, 1994; McGuire, 1999). There are also models aimed at accounting for the specificity of services (Fisk, 1981).

Differences between goods and services need to be taken into account. In contrast with search qualities applicable to goods (Nelson, 1970), services may be high in credence qualities (Darby and Karni, 1973). Service providers may provide utilitarian, temporal and spatial dimensions to their product, which can be augmented with social, emotional and other forms of value (Sheth *et al.*, 1991).

The selection of a service provider may occur before, after or simultaneously, with the selection of a service and may be influenced by consumers' personal values, personality, lifestyle, family, reference groups, economic situation and level of object knowledge. Hence, the selection process depicted in this model (Figure 10.2) does not provide sufficient detail to allow a prediction of a particular choice of brand or service provider even with adequate information on all the variables.[2]

Figure 10.3 combines the various contributions into a model of sequential choice that shows various sets that enter in the decision process. The model accounts for a total or universal set of choice items residing in a consumer's long-term memory. In ways not specified, this is updated by the addition of new items and, presumably, by the deletion of no longer available ones. This set includes all possible alternatives that could be considered by a consumer. These are then reduced to those the consumer is aware of, even if some may not be recalled on any given occasion. This knowledge contains lower hierarchy sets for each decision situation: an inert set (alternatives not recalled); an inept set (alternatives disregarded due to unsatisfactory past experience, negative or perceived as inferior in relation to current choices); and the alternatives actually considered by the consumer.[3]

The subsequent choice between alternatives is further reduced to a choice set through exclusion or rejection. The final consumer decision involves choosing, experiencing and appraising one item from those in the choice set. The model allows the reconsideration set to be updated at various decision stages, so that future selection takes past experience into account. Similar to the integrated model of consumer decision-making process (Figure 10.2), evoked sets and sequential choice theory do not seek to explain why consumers choose the way they do. They focus on

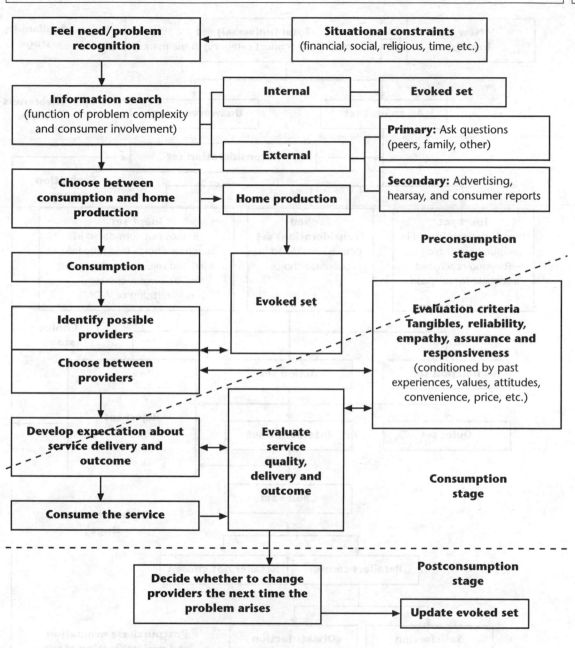

Figure 10.2 Integrated model of decision-making process.

the process and make no distinction between goods and services, brands, the retail outlet or the service provider (Spiggle and Sewall, 1987; Brand and Cronin, 1997), although the theory can be applied to selecting one service provider from a set.

Bringing together models of consumer decision-making and sequential choice theory of evoked sets provides a better understanding of the process of selection of

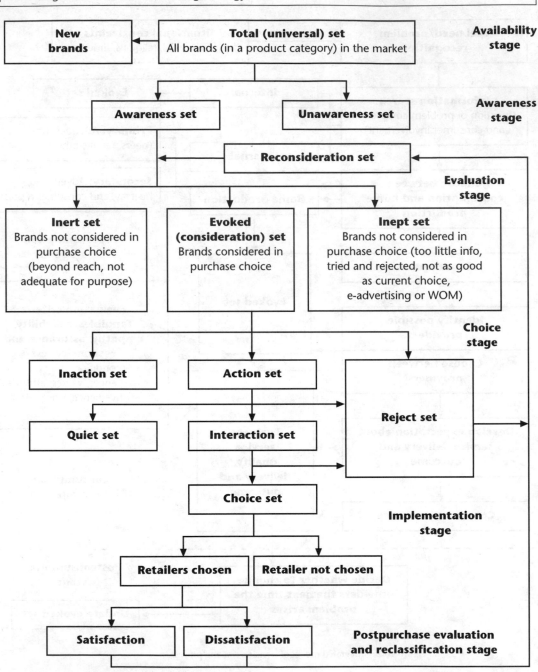

Figure 10.3 Integration of contributions to the sets model of sequential choice.

service providers. This understanding may be incomplete, because service characteristics necessitate different consumer evaluation processes from those used when assessing goods (Zeithaml, 1981). Identifying a consumption/evaluation process for services in three stages (identified in Figure 10.2 by the two broken lines) of pre-consumption, consumption and post-consumption, addresses this matter (Fisk, 1981).

10.4 Decisions about the Choice of a Service Provider

The *pre-consumption stage* of the decision process involves problem recognition, information search and selection of alternatives. All influence the evaluation that ensues. Information search and selection of alternatives involve a circular process of gathering and evaluating information using some undetermined criteria that culminates in a choice. Expectations are formed about the chosen service, marking the transition to the *consumption stage*. Service evaluation may follow, with purchase and consumption. Perishability then integrates service disposition with use – the last step in the consumption stage. Overall service evaluation occurs in the *post-consumption stage* and takes all preceding evaluations into account. If the result is satisfaction, the consumer experiences repurchase motivation that feeds back into the pre-consumption stage. This corresponds to the 'update evoked set' step in Figures 10.2 and 10.3. Subsequent research on the process of the consumption decision and evaluation applicable to services to date has added little to the representation of the Fisk model.

There are at least eight areas where the characteristics of services may lead to evaluation processes dissimilar to those for goods (Zeithaml, 1981):

- *Information search* – consumers may have limited access to information about services because external sources may be restricted due to regulation of professional services advertising, difficulty in communicating experiences and eventual limitations in communication skills and funding available to service providers.

- *Perceived risk* – intangibility and limited information may increase consumers' perceived risk in selecting a service alternative; service heterogeneity, fewer warranties or guarantees and a lack of personal technical knowledge limit consumers' ability to assess satisfaction even after consumption, so that perceived risk becomes even higher; perceived risk may be reduced by relying on word-of-mouth and on other independent sources, where the credibility of these sources is enhanced by personal references.

- *Size* – together with home production, self-service and the offer of fewer brands by individual service providers, fewer information sources may generate fewer alternatives for consumers to consider.

- *Composition of the evoked set of alternatives* – the evoked set may be smaller for services than for goods (Davis *et al.*, 1979; Brand and Cronin, 1997).

- *Adoption of innovation* – consumers may resist innovation because new services may be incompatible with existing values and behaviours.

- *Brand loyalty* – compared with goods, greater loyalty to service providers may result because switching service providers re-establishes risk and can be costly; switching costs identified in this context refer to search, transaction, learning, savings related to repeated use, habit, emotional and time associated with cognition.

- *Attribution of dissatisfaction* – inseparability of services relates to consumer involvement in the service production process, such that some of the blame for service failure is likely to be naturally appropriated by the consumer, whether the consumer is to blame or not (Bendapudi and Berry, 1997).
- *Evaluative criteria* – the characteristics of services lead to greater difficulty in assessing quality, satisfaction and, ultimately, establishing reliable evaluative criteria; price and the physical facilities housing the service are often the only cues available to judge quality and perceived value.

Linked to consumers' exchange decisions, perceived value is affected by three factors: (1) the experiential nature of services (i.e. services are difficult to evaluate prior to purchase and delivery); (2) co-production (influencing the evaluation of technical quality); and (3) direct service encounters influencing evaluations of service quality. Ultimately, these factors are argued to influence how consumers acquire information and consider alternatives; the criteria they use to choose between service providers, and how benefits are evaluated (McGuire, 1999).

10.5 How Consumers Select Service Providers

Consumers' decisions about service-products and brands are distinct because for many services the brand is the company rather than the particular service-product (McGuire, 1999). This explanation recognizes that service providers may often operate with a single brand or that the selection of service-brand and service provider may involve one and the same decision. These associations may apply, for example, in deciding between generalist or specialist medical services (the service-product), followed by a decision about the specific practitioner to provide the service (both service-brand and service provider). Indeed, decisions about the service-product and service provider may be separated, although not the procedure involved in these decisions. So, what do these decisions entail?

Drawing from perceived value theory, consumers decide between alternative offerings by comparing respective net perceived values. These correspond to the difference between all the perceived benefits and all the perceived costs associated with each of the offerings. How many offerings are considered depends on how many different providers consumers are aware of (McGuire, 1999). Prior experience, marketing communication, provider reputation and word-of-mouth recommendations, particularly in the case of services with high credence attributes, influence this awareness. Consumers may research the market to identify evaluation criteria for particular services and to compare competitors.

In summary to this point, the decision process model described by Figure 10.2 offers a general description without a particular focus. Different steps may be more or less important depending on that focus. For example, the difference between goods and services explains the greater importance devoted by consumers of services to evaluation in the post-consumption stage, while consumers of goods concentrate on pre-consumption evaluation. Excluding situational circumstances, the decision to seek more or less new information can be argued to depend on consumer knowledge and experience, as well as on the type, complexity and importance of the buying task. This also applies to which sources are selected. Consumers' motivation and evaluation criteria can be expected to vary with the stage in the overall decision-making process and decision task. All decisions involving information search internalize other auxilliary decisions regarding what and how much information is necessary and sufficient, and from where it will be sourced.

Evaluation by consumers of service delivery during the consumption and post-consumption stages is likely to be guided by five particularly conspicuous elements of the experience, originally identified by Zeithaml *et al.* (1990) as:

- *Tangibles* or *physical evidence* refer to the front-stage – whether physical facilities, equipment and appearance of the service personnel correspond to expectations.

- *Reliability* (also *technical* or *fuctional quality*, or *expressed performance*) refers to the basic expectation that a service provides, what it promises in a dependable and accurate manner (Gronroos, 1991; Swan and Comb, 1976).

- *Empathy* refers to the perception that the provider actually cares about consumers' needs, beliefs and reservations.

- *Assurance* refers to the perception that the provider is knowledgeable and courteous.

- *Responsiveness* refers to the perception that the provider is consistently willing to help.

While these are criteria that service providers need to address in developing their marketing strategies, experience by consumers with respect to these criteria can be expected to: (1) help determine whether to switch service providers; (2) help form expectations about service delivery; and (3) provide indicators of performance to take into account during provider selection.

This broad application of evaluation criteria is useful because consumers evaluate services by comparing expectations with perceptions of actual performance. It is reasonable to assume that criteria that has been used by providers to create expectations is used for subsequent evaluation by consumers (Keaveney, 1995). Ultimately, if perceptions match or exceed expectations, the consumer is satisfied, and there may be no motivation for switching service provider.

The conclusion so far is that the average 'rational' consumer can be expected to follow the various steps in the decision-making process more or less closely, depending on the decision unit, importance and complexity of the task, and related consumer experience and knowledge. These require decisions that may challenge consumers; however, how and why consumers actually do what they do is still a 'black box' that remains largely closed to our understanding (Lovelock *et al.*, 1998). The next section examines whether the basic process of service provider selection requires adaptation when applied to the case of EMCs.

10.6 How EMCs Select Service Providers

Market segmentation usually involves some level of critical mass that, in consumer markets, is unlikely to be met by any individual EMC, but may be at the reach of a MEG. An individual EMC becomes important, if at all, only when associated with other similar individuals, creating an identifiable, measurable and actionable group that is internally homogeneous in consumption and heterogeneous in relation to other groups. To be marketing relevant, individual EMCs may need to rely upon and behave similarly to other members of their MEG. The marketing relevance of the MEG depends on its membership mass and homogeneity, although its survival is separate from any one consumer. The MEG is a reference for EMCs. Their importance as targets depends on their association with the group. In turn, the group's importance depends on the individual's identification with the group.[4]

Some EMCs change their status and behaviour over time. Return migration, relocation to areas outside the reach of practical group influence, acculturation to the host or other cultures and consequent behavioural change are examples that come to mind. Some EMCs will leave a particular MEG and some new members will join. The consequence is that, in any given market and for any MEG, there is likely to be a consumer set with variable degrees of market knowledge. The more recent the arrival in the host country, the less the knowledge about the local market and the greater the difficulties faced, even for the satisfaction of common consumer needs.

10.7 Decision-making is More Difficult For EMCs

Reaching EMCs may not be easy, given the existence of ethnic communications networks (Laroche *et al.*, 1997); marketers' difficulty in understanding different cultures (Hotchkiss, 1996); language barriers and consumers' preference for ethnic brands; limited exposure to printed media; and difficulty with reading English (Kaufman, 1991). The consequences of these difficulties are addressed with reference to Figure 10.4. The Figure represents the process of selection of preferred service providers by inexperienced EMCs and depicts steps likely to be emphasized. Again, the process is depicted in the three stages (pre-consumption, consumption and post-consumption) shown earlier in Figure 10.3 and separated by two broken lines.

Pre-consumption Stage

All first-time potential purchasers of a product may face difficulties in learning about and appraising that product. Time and budgetary scarcities may limit available sources, and communication difficulties and limited knowledge of the marketplace may limit the ability to search for, and evaluate, product information. Inexperienced, communication-challenged EMCs may experience greater difficulty in perusing product literature and evaluating 'new' physical products and brand names, as well as discomfort in consulting with service staff. Inability or increased difficulty in acquiring risk-reducing information increases the perceived risk from making the wrong decision – a consequence that may be compounded when services are involved.

How might inexperienced EMCs reduce perceived risk? Trial and error consumption is a solution for some products. Home production is an option for some services (e.g. hairdressing). EMCs may also look for providers with a presence in their home country (e.g. international brands such as McDonald's or the Body Shop) or seek to reduce risk by searching for familiar ethnic brands. The more general answer is that for services difficult to appraise prior to consumption, perceived risk can be reduced by selecting providers from information sources that can be trusted. Because similar others (in

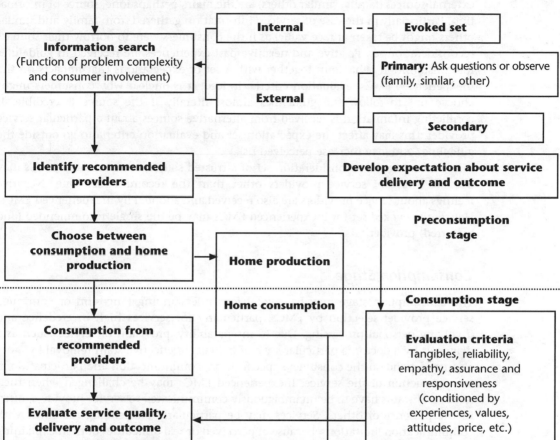

Figure 10.4 Preferred service provider selection by inexperienced EMCs.

values, attitudes, etc.) trust and are more trusted compared to dissimilar others (Dwyer *et al.*, 1987), inexperienced EMCs source consumption information from experienced similar others who can understand their needs and predicaments. Their recommendation may be adopted because it reduces perceived risk and because of the desire to conform to group behaviour.

For newly arrived EMCs, information search is conditioned by a lack of personal knowledge and poor access and exposure to secondary external sources. Primary external sources (family, similar others) are the main, perhaps lone, source of information. Particularly in the case of services, information gathered from family and similar others might be taken at face value, as if the consumers were to borrow their source's reconsideration set. Positive and negative past experiences are received in guidelines for consumption behaviour, together with a set of expectations that impacts on the inexperienced EMCs' evaluation criteria. Indeed, it is unclear why consumers might choose not to follow the guidelines almost literally if the source is credible. If conflicting information is received from alternative sources about a particular service provider, this may affect the expectation set and evaluation criteria to go outside the guidelines and may increase perceived risk.

In borrowing the reconsideration set of a trusted source, inexperienced EMCs may become aware of service providers other than the recommended one. Negative feelings about service providers are also received and adopted by inexperienced EMCs. Hence, the evoked set for inexperienced EMCs may be the single recommended (and preferred) provider.

Consumption Stage

The consumption stage may be pivotal for understanding long-term or continued service provider selection by EMCs, particularly for services high in credence and involving personal processing. Due to inseparability, provision of services such as a diagnosis by a doctor, a particular style of haircut, or effective stain removal by a dry cleaner, depend on the consumer's specification, communication and participation in the production of the service. Inexperienced EMCs may be challenged when their needs and wants have to be unambiguously communicated to service providers, often in the presence of others. Services may be particularly challenging for EMCs with communication limitations, because of perceived or real difficulties both in explaining their needs and responding to what may be required of them during their participation in the production process.

Communication difficulties involve more than language problems. Meaning and context are important in defining a 'normal' way of doing things, how service personnel and customers address each other, whether physical touch is allowed or how people with different ethnic backgrounds behave towards different others. By selecting the service provider recommended by experienced similar others, inexperienced EMCs reduce the perceived risk of service failure and conform, and are seen to conform to group behaviour. The outcome for EMCs may be the opportunity for social interaction with similar others.

From a different perspective, interaction with service personnel provides EMCs with the opportunity to make their needs and preferences known to service providers, together with additional personal information. Service providers may use such information for supplementing their core product. To the extent that the cultural awareness and sensitivity of the recommended service provider leads to responsiveness, customization and personalization may ensue. This involves adjusting the service so that it provides a better match for the particular needs of each customer at the time of service delivery (Hartman and Lindgren, 1993), as well as converting the commercial interaction into a de facto social interaction (Mittal and Lassar, 1996). Both create customer dependence on the preferred provider (Bowen and Jones, 1986).

In terms of evaluation, services intangibility, inseparability and heterogeneity create difficulties for all consumers. These may be greater for EMCs due to home country acquired expectations and evaluation criteria for similar services. Distinct expectations may emerge in the new market with new information sources. As a result, evaluation criteria may be less well articulated, and appraisal of the value received in the service encounter much more subjective. In addition, EMCs aware of their own communication difficulties may apportion at least part of the blame for service failure to themselves, contributing to performance ambiguity

In summary, in addition to the search costs incurred in the pre-consumption stage, inexperienced EMCs may invest considerable effort in the interaction process. *A priori*, preferred service providers may be considered credible due to recommendation by similar others. Combined with buyer–seller interaction, communication difficulties:

- Provide opportunities for customers' needs to be met more closely.
- Convert commercial encounters into social interactions.
- Possibly discount service delivery failure.

These outcomes also reinforce service provider credibility and promote customer dependence on that provider, resulting in lower perceived risk, social involvement and consequent continued patronage – all combining to reduce any incentive to switch service providers. Arguably, inexperienced EMCs may be loathe to change partners, because to do so is to re-establish risk.

Post-consumption Stage

Post-consumption evaluation takes all preceding evaluations into account and plays a major role in determining whether the service provider will have the consumers' continued patronage (Fisk, 1981). For inexperienced EMCs, the likelihood of switching providers may be very low. The consumption stage involves creation of perceived value through closer focus on customer needs via customization and personalization, culminating in increased customer dependence on a service provider with reinforced credibility. This outcome implies an alignment of perceptions with expectations and that the consumer is happy with the service provider. This leaves little incentive to switch. Continued customer satisfaction with provider performance promotes that provider to a preferred status. Preferred providers benefit from sustained EMC loyalty and a willingness by the EMC to recommend their services to others, namely their MEG.

The preceding propositions assume that consumers are rational in valuing risk and that the service provider is culturally aware, sensitive and, most importantly, responsive to customer needs. These assumptions can be defended, since (1) service provider recommendation is sourced from an experienced similar EMC; and (2) to the extent that they are perceived as a preferred provider to the MEG, service providers may perceive the long-term patronage of EMCs as particularly worth investing in. In reality, there will be service providers that meet the above criteria and others that do not, just as there will be satisfied and dissatisfied consumers. Whatever the case may be, the consumption experience can be visualized to result in the updating of the consumer's various sets (e.g. rejection set, reconsideration set). In extreme negative or positive cases, there may be voluntary feedback to the original source.

Finally, inexperienced EMCs do not remain inexperienced forever. Becoming experienced, they may pass their experiences, positive and negative, on to other ethnic group members, themselves potentially preferred sources of information for more inexperienced EMCs.

10.8 Challenges Arising from the Characteristics of Services

Not all analysts recognize the usefulness of separating goods and services for marketing purposes. The development of marketing strategies could be based upon the benefits provided by goods and services, rather than the development of classifications of goods and services based upon hypothetically unique characteristics (Enis and Roering, 1981). Although empirical evidence supporting the separate classification of goods from services is not abundant, the proposition that the uniqueness of services makes it difficult for customers to understand what is being offered, to identify potential providers and to evaluate alternatives (Legg and Baker, 1987), remains mostly undisputed. The view subscribed to here is that the unique characteristics of services necessitates different consumer evaluation processes from those used when assessing goods and therefore require unique marketing techniques (Zeithaml *et al.*, 1985).

The services marketing literature commonly grounds the uniqueness of services on four main characteristics, namely intangibility, simultaneity (and inseparability), heterogeneity (or variability, or inconsistency) and perishability. These characteristics are reviewed below in order to establish their implications for EMCs.

Intangibility

Intangibility refers to the non-physical nature of the core product, the basic, generic central thing that is exchanged (Levitt, 1973). It emphasizes service as performance resulting in service experience. Physical goods may be displayed and examined by prospective purchasers, often without interaction with the seller, beyond the act of exchange. As explained by Hartman and Lindgren (1993: 12) in retail stores, for example, a number of brands and a variety of models for each brand name may be displayed, providing the consumer with the opportunity to make physical comparisons and to set standards on which to make purchase decisions. Physical comparison may be insufficient for inexperienced consumers to evaluate a complex product conclusively. Reassurance may be sought from service personnel and free trials or the promise of 'satisfaction or money back guarantee' may go a long way in resolving evaluation and purchase difficulties.

EMCs who are inexperienced and challenged by communication in the host country language may face greater difficulties in the evaluation of 'new' physical products and brand names than other domestic consumers. Inability to peruse product literature and/or discomfort in consulting with service staff increases perceived risk, a consequence that may be compounded when ethnic consumers face highly intangible service-products.

Since intangible dominant service-products involve characteristics that can only be discerned after purchase or during consumption (such as taste or ease of handling), they can be described as high in experience qualities. Towards the pure service end, service-products such as surgery or technical repairs may be impossible to evaluate even after consumption, depending on how credible the service provider is in the eyes of the consumer. These services are described as high in credence qualities. The conclusion to be drawn is that inexperienced ethnic consumers can be expected to experience much greater difficulty than host consumers in acquiring risk-reducing information, both for goods and services, but especially for the latter. For this reason, risk-reducing information is likely to be highly valued once a reliable (even if non-expert) source is found. That value is likely to be linked to the source; in other words, the source is valued because of the consumer's continuing limitations. This source may be the service provider.

As long as the consumer is happy with the quality of the information, there may be no incentive to search for new sources. Service providers can develop an eventual source of competitive advantage by supplementing their core product with this information. Indeed, customers with less expertise may be reluctant to change partners because there is a perceived risk in doing so. The implication is that service provider credibility may be of crucial importance, particularly in the case of services high in credence qualities (Bowen and Jones, 1986). Inexperienced consumers, by definition, have no apparent grounds to assess service provider credibility.

Simultaneity

Simultaneity (or inseparability) is also a characteristic of services. As a performance results in a service experience, services have no existence apart from the interaction between the provider and consumer, who experience the service together (Friedman and Smith, 1993), although a customer and consumer may not be the same person (Shaw and Pirog III, 1997). Simultaneity implies that service production generally occurs at the same time as service consumption and the consumer is often an active partner in the production process. This is the case, for example, in most hairdressing services and in traditional education. A positive aspect associated with the customer–provider interaction is that it provides customers with the opportunity to make their individual needs and preferences known to service providers. Depending on a provider's degree of responsiveness – whether a provider is willing and able to respond to that information – inseparability provides the basis for customization; that is, for adjusting the service so that it provides a better match for the particular needs of each customer at the time of service delivery (Hartman and Lindgren, 1993).

The opportunity provided by the customer–provider interaction may not apply equally to all consumer groups. Inexperienced EMCs may be particularly challenged in situations where their needs and wants have to be unambiguously transmitted to service providers, often in the presence of others. In this context, for EMCs with communication limitations, services may be particularly challenging because of perceived or real difficulties both in explaining their needs and responding to what may be required of them during their participation in the production process.

Because of the simultaneous nature of services, the challenges faced by EMCs may be converted into marketing opportunities for firms aware of these difficulties. A lack of experience may increase dependence on the service provider and the interaction and exchange of information facilitates the collection of relevant knowledge about consumer attitudes, opinions and motivations (Friedman and Smith, 1993). Hence, in addition to customization benefits, simultaneity provides the grounds for personalization.[5]

The social support implied in the personalization process may ultimately provide firms with ethnic consumers' continued patronage. This is because social interaction in itself is a possible shopping motive or orientation, together with diversion from routine activities, exercise, sensory stimulation and learning about new trends; furthermore, the opportunity cost of switching service provider can be expected to increase for the consumer once a relationship has been established.

Heterogeneity

Heterogeneity (also variability or inconsistency) in services reflects the fact that active human involvement in the production or consumption of services limits the ability to perfectly reproduce or re-experience the service in subsequent service encounters. Services are performances that vary according to the mood of the service provider and service customer at the moment of service delivery. Personalization and the limited ability to replicate service performance can be expected to similarly limit service quality evaluation, particularly given intangibility. Indeed, the development of quality assessment measures such as SERVQUAL (Parasuraman *et al.*, 1988) do not escape criticism, and the services marketing literature clearly recognizes the difficulty faced by consumers in their evaluation of service quality. The more a market exchange approaches a pure service situation, the less its tangible element. Consequently, the difficulty in measuring service quality and the need for perceived provider credibility increase. These correspond to situations where customer satisfaction and repeat patronage may be determined solely by the quality of the personal encounter (Solomon *et al.*, 1985).

Intangibility, inseparability and heterogeneity can combine to create evaluation difficulties for all consumers, even those with substantial market knowledge. At least on two grounds, these difficulties may be greater for inexperienced EMCs:

- Evaluation criteria used by EMCs may not be articulated as clearly as mainstream consumers to potential providers and the appraisal of the value received (in the service encounter) may be much more subjective if the consumer is inexperienced.

- While experienced consumers may rely on what they have learned from past service encounters, probably with similar-others, inexperienced EMCs have no significant past in the new market.

These problems may give rise to a dependence on the provider for information. Awareness of their own communication difficulties may also induce inexperienced EMCs to apportion at least part of the blame to the provider in the event of service failure, contributing to performance ambiguity. Identification with a provider can offer guidance to the ethnic consumer. Similarity refers to the extent to which the dyad of provider and consumer are similar in personal attributes and characteristics. These may include one or all of life stage, gender, culture (ethnic background), work attitudes and personality. Interaction is likely to be easier and less challenging with others who have similar attitudes, values, activities and experiences (Smith, 1998). Communication difficulties may involve more than language problems. They may involve meaning and context, both important in defining a 'normal' way of doing things, and also include the way services personnel and customers address each other, whether physical touch is allowed, how people with different racial backgrounds behave towards different others (e.g. discrimination, paternalism, stereotyping) or, in a nutshell, how culturally-aware and sensitive are the parties to the service delivery.

Perishability

Perishability is a reinforcing characteristic of services. In contrast to physical goods, services are mostly intangible performances that cannot be stored. This may have some general implications for ethnic consumers, because consumers have been found to associate intangibility with availability (Hartman and Lindgren, 1993), a circumstance that may reduce a consumer's awareness of a service. Perishability also provides a possible explanation for the finding that consumers engage in more post-purchase evaluation than pre-purchase evaluation when selecting and consuming services (Friedman and Smith, 1993). Post-purchase evaluation involves consumers' recollections of their experiences throughout the service encounter. Hence, the consequences for inexperienced EMCs may be linked back, for example, to the difficulty in measuring service quality identified in discussing heterogeneity.

Other Characteristics

Intangibility, simultaneity, heterogeneity and perishability of services have been questioned on the grounds that they are not universally applicable to all services. For example, not all services require intensive customer–provider interaction, as in the case of car maintenance or furniture storage. As a result, alternative ways of characterizing services have been sought. One eight-fold classification is to distinguish services by:

- The nature of the product.
- Customer involvement in the production process.
- People as part of the product.
- A greater difficulty in maintaining quality control standards compared with goods.
- Greater difficulty for customers to evaluate compared with goods.
- An absence of inventories.
- The relative importance of the time factor.
- The structure and nature of distribution channels.

The applicability of these characteristics to all services is equally questionable. With the exception of the structure and nature of distribution channels, they are characteristics that arise with intangibility, simultaneity, heterogeneity and perishability.

In relation to the last characteristic, the structure and nature of distribution channels, services requiring customers to visit (or be visited by) a service point for the service delivery process to take place have the opportunity to use tangible elements (the physical environment) to impress and inform customers. Just like a play, scenarios may be created and behavioural roles and scripts developed to reach the customer and control service delivery.[6] Basic strategic requirements to create a positive impression in the potential customer are the management of own service personnel and other customers that may share the scene, and the development of physical environments that appeal to the customer. Colour, shape, smell, sound, objects and other media may be used for that purpose.

The concept of physically appealing front-stages may be quite challenging in culturally-diverse markets, even if political and social constraints usually involved in matters related to dealing with MEGs are disregarded. For example, the use by Australian firms of national flag colours (red, white and blue) to appeal to Australian consumers could be elusive to consumers from other countries, such as Italy (red, white and green) or Greece (white and blue). Similarly, incompatibility of meaning could occur if sound or most other media are preferred to colour. The conclusion is that what appeals to the host group may fail to cause an impression on other ethnic consumers. This is more likely for those new to the marketplace, given their probably lower degree of acculturation to the host culture. Information that is poorly targeted towards EMCs must affect their assessment of services and service providers.

So far, the analysis has focused on the differences between goods and services, pointing out that the uniqueness of services poses particular challenges to EMCs and inexperienced EMCs in particular. However, the fact that services can differ widely in terms of the key characteristics that define them leads to the conclusion that not all services equally pose the same challenges to all consumers or the same strategic opportunities for service providers.[7] Nonetheless, the challenges and opportunities identified from the discussion of service characteristics remain. EMCs with communication difficulties who are new to the marketplace are likely to experience significantly greater difficulties than mainstream consumers in the selection of service providers and in consuming services, basically because of a reduced ability to receive and convey risk-reducing information.

10.9 MEGs as References for Inexperienced EMCs

There are two basic sources of information for consumers: internal and external. Internal sources rely on memory scanning of past self-experience. Inexperienced EMCs by definition cannot rely on internal sources. External sources range from marketer-dominated to personal and impersonal. Starting from a pre-purchase situation, and comparing use of information sources by consumers of goods with usage by consumers of services, the evidence points to consumers of goods preferring direct product observation or trial, and consumers of services favouring personal sources (Murray, 1991). For services, due to their experiential nature, word-of-mouth is an important source of risk-reducing information. Because of clarification and feedback opportunities, there is a prominent role for opinion leaders and reference group members as well as family and friends (Childers and Rao, 1992). Word-of-mouth communications from these sources may be perceived as more reliable and trustworthy than others. (Clow *et al.*, 1997).

How do these findings apply to EMCs who have communication difficulties using the mainstream language and who are also new to a particular marketplace? Because their likely contribution to a firm's total revenue is likely to be small, an average individual consumer is unlikely to be individually targeted in a consumer market. Segment substantiality, one of the requirements for effective market segmentation, is unlikely to be met. Market segmentation is likely to involve some level of critical mass that, in consumer markets, is unlikely to be met by any one individual. Indeed, an individual becomes important, if at all, only when associated with other similar individuals, creating an identifiable, measurable and actionable group that is homogeneous within itself and heterogeneous in relation to other groups. This same reasoning may be applied to ethnic consumers.

For marketing purposes, an individual EMC is important as a member of the MEG with whom she or he identifies. An individual EMC is unlikely to be significant (to warrant a separate strategy) in isolation from a MEG. An EMC attracts the attention of marketers because he or she relies upon, and behaves similarly with, the MEG (that is, the MEG must be internally homogeneous in consumption). This conclusion is consistent with the argument that similar others (in terms of values and attitudes, etc.) trust, and are more trusted, compared to dissimilar others. Hence, members of a MEG exchange information and experiences with other members, and group consumer behaviour is a reference for that of the members. It follows that inexperienced EMCs are likely to source information about possible service providers from more experienced similar others (fellow EMCs that are knowledgeable about the marketplace). This provides the grounds for inexperienced EMC to assess service provider credibility, an issue earlier identified when discussing intangibility. Ultimately, recommendations from similar others are likely to be tried because this can reduce the individual's perceived risk. Positive or negative experiences that result feed back to the group, reinforcing or weakening group preferences.

10.10 Building a Service Provider Relationship with EMCs[8]

Individual exchanges of services are not assessed in isolation, but as a continuation of past exchanges likely to continue in the future (Bendapudi and Berry, 1997). EMCs draw on the experiences of similar others as a preferred source of market information, and this dependency has been recognized as influencing customer relationship maintenance (Sheth and Parvatiyar, 1995). This is consistent with the observation that consumers of services tend to exhibit a great propensity to maintain long-term relationships with service providers (Brand and Cronin, 1997).

From prior discussion, the interaction between EMCs and service providers involves two dimensions that can be usefully addressed by relationship marketing:

- The inexperience of individual EMCs within the new marketplace.
- The quality of the long-term relationship that MEGs develop and maintain with service providers.

Varying, but sometimes considerable, relationship-specific investment may be committed by customers to identify service providers and develop relationships with them. Whether informing a hairdresser about one's personal style and preferences or gathering financial records and participating in a series of in-depth discussions to educate a personal financial planner, these investments involve not only information, but also time, effort and money (Shaw and Pirog, 1997). From an economic perspective, such investments may be taken into account by consumers when considering whether to switch providers. In the case of EMCs, communication difficulties are likely to reduce access to information. Particularly in services high in interpersonal contact and credence, such as financial planning, customization, responsiveness and personalization have the potential to further differentiate the exchange object. This is likely to result in the dual effect of increasing switching costs and reinforcing dependence upon the provider. Greater dependency fosters the maintenance of the relationship (Ganesan, 1994).

The linkages that emerge between an inexperienced EMC and their MEG supports a long-term relationship emerging between the group's members and particular service providers, provided service experiences are not negative; that is, service providers remain credible. Inexperienced EMCs benefit from the support of the MEG through lower perceived risk and through their identification with that group, because they become important for service providers. However, continued group membership requires conformity to the group's values and attitudes. Belonging to a MEG is not enough; it is necessary to be seen to belong. In addition to economic costs, switching costs also needs to account for social or psychological costs, leading to a relationship that is constrained by a member's conformity to the group (Johnson, 1982).

Customers may stay in a relationship because of these constraints and/or as a result of customer satisfaction, which may be attributed to service provider dedication to customer orientation. Continued support and referral by a MEG implies consistently positive service experiences, together with switching constraints. Hence, the combination of the uniqueness of MEGs and services marketing may result in greater loyalty by EMCs.

10.11 Implications for Marketing Practice

This review of the distinctive characteristics of services and their implications for marketing to EMCs raises many points of different emphasis in the treatment of EMCs that need to be acknowledged. The following provides an indication of the variety of issues that need to be taken into account.

Perhaps the most attractive opportunity in serving MEGs is to invest in the establishment of rewarding long-term relationships that will maximize customer lifetime value (Bolton, 1998). Because the cost of retaining an existing customer is less than the cost of acquiring a new customer,[9] and because one customer retained is one less customer for competitors, promoting customer loyalty is an absolute must. Disregard for the building of loyalty among customers is likely to cause eventual decline to a service firm, although loyalty may be undesirable if it means keeping unprofitable customers (Duboff and Sherer, 1997). MEGs are likely to invest in long-term relationships. Firms need to take this into account if they want to identify those customers who are likely to remain in long-term relationships with the firm (Bendapudi and Berry, 1997).

Customer loyalty is not easy to achieve, particularly in the case of services where the subjectivity of intangible experiences is compounded by customer–provider interactions for which ethnic consumers may not be prepared. The marketers' problem is to determine how to provide consumers with memorable service experiences and positive value perceptions that they will evoke every time the need for the service arises. Customization, responsiveness and personalization are effective tools that marketers may use to reach EMCs.

Effective customization, responsiveness and personalization, however, depend on the ability of service personnel to interact with consumers. Marketers need to encourage internal cultural sensitivity and awareness in personnel to bridge the understanding gap between culturally different actors. Possible avenues include training and, when appropriate, reducing dissimilarity in the interaction through the employment of ethnically-identified service personnel (Danowski, 1993). Ultimately, progress towards a relationship depends on the characteristics of the participants, on the quality of the service encounters and on the adoption of a customer orientation. This strategy concentrates on satisfying customer needs at the level of the employee–customer interaction (Kelley, 1992).

Service encounters often occur in a front-stage that may be strategically designed to appeal to customers. Culturally-sensitive service personnel and a customer orientation may succeed in reducing consumers' perceived risks by developing user-friendly service delivery systems (Hartman and Lindgren, 1997). Because inexperienced EMCs may face difficulties mostly outside their control, service provider initiated activities that result in a reduction of a consumer's perceived risk may promote goodwill towards the service provider.

The service encounter determines overall satisfaction with the service, a factor that in the case of EMCs may be also influenced by the setting of standards (expectations regarding service performance) and positive recommendations by peers. It has been argued that it is the service experience that distinguishes one service organization from another (Booms and Nyquist, 1981). Combined with a reduction in perceived risk, the increase in switching costs stimulates customer dependence on the service provider that converts into competitive advantage. The service encounter with EMCs is, therefore, well worth the service provider's attention. There appear to be sufficient differences in the nature of the difficulties faced by ethnic and mainstream consumers of services for specialization opportunities to be considered by firms.

A key challenge facing providers of services to EMCs may be the consumer's communication difficulties. Marketers have identified ethnic communication networks as a barrier; however, there is no apparent reason why these networks should not be used as promotional vehicles.

Services firms need to understand that they are not dealing with isolated EMCs but with potentially important MEGs through individual consumers. Marketing strategies directed to the MEG at large (such as sponsorship of, and conspicuous participation in, important community events, together with social bonding and endorsement of ethnic group societal attitudes and concerns) may shape a firm's profile to a status of credible perceived similar other (Bendapudi and Berry, 1997). Again this fosters close long-term relationships and competitive advantage.

Focusing on the MEG at large is likely to be ineffective if service encounters with individual EMCs are allowed to deteriorate. Firms must match and preferably exceed consumer expectations, ensuring that the consumer's feedback to the group is positive. Contrast effects determine that firms with good prior service levels will suffer the most when consumers perceive a loss from service deterioration (Bolton, 1998). In contrast, positive experiences trigger positive feedback that raises the firm's profile or image in terms of its reliability and credibility. Reliability has been cited as the most influential determinant of overall service quality or of customer satisfaction with the service (Mittal and Lassar, 1998).

Reliability and credibility can be expected to help retain most clientele (some switching can be expected to occur regardless of service levels), and to foster recommendations to new consumers. The ultimate test of the customer's relationship with the service may be whether the customer is willing to become an advocate for the service, promoting the service to others, and even defending it against detractors (Cross and Smith, 1995).

Finally, all of the above contribute to a preferred service provider's achievement of sustainable competitive advantage. This is because greater dependence on existing service providers becomes an obstacle for new entrants in the market. Hence, being first in the market is important (Bolton, 1998; Sriram and Mummalaneni, 1990). This promotes 'new' inexperienced EMCs as a strategic target for service providers.

10.12 Conclusion

Services cover a continuum ranging from products with a highly intangible element to products with a very high tangible element. Selecting a service provider is difficult for credence based services high in intangibility. There are at least eight areas where the characteristics of services may lead to evaluation processes dissimilar to those for goods. Marketing to EMCs in a culturally diverse economy is likely to be complicated by the difficulties marketers may have in understanding different cultures, in communicating and in using ethnic communication networks. Reaching EMCs may not be easy given the existence of ethnic communications, marketers' difficulty in understanding different cultures, language barriers and consumers' preference for ethnic brands, limited exposure to printed media and difficulty with reading English.

The decision process that EMCs may face when choosing a first time service provider can be modelled in three stages of pre-consumption, consumption and post-consumption. For EMCs, information sources used and the criteria that lead to the selection of a particular service provider may involve strong reliance on the networks that exist within the MEG and the use of providers that the MEG favour. Difficulties may be complicated by difficulties EMCs may face in reading or speaking the dominant host country language and a consequent limited exposure to mass media.

Services consumption decisions by inexperienced EMCs are constrained by their limited knowledge of the marketplace, their communication problems, and a time and budget constraint which, if the same as other consumers, will restrict their available choices. Examination of the characteristics of services consumption, and how these may impact on the process of selection by inexperienced EMCs, suggests they will experience or confront a very wide range of specific difficulties. These include a restricted ability to read all product literature and a discomfort in consulting with service staff and different others. There will be an inability to draw on past experience as well as differences in meanings and contexts.

Difficulty in obtaining information from available sources and limited sources of information are likely to increase perceived risk. Due to perishability, reduced awareness and greater difficulty in assessing provider credibility are likely. There is also likely to be greater difficulty in participating in service encounters and a more subjective assessment of value and quality. As a result of such difficulties, identified outcomes include increased post-purchase evaluation, less information gathering from the front-stage, an increased dependence on service providers, a decreased incentive to search for information and to switch service providers and, consequently, greater loyalty.

REVIEW QUESTIONS

1. Discuss the kinds of difficulties that EMCs may face in selecting a service provider. How can marketers convert these difficulties into marketing opportunities?

2. On what grounds can we argue that a MEG's consumer behaviour is a reference for the behaviour of its members?

3. How can the integrated model of the decision-making process be used to assist marketers in their targeting of EMCs?

4. Explain how the different characteristics of services challenge EMCs.

5. The evoked set has been argued to be potentially smaller for services relative to goods. Explain why. What can be said in relation to the evoked set for an EMC, compared with a mainstream consumer?

6. What is the meaning of 'physically appealing front-stages'? How can this concept be applied to minority and mainstream consumers?

7. Why is it that the combination of the uniqueness of MEGs and services marketing may result in greater loyalty by EMCs?

8. How can we use EMCs' consumer behaviour as an illustration for the concept of 'maximization of customer lifetime value'?

Notes

1. See Nicosia, 1966; Engel *et al.*, 1968 and 1986; Howard and Sheth, 1969; Sheth *et al.*, 1991.
2. Various researchers have looked for solutions in the investigation of particular aspects of the overall decision-making process (Fishbein, 1963; Ajzen and Fishbein, 1973; Chan and Lau, 1998; Sheth, 1974; Bettman, 1979; Shaw and Pirog, 1997). Others have focused on a theory of consumer choice sets, perceived as outcomes of consumer decision-making processes (Narayana and Markin, 1975; Shocker *et al.*, 1991).
3. These alternatives form the evoked (or consideration) set referred to in Figure 10.2.
4. The term 'reference group' indicates any collective influencing the attitudes of the individuals using it as a reference in evaluating their own situation (Hyman, 1942). Group membership influences individual behaviour for products varying widely in their characteristics (Brady, 1952; Hechter, 1978; Boume, 1957; Bearden and Etzel, 1982; Stafford, 1966). Consumers actively attempt to observe the group's consumption behaviour as a lead for evaluating consumption alternatives and as a source of product information (Moschis, 1976). In addition, reference group pressure and/or high group cohesion contribute to group conformity. Cultural and subcultural identification is an effective determinant of consumer choice behaviour (Wallendorf and Reilly, 1983).
5. Personalization refers to the social content between customer and service provider (Mittal and Lassar, 1996), ranging from alleviation of mild boredom to empathy and comfort in grief.

6. This dramaturgical perspective (Grove and Fisk, 1983) recognizes the augmented characteristics of the service product, using the physical environment and creative actors (service personnel, other customers) to enhance the perceived quality of the service delivery.

7. Because not all services equally pose the same challenges to all consumers or the same strategic opportunities for service providers, it is important to identify possible regularities (similarities across service industries) in order to further understand the uniqueness of services and thereby to improve the marketing of services. To this end, Lovelock (1996) identified a set of six major, non-exclusive, service classifications or frameworks that could be used to help formulate marketing strategy: (1) service as a process addresses the degree and type of consumer involvement in the service delivery, the scope for customization, responsiveness, personalization, and front-stage strategy; (2) the mode of service delivery recognizes differences in distribution strategy and front-stage activities; (3) the ability of service providers to customize their offering again includes their ability to be responsive and to be able to personalize this offering; (4) addressing differences in the nature of the demand for services recognizes that aggregate demand for the provider's services may be made more stable if a service provider is aware of a consumer's consumption pattern; (5) addressing attributes of the service experience deals with the relative intensity with which service personnel and the front-stage participate in the service experience; (6) the nature of the relationship between service provider and customer may vary across different service activities – for example, a greater dependence by an ethnic group on a service provider may create a quasi-membership reflected in continuous service delivery.

8. The study of long-term marketing relationships is the focus of relationship marketing (Wilson, 1995).

9. Arguably five times less (Mittal and Lassar, 1998).

References

Ajzen, I. and Fishbein, M. (1973) 'Attitudinal and normative variables as predictors of specific behaviours', *Journal of Personality and Social Psychology* 27(1): 41–57.

Bendapudi, N. and Berry, L. (1997) 'Customers' motivations for maintaining relationships with service providers', *Journal of Retailing* 73(1): 15–37.

Bettman, J. (1979) *An Information Processing Theory of Consumer Choice*, Sydney: Addison-Wesley Publishing Company.

Bolton, R. (1998) 'A dynamic model of the duration of the customer's relationship with a continuous service provider: the role of satisfaction', *Marketing Science* 17(1): 45–65.

Booms, B. and Nyquist, J. (1981) 'Analysing the customer/firm communication component of the services marketing mix', in J. Donnelly and W. George (eds), *Marketing of Services*, Chicago: American Marketing.

Bowen, D. and Jones, G. (1986) 'Transaction cost analysis of service organization–customer exchange', *Academy of Management Review* 11(2): 428–441.

Brand, R. and Cronin, J. (1997) 'Consumer-specific determinants of the size of retail choice sets: an empirical comparison of physical goods and service providers', *The Journal of Services Marketing* 11(1): 19–38.

Chan, R. and Lau, L. (1998) 'A test of the Fishbein–Ajzen behavioural intentions model under Chinese cultural settings: are there any differences between PRC and Hong Kong consumers?', *Journal of Marketing Practice: Applied Marketing Science* 4(1): 85–101.

Childers, T. and Rao, A. (1992) 'Influence of familiar and peer-based reference groups on consumer decisions', *Journal of Consumer Research* 19 (September): 198–211.

Clow, K., Kurtz, D., Ozment, J. and Ong, B. (1997) 'The antecedents of consumer expectations of services: an empirical study across four industries', *The Journal of Services Marketing* 11(4): 230–248.

Cross, R. and Smith, J. (1995) *Customer Bonding*, Chicago, IL: NTC Business Books.

Danowski, A. (1993) 'Ethnic markets', *Journal of Bank Marketing*, November, 65–66.

Darby, M. and Karni, E. (1973) 'Free competition and the optimal amount of fraud', *Journal of Law and Economics* 16 (April): 67–86.

Davis, D., Guiltinan, J. and Jones, W. (1979) 'Service characteristics, consumer search and the classification of retail services', *Journal of Retailing* 55(3): 3–23.

Duboff, R. and Sherer, L. (1997) 'Customized customer loyalty: in the real world, all customers are not created equal', *Marketing Management*, Summer, 21–27.

Dwyer, F., Schurr, P. and Oh, S. (1987) 'Developing buyer–seller relationships', *Journal of Marketing* 51(2): 11–27.

Engel, J., Kollat, D. and Blackwell, R. (1968) *Consumer Behaviour*, New York: Holt, Rinehart and Winston.

Engel, J., Kollat, D. and Miniard, P. (1986) *Consumer Behaviour*, Hinsdale, IL: Dryden Press.

Enis, B and Roering, K. (1981) 'Services marketing: different products, similar strategy', in J. Donnelly and W. George (eds), *Marketing of Services*, Chicago: American Marketing Association, pp. 1–4.

Fishbein, M. (1963) 'An investigation of the relationship between beliefs about an object and attitude toward that object', *Human Relations* 16: 233–240.

Fisk, R. (1981) 'Toward a consumption/evaluation process model for services', in J. Donnelly and W. George (eds), *Marketing of Services*, Chicago: American Marketing Association, pp. 191–95.

Friedman, M. and Smith, L. (1993) 'Consumer evaluation processes in a service setting', *Journal of Services Marketing* 7(2): 47–61.

Ganesan, S. (1994) 'Determinants of long-term orientation in buyer–seller relationships', *Journal of Marketing* 58 (April): 1–19.

Gronroos, C. (1991) 'Strategic management and marketing in the services sector', *Studentlitteratur*: Lund, Sweden.

Grove, S. and Fisk, R. (1983) 'The dramaturgy of services exchange: an analytical framework for services marketing', in L. Berry, G. Shostack and G. Upah (eds), *Emerging Perspectives on Services Marketing*, Chicago: American Marketing Association.

Hartman, D. and Lindgren Jr., J. (1993) 'Consumer evaluations of goods and services: implications for services marketing', *Journal of Services Marketing* 7(2): 4–15.

Hawkins, D., Best, R. and Coney, K. (1994) *Consumer Behaviour: Implications for Marketing Strategy*, 5th edn., Boston: Irwin.

Hoffman, K. and Bateson, J. (1997) *Essentials of Services Marketing*, New York: The Dryden Press.

Hotchkiss, D'Anne (1996) 'Weaving cultural sensitivity into marketing', *Journal of Bank Marketing*, June, 26–33.

Howard, J. and Sheth, J. (1969) *The Theory of Buyer Behaviour*, New York: Wiley.

Jeannet, J. and Hennessey, H. (1995) *Global Marketing Strategies*, 3rd edn., Boston: Houghton Mifflin.

Johnson, M. (1982) 'The social and cognitive features of the dissolution of commitment relationships', in S. Duck (ed.), *Personal Relationships: Dissolving Personal Relationships*, New York, Academic Press, pp. 51–73.

Kaufman, C. (1991) 'Coupon use in ethnic markets: implications from a retail perspective', *Journal of Consumer Marketing* 8(1): 41–51.

Kearney, S. (1995) 'Customer switching behaviour in service industries: an exploratory study', *Journal of Marketing* 59 (April): 71–82.

Kelley, S. (1992) 'Developing customer orientation among service employees', *Journal of the Academy of Marketing Science* 20(1): 27–36.

Laroche, M., Kim, C. and Clarke, M. (1997) 'The effects of ethnicity factors on consumer deal interests: an empirical study of French-English-Canadians', *Journal of Marketing Theory and Practice* 5(1): 100–111.

Legg, D. and Baker, J. (1987) 'Advertising strategies for service firms', in C. Surprenant (ed.), *Add Value to Your Service*, Chicago: American Marketing Association, pp. 163–168.

Levitt, T. (1973) 'What's your product and what's your business?', in *Marketing for Business Growth*, New York: McGraw-Hill, p. 7.

Lovelock, C. (1996) *Services Marketing*, 3rd edn., New York: Prentice Hall International.

Lovelock, C., Patterson, P. and Walker, R. (1998) *Services Marketing – Australia and New Zealand*, Sydney: Prentice Hall.

McColl, R., Callaghan, B. and Palmer, A. (1998) *Services Marketing: A Managerial Perspective*, Sydney: McGraw-Hill.

McGuire, L. (1999) *Australian Services: Marketing and Management*, Sydney: MacMillan.

Mittal, B. and Lassar, W. (1996) 'The role of personalization in service encounters', *Journal of Retailing* 72(1): 95–109.

Mittal, B. and Lassar, W. (1998) 'Why do customers switch? The dynamics of satisfaction versus loyalty', *The Journal of Services Marketing* 12(3): 177–194.

Murray, K. (1991) 'A test of services marketing theory: consumer information acquisition activities', *Journal of Marketing* 55 (January): 10–25.

Murray, K. and Schlacter, J. (1990) 'The impact of services versus goods on consumers' assessment of perceived risk and variability', *Journal of the Academy of Marketing Science* 18(1): 51–65.

Narayana, C. and Markin, R. (1975) 'Consumer behaviour and product performance: an alternative conceptualization', *Journal of Marketing* 39 (October): 1–6.

Nelson, P. (1970) 'Advertising as information', *Journal of Political Economy* 81 (Jul–Aug): 729–754.

Nicosia, F. (1966) *Consumer Decision Processes*, Englewood Cliffs, NJ: Prentice Hall, pp. 151–192.

Parasuraman, A., Zeithaml, V. and Berry, L. (1988) 'SERVQUAL: a multiple-item scale for measuring consumer perceptions of service quality', *Journal of Retailing* 64(1): 12–40.

Penaloza, L. (1989) 'Immigrant consumer acculturation', in T. Srull (ed.), *Advances in Consumer Research*, Vol. XVI, Association of Consumer Research, pp. 110–118.

Shaw, E. and Pirog III, S. (1997) 'A systems model of household behavior', *Journal of Marketing Theory and Practice*, Summer, 17–29.

Sheth, J. (1974) 'Family decision-making model', in *Models of Buyer Behaviour: Conceptual, Quantitative and Empirical*, New York: Harper & Row, pp. 17–33.

Sheth, J., Newman, B. and Gross, B. (1991) *Consumption Values and Market Choices: Theory and Applications*, Cincinnati: South-Western Publishing Co.

Sheth, J. and Parvatiyar, A. (1995) 'Relationship marketing in consumer markets: antecedents and consequents', *Journal of the Academy of Marketing Science* 23: 255–271.

Shocker, A., Ben-Akiva, M., Boccara, B. and Nedungadi, P. (1991) 'Consideration set influences on consumer decision-making and choice: issues, models, and suggestions', *Marketing Letters* 2(3): 181–197.

Smith, J. (1998) 'Buyer–seller relationships: similarity, relationship management, and quality', *Psychology & Marketing* 15(1): 3–21.

Solomon, M., Surprenant, C., Czepiel, J. and Gutman, E. (1985) 'A role theory perspective on dyadic interactions: the service encounter', *Journal of Marketing* 49 (Winter): 99–111.

Spiggle, S. and Sewall, M. (1987) 'A choice sets model of retail selection', *Journal of Marketing* 51 (April): 97–111.

Sriram, V. and Mummalaneni, V. (1990) 'Determinants of source loyalty in buyer–seller relationships', *Journal of Purchasing and Materials Management*, Fall, 21–26.

Swan, J. and Comb, L. (1976) 'Product performance and consumer satisfaction: a new concept', *Journal of Marketing* 40 (April): 25–33.

Wilson, D. (1995) 'An integrated model of buyer–seller relationships', *Journal of the Academy of Marketing Science* 23: 335–345.

Zeithaml, V. (1981) 'How consumer evaluation processes differ between goods and services', in J. Donnelly and R. George (eds), *Marketing of Services*, Chicago: American Marketing Association, pp. 39–47.

Zeithaml, V., Parasuraman, A. and Berry, L. (1985) 'Problems and strategies in services marketing', *Journal of Marketing* 49(2): 33–46.

Zeithaml, V., Parasuraman, A. and Berry, L. (1990) *Delivering Quality Service*, New York: Collier MacMillan.

CHAPTER 11

Relationship marketing in cross-cultural contexts

Poul Houman Andersen

LEARNING OBJECTIVES

At the end of this chapter readers will be able to:

▶ Gain a deeper insight into the nature of cross-cultural marketing relationships and networks.
▶ Gain an understanding of the role of national culture in cross-cultural marketing relationships.
▶ Appreciate the different concepts of culture and how these impact on cross-cultural relationship marketing research.
▶ Understand the model-building process and the attendant parameters for analyzing aspects of cross-cultural relationship marketing management and the managerial implications arising therefrom.

11.1 Introduction

Along with the internationalization of trade and investment, developing and maintaining business relationships across cultural contexts has become an increasingly important aspect of contemporary industrial marketing. The expansion of international production networks, where companies source internationally for world-class suppliers in specific technological areas, along with the internationalization of industrial producers, are among the important drivers for the increased focus on this area.

Relationship marketing is an important aspect of international as well as domestic industrial marketing. Initiating and managing relationships across cultural contexts adds considerably to the complexity of the relationship marketing process. There are two central reasons for this: the psychic distance of decision-makers; and the embeddedness of partners in existing networks of both buyers and sellers. Therefore, the central challenge in the formation of business relationships is not only on learning to adopt to the culture-related differences in business practice across business contexts, but also to balance the formation of new relationships with the existing portfolio of business relationships. This calls for learning as well as careful navigation in the relationship marketing process.

Although several studies have been made on various aspects of marketing management in cross-cultural contexts, this literature has only been briefly addressed in the literature on business relationships and networks. Only a few attempts have been made to couch relationship marketing in a cross-cultural context. This contribution provides a model for encompassing the various dimensions of initiating and developing relationships in cross-cultural business contexts. The structure of this contribution proceeds as follows. First, the concepts of business relationships, networks and culture are discussed and the literature on international relationship marketing is reviewed. Next, a model for addressing three aspects of cross-cultural relationship marketing management is presented. A case is analyzed, using the model. Finally, managerial implications are discussed.

11.2 Cross-cultural Relationship Marketing, Networks and the Importance of Meaning Systems

There are several research strands within the field of relationship marketing (Ricard and Perrien, 1999). In the following, the focal point is the IMP tradition of industrial marketing research. However, elements from other traditions (such as the strategic relationship marketing perspective) are also integrated.

A dominant part of the industrial marketing activities of a firm is characterized by long-term relationships to specific other firms. In one of the earliest encounters of this perspective, Arndt (1979), suggested that markets become 'domesticated', as regulations increasingly surround repeated exchange activities in order to reduce purchasing and selling costs. The basic idea of relationship marketing is that both buyers and seller can benefit from a durable relationship by attaining a larger proportion of each other's exchange activities, rather than maximizing on single transactions. By retaining customers and suppliers over several transactions, both parties may profit from experiences gained through previous transactions. Thus, the development of customer–supplier relationships may be described as a set of cumulative phases where the trustworthiness of suppliers and buyers are tested, and mutual norms concerning exchange activities are developed. The benefits of relationship marketing are expected increase with the complexity of interaction as complex exchange patterns necessitate information exchange across many levels of organization (Dwyer, Schurr and Oh, 1987).

The formation and development of international marketing relationships is a complex process involving multiple actors, activities and resources at both sides of the exchange dyad. Moreover, managing initiating relationships across cultural contexts is seen as more complex than relationship marketing within a specific cultural context such as a national culture (Haugland, 1999). A central aspect of establishing and maintaining market relationships concerns the actors' learning and adaptation processes. Especially in industrial markets characterized by a high degree of heterogeneity and continuous adaptations to new technologies and market situations, decision-makers are unable to determine the potential benefits of establishing such relationships ex ante. Marketing relationships are therefore developed through processes of trial and error, where decision-makers gradually expand the knowledge of their counterpart and increase their understanding of their motives and norms (Dwyer, Schurr and Oh, 1987).

The knowledge of decision-makers and their discrete choices are at the core of the relationship marketing process. Research in managerial cognition has convincingly argued that managers rely on their established knowledge structure when framing reality into recognizable situations to which specific actions can be assigned (Fiol and Huff, 1992; Weick, 1979). We refer to this existing cognitive structure as a meaning system, as the mental process of cognition. Managers differ on how they 'see' specific situations and how they assign actions to them. In essence, the interplay between the actors' meaning systems and their entrenchment in established patterns of meaning conceptualize the fundamental dynamics of creating relationships.

Differences in meaning systems are allegedly closely related to concepts of national cultural affiliation, as an important element in shaping cognitive diversity. Clearly, differences in managerial cognition can also be found within a certain national context. However, different cultural contexts add considerably to the diversity of managerial thought, as different cultures promote different aspects of management, e.g. leadership styles (Hofsteede, 1980).

11.3   Relationship Marketing in Cross-cultural Contexts: The Notion of Cultural Spheres of Influence

As already pointed out, there are different dimensions of the firm's existing cultural and business context that must be taken into consideration when developing relationships across cultures. In order to address these issues, a definition of what constitutes culture is called for.

There are certainly numerous definitions of culture in the social science literature, dealing with different conceptions of what should be included in cultural analysis. At the core of virtually all definitions of culture is a reference to shared values, norms, beliefs and practices evolving among a group of humans. This is close to the widely-used definition of culture as collective mental programming of the mind, distinguishing members of one group from another (Hofstede, 1980). However, rather than seeing culture as a given programme once and for all, defining the mental patterns of individuals, culture is here seen as an evolving meaning system, as individuals (and even collectives of individuals) interact and learn throughout their lifetime, developing their identity and perception of self. Therefore, the notion of identity- (identities) created learning and interaction among a collective of people is at the heart of cultural analysis.

Culture can be analyzed at various levels of society, relating to particular organizing institutions or 'spheres of cultural influence' (Sparrow, 2000; Bernheim and Whinston, 1990). The spheres are distinguishable to the extent that the underlying mandates for forming these spheres of influence differ. In particular, spheres differ with respect to what constitute them as cultural groups in the first place. However, they are interdependent at the same time, as a person's cultural identity formed in one specific cultural setting will affect how they view other situations in other cultural settings. We will take four such interdependent spheres of influence of collective interaction into account, relevant for this study:

- The national sphere.
- The network pattern sphere.
- The relationship sphere.
- The corporate sphere.

The latter three spheres resemble closely the level of analysis used in IMP research, focusing on change processes in business relationships and networks (Hakansson and Lundgren, 1995).

The national cultural sphere refers to the patterns of meaning, which are common amongst a majority of citizens in that country. A citizen shares fundamental rights and obligations with a collective of persons governing large parts of social life, which also affects the development of shared identity. Education systems, national laws, occupational experiences, etc. all play an important role in socializing individuals into a specific pattern of beliefs. Several studies have confirmed the importance of national cultures in explaining differences in firm as well as management behaviour (Van Oudenhoven, 2001; Hofstede, 1980).

The national identity can be distinguished from the cultural identities of a network pattern, which essentially relate to the evolving shared norms and practices in a set of interrelating firms, and are mutually dependent on access to each others' resources and activities. Hence, individual changes coincide and gradually create specific evolutionary processes within the network (Hakansson and Lundgren, 1995). In this setting, shared beliefs and experiences, stemming from repeated interactions and interconnectedness, form a system of shared norms and practices which guides patterns of coordination and decision-making. This is sometimes referred to as network embeddedness, signalling that business actors in networks are interlocked in shared systems of values and norms (Andersson and Molleryd, 1999). In some cases, networks transcend national borders to an extent where it is not meaningful to separate a specific part of the network in terms of national identity. However, truly global networks are not common in industrial markets (Wilkinson, Mattson and Easton, 2000).

On the relationship sphere, a dyad of actors may have formed a specific pattern of norms and belief system through repeated interactions. As compared to the network sphere, it is reasonable to believe that the shared belief system and the repertoire of shared norms and practices are more developed within the specific relationship, although it may reflect both national as well as network pattern aspects. We refer to this development of shared belief system as a relationship atmosphere (Hallen and Sandstrom, 1991). The relationship atmosphere refers to the shared beliefs and emotions of the partners, and has been described as the social or emotional superstructure of the relationship (Cova and Salle, 2000). Here, interpersonal relationships play a strong role as facilitators of developing a network culture over time. In face-to-face interactions, buyers and sellers engage in dynamic bargaining and communication processes that can dramatically change the attitudes, intentions and behaviours of all involved (cf. Jap, Manolis and Weitz, 1999: 303). Through repeated interactions and shared experiences, relations between decision-makers may evolve from professional acquaintances into private friendships, and act as lubricants for the relationship or even as carriers of trust (Toye and Ford, 1999). Again, at the level of analyzing the relationship atmosphere, traits from other cultural spheres are found. Influencing factors, both in terms of professional codes of conduct, as found in business networks or in terms of basic values of interpersonal interaction rooted in a society, may eventually decide on the direction and form of interpersonal relationships that are likely to be formed.

Finally, on the firm level of analysis, the role of the corporate sphere as identity-shaping has been thoroughly discussed in literature (Barley, 1983; Desphande and Webster, 1989). Organization culture may be defined as 'the pattern of shared values and beliefs that helps individuals understand organisational functioning and thus provide them norms for their behaviour in the organisation' (Desphande and Webster, 1989: 4). For the individual, the firm is a strong influencing factor, as a large proportion of a working person's life is spent with a particular firm. Consciously as well as unconsciously, organizations are bearers of value and belief systems to which individuals are socialized. These systems are often evolving through shared past experiences, and although they are efficient institutions for guiding actions within the organization, they may be difficult to apply outside the organization.

11.4   A Model of Cross-cultural Relationship Marketing Dimensions

Taking into account the various dimensions of culture introduced in the section above, a model for identifying the dimensions of cross-cultural relationship marketing can be developed. As outlined in Figure 11.1, these dimensions concern: (1) the initiation of international business relationships; (2) developing and managing the relationship atmosphere in international relationships; and (3) managing network interconnections between international relationships and existing internal and external relationships between actors.

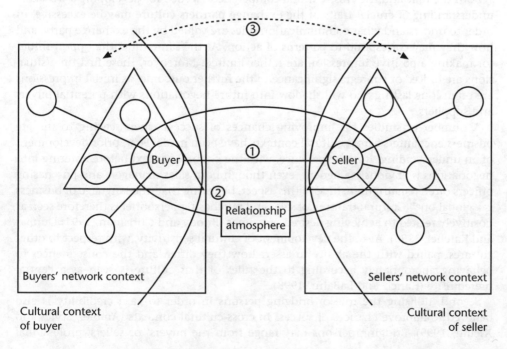

Figure 11.1 Dimensions of cross-cultural relationship marketing.

The initiation of new relationships across cultural contexts carries with it a number of problems which are specific to international business. First, the role of domestic social networks in supporting the salesperson is substantially reduced, if not entirely lacking. Credentials, personal referrals and other sources of reputational information are important if not crucial in several business cultures (Andersen and Soerensen, 1999).

In relation to this, sales and purchasing managers are faced with problems of psychic distance, as decision-makers may find it difficult to understand and learn about the overt and/or subtle signals and understand business situations diverse from their own, when communicating with persons from another culture (Johanson and Widersheim-Paul, 1975). In this context, identifying and understanding the culturally-related demands of the other party and how to respond to them becomes critical (Schultz, Evans and Good, 1999). Culturally defined procedures include:

- Who is supposed to participate in discussions and make decisions on marketing exchange possibilities.
- When decisions on going ahead or termination of further negotiations are to be made and by whom; and
- What information to be shared and when.

For instance, there are numerous accounts of Danish marketing managers who do not understand the business etiquette of Mediterranean buyers, and are frustrated over their potential customers seeming unwillingness to 'talk business'. On the other hand, Mediterranean managers often find Danish business people rude and impolite as they seem to have little understanding of the social norms underpinning business life in their national culture(s).

Both the time and the cross-cultural competences needed for developing a workable understanding of crucial traits of the exchange partners culture may be excessive, in order to understand what communication rules are valued by the exchange party, and how they may correspond to patterns of action. At the same time, the opportunities for making a positive impression are rather limited. Moreover, these first-time situations are indeed of strategic significance to the further outcome, as initial impressions are often long lasting and will shadow into future negotiations with potential buyers and suppliers.

A number of studies for improving chances of success when seeking to initiate business encounters across cultural contexts have been made. First, prior development of an understanding, if not experience, with the cultural context before entering into negotiations is obviously a benefit, even though both sales managers and purchasing officers often remain insensitive to this aspect, believing that 'the language of business is a global one'. Cultural training of sales and purchasing personnel is therefore seen as positively related to achieving desired outcomes (Briody and Chrisman, 1991; Dunbar and Katcher, 1990). Also, the development of cultural sensitivity, with respect to other cultures, paired with the ability to assert how they differ, and the consequences to behaving appropriately according to the rules of that culture is seen as a central prerequisite (Harich and LaBahn, 1998).

Second, utilizing the role of bridging persons in order to gain credibility is also believed to improve chances of success in cross-cultural contexts (Ambler, Styles and Xicum, 1999). Bridging persons may range from the buyers' or sellers' professional network, e.g. colleagues in- and outside the organization, or using a local person as mentor, with knowledge of both the local business culture and that of the purchasing or sales manager.

Managing Relationship Atmosphere in Cross-cultural Business Relationships

The social influence from the relationship atmosphere is often downplayed in relationship marketing investigations, although it plays a powerful role in forming adaptation of resources and activities among actors (Fang, 2001; Cova and Salle, 2000). In developing relationships, the personal encounters between buyers and sellers play a prominent role in forming expectations of both parties and their willingness to pursue further commitment into the business relationship. These encounters are even more critical in cross-cultural contexts, as actors are less likely to meet often in person, given the larger physical distance. This also increases the importance of critical episodes, where network participants use exceptional situations to test the bounds of their exchange party's willingness and ability to collaborate. For instance, when a French retailer of dairy products discovered that a product sample from Nordex Food (a Danish producer of dairy products) to be used at a trade fair had been damaged, Nordex thought it of crucial importance to ensure that the French retailer understood the gravity of the situation and were able to help accordingly. Therefore, the managing director of Nordex took the plane to Paris directly, together with the product sample, and delivered it personally. Even though there was no need for the Nordex managing director to show up in person, this episode signalled a high degree of commitment and willingness to serve a customer's needs, which eventually also helped Nordex in developing the relationship further.

Hence, there is also an increased focus on other means of social exchange between periods of meeting (Tikkanen, 1998). Gift giving, notification on holiday and birthdays and invitation of key persons in the buyer's or seller's decision-making unit to social events hosted by the other party are all elements that may contribute to the development and sustainment of the relationship atmosphere (Cova and Salle, 2000). Conventions and trade fairs often function as stages for this type of interaction, as key account managers and purchasing officers can economize on time and travelling costs by interacting with a large group of persons over a short period of time (Munuera and Ruiz, 1999).

In relation to this, communicative abilities are of vital importance, both with respect to listening and responding to customers. Each partner brings their own meaning system, representing reality to them, and originating in their cultural as well as personal values. Comprehension of the signals received from the other, as well as emphatic ability to understand how one's own signals are comprehended and linked to action patterns by the other party, are crucial for achieving a positive relationship atmosphere. Development of dialogical communication skills is therefore a significant prerequisite for the successful development of a positive atmosphere between the parties (Casrnir, 1999)

A central issue in developing and maintaining a relationship atmosphere relates to managing internal marketing relationships in the firm. Initiating and establishing cross-cultural relationships often calls for greater autonomy and individual decision-making abilities for those involved in this process. Having reached an agreement on pursuing the exploration of a relationship (or at least taking the first steps towards doing so) immediately evokes a number of other tasks with respect to convincing the organizations to which these persons belong. This is the classical 'double-sell' dilemma of boundary spanning personnel, as discussed in the industrial sales management literature (Moller and Rajala, 1999; St. John, Young and Miller, 1999). Lack of organizational support from the domestic organization to expatriate sales personnel is frequently discussed as a central reason for poor performance in relational selling (Guy and Patton, 1996). Marshalling support internally in the firm is therefore a crucial issue, when handling what are called critical issues in the development or relationship atmosphere.

Navigating Network Interconnectedness in Cross-cultural Business Relationships

In processes of establishing, managing and developing business relationships, decision-makers must take into consideration existing relationships with other firms. New relationships may be positively or negatively connected to existing relationships, strengthening or weakening the strategic manoeuvrability of the firm (Blankenburg and Johanson, 1991; Cook and Emerson, 1978). First, relationships may be positively or negatively interconnected. By positive interconnections is meant situation, where adding a relationship to the existing relationships of a firm will help the focal firm in improving its overall position in a network. For instance, the addition of a new supplier may strengthen the assortment of technologies that the focal firm already holds and increase the value as perceived by the companies which have formed relationships as sellers, or make it possible to better utilize existing technologies. Negative interconnections, on the other hand, refer to situations where a firm, by linking up with other firms, may weaken its network position or eventually exclude it from exchange relationships. For instance, forming relationships with one pharmaceutical company may be incompatible with having relationships with other car producers, as they perceive the indirect link to other producers as a potential source of knowledge spillover. In a cross-cultural context, links with competing networks situated in different cultural contexts, are a potential source of knowledge generation, as both parties may find mutually beneficial interactions occur, which have the potential of creating benefits for both parties. However, such linkages may also be seen as potentially threatening by the buying and/or selling party, and may lead to relationship termination.

Interconnectedness does not only affect the possibility of initiating relationships. Networks are dynamic by nature, as individual actors develop, transform or terminate relationships with each other, excluding existing partners and including new ones (Anderson *et al.*, 1998). Because of their emergent properties, firms may be navigating according to the changing nature of relationships and the opportunities and threats they encounter from these changes (Andersson and Moelleryd, 1999). Firms may decide to follow a network-integrative strategy where they seek to bridge relationships, overcoming temporary and/or permanent tensions between partners. However, firms may also choose a network changing strategy, where they manipulate the network structure in order to achieve a specific aim, by breaking old relationships and/or forming new ones.

From a cross-cultural point of view, negative and positive interconnections may relate to specific procedures or ways of doing things. As networks represent spheres of influence, involving specific patterns of interaction, norms and regulations, some forms of behaviour, which may be seen as inappropriate in one context, may be deemed acceptable in others. For instance, in certain networks price negotiations, fixed contracts are a central part of the network pattern, whereas in other network patterns, such dealings are not acceptable. For the actor inbetween these network patterns, it can be difficult to emulate both postures at the same time, as different rules for forming and managing relationships influence the delegation of roles and responsibilities inside the organization. This can create tensions and incompatible alignment of incentive structures and management routines internally in the firm. Hence, whereas a salesperson in one context is working fairly autonomously, this policy may not be advisable to follow in other contexts. As the salespersons are a central part of striking a deal with the customer, they may promise early delivery times or extended tailorization of products, essentially competing over scarce resources (such as production capacity), but not following the same set of rules for doing so. One consequence, if problems are persisting and cannot be solved through integration or development strategies, may be to divisionalize the focal actor in an attempt to reduce interdependencies of network interconnections. For instance, in order to overcome internal and network resistance towards the development and e-trade of new interactive, Lego products by the existing network of retailers, Lego decided to develop a new division, Lego Direct. This division has developed a range of new relationships to customers and cyber-retailers and maintained some of the old relationships as well to suppliers.

Networks of established relationships support as well as lock in the firm into specific administrative routines. These routines may not square easily with those emerging from international relationships. As international relationships evolve, they form a third culture in terms of a sphere of influence, which contain values, norms and procedures mutually acceptable for both parties. Both buying and selling organizations need to oversee the activities of salespeople to ensure these strategies are consistent with activities in existing networks.

Consequently, a central issue in managing the presence of numerous business contexts therefore concerns striking the right balance between different relationship postures. Flexibility to operate and take into account changes in multiple business contexts is a dominant feature of effective relationship management across cultures. Striking this dynamic balance also means avoiding over-designed relationships, in terms of linking activities and resources too tightly to specific customers or suppliers.

Managerial Implications of Navigating in Contexts: Towards a Holistic Understanding

The multidimensional model proposed here suggests that a range of aspects must be taken into account when firms are initiating and developing relationships across cultural contexts. These elements are shown in Table 11.1.

Clearly, not all elements of the model are equally important in all situations of creating international marketing relationships. However, as shown in two cases in the next section, the model can be used in order to capture the evolving dynamics of international market relationships.

	Initiating relationships	*Developing relationship atmosphere*	*Managing network interconnectedness*
Strategic challenge	Overcoming psychic distance and coping with culture shock	Ensuring continuous communication and organizational backup	Bridging diverse and sometimes incompatible business norms, handling positive and negative interconnections
Managerial implication	Cultural training Use of mentors and actor bonds	Developing policies for expatriate sales force, building policies for maintaining communication and managing critical events	Network integration and change strategies

Table 11.1
An overview of issues, challenges and managerial implications of cross-cultural relationship management.

11.5 Relationship Marketing in the Pharmaceutical Industry: Novo Nordisk Case

In the following, the framework developed is used in analyzing international relationship marketing processes. The initiation and development of the business relationship is primarily seen from the buyer's point of view. The data collection for the case involves interviews with Nissho and Novo personnel, as well as archival data, internal memos, newspaper articles and observations. More than 150 pages of interviews have been transcribed and sent to interviewees for approval.

Novo Nordisk is a multinational company within the pharmaceutical and biochemical industry, with headquarters in Denmark. It was established when two leading insulin producers, Nordisk Gentofte and Novo, merged. Novo Nordisk is a leading producer of insulin for diabetics, providing more than 40 per cent of the global production.

The case story begins before this merger took place. Therefore, in the first part of the case the company is referred to as 'Novo', whereas in the post-merger part of the case the company is referred to as Novo Nordisk. As all interviews have been carried out after the merger, the respondents from this company are all referred to as employees of Novo Nordisk.

In the 1970s, researchers became aware that diabetic complications might be reduced through smaller and more frequent doses of insulin. However, if diabetics were to benefit from this new kind of treatment, they were to bring with them a bulky assortment of syringes, needles and insulin. After some attempts, interest began to emerge around the cartridge concept. In 1981, Novo started a pilot project with the intention of developing an injection system based on the cartridge technology. The NovoPen was launched in 1985. It was an insulin syringe, the size and shape of a ball point pen, which diabetics could keep in their shirt pocket. Prior to the product launch, both the technical staff at Novo and their external partners had put considerable effort into developing the pen systems. The use of external partners was a necessity, as the development and production of the injection system called for capabilities that were not available within Novo.

The Initiation of the Search Process

In 1981, while developing the initial sketches of the pen, the product development team focused on developing a foolproof system for dispensing insulin in correct doses. Initially, when NovoPen was launched for testing, it was equipped with a pilot version of the needle ground by a local manufacturer of needles. Novo soon realized that the quality and production capacity of this supplier were not sufficient to meet the demands of Novo. In 1983, they initiated a global search for qualified subcontractors who were willing to participate in the development of the needle component. Novo technicians believed that if they were to meet the subcontractor's engineering department, they would be able to explain and clarify their ideas for the needle component, without revealing the product concept they were working on.

Initiation and Development of the Relationship with Nissho Medical Industries

As the range of prospective subcontractors gradually shrank, the Novo team eventually met with a group of marketing representatives from Nissho Medical Industries (Nissho). The Nissho representatives were very interested in the product concept:

> Nissho was strictly business-minded. Naturally, they would like to know what the product concept was. At that time I suspected that they were trying to get our idea and use it for themselves. However, we had been very cautious when we developed the drawings and specifications for the pen, so that the total product concept was not revealed from the drawings of one component (Jørn Rex, Product Development Manager, Novo Nordisk).

On the one hand, the representatives from Novo were unwilling to provide this information, while on the other hand, they wanted to maintain Nissho's interest. So, they hinted to the Nissho representatives that a production of no less than 50 million items annually was planned. This was clearly overstated, but it helped to increase Nissho's interest. However, the representatives from Nissho wanted more information on the product if they were to engage in the project and present the business proposal to management. Finally, the representatives from Novo stated that the product concept would be revealed if Nissho would commit itself to collaborate under a secrecy agreement. Novo was willing to make the necessary investments in production facilities, while Nissho's contribution was mainly to provide the necessary expertise and to contribute towards a further refinement of the product. After the negotiation team had returned to Denmark, Nissho wanted a new meeting with Novo, and contacted them based on the information concerning the production volume. This time the representatives from Novo visited Nissho's production plant, where they had discussions with several production engineers concerning how to produce the component. The initial reaction from the Nissho engineers was that Nissho could not manufacture the product. Although this seemed like a blank rejection, the negotiation team from Novo had learned from their first visit that such absolute stances were negotiable. Moreover, at that point in time, the Japanese partner was not experienced in doing business with foreign customers and, therefore, had limited skills in communicating in English.

The negotiation team from Novo explained to the Nissho engineers that Novo was here at their invitation, and that Nissho had already seen the drawings of the needle.

If the engineers from Nissho were able to flatly reject the idea, then why did they invite Novo in the first place? During the discussion, Jørn Rex, who was responsible for the development of the Novo Cartridge, showed a needle component to the Nissho engineers, which he had picked up during a round trip of the factory. While doing so, he pointed out that Nissho was already producing a component which was similar to that of the Novo concept in many respects. This point increased Nissho's interest, and the meeting ended with an agreement to pursue production. In September 1983, only two months after the meeting at the Nissho factory, Novo received the first trial batch. Following this initial contact period, production staff from Novo and Nissho visited each other two or three times a year for six years, parallel to the clinical testing activities of the device on Danish diabetics.

During this period, the NovoPen, including the needle component, was modified several times in order to increase its user-friendliness. Novo had designed a short, thin needle, with a connecting device to the pen, and they gradually improved the functionalism of this needle in collaboration with Nissho. The producer possessed excellent skills concerning product modification, while maintaining low costs as well as product quality, even in mass production. Novo later perceived these collaborative efforts as critical when designing the new versions of the pen. Thus, a lot of joint effort and participation from the construction and production departments of both Nissho and Novo finally produced the results.

The Emergence of Distrust: A Critical Episode

In the midterm stage of the subcontractor relationship with Nissho, Novo invested in a production line for needles to the pen. The line was staffed with Nissho's employees. Through these mutual investments, Nissho and Novo both demonstrated a shared commitment to the relationship, very much in line with the Japanese tradition of subcontractor relationships. Shortly thereafter, Novo merged with its largest competitor, Nordisk Gentofte. Because of the merger of NOVO and Nordisk Gentofte, the new company Novo Nordisk took over a needle fabrication plant. Partly based on semi-manufactured needle tubes from Nissho, this plant manufactured needles for the pen launched by Nordisk Gentofte in 1986. After the merger Novo Nordisk equipped the plant to produce needles for NovoPen and the NovoLet. When Nissho realized this it caused a great deal of confusion and disappointment in Nissho:

> The introduction of a new supplier was unexpected for us. We had been treating our customer loyally and respectfully – they never found reason for complaint (Sales manager at Nissho, medical division).

They feared that Novo Nordisk would phase out their production line at Nissho and in the end transfer the knowledge of grinding thin needles to their in-house plant. The result was that Nissho became less committed towards participating in development activities. In the words of a Novo Nordisk manager:

> They saw the Danish facilities as a direct competitor and did not want to give anything before Novo Nordisk gave something to them (Subsidiary Manager, Novo Nordisk Japan).

First, Nissho suggested that its new plant in Taiwan could function as a secondary source of supply. However, Novo Nordisk needed to ensure that delivery would continue, even if Nissho went bankrupt. The relationship climate gradually worsened. In 1990, Novo Nordisk found out that Beckton and Dickinson (B&D), a world leading manufacturer of needles and injectors, had started developing a cartridge model, conceptually similar to the NovoPen, and using Nissho as a needle supplier. Although Novo Nordisk did not approve of it, neither did they prohibit it. One reason for this was that Novo Nordisk and B&D considered forming a partnership at the time. The potential risk of transferring strategically important assets in terms of knowledge to a possible rival was not acknowledged in this context. It was the belief among managers responsible for the production that the B&D operations had been cleared somewhere in the organization. Moreover, the marketing and top management did not equally acknowledge the importance of protecting strategically important knowledge from rival competitors' decision-makers. A lack of communication and exchange of knowledge between these divisions therefore blocked the possibilities of a coordinated response.

Finally, the top management of Novo Nordisk announced that they would discontinue doing business with Nissho unless its relation to B&D was terminated. It took serious time and effort before Novo Nordisk could convince Nissho management that the Danish subsidiary mainly worked as a secondary supplier to ensure delivery, rather than being a threat to Nissho. The fact that the Danish plant only had a fraction of the production capacity needed, and that it had insufficient development capabilities, helped to convince the Nissho managers. All development activities were still to be conducted with Nissho. Finally, Novo Nordisk is now using long-term delivery contracts in which the purchased amount is settled up to five years ahead.

The Relationship Today

The collaboration between Nissho and Novo Nordisk has regained its strength and has become more extensive during the course of the successful launch of NovoPen. The latest result of the collaboration between the two companies is the NovoFine: the thinnest and shortest needle available for insulin injection worldwide. Frequent visits and exchange of staff members have continued over the years, and today all of Novo Nordisk's product improvement activities regarding the needle involve Nissho. This collaboration has now worked for 20 years.

Both Nissho and Novo Nordisk have improved their ability to collaborate over wide cultural as well as physical distances. At the present time, four staff members from Novo Nordisk are working together with Nissho on a regular basis, to improve the needle. Novo Nordisk has developed a culture sensitivity seminar for employees who are to encounter their Japanese partners for the first time. Moreover, a person who has already developed personal relations with his/her Japanese colleagues, always accompanies employees who need to be introduced to the Japanese for the first time. On the other hand, Nissho has also developed its collaborative skills. To begin with, Nissho employees who were directly involved with Novo Nordisk, improved their English-speaking capabilities. And what is more, the Japanese partner gradually became more aware of the business culture of Novo Nordisk. Thus, discussions between Danish and Japanese engineers have become more open-ended and informal than before, signalling a higher level of confidence between the partners. Over the years of collaboration, an entangled web of personal relationships has emerged. Although both companies encourage close personal relationships, such relationships can also be an obstacle for the development of the relationship between the companies. Individual staff members could make deals and agreements which would not be in agreement with the overall mission of the respective firms, or decisions may not be communicated to all persons involved. For this reason, Novo Nordisk has developed a procedure where all formalized agreements must be cleared. At Novo Nordisk, two persons are responsible for this procedure: one takes care of the technical aspects, including alterations of designs, development projects, etc., while the other is in charge of the commercial aspects of a relationship. As well as these arrangements, a yearly meeting is held at both top and middle management levels in order to ensure the smooth functioning of the relationship.

11.6   Analysis of the Case

As illustrated here, the initiation and development of international relationships across cultures is a challenging obligation for both buyers and sellers. Also, the case illustrates some of the elements of the framework that the actors took into consideration in order to promote the process of relationship building. In particular, the role of the Novo expatriate purchasing force and the development of support functions in both organizations, in order to smooth apparent culture shocks, and the development of a forum where top management can address divergent views and interests, correspond with previous findings.

Complexity of learning and navigation, however, arise not only from the differences among actors on the national level, but are also affected by corresponding developments on the organizational and the network level. Different expectations and interpretations are reflected by culture-bound meaning systems, and cultural spheres of influence may work in opposite directions, causing tensions and promoting changes in business relationships. Hence, an event may evoke very different streams of actions, or may be viewed very differently by actors. In Table 11.2 below, an overview of the observations in the case are presented, using the spheres of influence to address critical events in each of the dimensions of international relationship (initiation, relationship atmosphere management and navigation of network interconnectedness).

As can be seen from this presentation, not all spheres of influence were equally important to all aspects of developing international market relationships in this particular case. An alternative case may breed a very different configuration of the cells. Another issue concerns the interlinkages of cultural spheres in different situations. One such situation concerned the initiation of the relationship between Nissho and Novo. The language and communication barriers that Novo and Nissho faced during their initial negotiations were somewhat relieved by the extended negotiation rights given to the Novo expatriate purchasing team, which allowed them to accommodate better with the business practices of the Japanese supplier. Moreover, the Novo policy well reflected the value system of Novo, which allowed for a strong degree of delegation and lateral networking (a feature which has been repeatedly noticed as a distinguishing feature of Danish management – Hofstede, 1980; Oudehoven, 2001). In this case, cultural spheres act as supportive levers. However, in the situation where a merger between Novo and Nordisk Gentofte led to the establishment of an internal supplier, different conceptions of the roles and obligations of

Table 11.2 A schematic overview of the case analysis.

	National level	Network level	Relationship level	Organizational level
Initiation of relationship	Language barriers and communication problems created psychic distance in initial negotiatons between Novo and Nissho			An expatriate purchasing team searching for viable suppliers is established. The team has extended negotiation rights and is supported by Novo
Relationship atmosphere	Different expectations on the roles and obligations of Novo as a contractor and Nissho as a buyer emanating from a different (culture-dependent) business logic	The regained collaborative atmosphere between Nissho and Novo Nordisk allows the transfer knowledge from Nissho to internal Novo supplier	Procedures are developed for internal knowledge transfer in both Novo and Nissho positively affecting communication abilities

Personal friendships beyond initial negotiations gradually form between Novo and Nissho managers | Inter-departmental differences in Novo Nordisk concerning the importance of needle supplier and how internal production and how it affects relationship |
| Network interconnect-edness | | Merger between Novo and Nordisk Gentofte created reactions in terms of network change | Merger between Novo and Nordisk Gentofte created tensions and affected atmosphere negatively as event was enacted differently in Novo Nordisk as compared to Nissho | Lack of trust toward Novo Nordisk leads Nissho into initiating relationship with Beckton & Dickson |

buyers and suppliers in a business relationship clashed. Here, changes in interconnectedness between Novo and Nordisk Gentofte, together with different priorities and understandings within Novo Nordisk, caused problems at the relationship level.

11.7 Conclusion

Developing and managing cross-cultural business relationships calls for managers to consider a range of issues, with respect to psychic distance and differences related to diverging network patterns, national and organizational cultures. Some of these issues are unique to cross-cultural management and are a part of the learning process of internationalization (Johanson and Vahlne, 1977). The idea put forward in this contribution is that management can address these issues in terms of spheres of influence and may adopt their actions and foresee a range of potential challenges accordingly.

This framework is an attempt to address the complexity at different levels of cross-cultural relationship management, using previous research on cross-cultural industrial marketing. There is obviously much work to be done with respect to developing cultural aspects of each level of analysis and in discerning the specific patterns of interrelations between levels. In particular, the development of cross-cultural relationships may be linked to the growing literature on the internationalization of firms in networks (Chetty and Blankenburg, 2000; Wilkinson, Mattson and Easton, 2000). This is an issue for future investigation in this field.

REVIEW QUESTIONS

1. Discuss the role of national culture in cross-cultural market relationships.

2. What is the difference between static and dynamic conceptions of culture and how does it matter in relation to market research?

3. Describe the relationship between a designated behaviour pattern of your own and the underlying norms in a series (two or more) of international encounters with a person or a group of people from another culture (national, corporate, educational or otherwise).

4. Using the notion of cultural spheres, describe any type of communication failures to occur and try to analyze the possible reasons for these.

References

Ambler, T., Styles, C. and Xicum, W. (1999) 'The effect of channel relationships and Guanxi on the performance of inter-province export ventures in the People's Republic of China', *International Journal of Research in Marketing* 16: 75–87.

Andersen, P. H. and Sørensen, H. B. (1999) 'Reputational information and interorganizational collaboration', *Corporate Reputation Review* 2(3): 215–230.

Anderson, H., Havila, V., Andersen, P. H. and Halinen, A. (1998) 'Position and role: conceptualizing dynamics in business networks', *Scandinavian Journal of Management* 14(3): 167–186.

Andersson, P. and Moelleryd, B. (1999) 'Channels of network change and behavioural consequences of relationship connectedness', *Journal of Business Research* 46: 291–301.

Arndt, J. (1979) 'Toward a concept of domesticated markets', *Journal of Marketing* 43 (Fall): 69–75.

Barley, S. T. (1983) 'Semiotics and the study of occupational and organisational cultures', *Administrative Science Quarterly* 28: 393–413.

Bernheim, D. and Whinston, M. D. (1990) 'Multimarket contact and collusive behaviour', *Rand Journal of Economics* 21: 1–26.

Blankenburg, D. and Johanson, J. (1992) 'Managing network connections in international business', *Scandinavian International Business Review* 1(1): 5–19.

Briody, E. K. and Chrisman, J. B. (1991) 'Cultural adaptation in overseas assignments', *Human Organization* 50(3): 264–282.

Casrnir, F. L. (1999) 'Foundations for the study of intercultural communication based on a third-culture building model', *International Journal of Intercultural Relations* 23(1): 91–116.

Chetty, S. and Blankenburg, D. (2000) 'Internationalisation of small to medium-sized manufacturing firms: a network approach', *International Business Review* 9(1): 77–93.

Cook, K. and Emerson, R. M. (1984) 'Exchange networks and the analysis of complex organizations', *Sociology of Organizations* 3: 1–30.

Cova, B. and Salle, R. (2000) 'Rituals in managing extra business relationships in international project marketing: a conceptual framework', *International Business Review* 9: 669–685.

Desphande, R. and Webster, F. R. (1989) 'Organisational culture and marketing: defining the research agenda', *Journal of Marketing* 53: 3–15.

Dunbar, E. and Katcher, A. (1990) 'Preparing managers for foreign assignments', *Training and Development Journal*, September, 45–47.

Dwyer, Schurr and Oh (1987) 'Developing buyer–seller relationships', *Journal of Marketing* 51: 11–27.

Fang, T. (2001) 'Culture as a driving force for interfirm adaption: a Chinese case', *Industrial Marketing Management* 30(51): 51–63.

Fiol, C. M. and Huff, A. S. (1992) 'Maps for managers: where do we go from here?', *Journal of Management Studies* 29: 267–285.

Guy, B. S. and Patton, W. E. (1996) 'Managing the effects of culture shock and soujourner adjustment on the expatriate industrial sales force', *Industrial Marketing Management* 25: 385–393.

Hallen, L. and Sandstroem, M. (1991) 'Relationship atmosphere in international business', in S. J. Paliwoda (ed.), *New Perspectives on International Marketing*, London: Routledge.

Hakansson, H. and Lundgren, A. (1995) 'Industrial networks and technological innovation', in K. Moller and D. Wilson (eds), *Business Marketing: An Interaction and Network Perspective*, Dordrecht: Kluwer Academic Publishers.

Haugland, S. A. (1999) 'Factors influencing the duration of international buyer–seller relationships', *Journal of Business Research* 46(3): 273–280.

Harich, K. R. and LaBahn, D. W. (1998) 'Enhancing international business relationships: a focus on customer perceptions of salesperson role performance including cultural sensitivity', *Journal of Business Research* 42: 87–101.

Hofstede, G. (1980) *Culture's Consequences: International Differences in Work-related Values*, Beverly Hills, CA: Sage Publications.

Jap, S. D., Manolis, C. and Weitz, B. A. (1999) 'Relationship quality and buyer–seller interactions in channels of distribution', *Journal of Business Research* 46: 303–313.

Johanson, J. and Vahlne, J. (1977) 'The internationalization process of the firm: a model of knowledge development and increasing foreign commitments', *Journal of International Business Studies* 8(1): 23–32.

Johanson, J. and Wiedersheim-Paul, F. (1975) 'The internationalisation of the firm – four Swedish case studies', *The Journal of Management Studies* 12(3): 305–322.

Moller and Rajala (1999) 'Organizing marketing in industrial high-tech firms – the role of internal marketing relationships', *Industrial Marketing Management* 28: 521–535.

Munuera, J. L. and Ruiz, S. (1999) 'Trade fairs as services: a look at visitors' objectives in Spain', *Journal of Business Research* 44: 17–24.

Ricard, L. and Perrien, J. (1999) 'Explaining and evaluating the implementation of organizational relationship marketing in the banking industry: clients' perception', *Journal of Business Research* 45: 199–209.

Sparrow, L. M. (2000) 'Beyond multicultural man: complexities of identity', *International Journal of Intercultural Relations* 24(2): 173–201.

Schultz, R., Evans, K. R. and Good, D. J. (1999) 'Intercultural interaction strategies and relationship selling in industrial markets', *Industrial Marketing Management* 28: 589–599.

St. John, C. H., Young, S. T. and Miller, J. L. (1999) 'Coordinating manufacturing and marketing in international firms', *Columbia Journal of World Business* 34(2): 109–127.

Tikkanen, H. (1998) 'Research on international project marketing', in H. Tikkanen (ed.), *Marketing and International Business – Essays in Honour of Professor Karin Holstius on her 65th Birthday*, Turku School of Business.

Toye, S. and Ford, D. (1999) 'Interpersonal interaction in business relationships: an asset management problem', Proceedings of the 15th IMP Conference, University College, Dublin.

Van Oudenhoven, J. P. (2001) 'Do organizations reflect national cultures? A 10-nation study', *International Journal of Intercultural Relations* 25: 89–107.

Weick, K. E. (1979) *The Social Psychology of Organizing*, New York: Doubleday Books.

Wilkinson, I. , Mattson, L.-G. and Easton, G. (2000) 'International competitiveness and trade promotion policy from a network perspective', *Journal of World Business* 35(3): 275–299.

CHAPTER 12

Corporate social responsibility

Ven Sriram and Franklyn Manu

12.1 Introduction

The issues surrounding corporate social responsibility (CSR) have been discussed and debated in Western societies for several years now. As these countries have achieved a level of economic well-being for the bulk of their populations, the focus has now shifted from the pure, immediate economic consequences of corporate actions to include the long-term impact of these actions on the society as a whole. Domestic concerns over environmental pollution and working conditions are being aggressively articulated and corporations are feeling the pressure to respond to them. However, as companies globalize and move production from developed to developing countries, CSR issues have also begun to become a global concern. The strength of the anti-globalization protesters at the WTO meeting in Seattle in 1999, the IMF meetings in Prague in 2000, the World Economic Forum in Switzerland in 2001, and more recently at the G–8 meeting in Genoa indicate that there is a deep concern among many regarding the social responsibility of multinationals as they expand globally.

While corporate leaders have become more sensitive to public concern over these issues, they have yet to formulate a consistent response. Some companies have attempted to develop a code of conduct and apply that to their actions, whereas others are more reactive and respond in an *ad hoc* fashion when pressure mounts from external groups and legislative bodies. What this chapter tries to do is to develop a model of corporate response, from the corporate point of view, in order to create a framework which will help us understand the nature of external pressures on companies to behave responsibly, the internal decision-making process, and finally, corporate actions and their outcomes.

We begin with a discussion of this model in general terms, explaining its links and the process involved. We also use cross-cultural examples to illustrate each of these linkages. Finally, we use the example of an important global concern, containing the spread of AIDS, to show how the model works. We conclude with some questions for discussion to help readers apply some of the concepts.

12.2 The Model: A Conceptual Framework

The model presented in Figure 12.1 consists of three parts. The first deals with the elements that are antecedent pressures which trigger corporate concern about the social impact of their actions. These pressures can originate either from within or outside the organization. The second describes the decision process by which these pressures are processed and a course of action determined. The third discusses the anticipated outcomes of this action and the impact of those outcomes on the triggering forces themselves. It is argued that while the specific nature of the elements in the model may vary from country to country, the overall concepts are applicable to organizations the world over.

12.3 External Pressures

Pressures for the organization to act in a socially responsible manner may originate from several sources. Initially, individual consumers and citizens may take private action, such as boycotts, to signal their protest regarding certain corporate activities. While these are often not recognized by companies, or are minimized, if the root cause of the action has enough public support and the action is led by a strong and charismatic leader, the number of supporters may swell enough for a pressure group to be formed. In developed countries, many well-funded and powerful interest groups, often non-governmental organizations (NGOs), have emerged over the years and are actively involved in putting pressure on corporations to consider the social consequences of their actions. Many of them are single-issue groups focused on activities such as stopping deforestation caused by clear-cutting of trees or protecting endangered species. Others tend to be more broad-based, their concern being corporate employment practices, for example. As corporations have globalized and expanded their operations into developing countries in search of cheap labour and raw materials, many of these interest groups have also followed, expanding their reach either directly or via alliances with similar groups in the countries hosting corporate foreign investments. In

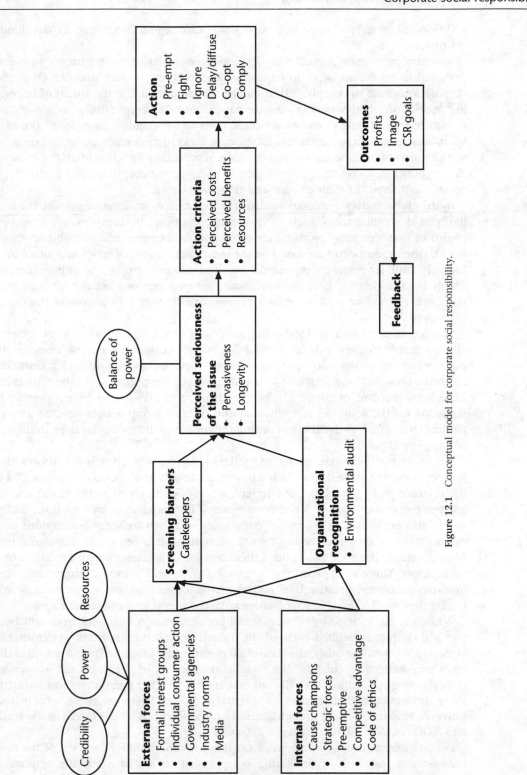

Figure 12.1 Conceptual model for corporate social responsibility.

addition, home-grown interest groups have also begun to emerge in developing countries.

Governments, again initially in developed countries, have begun to pass laws designed to force companies to behave in a socially responsible manner. Of course, corporations need to comply with these laws, once passed, but the threat of impending legislation often serves as an external pressure for corporations to act. If they recognize these pressures early they often offer to self-regulate in order to pre-empt what they see as more restrictive regulation. In areas such as environmental pollution, working conditions and truth-in-advertising, several laws are already on the books in many countries. Increasingly, developing country governments are also beginning to act in the interests of their citizens and their well-being.

In the global context, industry norms are often created in situations where the issue has global significance – such as working conditions in factories in developing countries manufacturing products for companies and consumers from the developed world. Often these norms are based on the recommendations of task forces made up of industry and government representatives and interest groups, usually under the umbrella of a global organization. Again, their prescriptions usually set minimum standards of conduct and are often a pre-emptive strategy on the part of the parties concerned.

The media also plays an interesting role, both direct and indirect, as an external change agent. In their role as a watchdog, they occasionally expose questionable practices of companies both home and abroad. Investigative reporting by journalists has often brought these activities to the attention of the public who otherwise might have been ignorant of them. The media also brings pressure to bear indirectly by reporting on the activities of individual and interest group action directed at companies. This again has the effect of raising the profile of the particular issue in the eyes of the general public.

The impact of these external forces on the industry or company is not always high. It is dependent to some degree on the power, credibility and resources commanded by the relevant party. Typically, government actions or threats of action command the greatest corporate attention for obvious reasons. The same holds true for independent media and explains why individual companies and their industry associations dedicate so much of their money and time to lobbying legislators and in managing their press coverage. The ability to control these two forces is often a major determinant of their power. This also explains the seriousness with which interest groups take their fund-raising efforts, because they realize that in order for them to get their desired results they need to be able to influence both the media and the legislatures.

While the tactics used by these external pressure groups may vary from collaborative and cooperative efforts with private industry on the one hand, to confrontation and disruption on the other, these external pressures are often the primary trigger that force corporations to consider the social consequences of their actions. As a result, they also frequently have the effect of making the targeted companies and industries more introspective. This creates an internal pressure. There are those who believe, however, that the pressure brought to bear on corporations by the nexus of the media and NGOs could backfire (Kapstein, 2001).

Public interest groups have been in existence for some time now. One of the more talked-about instances of pressuring corporations to act in a socially responsible manner dates back to the 1970s, when a coalition of groups engineered a boycott of the Swiss multinational Nestlé in a dispute over how it marketed its infant milk formula in developing countries. Subsequently, other groups such as People for the Ethical Treatment of Animals (PETA) have mounted action against companies in protest at their treatment of animals in product research and testing. PETA's actions were also instrumental in raising consumer consciousness against wearing furs, sometimes through very aggressive means. Perhaps the best indicator of their success is that while they started as 'fringe' groups with somewhat radical ideas, many of them have become well-organized and several of the causes they espouse are now perceived as more mainstream. They have also become more sophisticated in their use of technology to mobilize support for their causes. Groups that are fighting for improved working conditions in developing country sweatshops and have targeted companies such as Nike for its labour practices have websites to counter corporate PR efforts (e.g. <www.saigon.com/nike>; <www.globalexchange.org>).

While such groups sometimes wield enormous clout, actions by committed, passionate and articulate individuals can also be a source of pressure on organizations. Ken Saro-Wiwa organized and led a protest against Royal Dutch/Shell and its activities in Nigeria for its role in the pollution of rivers and deforestation in land belonging to his Ogoni tribesmen (*Economist*, 13 February 1999). Two activists in the UK were sued for libel by McDonald's for accusing the company of various activities including rainforest destruction, food poisoning, starvation in the Third World, heart disease and cancer, and bad working conditions. After a lengthy trial, the court ruled that the pair had not provided sufficient evidence to support their accusations, but did find the company 'falsely advertise their food as nutritious', risk the health of their long-term regular customers, are 'culpably responsible' for cruelty to animals reared for their products, are 'strongly antipathetic' to unions and 'pay their workers low wages' (<www.mcspotlight.org>). The trial became somewhat of a *cause celebre*, because it was seen in some quarters as a David versus Goliath situation. There are other examples of individual consumers boycotting products of companies they believe to have behaved irresponsibly with regard to the society, such as Exxon's perceived lack of an appropriate response over the Alaska oil spill or Firestone and Ford's problems with recalled tyres (Alsop, 2001).

In many countries, governments and courts have also begun to play a more activist role as external pressure points. In India, for example, the courts have ruled in favour of public-interest litigants who have argued for the enforcement of clean-air statutes by requiring that diesel buses in New Delhi be replaced with pollution free ones powered by compressed natural gas. In others, the election success of parties such as the Greens in Germany means that proponents of various social causes have a sympathetic ear in the seats of power. When governments sign global accords, such as the Kyoto treaty to curb global warming, this can have a trickle down effect on companies as they may be forced to adhere to stricter environmental standards.

Industry associations have begun to develop normative standards of conduct for their members, which in turn puts pressure on individual organizations to adhere to them. Also, consortia representing a cross-section of interested parties – companies, human rights, labour, religious and consumer groups – such as the Fair Labor Association (FLA), develop and require adherence to codes of conduct. The FLA's code encompasses issues such as 'human rights, including freedom of association and collective bargaining, wages, hours, and benefits' (<www.nikebiz.com>).

There are several instances of the media creating pressure on organizations by reporting on their business activities that show them in an unfavourable light. For example, in the US, the *Baltimore Sun* newspaper reported how the large poultry companies exploit the contract farmers who raise the birds (Fesperman and Shatzkin, 1999).

12.4 Internal Pressures

As external pressure has mounted on organizations to explicitly incorporate social responsibility concerns into their strategic thinking and planning, this issue has become one for which there is also internal pressure for action. In addition, several business schools have also begun to sensitize their students about the need for such thinking. Professional managers, often the products of such schools, have therefore started to champion these causes from within their organizations. As these cause champions emerge, the issue of CSR is brought to the forefront. As a consequence, many firms have begun to develop a code of ethics to govern their behaviour. This may be a quite distinct standard for individual corporate action from industry-wide norms that are developed from outside the organization, albeit with the participation of the specific company concerned.

While some managers may therefore see the need for their organizations to be socially responsible as the 'right' thing to do, there may also be another, perhaps more calculated, internal pressure. This is when executives recognize the potential strategic pay-offs that can accrue from taking a proactive stance with respect to CSR. Just as there are first-mover advantages from other strategic actions, such as investments in technology or forming certain strategic alliances, by establishing itself and being recognized as a socially responsible organization a company may pre-empt others within its industry from staking claims to that position. This can raise the profile of the company in a positive way among its publics, including its customers and external pressure groups. Also, as suggested earlier, this strategic move may insulate it by pre-empting potentially more restrictive legislation.

Several companies have established clear guidelines and codes of conduct for their global operations. For example, Levi Strauss & Co.'s website (<www.levistrauss.com>) details the principles that drive its relationship with its contractors. They have set standards for employee working hours, minimum age, health and safety, and in other areas. This code also provides for periodic evaluation of contractor adherence to the code and a compliance mechanism is in place that allows Levi's to terminate the relationship if the contractor fails to comply. The company believes that as a result of this evaluation process they have begun to make a significant improvement to the lives of workers in Bangladesh, Colombia, Indonesia and other such countries where several companies have been accused of running sweatshops. Nike is another company that has a code of conduct and, along with Reebok, has hired independent auditors to assess its contractors' compliance with this code (<www.nikebiz.com>).

The other major internal force is when corporations attempt to emphasize their CSR credentials for strategic reasons. Some companies such as Benetton have historically taken provocative and controversial positions in their advertising – arguing against the death penalty in the US, against racism and running anti-war messages, for example. While some of these arguably will have little negative fallout, others, like the anti-death penalty message that included interviews with prisoners on death row, did affect their sales. Stores such as Sears stopped carrying their products in protest that Benetton's position ignored victims' rights (*Wall Street Journal*, 17 February 2000). It is possible that taking such a stand on social issues is based on the calculation that the cost in terms of lost sales is more than made up by increased name recognition and sales from supporters of their position.

Other companies have taken stands on more specific issues and tried to use this as a source of competitive advantage. For example, Body Shop has tried to emphasize their environmental friendliness by using natural ingredients and their decision to not test their cosmetic products on animals. Others such as Shell and BP have attempted to build a corporate identity around being known as environmentally conscious corporations. By using environmental symbols, changing its corporate logo from a shield to a sunburst and using the slogan 'Beyond Petroleum', BP has tried to emphasize its environmental credentials. It also started reducing its own emissions and promoting solar power. By staking its claim as an environmentally friendly company and building its identity on this claim, BP is trying to use its socially responsible positioning as a basis for competitive advantage (Bahree, 2001). Radio 702 is another example of a company taking a socially responsible position which it then used as a means of building competitive advantage. This is a radio station in South Africa that in the pre-apartheid days took a very aggressively anti-apartheid stance in its broadcasts and positioned itself as a fighter for justice. This drew listenership as people began to see it as a champion of the underdog. In those days, there were some risks in taking on the government, but it is arguable that Radio 702 benefited, and still continues to do so, from its strategy.

Sometimes, external pressures can create a source of internal pressures. An example is the employment discrimination suits filed against companies such as Coca-Cola, Texaco and Denny's in the US. As part of Coca-Cola's settlement of the suit, an external pressure brought by a class of employees, the company agreed to 'have its employment policies and practices, from promotions to performance evaluations, overseen by a seven-member task force' (McKay, 2000). Thus, the external pressure resulted in the formation of an internal group charged with the responsibility of reviewing human resource practices and reporting annually on Coca-Cola's compliance with the settlement.

12.5 Screening Barriers and Organizational Recognition

In order for the two sets of pressures outlined above to have any impact and even be taken seriously by the targeted organization, they will have to pass certain screening barriers. For both internal and external forces, their strength will largely be determined by the credibility of the source. While it is not often that external pressure from interest groups, with the participation of the media, can be sustained for very long regarding generalized expectations of socially responsible corporate action, issue-specific pressure (e.g. pollution, labour practices, layoffs) can become a legitimate threat that penetrates these screening barriers. Credibility may also be a function of the perceived knowledge of the source and its ability to generate information.

The issue of source credibility is an important determinant of whether internal pressures are screened out as well. The status of the cause champion within the organization is a major factor impacting its credibility. The power of these individuals, both formal and informal, and the resources they command play a big role in whether the causes they champion are accorded serious consideration. The commitment of top management is frequently cited as significant factor in whether organizations embrace innovative ideas such as business process re-engineering. Raising the internal profile of CSR is no exception and is likely to be highly dependent on the relevance of the issue.

Once the pressures to act in a socially responsible manner pass these screening barriers, they will then be subjected to internal scrutiny. The business literature is replete with calls for organizations to maintain a close fit with their environments in order for them to be successful. As a result, organizations have accorded great importance to the environmental scanning function and have become much more adept at monitoring and picking up signals from the environment. Additionally, as expectations of CSR increase, corporations will be even more alert to suggestions of adverse social impact of their actions. Many companies have in the recent past put into place an environmental audit process that seeks to constantly assess these impacts. With organizations that have internal codes of conduct, these audits are frequently an ongoing and coordinated effort to assess compliance with CSR goals. The formalization of such audit processes means that CSR issues are given a level of legitimacy within the company and, even if no action results, their mere existence reduces the chances of external and internal pressures being screened out from the decision-making process.

One of the ways that companies scan their environment is by conducting periodic audits such as the one done on behalf of Nike and Reebok by Verite in Mexico (<www.nikebiz.com>). These represent proactive attempts by companies to monitor compliance with their codes of ethics. These audits also identify potential problems with workplace and employee issues and can be dealt with internally before they become a major issue for interest groups and other external agencies.

One organization where a leader has articulated the need for the company to be more socially responsible is Ford Motor Company. Its chairman, William Ford Jr., in a Corporate Citizenship Report articulated the need for the company to become more environmentally conscious. He also said that 'SUVs, engine of the company's profits, were environmental disasters that gobbled fossil fuels, spewed emissions and threatened the lives of drivers in smaller cars' (Goldman, 2000). While this hasn't slowed down the company's emphasis on the profitable SUV market, partly because consumers may not be as environmentally-conscious as they may claim, it is still an important statement by an influential person.

By appointing a vice president for global diversity, the US-based Delta Airlines has signalled the importance it places on fairness in global employment practices (Brannigan, 2000). By elevating the importance of this issue within the organization, it strengthens the organization's ability to recognize threats and increases their chances of being taken seriously.

12.6 Perceived Seriousness of the Pressures

Once the pressure is recognized, the natural first response will be to assess how serious it is before deciding whether to respond and, if so, how. Ultimately, it will be the anticipated long-term impact on the organization that will be the main determinant of any response. Some threats enjoy heightened attention when they initially occur but this attention begins to wane if the media loses interest or if the relevant interest groups are not successful in maintaining sustained pressure. In these circumstances, although the pressure may be intense for a short period of time, the organization may be able to ride it out as the threat begins to lose steam. In other situations, it may pose a credible danger of seriously disrupting the normal functioning of the business. Others may start small, but can pick up momentum if the organization does not move quickly to neutralize them. The tricky issue is being able to make accurate judgements about their longevity. This difficulty is further compounded by the fact that while some short-term costs (in terms of lost sales due to consumer boycotts for instance) may be easy to calculate, the long-term consequences of adverse publicity and damage to reputation may be much more difficult to forecast precisely, particularly in monetary terms. As a consequence, this decision is inherently risky, because it depends to a very great extent on the outcome of a calculated gamble on the threat's pervasiveness, longevity and potential cost.

A further complicating factor in the determination of the seriousness of the threat is the relative balance of power between the organization and the sources of the pressures. The degree to which the organization perceives a threat to its competitive position from the actions of the pressure sources is likely to affect the nature of its response. Large corporations and industry groups traditionally have been able to out-manoeuvre and blunt the external pressure groups by deploying their larger resources with greater sophistication and effectiveness. They generally have become more nimble in responding to external pressures, and also have managed the media and political establishment better than their usually less well-funded adversaries. However, anecdotal evidence suggests that individual consumers and consumer interest groups have also become more adept in getting support for their positions. They have also become more effective at raising funds, mobilizing protests (e.g. at the WTO meeting in Seattle), and at garnering media coverage. As a result, the ability of corporations to out-muscle or minimize the agendas of these groups is diminishing and the power asymmetry is starting to reduce. Part of the reason for the enhanced effectiveness of external interest groups is undoubtedly technology: for instance, the fact that they have been able to use the Internet to advance their positions and articulate their stand on their websites without being screened out by the gatekeepers that control traditional media outlets. As consumers increasingly look to web-based sources for their information, these groups will definitely benefit, thus tipping the power imbalance more in their favour. Consumers may also become better informed and more knowledgeable about CSR issues, thus elevating the profile of many issues that currently do not even appear on corporate radar screens. What this may mean is that in the future large corporations will have to deal with some issues that today they may be able to ignore. The assumption that pressure groups will not be able to sustain their pressure in the face of the corporations' ability to manage and minimize it may not hold true any more.

One example of the power asymmetry changing in favour of external interest groups concerns the World Bank project to dam the Narmada river in India. Although the pressure was not directed specifically at a company, it did take on two large organizations – the World Bank and the Indian government. Traditionally, 'Asia's heavy-handed governments bothered little about the unfortunates displaced by dams;

usually, officials merely made grand promises of cash or land' (*Economist*, 20 November 1999). What was telling in this instance, however, was how various interest groups, representing displaced villagers, tribal populations and citizens concerned about the environment were able to stop the project with the participation of the media. The protesters were able to maintain sustained pressure and this in turn helped increase the seriousness of the threat. Ultimately, the World Bank withdrew from the project and the Indian Supreme Court banned further construction until the 'human problems' were resolved (Appa and Sridharan, 2000).

12.7 Action Criteria

The model suggests that once CSR pressures pass these screening stages, the decision will be made to respond in some fashion. What form this action will take will depend on the criteria used. Typically, managers will weigh several different options before deciding on a course of action. Three factors will dictate the course pursued: (1) the costs of the proposed action and the costs of not taking any action; (2) the benefits that will accrue to the organization from its response; and (3) the resources available to the organization. Each of these three considerations has a monetary as well as a non-monetary angle to it. As mentioned earlier, the monetary factors are very difficult to calculate and depend at least partially on certain assumptions.

The primary monetary cost calculation is the cost of the activities in which the corporation will have to engage in order to respond to the external pressure. In the case of issue-specific and immediate pressures, this will involve all-out efforts to build public support and lobbying the relevant legislators. Much of this cost will of course not be incremental, but will be more a case of the corporation deploying its already-existing PR machinery. In the case of more sustained and long-term pressure on corporations to change certain practices, the costs may well be incremental. For instance, one of the major pressures on US corporations that have shifted labour-intensive manufacturing and assembly operations to developing countries, where standards on working conditions are either non-existent or not enforced, will require significant additional financial commitments. These may include higher wages, shorter working hours, contributions to employee health care and improved safety. In addition to the very real costs, corporations will also need to take into account the opportunity costs of not responding to these pressures. It is conceivable that if the pressure groups perceive that the offending companies are not taking the appropriate action, they may organize media and consumer campaigns that may hurt the company's image and sales and ultimately, it's bottom line. Various such interest groups issue periodic 'report cards' of companies' performance on CSR and these, if negative, are a potential cost to be taken into account.

Unlike some of the costs that are calculable, most of the benefits are notional. These are the other side of the coin of opportunity costs discussed earlier. Companies seen to be responsive and proactive will gain from enhanced reputations and this goodwill is a distinct benefit. As consumers become increasingly aware of CSR issues, partly due to the increased availability of and access to information, segments of consumers may emerge who make their spending decisions based on the company's record on issues related to CSR.

The last criterion is the availability of resources. Assuming that the organization's cost-benefit assessment indicates that some type of response is necessary, but it is faced with a resource constraint, what should it do? Here's where the fact that some of the costs and virtually all of the benefits from a particular course of action cannot easily be monetized, takes on importance. Given the economic nature of most decision-making in for-profit companies, how can they justify an action if the outlays are specific but the gains nebulous, particularly in a resource-constrained situation? Some authors have suggested a new 'environmental accounting' method where some of these calculations may become possible. Clearly, under current accounting practices, unless there is a change in the use of traditional performance measures, CSR decisions will largely be made based on their immediate economic consequences and will be hard to justify based on future, and unspecified, gains.

The case of Enron in India is illustrative. Enron agreed to build a power plant in India's Maharashtra state in 1992, but the deal was fraught with problems from the start. Political pressure mounted on the company to renegotiate the deal, largely from the state government which was different from the one with whom Enron signed the deal. The company was accused of charging too much and damaging the environment (Karp, 1999). The deal was subsequently renegotiated and despite its 30 per cent return on investment (Kripalani, 2001), the company decided that the costs – the political uncertainty and having to invoke an Indian government guarantee to get paid (Pesta, 2001) – did not justify the gains.

When its African-American employees sued Coca-Cola for employment bias, the company settled the suit for almost $200 million. While this was a very explicit cost, some of the costs and most of the benefits of this settlement were not as clear. A major cost to be taken into account as an action criterion was the damage to its image and the potential loss in sales if consumers began to boycott Coca-Cola products. The benefit, again hard to calculate, is the easing of the pressure and its ability to salvage its image before even more serious damage was done. The company is getting favourable press and is being cited as an example for others for bringing the glass ceiling down, as well as being credited with putting diversity management on the corporate agenda (King, 2001).

Owens-Corning and W. R. Grace are examples of companies under threat from asbestos-related lawsuits in the US. The resource issue was a factor in the decision by both companies to file for Chapter 11 bankruptcy protection. In Grace's case, it experienced an 81 per cent increase in suits between 1999 and 2000, and felt that it needed some predictability in the settlement process (Walsh, 2001).

12.8 Corporate Response

A menu of possible actions is available for corporations in response to pressure to behave in a socially responsible manner. The following list is by nature general, although the specific nature of each option may vary depending on the issue(s) for which pressure is being put:

- *Pre-empt*: if the internal cause champion is powerful and the organization's environmental scanning is able to accurately forecast an issue(s) likely to create pressure, it may be able to reduce the threat by taking pre-emptive action. This may include making changes likely to satisfy potential pressure groups and/or strengthening any existing codes of conduct to proscribe actions that may bring on pressure. Lobbying for industry-wide regulation is another effective pre-emptive move.

- *Ignore*: when the corporation feels that the issue is not serious, either because it is inherently minor or temporary, or that there is a power asymmetry in favour of the corporation relative to the groups exerting the pressure, ignoring it may be the best option. This may also be revealed by a cost-benefit analysis when weighing the other response options. This option involves doing nothing and waiting for the pressure to abate. The consequences of miscalculating the magnitude of the threat can be serious.

- *Fight*: if the corporation feels that it is in the right, it may choose to fight back by presenting its side of the issue, correcting facts it may feel have been mis-stated, threatening and/or taking legal action, undertaking aggressive publicity campaigns and the like. They sometimes use seemingly independent groups, in reality supported by industry and corporate funding, to present the corpora-tion's viewpoint and to fight external interest groups.

- *Delay/Diffuse*: when the costs of responding are very high, the corporation can adopt delaying tactics. These may include filing for bankruptcy protection to stave off lawsuits and allow the firm to reorganize while it determines another course of action. These tactics may also include attempts to buy time by offering to engage in dialogue with the interested parties, appointment of independent bodies to study the issue, etc.

- *Co-opt*: when the external pressure groups enjoy a power advantage, the best course of action often is to co-opt them. This can be done by getting them involved in setting standards, allowing their representatives to be part of fact-finding teams investigating situations where corporations have been accused of not being socially responsible, etc.

- *Comply*: cooperation with the pressure group and compliance with their demands may make sense when the pressure groups have a power advantage and the issue appears serious and long-standing. As pressure builds, and the corporation finds itself unable to defend its position credibly, exercising this option may be necessary to relieve the pressure.

It is important to note that these options are not mutually exclusive and that they each may be evoked at different points, often in sequential order. A further confound-ing factor is that the corporation and its adversaries will often see their position as being 'right'. However, once pressure is brought to bear, and media coverage intensi-fies, objective determinations of 'right' and 'wrong' become difficult. The key issue from the corporation's point of view is to make its position known and defuse the pressure as quickly as possible.

The most effective pre-emption strategy is to create an effective environmental scanning function that can forecast threats far enough in advance to enable the corporation to take the necessary action. Delta's diversity initiative and Nike's audit of its developing country manufacturing facilities should enable them to put systems in place that can pre-empt most pressures in these areas.

The decision to ignore a pressure is taken if the pressure is seen as temporary or if the sources are perceived as being weak. It is arguable that Exxon's decision not to respond immediately to the Valdez oil spill in Alaska exacerbated the problem. Similarly, the seven-day delay between the first media reports of children getting sick in Belgium after drinking Coca-Cola and the company's response badly damaged the brand (Schmidt, 1999). These companies may have miscalculated the seriousness of these threats and subsequently had to take aggressive damage control measures.

In the biotech industry, firms have chosen to fight critical external pressure from interest groups such as Friends of the Earth regarding genetically modified (GM) foods. Recognizing public concern over the safety of these foods, companies such as Monsanto have launched major public relations campaigns, touting the benefits of GM foods while at the same time providing scientific evidence to back their claims. They are also lobbying the US and other governments not to pass legislation labeling GM foods as such (although Japan and the EU have such requirements and are aggressively fighting calls to ban GM foods). On another front, they are also using price subsidies to encourage farmers to use GM seeds (Moore and Scott, 1999). Ultimately both the industry and their opponents are fighting to get consumers to support their respective points of view.

The Chapter 11 bankruptcy filings by Owens-Corning and W. R. Grace referred to earlier are examples of companies attempting to buy time in order to formulate an appropriate response to the asbestos-related lawsuits that have the potential to seriously damage the companies.

Action organizations frequently respond to pressure by co-opting the pressure sources. For example, by involving three plaintiffs from the employment discrimination lawsuit in the seven-person task force created to assess compliance of the settlement, Coca-Cola has essentially co-opted them. Similarly, in addition to the companies themselves, the FLA comprises parties that have traditionally been critical of the employment practices of companies in developing countries – human rights, religious, consumer and labour groups. By getting them involved, companies can incorporate their views into the development of codes of conduct and in monitoring their activities. Forming a partnership with these organizations also enhances the credibility of the company in the eyes of the public and eases the pressure from these groups as they get 'certified' through NGO social audits and are recognized as 'responsible' firms by portfolio managers. Some critics (Kapstein, 2000) suggest that it is incumbent on the 'ethics crusaders' to use their power responsibly when they forge linkages with corporations or else such relationships can become counterproductive.

There are examples of other situations where corporations resort to a combination of these actions. When Dole Food Inc. was criticized for its employment and environmental practices at its flower farms in Colombia (Maharaj and Hohn, 2001), it responded on several fronts. It said that its farms were certified by the International Standards Organization's ISO 14001 environmental-management standard. It also claimed that its workers were among the best paid and that it contributed to the community by, for instance, financing schools (Hayes, 2001). The Society of American Florists (SAF) – representing growers, wholesalers, importers and retailers – responded by saying that employees at Colombian flower farms receive above-average pay and extended benefits according to the International Labour Organization (ILO) (Moran, 2001). The industry critics argued that even the above-average wages were not a living wage and that those hired by subcontractors earned even less. They cited ILO reports that the industry's occupational safety and environmental practices were not being enforced. They also believed that ISO 14001 was an industry-run programme and essentially a PR exercise (Hohn, 2001). This situation illustrates a fundamental point about CSR issues. Regardless of who is in the right, and here each side feels they are, if the issue is not properly managed it can create enormous pressure on corporations to respond. As the above discussion illustrates, corporations may adopt several responses simultaneously, including fighting, diffusing and co-opting, and perhaps complying partly or wholly to ease the pressure.

12.9 Outcomes

Clearly, whether or not the pressure abates is a function of the success of the corporation's initial response. As discussed earlier, this response may well have to be modified if the desired outcome does not occur. If the response is effective, the firm can expect to see an impact in several key areas, both financial and non-financial. The most immediate will be an easing of the external pressure. Subsequently, there should also be an impact on the bottom line. As discussed earlier, the costs associated with any of the above response options will be felt in the near-term while the benefits will accrue in the long-term. These costs include PR and lobbying costs, compliance costs of any additional expenses such as wage bills, anti-pollution measures or those associated with improving working conditions. Consequently, traditional perform-ance outcomes such as profits and returns may be difficult to compute. However, there may be an immediate impact on the top line as sales increase when interest group-sponsored actions such as boycotts are lifted.

The firm should also attempt to assess other, less tangible, outcomes of their response. These may include enhancements to its corporate identity and public image. In addition, it should also evaluate how its response complies with its own internal code of conduct and its social responsibility mission. When the outcomes are positive, they will also have the affect of strengthening this code and will sensitize other corporate actors about the need to specifically and formally incorporate CSR thinking into their missions. This will, in turn, presumably empower the internal cause champions and enable them to ensure that the social outcomes of corporate actions are fully considered as part of the decision-making process.

Early in the chapter we discussed the pressure faced by Nestlé over its marketing practices for infant formula in developing countries. Initially, it successfully sued for libel over reports that argued that its infant formula was not healthy for infants. While it won in court, it began to lose the PR war. Subsequently, the company was able to manage this threat by negotiating an end to the worldwide boycott. It became a leader in implementing the WHO code of International Marketing of Breast Milk Substitutes and changed its marketing practices. By developing relationships with the pressure groups and other actions, it was able to build back its corporate image (Sethi, 1994). Perhaps the most telling evidence of Nestlé's re-emergence is that it has developed from being known largely for its infant formula to becoming a diverse corporation manufacturing some of the world's best-known food brands.

REVIEW QUESTIONS

1. Was the South African government justified in the stand it took? Discuss the criteria you would use in making that assessment.

2. Do corporations have any responsibility other than making profit in the short term? Discuss with reference to the corporate social responsibility (CSR) debate in a contemporary business organization.

3. Discuss the nature of social responsibility in a dynamic business enterprise. Identify the external environmental factors shaping CSR in a rapidly changing industry (e.g. the computer software industry).

4. How can a corporation assess the level of pressure on its operation and performances? Give examples from your own experience.

5. Identify the patterns of corporate response to CSR. Which of these actions are strategically important for firms operating in industries that are vulnerable to social issues?

References

Alsop, R. (2001) 'Survey rates companies' reputations, and many are found wanting – respondents disparage AT&T, Bridgestone, Philip Morris; highest marks go to J&J', *Wall Street Journal*, 7 February.

Appa, G. and Sridharan, R. (2000) 'OR helps the poor in a controversial irrigation project', *Interfaces*, Mar/Apr, pp. 13–28.

Bahree, B. (2001) 'As BP goes green, the fur is flying – oil giant's bid to be seen as more environmental draws critics' scrutiny', *Wall Street Journal* 16 April: A 10.

Brannigan, M. (2000) 'Delta, facing discrimination complaint, creates global-diversity executive post', *Wall Street Journal* 2 August: A13.

Brubaker, B. (2000) 'The limits of $100 million', *Washington Post*, 29 December: A01.

Crossette, B. (2001) 'Fungus drug offered to poor nations', *New York Times*, 7 June: A3.

The Economist (1999a) 'International: Delta blues', 13 February: 44–45.

The Economist (1999b) 'Asia: the dry facts about dams', 20 November: 46.

Fesperman, D. and Shatzkin, K. (1999) 'The new pecking order', *Baltimore Sun*, 28 February.

Gellman, B. (2000) 'A turning point that left millions behind; drug discounts benefit few while protecting pharmaceutical companies' profits', *Washington Post*, 28 December: A01.

Goldberg, R. M. (2001) 'Fight AIDS with reason not rhetoric', *Wall Street Journal*, 23 April.

Goldman, D. (2000) 'Consumer republic', *Adweek*, 22 May: 24.

Hayes, S. (2001) 'Letter to the editor', *Harper's Magazine*, 17 May.

Hohn, D. (2001) 'Response to letters to the editor', *Harper's Magazine*, 17 May.

Inter Press Service (2001) Release dated March 13 at <www.commondreams.org/headlines01/0313-03.htm>

Kapstein, Ethan B. (2001) 'The corporate ethics crusade', *Foreign Affairs*, September/October: 105–199.

Karp, J. (1999) 'Enron facility again becomes political target in Indian race', *Wall Street Journal*, 8 September: A19.

King, A. (2001) 'Coca-Cola takes the high road', *Black Enterprise*, February: 29.

Kripalani, M. (2001) 'Enron switches signals in India', *Business Week*, 8 January: 58.

Maharaj, N. and Hohn, D. (2001) 'Fleurs du mal', *Harper's Magazine*, February.

McGreal, C. (2001) 'Firms split over deal in cheap drugs lawsuit', *The Guardian*, 18 April.

McKay, B. (2000) 'Coke settles bias suit for $192.5 million – outside panel will monitor company's activities; "painful chapter" closes', *Wall Street Journal*, 17 November.

Moore, S. and Scott, A. (1999) 'Biotech battle: waging a war for public approval', *Chemical Week*, 15 December: 23–26.

Moran, P. (2001) 'Letter to the editor', *Harper's Magazine*, 17 May.

Munusamy, R. (2000) 'US firm joins local battle against AIDS', *Sunday Times (South Africa)*, 23 January.

Pesta, J. (2001) 'Enron calls on guarantee by India to collect debts – unit's main customer owes $17 million for November, "we're obliged to pay" ', *Wall Street Journal*, 7 February: A21.

Petersen, M. (2001) 'Lifting the curtain on the real costs of making AIDS drugs', *New York Times*, 24 April: C1.

Pollack, A. (2001) 'Defensive drug industry: fueling clash over patents', *New York Times*, 20 April: A6.

Schmidt, K. (1999) 'Coke's crisis', *Marketing News*, 27 September: 1, 11.

Sethi, S. P. (1994) *Multinational Corporations and the Impact of Public Advocacy on Corporate Strategy: Nestlé and the Infant Formula Controversy*, Boston: Kluwer Academic.

Wall Street Journal (2000) 'Business brief – SEARS, ROEBUCK & CO.: pact with Benetton ends due to an ad campaign', 17 February.

Walsh, K. (2001) 'Grace files for Chapter 11', *Chemical Week*, 11 April: 7.

Warner, Susan, 'GlaxoSmithKline says AIDS drugs prices in Africa won't impact other markets', *Philadelphia Inquirer*, 25 April.

Electronic References

www.bms.com/news/press/data/fg_press_release_1163.html
www.cptech.org/ip/health/sa/pharmasuit.html
www.cptech.org/ip/health/sa/sa-timeline.txt
www.globalexchange.org
www.levistrauss.com
www.lists.essential.org/pipermail/pharm.policy/2001-April/000944.html
www.mcspotlight.org
www.nikebiz.com
www.oxfam.org.uk/policy/papers/safrica2.htm
www.oxfam.org.uk/policy/papers/safrica3.htm
www.phrma.org/publications/documents/backgrounders/2001-03-20.207.phtml
www.saigon.com/nike

CHAPTER 13

Internal marketing

Paul Matthyssens and Huib Wursten

LEARNING OBJECTIVES

At the end of this chapter readers will be able to:

▶ Grasp the complexity and diversity of cultures in terms of six metaphoric 'mental images'.
▶ Understand the impact of these culture types on the way successful management is conceived.
▶ Understand the impact of culture on the thrusts of relationship marketing management.

13.1 Introduction

The authors explore the impact of culture on relationship marketing. A typology of cultures is introduced and is crossed with the different dimensions of relational marketing exchange. First, the concept of relationship marketing is discussed. Next, the different modes to look at cultures are described briefly, as are reflections on cultural metaphors and typologies. The third section introduces a new, six-cluster typology of national cultures. In the fourth section the impact of the six culture types on relationship marketing is explored. The chapter concludes with managerial implications.

'The goal of marketing is to own the market, not just to sell the product.' This sentence of McKenna (1991: 7) is representative for the birth of relationship marketing (RM), an approach deemed necessary for high-tech, industrial and services markets.

Cram (1994: 19) described RM as follows: 'Relationship marketing is the consistent application of up-to-date knowledge of individual customers to product and service design which is communicated interactively, in order to develop a continuous and long term relationship, which is mutually beneficial'. According to this author, such an approach consists of loyal staff, loyal customers, a learning organization, relational pricing, communications (dialogue), staff training (improved service level) and relationship management (to stimulate collaborative activities and commitment).

In the same vein, Payne (1995) argues that relationship marketing implies three core issues: cross-functionally based marketing, an emphasis on customer retention and a relationship management approach that addresses six markets rather than just the traditional customer market. Cross-functional cooperation is necessary in order to solve the customer's problem in an efficient and effective way. In many industrial and business-to-business markets and in service transactions, the customer interacts with employees from diverse functional departments. Moreover, the order fulfilment process requires that, as in a relay race, each department does its part of the job with excellence, before 'handing over' to the next department until the external customer is reached. Internal quality and integration guarantees the customer's problem will be solved smoothly.

Both aspects – multiple interactions and the participation of many functions in the order process – make the concept of *internal marketing* a key issue in relationship management. It covers a wide range of activities to motivate employees, make them cooperate in line with the mission and empower them to deliver value to internal and external customers. This means that internal marketing is an umbrella concept for a range of internal activities used in the management of attitudes and communications (Stershic, 1995). For instance, the (meaningful) mission must be clarified and internalized by all employees. After the mission is made real, it should often be reinforced and backed by training and internal communication. Internal marketing also implies that all employees are linked to the customer. Further, employees who have no direct link to customers must be willing to serve other employees who serve the external customer.

Customer retention implies different actions (Payne, 1995). First, it starts with the measurement of customer satisfaction and retention rates and the communication of these findings. Second, the root causes of customer defections have to be identified and addressed. Third, service quality and customer value have to be corrected/increased, backed by a customer-focused culture and managerial attention. Next, internal marketing must be applied to generate employee satisfaction and loyalty.

Authors have introduced process-oriented views on marketing. For instance, Heskett *et al.* (1994) introduced the 'service profit chain' and Payne (1995) the 'relationship management chain'. Approaches like these identify a series of activities, relations and outcomes generating value to customers which will eventually result in customer satisfaction and loyalty. Matthyssens and Van Den Bulte (1994) describe how the establishment of enduring relationships with business customers begins with a deliberate *selection* of customers. Furthermore, they argue that key account management practices and consultative selling are major tools to build long-term relationships.

Ford *et al.* (1998) argue that buyer–seller relationships in business markets develop gradually through different stages. In the first stage (the pre-relationship stage), a high degree of inertia and uncertainty has to be reduced by the two parties who still are very distant from each other. During the exploratory stage, buyer and supplier engage in serious discussions and/or tests. Both partners show overt communication and mutual learning. As such, they invest a lot of time 'to learn about each other *as people* to reduce the considerable "distance" between them' (p. 34). Demonstrating commitment and building trust via mutual investments are key issues to develop the relationship from the stage of exploration. The third stage is called the developing stage, in which both partners intensively learn, interact and adapt. Mainly informal adaptations (e.g. when a salesperson agrees on a change in delivery schedule) will make the partnership grow. Ford *et al.* (1998) stress such development does not continue inevitably and may slow down due to one partner's conscious or unconscious actions.

During the last stage, the stable stage, routines allow the relationship to operate at low cost. However, a growing inertia ('institutionalization') may endanger the relationship. Sometimes a relationship might move back to an early stage and can be revitalized or stopped. In the case of successful relationships, however, the gradual process will lead to increasing levels of trust and commitment, thereby reducing the distance between the partners. An important type of distance between the (potential) partners is cultural distance, referring as well to differences in national, industry and corporate cultures.

The conception of a relationship management approach in six markets (Payne, 1995) introduces the following markets besides the traditional customer market:

- Referral markets: intermediaries, connectors, multipliers and so on.
- Supplier markets: suppliers and outsourcing partners.
- Recruitment markets.
- Influence markets: venture capitalists, lobbyists, litigators and so on.
- Internal markets.

Marketers should identify the key participants in their network and define a relationship strategy for each strategic relation. Anderson and Narus (1999) speak of an *alliance network* 'which is a cligne of interrelated and coordinated business relationships' (p. 27), organized around marketplace opportunities. Such networks show a high degree of complexity (Anderson and Narus, 1999; Ford *et al.*, 1998) due to multiple relations, evolving network positions, diverse activity links, resource ties and actor bonds that arise from them. The network does not have a centre nor clear boundaries.

It must be clear from the above discussion that RM consists of a stepwise approach of selecting and targeting customers and network partners with strategic relationship potential, building trust, growing the relationship via excellent problem-solving solutions and the showing of commitment. Such an approach can only be realized when backed by a network strategy toward key partners and excellent internal relations among divisions and functions. It might be argued that such an approach is not always necessary or useful. A relationship continuum exists. Matthyssens and Van Den Bulte (1994) identify three types of exchange and relationship strategies. At one end of the spectrum is the transactional relationship, in which a power and antagonistic relational strategy is applied and where a simple transfer of goods or services for money is realized. At the other end of the spectrum is a purely cooperative exchange, where the partners exchange competencies and performances through multiple interactions. In the middle is an intermediary position in which partners 'tune' their (logistical) processes in order to reduce total cost of ownership or try to increase the efficiency of the order cycle.

There is no doubt that culture might play a role in the expectations of each partner regarding the type of exchange and relationship strategy. For instance, a Belgian or Spanish partner might expect at least a tuning approach even for a commodity, whereas a Dutch or a Scandinavian client might consider a simple functional exchange good enough in that situation. In the next section it will be demonstrated how culture impacts on relational marketing.

13.2 Understanding Cultures

Business-to-business networks are increasingly international in composition, with partners often originating from Japan, the USA and Europe. Numerous studies have demonstrated that cultural differences are among the key reasons for the failure of cross-border deals. In fact, cultural distance might largely explain why many international mergers actually destroy shareholder value. Others pinpoint that three out of ten expatriates have to return home due to poor performance or failure to adapt to the foreign culture (Management Centre Europe). It is amply illustrated how different cultural assumptions and business practices endanger both internal and external cross-border business relations (Hoecklin, 1995; Usunier, 2000).

Culture is a shared system of meanings that is relative, learned and describes group behaviour (Hoecklin, 1995). As such, managers from different departments or subsidiaries have learned a common 'value system' which is difficult to understand for outsiders. Cross-cultural psychologists and cultural anthropologists have tried to characterize the differences between cultures (Gannon, 1994; Schneider and Barsoux, 1997; Hoecklin, 1995). The following dimensions are frequently used to describe culture:

- Assumptions about the nature of people: basically good or bad.
- Assumptions about the relationship with nature: harmony vs subjugation.
- Primary mode of activity: being vs doing.
- Conception of space: private vs public.
- Attitudes toward time: monochronism vs polychronism; past, present or future orientation.
- Context and the amount of explicit communication needed: high vs low context cultures.
- Assumptions about the relationship between people: individualism vs collectivism.
- Power distance: the degree to which people accept unequal distribution of power in organizations or society.
- Uncertainty avoidance: the degree to which people try to contain risk and uncertainty.
- The degree to which a society looks favourably towards assertive and materialistic behaviour (i.e. masculinity) or otherwise favours nurturing and well-being (femininity).

Characterizing cultures with such dimensions can be insightful but, as Gannon (1994) rightfully asserts, they lead to somewhat lifeless and narrow descriptions as such an approach leaves out many facets of daily life. For instance, religion, education, leisure activities, lifestyle and so forth are not considered, although they play important roles in describing societies. A way out of this is the construction of multidimensional cultural metaphors (Gannon, 1994).

Besides these approaches to describe the diversity between and the uniqueness of countries' cultures, effors have been made to cluster countries with similar cultures and worldviews. As we use such a so-called nomological net approach, we mention two other parallel approaches. Ronen and Shenekar (1985) identified eight clusters of countries with common worldviews. Schneider and Barsoux (1997: 84), building on prior work from Stevens at INSEAD, constructed cultural profiles of organizations. The following four types emerged:

- *Anglo/Nordic 'village market':* decentralized organizations with output control and informal communication, a generalist management style, people as free agents, an entrepreneurial style stressing flexibility.
- *Asian 'family or tribe':* centralized and paternalistic organizations, patriarchal authority, generalist managers, networking based on loyalty and personal relations, social controls.
- *Germanistic 'well-oiled machine':* decentralized decision-making, narrow span of control, specialist and technical competence highly appreciated, strong role of expertise, functional organization (chimneys), coordination through routines and rules, efficiency-driven mentality, structural solutions, throughput control.
- *Latin 'traditional bureaucracy' (or 'the pyramid of people'):* elite, centralized decision-making, low degree of delegation (hierarchy), strong role of staff, specialist and analytic ability, a parallel decision-making system ('système D') through strong informal ties, input control.

It must be clear that when two companies belonging to a different cultural cluster form business relationships, they will have difficulties streamlining their strategic decisions and implementing strategy. At least, they should be aware of the other partner's cultural background and its business practices. In the same vein, it is clear that two partners from the same culture type, although belonging to different nations, will more easily cooperate. In this chapter we will use another, more refined typology, presented in the next section.

13.3 Typology of National Cultures

Starting from the four dimensions introduced by Hofstede (see Hoecklin, 1995), Wursten (1997) began clustering countries into relatively homogeneous clusters. Based on his experience from consulting global companies on cross-cultural conflicts and management, he came to six culture types sharing common mental images (Table 13.1).

The Contest Model

The cultural context of the Anglo-Saxon mental image is: low power distance, relatively low uncertainty avoidance and a high individuality. The central assumption of this mental image is: if you give people and organizations the freedom to compete with each other, something good will always come out of it. The characteristic of this

Contest	Network	Family	Pyramid	Solar system	Machine
AUL,CAN, GBR, IRE, NZ, USA	DEN, NET, NOR, SWE	CHI, HK, IND, IDO, MAL, PHI, SIN	BRA, CHL, COL, ECA, SAL, GRE, GUA, ITA SOUTH, KOR, MEX, PER, POR, RUS, TAI, THA, TUR, URU, VEN	BEL, FRA, ITA NORTH, SPA, SWI (FRENCH)	AUT, CZE, FIN, HUN, GER, SWI (GERMAN)
Competition	Consensus	Loyalty and hierarchy	Loyalty, hierarchy and implicit order	Hierarchy and impersonal bureaucracy	Order
−PDI	−PDI	+PDI	+PDI	+PDI	−PDI
+IDV	+IDV	−IDV	−IDV	+IDV	±IDV
−UAI	−UAI	−UAI	−UAI	+UAI	+UAI
+MAS	−MAS				

Table 13.1 Mental images. (Copyright ITIM Wursten 1998)

PDI = power distance index; IDV = individualism; UAI = uncertainty avoidance index; MAS = masculinity

organization outline is that hierarchy is not seen as an existential difference between people, but something that is agreed between people to facilitate the work in organizations: it should be clear who is delegating to whom and who is reporting to whom.

In principle, managers and subordinates negotiate about objectives, targets and the work-content. Targets are very important because people experience them as a challenge. No-one can fiddle with targets once they have been formulated, as they function as the central element of performance-monitoring. The assessment with respect to the targets formulated beforehand is the foundation for work motivation. People are rewarded by measurement against the fixed targets. The reward is given in the form of bonuses or career moves.

Solutions to problems are obtained by communicating with each other. Open competition is central in this model. In order to motivate people, they must be able to compete with others, but also with themselves. Important concepts in this model are: achievement, orientation, target setting, winners and losers, making it, career, bonus systems as a reward for competition, special career paths for 'high potentials', etc.

The trap is that there is a tendency to give these theories and concepts a universal value. In fact, the management theories that are taught at universities and business schools around the world mainly stem from Anglo-Saxon scholars. The explanation for this is a general human one. The inclination exists to imitate the conduct of (economically) successful people. This is true globally with respect to the American culture. All over the world people drink Coca-Cola. There is even a McDonald's on the Square of Heavenly Peace in Beijing. They constitute, as it were, a symbol for progress and success. American management ideas are blindly adopted by managers everywhere.

Some well-known consequences for organizations are the introduction of tools such as flexible reward systems, career-oriented management development systems, management by objectives, special training courses for 'high potentials', etc. The consequences are that people partly adjust to the new rituals. It is a common human tendency to act according to what is expected by your environment. However, this does not mean that this is corresponding with people's own inner motivation. The rituals are not 'internalized'.

The Network Model

This model is a combination of low power distance, high individualism and femininity. In actual practice of working for international companies like IBM, Boskalis, Heineken, Shell and Philips, we discovered that there is a big difference between the Anglo-Saxon view on leadership, motivation and negotiation, on the one hand, and the Scandinavian-Dutch way on the other. For instance, in the latter countries practically everyone agrees with the proposition that 'the biggest punishment one could be given at work would be to be rewarded in the American way: a portrait on the wall as "employee of the month" '. It would be a punishment in these countries because it would be the immediate cause for cynical remarks and jokes by coworkers.

The Scandinavian countries and The Netherlands are found to share mental models characterized by sayings like: 'just act normal, that's mad enough' and 'if your head sticks out above the ground level, it will be chopped off'. It is not appreciated if you try to profile yourself as the 'winner'. People who try to do this give other people the feeling that something is quite wrong with them. This is known as the 'Jante law' in Sweden, Denmark and Norway: don't think you are better than any other person in your environment, a practice regarded as normal behaviour in the competitive countries of culture type one.

A fundamental difference between the network model and the competition model is the feminine character of the cultures concerned. Competition, career and external material rewards are not central issues. This is in sharp contrast to the core theories on management, leadership and organizations, which originate from the masculine worldview of type one cultures. Here, other elements are important for work motivation: having autonomy in your subject field, the work-content, quality of the relations network, cooperation, the work environment and the feeling of mutual independence and the harmonization of interests between heterogeneous groups. Decisions are normally made by involving all the relevant stakeholders and trying to develop consensus among them. The countless meetings that take place in organizations are the consequence of this.

The most important characteristic of these meetings is the objective to find 'support': consensus between the main stakeholders on what should be done. The major criterion for evaluating good policy is 'stakeholder-satisfaction', with respect to the manner in which their interests are covered by the decisions taken. That is why it is allowed to retract decisions that have already been reached. In principle, if the stakeholders after a meeting have second thoughts, it is not regarded as strange to allow them to return to the organization and say to a colleague: 'I've been giving it a lot of thought and have decided that it is not a good idea. Can't we do it in another way?' In a country like The Netherlands, this means that decisions that have been taken tend to be open for further development the following day. This takes place on a macro-level, in politics at the meso level and in micro-organizations. An example of this is the Dutch part of the bank conglomerate from the opening case. Another example is the public and political debate in Oslo on the best destination for the open space in front of the royal palace, a discussion that has continued for one hundred years!

The Organization as a Family

This is the dominant image in some countries in Asia, especially the Chinese-dominated cultures and in some of the Caribbean countries. This image is formed by a combination of high power distance, collectivism and a low score for uncertainty avoidance. The characteristics are as follows. First, there is a strong acceptance of hierarchy. In general, this is linked to old age or seniority. Old age is usually synonymous to wisdom. Furthermore, as in the pyramid model, there is a 'moral' relation between employers and subordinates. In exchange for loyalty from the side of the employees, the employer will ensure his employees' well-being. This means that in a way he or she acts like a 'father of a family'. The employees can always go to the boss if they have good ideas, personal wishes or problems. In principle, they can do this in- and outside office hours. This can be about anything from money problems to family problems. Any boss who backs out of this care is a bad boss.

In contrast to the pyramid model below, communication between managers and their subordinates is not well-formalized. This system is very flexible. The 'boss' decides everything and can change strategic intents instantaneously.

The Pyramid of People

The next image that was found was that of organizations as a pyramid of people. The main dimensions of culture are power distance, uncertainty avoidance and collectivism. In principle, this is the system in the majority of countries in the world. Almost all Asian countries, all Latin American countries, all Arab countries and some European countries like Portugal, Greece and Russia have this in common. The decision-making process is top-down. Hierarchy is important and essentially acknowledged and accepted by everyone . There is a strong need for centralization by government .

A frequent reference point for the legitimation of actions is the 'general interest', as formulated by the people at the top. There is a strong need to formalize the communication between the various levels in the organization, and there is also a need to formalize the relationship between colleagues. In such countries, the way to evaluate policy is to inspect in a direct way whether the people lower in the hierarchy have effectively and efficiently implemented the decisions taken at a higher hierarchy level.

The Solar System

This is the culture of countries like France, Belgium, the North of Italy and Spain. The features are: high power distance, high individualism and high uncertainty avoidance. The main difference between these cultures and the pyramid system (type three) is the high degree of individualism. This leads to a tendency never to contradict power-holders in their presence, but to 'draw your own plan' outside their reach (the so-called 'système D'). Because of the individualistic element, leadership is not so much being the 'father of the family', but being a highly-visible intellectual technocrat. Delegation and control are the same as in the pyramid system.

The Well-oiled Machine

A sixth image was found that fits countries like Germany, Austria, the German-speaking part of Switzerland and Hungary. It is related to a low score on power distance and a high score on uncertainty avoidance. In principle, people in these countries feel autonomous and want to perform tasks independently. The condition, however, is that all obscurities around expectations with respect to task-completion and task-description are reduced. Clarity in the structure and explicit procedures form the core of the internal discussion about the organization. Decentralization within clear, 'unshakeable' agreements is the natural form of leadership and management. An example is the autonomous position of the 'States' in Germany with respect to the central authority in Berlin. The reference point for evaluation is: have all the parties involved observed the previously formalized planning procedures and acted according to the plan?

Examples of some implications of the differences in cultures can be found in Table 13.2. We focus on issues that definitely have an impact on strategic partnerships of companies with actors in their six markets.

13.4 Impact of Culture on Relationship Marketing

The impact of culture on RM cannot be overestimated. The literature highlights diverse aspects of this impact. Hoecklin (1995) used case studies describing the (lack of) cooperation between an Italian affiliate and its headquarters in the UK, as well as the cultural learning from Japanese companies in the USA, to illustrate different cultural assumptions. She introduces a value-added perspective on managing across cultures. Managers should decipher and appreciate these differences in each phase of building partnerships: understanding objectives and expectations of the potential partner, the negotiation process, the integration process and the management process.

Schneider and Barsoux (1997) demonstrate how culture influences (internal) organizational processes, such as the nature of policies and procedures, planning and control, information processing, communication and decision-making. For instance, in some cultures a lot of decision-making is accomplished in a parallel, informal 'circuit', whereas in others the formal planning system is key. Usunier (2000) focuses on the different stages in the development of a relational exchange: awareness, exploration, expansion, commitment and dissolution. He argues that this model is valid across cultures. At the same time, however, he shows that each phase is influenced by cultural values and norms.

Table 13.2 Impact on management of the six culture types.

	Context	Network	Family	Pyramid	Solar system	Machine
Organizational principle(s)	▲ Self-interest	▲ Shared interest of stakeholders	▲ In-group interest ▲ Interest of the boss	▲ In-group interest ▲ Interest of the boss	▲ Public interest ▲ School system ▲ Professional group	▲ Balanced interest
Effective manager	▲ Decisive ▲ Selling the decision in a consultative way ▲ Hero ▲ Have data available to inform and instruct people ▲ 'In control'	▲ Consultative ▲ Supportive ▲ Decisive at last resort ▲ Colleague ▲ Negotiating decisions ▲ Recognize all the stakeholders	▲ Benevolent and strict father ▲ Giving clear briefings regularly ▲ Play internal and external network ▲ Overlook the moral stance of your people ▲ People respect what you inspect ▲ Can improvise at last moment	▲ Benevolent and strict father at a distance ▲ Giving clear briefings and inspecting results ▲ Play external network ▲ Take care of your people 'moral competence' ▲ 'People respect what you inspect'	▲ Highly visible ▲ Technocrat ▲ Giving clear direction ▲ 'People respect what you inspect' yet resist inspection ▲ Politician; play internal and external network ▲ 'Noblesse oblige'	▲ Proven expert ▲ Give scenarios for solutions ▲ Don't say 'I don't know' ▲ Ensure competence of subordinates
Delegation	▲ Empowerment around objectives ▲ Co-produce task/performance descriptions ▲ Monitor progress against objectives either formally (US) or informally (GB) ▲ Provide feedback and coaching	▲ Autonomy within specific and meaningful content areas ▲ Set objectives at beginning of year to set direction ▲ Negotiate individual objectives ▲ Organize regular assessment meetings	▲ Within framework of limited mandates ▲ Give clear briefings to set expectations ▲ Inspect at end of day	▲ Within framework of limited mandates ▲ Give clear briefings to set expectations ▲ Inspect at end of the day	▲ Within task description and according to mandate ▲ Give clear briefings regularly ▲ Inspect indirectly	▲ Within framework of clearly defined structure ▲ Explain the plan ▲ Check against plan without interference in on-going work ▲ 'Management by exception'
Motivators	▲ Career and earnings ▲ Challenges ▲ Public praise and recognition ▲ Increase of status ▲ Success of own unit/company	▲ Autonomy within meaningful content ▲ Pleasant work ambience ▲ Nice colleagues	▲ Good boss and harmonious group ▲ Climbing the societal ladder	▲ Good boss, harmonious group and clear standards and procedures ▲ Climbing the societal ladder	▲ Effective boss and clear standards and procedures ▲ Success and continuity of the employer to safeguard job ▲ Identification with trade/professional group	▲ Good rules ▲ Success and continuity of the employer to safeguard one's job ▲ Recognition of competence

In this section we will explore how the aspects of RM introduced in the first part of this chapter (i.e. cross-functional cooperation, customer retention and relationship management) will get a different 'loading' for the six cultural types. Due to their clear impact on managerial practices, their impact on relational marketing management can be taken for granted. Table 13.3 can be used as a guide. In general, the 'agent' can be a supplier, principal, initiator, licensor, etc., and the 'client' (or in more general terms, the 'partner') will show a different interaction pattern along the six types of culture. Rather than expanding on each type in detail, we highlight major differences.

The first three types allow an agent to say that it cannot solve a problem on the spot but will come back to the client after gaining insight. In the latter three types, the agent has to demonstrate a continuous capacity to solve problems. In some cultures, the client wants to sit in the driver's seat, whereas in others the agent is 'part of the team' (e.g. network culture). In the pyramid and solar system culture, the availability or scarcity of the product will dictate the power balance. Also, the 'content' of the 'ideal' interaction will differ, ranging from precise and factual (contest, machine culture), over flexible and modest (network culture) to personal relation (family and pyramid culture). It can be seen from Table 13.3 that the three RM thrusts show large differences across the six types. Some main issues follow.

Cross-functional cooperation requires open communication, interaction, cooperation and the pursuit of synergy and internal marketing. Due to their low degree of power distance, both contest and network cultures enable open, constructive communication between key players regardless of their position in the hierarchy. In the former, however, the individualistic orientation will make synergetic thinking in a partnership more difficult than in the latter type of culture.

In both the family and pyramid models, teamwork and partnership is easy for in-group members, but might be much more problematic for outsiders. Due to high power distance, family, pyramid and solar system cultures are all showing extensive, multi-level decision-making units, and (on the selling side) extensive problem-solving account teams. Also, the hierarchy has to be strictly respected. Due to opportunistic behaviour in the solar system, synergy will often remain unrealized. In the latter three types, open communication is difficult. The well-oiled machine requires small teams of experts, but integration of even this small team is not easy.

Customer retention is facilitated by assertive problem signalling, joint innovation projects and the upfront selection of partners. The high degree of masculinity from the contest model facilitates problem-solving due to assertive problem signalling by partners. The low degree of uncertainty avoidance of the first three culture types makes it relatively easy to start joint innovation and investment programmes. For the last three types (pyramid, solar, machine), large projects will have to be split into a series of small projects (salami approach). Customer selection is more feasible for contest, network and machine cultures than for the other types, as these latter will always introduce personal connections as an important 'entry' (hence, it is difficult to refuse a new partner introduced by a good, old relationship).

Relationship management with partners from the six cultures outlined above will also be coloured differently. Contest and machine cultures are focusing on hard objectives (financial and market performance). Network cultures will seek stakeholder satisfaction, emphasizing soft values. Building partnerships will be slow in network and solar system cultures, due to gradually growing insight processes and a need to consult all

Table 13.3 Impact of the six culture types on relation marketing management.

	Contest	Network	Family	Pyramid	Solar system	Machine
Agent-client pattern	▲ Agent allowed to say: 'I'll find out' ▲ Clients want to steer ▲ Precise, factual, flexible approach ▲ 'Success breeds success'	▲ Agent allowed to say 'I'll find out' ▲ Agent is seen as 'colleague', who can help you in defining your own choices ▲ Approach should not be too 'flashing' ▲ Flexible attitude is appreciated. Not too serious	▲ Agent allowed to say: 'I'll find out' ▲ Client expects agent to outline path ▲ Client wants to be seen as in control ▲ Relationship building is essential for effectiveness	▲ Agent is expected to have all the answers and to outline path ▲ Agent is expected to run like hell if the product is easily available ▲ Agent can act like a king if the product is sparse ▲ Relationship building is essential for effectiveness	▲ Agent is expected to have all the answers and to outline path ▲ Agent is expected to run like hell if the product is easily available ▲ Agent can act like a king if the product is sparse	▲ Agent is expected to have all the answers and to outline path ▲ Client wants to steer ▲ Emphasis on expert behaviour ▲ Precise and factual; structured approach, the only and best solution, formal serious
Relation management thrusts	▲ Open, constructive communication between key persons, regardless of position ▲ Joint innovation projects possible ▲ Individualistic motivations ▲ High empowerment possible ▲ Materialistic drivers ▲ Fast, factual decision cycle	▲ Open, constructive and recurring communication between all stakeholders ▲ Search for synergy ▲ Also soft drivers ▲ Joint innovation projects possible ▲ Long decision processes	▲ Indirect and contextual communication ▲ Hierarchy must be respected ▲ Willingness to cooperate among Chinese high (not as much with outsiders) ▲ In-group feeling strong	▲ Formalized communication ▲ Synergy enforced top-down ▲ Slow trust generation processes ▲ Big projects must be split into less risky parts ▲ Formalized approaches	▲ Formalized communication ▲ Opportunism by all parties ▲ Lots of 'politicking' and 'système D' ▲ Trust seeking is long process ▲ Indirect communication through personal connections ▲ Small projects needed	▲ Group of experts difficult to integrate ▲ Small team of specialists needed ▲ Sequence of small projects rather than one large one ▲ Formalized communication and planning

stakeholders in the former, and lots of 'politicking' and 'système D' (Schneider and Barsoux, 1997) in the latter. In family and pyramid cultures the process of establishing alliances will also be slow due to difficulties related to gaining trust. The leader of the project should be a strong 'father' (seniority is key), taking time for building rules and procedures. As in the solar system and machine cultures, a tight organization and good cooperative planning are required.

13.5 Conclusion

Cultures can be clustered into six 'gestalts'. These mental images differ in organizational principles and in the expectations regarding effective management. As such, it can be argued that relationship marketing has to take into account these differences in mental images as well. Indeed, partnerships gradually grow, someone takes the lead in this process and objectives and working principles have to be decided upon. It was shown in this chapter how the six culture types impact on these relational issues. This contribution has clear managerial implications.

Managers from one culture type have to analyze 'upfront' in the relationship-building process how a (potential) partner from another culture type differs with respect to the dimensions identified here. Adaptation to and/or communication about these differences will result in a stronger partnership. Members from the account team can be trained, working principles adapted, and so forth. Further, cultural diversity can be exploited. For instance, the more risky parts of a long-term project can be better accommodated in a contest or network cultural environment. Culture is a complex 'mosaic'. The building and use of cultural types can be useful in our dealings with 'other' people. A caveat must be added, though. Culture research remains largely dominated by national boundaries. In real life, subcultures will exist and make any effort of classifying cultures always somewhat arbitrary. Someone can be working for the Chinese affiliate ('family'), a German company ('machine'), who studied previously in the US ('contest') and might have a French partner for life ('solar system'): how do you classify such a person from a cultural point of view? Notwithstanding this criticism, we feel confident that our analysis will be a first step toward a professional approach for managing relational marketing across cultures.

REVIEW QUESTIONS

1. What are the three core elements of a relational marketing approach? Can you give real examples of these?

2. In what way are these three aspects influenced by cultural differences?

3. By talking with fellow students, compare cultural influences.

4. Starting from your own cultural background and the mental image to which your country belongs:
   (a) what differences would you expect in negotiating a joint venture with a business-to-business customer for the next two culture types in Table 13.1?
   (b) running a business-to-consumer relational marketing campaign for a bank in the preceding two types to your country in Table 13.1? *continued* ☞

REVIEW QUESTIONS cont.

5. What adaptations does an American manager need to make to his management style when getting an expat assignment in Belgium, China and Austria respectively?

6. What would be demotivators (the opposite of motivators) for collaborating partners in each of the six culture types?

7. What would be the ideal organization form for a collaboration with multiple supply chain partners in the six types?

References

Anderson, J. C. and Narus, J. A. (1999) *Business Market Management*, Upper Saddle River, NJ: Prentice Hall.

Cram, T. (1994) *The Power of Relationship Marketing*, London: Pitman Publishing.

Ford, D., Gadde, L.-E., Hakansson, H. *et al.* (1998) *Managing Business Relationships*, Chichester: John Wiley.

Gannon, M. J. (1994) *Understanding Global Cultures*, Thousand Oaks, CA: Sage Publications.

Heskett, J. L., Hart, C. W. L. and Sasser, W. E. (1994) 'Putting the service-profit chain to work', *Harvard Business Review* 72(2): 164–174.

Hoecklin, L. (1995) *Managing Cultural Differences*, Wokingham: Addison-Wesley.

Management Centre Europe, Brussels, Belgium, <www.mce.be>, telephone 32/2/543.21.00

Matthyssens, P. and Van Den Bulte, C. (1994) 'Getting closer and nicer: partnerships in the supply chain', *Long Range Planning* 27(1): 72–83.

McKenna, R. (1991) *Relationship Marketing*, Reading, MA: Addison-Wesley.

Payne, A. (ed.) (1995) *Advances in Relationship Marketing*, London: Kogan Page.

Ronen, S. and Shenekar, O. (1985) *Understanding Global Cultures*, Thousand Oaks, CA: Sage Publications.

Schneider, S. C. and Barsoux, J. L. (1997) *Managing Across Cultures*, London: Prentice Hall.

Stershic, S. F. (1995) 'Internal marketing', in J. Heilbrunn (ed.), *Marketing Encyclopedia*, Chicago: American Marketing Association, pp. 101–106.

Usunier, J.-C. (2000) *Marketing Across Cultures*, Harlow: Pearson Education.

Wursten, H. (1997) 'Mentale beelden. De gevolgen van cultuur voor organisaties', in *Instituties, waarden, normen en groei*, vier studies naar de relatie tussen economie en cultuur. [Dutch text] NYFER, speciale studie 9, Breukelen.

The pharmaceutical industry and AIDS

Ven Sriram and Franklyn Manu

C5.1 Introduction

On 19 April 2001, 39 pharmaceutical companies abandoned a lawsuit they had brought against the government of South Africa concerning its 1997 Medicines Act. The Act was passed by the South African Parliament in 1997 and signed by then President Mandela to provide South Africans with more affordable pharmaceutical drugs. This was to be achieved by permitting sourcing of lowest-priced patented drugs from anywhere in the world, as well as allowing imports of generic versions of patented drugs. The companies' filed the lawsuit to prevent the South African government from depriving them of their property rights and to force it to adhere to World Trade Organization patent rules (<http://ww.oxfam.org.uk/policy/papers/safrica3.htm>). The full text of the lawsuit is provided at <www.cptech.org/ip/health/sa/pharmasuit.html>, which also gives a full list of applicants and respondents.

From the companies' perspective, the Act ignored the fact that price was not the major factor determining access to AIDS drugs, and that, by ignoring patent protection, it would have a deleterious effect on research and development. The lawsuit was the ultimate response of the pharmaceutical companies to what they viewed as the intransigence of the South African government. What brought about this change in the behaviour of the pharmaceutical companies? Using the model depicted in Figure 12.1, p. 229, we can outline and highlight the major aspects of events leading to this change in behaviour.

Much pressure was brought to bear on this issue from a variety of external forces including the following: Oxfam, the South African government, Doctors Without Borders (MSF), Treatment Action Campaign (TAC), Consumer Project on Technology (CPT), Brazilian government, various African and other developing country governments and institutions, mass protests against the Pharmaceutical Research and Manufacturers of America (PhRMA), politicians in developed countries and the media in general (<http://www.lists.essential.org/pipermail/pharm.policy/2001-April/000944.html>). Obviously, governmental pressures were the greatest, given their resources and ability to attract public attention. In particular, the South African government had a major influencing role, being the defendant in the lawsuit and yet having the ability to assert sovereignty over issues affecting South Africans in South Africa. Groups like TAC, MSF and Oxfam were also able to exert a great deal of pressure, because of their experience in social activism and humanitarian aid that enhanced their credibility, as well as their ability to make use of the media.

The pressures exerted by these groups were mostly in the public sphere, as they engaged in very comprehensive public relations efforts aimed at showing the horrendous effects of AIDS and how the position of the pharmaceutical companies would hinder the fight against it. The basic thrusts of their campaign were that the companies were greedy and immoral. Thus, there was more confrontation and disruption than cooperative effort from the external forces. Resulting media reports created a backlash against the companies and hurt their public images, and people saw them as socially irresponsible and trying to make obscene profits (Goldberg, 2001).

Given the lock-step approach of the pharmaceutical companies and the typical lack of transparency in their operations, whatever internal pressures existed were not as clear. They were probably masked by the need for a united front. However, it appears there were some differences in perspective that led to a split between Glaxo Smith Kline, (GSK), Bristol-Myers Squibb (BMS) and Merck and 36 other companies that had filed the lawsuit (McGreal, 2001). According to the report, GSK had tried to distance itself from the lawsuit by using its South African subsidiary as a participant in the lawsuit, and had also offered cheaper life-saving drugs to developing countries. BMS in turn also said it would not try to prevent the production of generic versions of its drugs in Africa and proposed selling its anti-retrovirals for $1 each. Merck, which was said to be uncomfortable with the lawsuit, also proposed selling its two anti-AIDS drugs to developing countries at cost. This split could have been a major precipitating factor in the change in the industry position. A withdrawal of the three firms would have put the other 36 in a very bad light if they had continued with the lawsuit.

While there are no published reports on the methods used by the companies to screen their environments for CSR issues, it is clear that the companies misread the situation. The companies felt the stakes and seriousness of the pressures were quite high. Tom Bombelles of PhRMA, in a radio interview in South Africa, indicated that the dispute over the Medicines Act was 'the single most important economic or trade issue'. He further alleged 'that South Africa is being used by India and Argentina as a test run to see how worldwide agreements could be broken relating to the protection of intellectual property rights' (<www.cptech.org/ip/health/sa/sa-timeline.txt>). Other arguments by the companies included their position that a resolution of the dispute against them would have negative impacts on research and development and the search for new drugs. As the CEO of Merck put it, 'If we don't solve the drug access problem then our intellectual property is at risk' (<www.oxfam.org.uk/policy/papers/safrica2.htm>). Similarly, the CEO of GSK indicated 'There was a feeling that if a country deliberately went against Trips, there would be a castle-of-cards effect. Without patents, the industry ceases to exist' (Pollack, 2001).

Given the perceived seriousness of the pressures, it is not surprising that the companies' undertook a forceful response. In terms of action criteria, it can be inferred that the companies felt that the benefits of responding would outweigh their costs. Some of the costs that were evident if they had not responded may have been the loss of business to Cipla and similar generic manufacturers, the inability to fully appropriate investments in R&D and reduction in profits. However, these had to be weighed against the negative public image that they acquired.

Not surprisingly, the companies engaged in a variety of actions to put their case across and secure a positive outcome. First and foremost in their response strategy was an attempt to fight through political lobbying of the governments of the developed countries, mainly the United States and Britain. In the United States, this lobbying cut across federal and state governments, political parties, and different political groupings such as the Hispanic and Black caucuses (<www.cptech.org/ip/health/sa/sa-timeline.txt>). Then Vice-President Gore seemingly became the point man for the pharmaceutical manufacturers in negotiations with the South African government. Lobbying was intense and involved donations to political groups. Sponsored seminars and position papers were developed by the industry and given to various political institutions for presentation. Lobbying was aimed at explaining the companies' position and to get governmental support.

The industry also continued its 'fighting' by engaging in a public relations campaign to counter its image of a greedy immoral outfit. Examples of some of the actions taken were as follows:

- Merck, the leading producer of anti-HIV drugs, slashed the prices of two important ones (Crixivan and Stocrin) in South Africa and other developing countries in March 2001. The new prices were $600 and $500 per patient per year (reduced from $6000 and $4700 respectively) and the company claimed that at such prices there was no profit.

- Pfizer donated $50 million worth of its drug Diflucan (fluconazole) to the South African government in December 2000. Interestingly, the drug's patent was set to expire on 6 June 2002. Its price in September 1999 was $9.34/unit compared to $0.60/unit in Thailand.

- Boehringer Ingelheim announced in July 2000 the donation of Viramune free of charge for five years, for the prevention of mother-to-child transmission of HIV-1 in developing countries.

- Bristol Myers Squibb launched the 'Secure the Future' initiative in January 2000. This initiative was funded with a five-year $100 million commitment to help women and children with HIV/AIDS in five southern African countries (Botswana, Namibia, Lesotho, Swaziland and South Africa). The initiative would provide grants for medical research, orphan and home care, and AIDS education programmes (Munusamy, 2000).

This public relations campaign failed to mollify the industry's critics. It was argued that the offers of discounts came with many conditions that limited the amount of drugs African countries would get. For example, only about 1000 people in Senegal would get access to the medication under the programme agreed to with the industry (Inter Press Service, release dated 13 March 2001 at <www.commondreams.org/headlines01/0313-03.htm>). Paul S. Zeitz, a doctor with twelve years of experience working on AIDS in Africa, had this to say about such programmes: 'a strategy to block access to generically manufactured drugs.' He further commented as follows: 'We don't know the details of the written deal. . . . What kind of influence are they buying with this? Are there unwritten ways that the pharmaceutical companies are influencing the governments? We think there should be open, fair competitive bidding between generics and competitive brands. A free donor program effectively blocks the demand for the generically manufactured drugs' (Crossette, 2001).

The public relations campaign was further undercut by media reports on the companies' operations, examples of which are mentioned below:

- In 2000, GSK spent 37.2% of revenue on marketing and administrative costs and 13.9% on research. BMS spent 30.4% of revenue on advertising, marketing and administration and 10.6% on research (Petersen, 2001).

- 77 per cent of the money committed by BMS to the 'Secure The Future' initiative went to US-based charities and medical research institutions. Additional money went to US-based consultants, including the so-called independent monitor of the programme. Other concerns were raised about the focus of the initiative (Brubaker, 2000).

- GSK sold its drug Combivir for about $7000 a year in the US, but the active ingredients cost about $240 on the international generic market. Cipla of India offered a generic version for $275 a year. BMS sold Zerit in Africa at $55 a year, supposedly below cost. The active ingredient cost $23 and Cipla offered the generic (stavudine) for $40 a year. In the US it cost $3400 a year (Petersen, 2001).

In fact, it seemed there was a certain degree of ambivalence on the part of the industry itself with regards to the pricing issue. A quote from one of its publications *The Issue of Discounted Pricing in Developing Countries*, is illuminating in this regard: 'It should be noted, however, that pricing practices reflect individual company decisions, and that there can be no unified industry policy or agreement on such a practice, as this would contravene antitrust and competition policies.' This was in response to suggestions to broaden access by discounting prices of pharmaceutical products sold to the public sectors of developing countries (<www.phrma.org/publications/documents/backgrounders/2001-03-20.207.phtml>). Yet, the CEO of GSK indicated in an interview that reducing the price of AIDS drugs in Africa would not lead to lower prices in its key Western markets (Warner, 2001). So why did the companies become so intransigent? After all, more than 90 per cent of worldwide sales of AIDS drugs in 2000 were concentrated in only five countries – the USA, Italy, Germany, France and Britain (Petersen, 2001). Furthermore, these drugs were only a minor percentage of the major companies' sales revenue. The intransigence can be seen within the context of fighting as depicted in the model shown in Figure 12.1, a strategy that was adopted given the importance of the stakes as the companies viewed them.

The companies initially rejected the idea of lowering prices in poor countries in order not to undercut profits in the rich ones. They argued that the real obstacles to AIDS treatment in Africa and other poor regions were not drug prices but rather socioeconomic and political barriers, as well as inadequate managerial and other resources which resulted in a lack of basic health care. They further argued that high profits were crucial for continued research and development. These attempts at delay/diffusion failed to work and so the companies decide to go on the offensive and tried to co-opt two of the major external forces, the United Nations (UN) and the World Health Organization (WHO). As reported by Gellman (2000), they initiated a number of discussions with these two international organizations that resulted in a joint statement with the UN in May 2000. The statement suggested that the companies would reduce drug prices significantly in developing countries if the following five conditions were met:

- Unequivocal and ongoing political commitment by national governments.
- Strengthened national capacity.
- Engagement of all sectors of national society and the global community.
- Efficient, reliable and secure distribution systems.
- Significant additional funding from national and international sources.

Throughout the entire process, WHO and the UN expressed reservations about various aspects of the plan. As public pressure mounted, cracks began to appear among the companies, resulting in the previously mentioned individual company public relations initiatives. It was at this juncture that Cipla entered the scene with its offer of much cheaper generics. The stakes went up considerably for the companies, but at the same time eroded the basis of one of their key arguments relating to the costs of developing these drugs.

In the end the lawsuit became unsustainable. Publicity had brought about a kind of price war among the pharmaceutical companies themselves, and between them and manufacturers of generic drugs in developing countries. Price cuts failed to blunt offers from the generics manufacturers and did not garner much public support. When additional information came to light in the media, showing that the firms had exaggerated their research costs and failed to take into account the role of public sector institutions (e.g. US National Institutes of Health) in developing some of the major drugs, and spent more on marketing than on R&D, their position became untenable. The balance of power had shifted from the drug companies to developing countries. All that was left was for them to find a face-saving exit from their conundrum. The Secretary-General of the United Nations, Kofi Annan, provided such a cover and on 19 April 2001 an 'agreement' was reached. Basically, the pharmaceutical companies had capitulated. Given the seriousness of the AIDS crisis, the fact that the issue was likely to be long-lived in the absence of a cure, and the negative image the companies became associated with, it was clear they had no further option but to comply.

It remains to be seen if this compliance will generate the kind of outcomes that the companies may have hoped for. What is the likely impact on their profits? Have their shattered corporate images taken a turn for the better? Whatever the case, it is clear that corporate social responsibility remains an area in cross-cultural marketing practice that many companies still have a problem pursuing.

ACTIVITY

1. Was the South African government justified in the stand it took? Discuss the criteria you would use in making that assessment.
2. Critically evaluate the strategies adopted by the pharmaceutical companies.
3. Identify and discuss some of the internal pressures that may have brought about the capitulation of the pharmaceutical corporations.
4. Assess the usefulness of the model shown in Figure 12.1 for analyzing the events surrounding the AIDS drugs case.

References

Alsop, R. (2001) 'Survey rates companies' reputations, and many are found wanting – respondents disparage AT&T, Bridgestone, Philip Morris; highest marks go to J&J', *Wall Street Journal*, 7 February.

Appa, G. and Sridharan, R. (2000) 'OR helps the poor in a controversial irrigation project', *Interfaces*, March/April: 13–28.

Bahree, B. (2001) 'As BP goes green, the fur is flying – oil giant's bid to be seen as more environmental draws critics' scrutiny', *Wall Street Journal*, 16 April: A10.

Brannigan, M. (2000) 'Delta, facing discrimination complaint, creates global-diversity executive post', *Wall Street Journal*, 2 August: A13.

Brubaker, B. (2000) 'The limits of $100 million', *Washington Post*, 29 December:A01.

Crossette, B. 'Fungus drug offered to poor nations', *New York Times*, 7 June: A3.

The Economist (1999a) 'International: Delta blues', 13 February: 44–45.

The Economist (1999b) 'Asia: the dry facts about dams', 20 November: 46.

Fesperman, D. and Shatzkin, K. (1999) 'The new pecking order', *Baltimore Sun*, 28 February.

Gellman, B. (2000) 'A turning point that left millions behind; drug discounts benefit few while protecting pharmaceutical companies' profits', *Washington Post*, 28 December: A01.

Goldberg, R. M. (2001) 'Fight AIDS with reason not rhetoric', *Wall Street Journal*, 23 April.

Goldman, D. (2000) 'Consumer republic', *Adweek*, 22 May: 24.

Hayes, S. (2001) 'Letter to the editor', *Harper's Magazine*, 17 May.

Hohn, D. (2001) 'Response to letters to the editor', *Harper's Magazine*, 17 May.

Inter Press Service, release dated 13 March 2001 at <www.commondreams.org/headlines01/0313-03.htm>

Kapstein, E. B. (2001) 'The corporate ethics crusade', *Foreign Affairs*, September/October: 105–199.

Karp, J. (1999) 'Enron facility again becomes political target in Indian race', *Wall Street Journal*, 8 September: A19.

King, A. (2001) 'Coca-Cola takes the high road', *Black Enterprise*, February: 29.

Kripalani, M. (2001) 'Enron switches signals in India', *Business Week*, 8 January: 58.

Maharaj, N. and Hohn, D. (2001) 'Fleurs du mal', *Harper's Magazine*, February.

McGreal, C. (2001) 'Firms split over deal in cheap drugs lawsuit', *The Guardian*, 18 April.

McKay, B. (2000) 'Coke settles bias suit for $192.5 million – outside panel will monitor company's activities; "painful chapter" closes', *Wall Street Journal*, 17 November.

Moore, S. and Scott, A. (1999) 'Biotech battle: waging a war for public approval', *Chemical Week*, 15 December: 23–26.

Moran, P. (2001) 'Letter to the editor', *Harper's Magazine*, 17 May.

Munusamy, R. (2000) 'US firm joins local battle against AIDS', *Sunday Times (South Africa)*, 23 January.

Pesta, J. (2001) 'Enron calls on guarantee by India to collect debts – unit's main customer owes $17 million for November, "we're obliged to pay" ', *Wall Street Journal*, 7 February: A21.

Petersen, M. (2001) 'Lifting the curtain on the real costs of making AIDS drugs', *New York Times*, 24 April: C1.

Pollack, A. (2001) 'Defensive drug industry: fueling clash over patents', *New York Times*, 20 April: A6.

Schmidt, K. (1999) 'Coke's crisis', *Marketing News*, 27 September: 1, 11.

Sethi, S. P. (1994) *Multinational Corporations and the Impact of Public Advocacy on Corporate Strategy: Nestlé and the Infant Formula Controversy*, Boston: Kluwer Academic.

Wall Street Journal (2000) 'Business brief – SEARS, ROEBUCK & CO.: pact with Benetton ends due to an ad campaign', 17 February.

Walsh, K. (2001) 'Grace files for Chapter 11', *Chemical Week*, 11 April: 7.

Warner, Susan, 'GlaxoSmithKline says AIDS drugs prices in Africa won't impact other markets', *Philadelphia Inquirer*, 25 April.

Electronic References

www.bms.com/news/press/data/fg_press_release_1163.html
www.cptech.org/ip/health/sa/pharmasuit.html
www.cptech.org/ip/health/sa/sa-timeline.txt
www.globalexchange.org
www.levistrauss.com
www.lists.essential.org/pipermail/pharm.policy/2001-April/000944.html
www.mcspotlight.org
www.nikebiz.com
www.oxfam.org.uk/policy/papers/safrica2.htm
www.oxfam.org.uk/policy/papers/safrica3.htm
www.phrma.org/publications/documents/backgrounders/2001-03-20.207.phtml
www.saigon.com/nike

CASE 6

Cadbury Schweppes

Frances Ekwulugo

C6.1 Introduction

Over the past decade, Cadbury Schweppes has been transformed into a truly global player. Through a process of organic growth in new markets such as Eastern Europe and Asia, and a series of acquisitions all over the world, it has gone from being a UK-dominated operation with traditional overseas markets in the commonwealth, to a truly international company with less than half of its profits coming from the UK.

Current chairman, Sir Dominic Cadbury, masterminded the re-focusing of the group in the mid-1980s. The food, health and hygiene businesses were sold off to concentrate on the core streams of confectionery and beverages. 'We decided that we needed to compete with those large organisations already established in the world's major markets, so we needed to be global ourselves', said group chief executive, John Sunderland.

The Cadbury master brand is our biggest brand world wide which covers products like Cadbury's Dairy Milk, Picnic, Timeout and Roses. In beverages, Schweppes is more of a nice brand but nevertheless has global representation. We are now developing Dr Pepper as an international brand, which we acquired in the US two-and a-half years ago. It had little representation previously outside the US, and is now in 16 markets, including the UK.

Unlike many other food products, confectionery and beverages have underlying average growth rates of about five per cent, driven by levels of two to three per cent in mature markets and, although fluctuating, are considerably higher in developing markets. The growth markets are Eastern Europe and Asia-Pacific Rim, also Africa too. However, because of the sheer size of the mature markets an impact of just two per cent on such a huge market base can be as great as 20 per cent in developing countries.

Certain considerations are common to all exporters, regardless of their size. For example, the power of indigenous taste is a critical factor to recognize.

Niche categories may be developed for foreign Western tastes. Of course, you can sell marmalade and chocolate to Japan, but it will be on a low volume, high margin basis, which is good for small operators. At Cadbury Schweppes, we are more interested in tapping into mass market appeal, which is a far bigger challenge because you are right up against the indigenous factor.

Russia is an interesting example. With huge import growth in the early 1990s, it seemed the taste for Western confectionery was going to supercede what went before. However, once Russian companies got their own brands back to consumers with updated packaging, the indigenous brands came back strongly.

It is ironic, because on the one hand you are looking to standardise to take advantages of easy movements between markets, but you also have to cater for local demand and taste characteristics. It is an interesting trade-off.

Among other factors to consider is infrastructure. How do you develop a route to market? You may have a product for which there is no existing consumer franchise and you probably don't have a robust route to market. You may decide to do this on a greenfield basis, as Cadbury Schweppes did in Russia and China, or you can do it through acquiring companies.

The high rate of sterling is affecting exporters, but what difference will the introduction of the Euro make?

The fluctuating exchange rate is a concern. There is nothing you an do except manage through it – perhaps with lower margins, or in more profitable regions, or maybe not at all.

I believe the immediate implications of introducing the Euro will be disadvantageous. There is concern as to where, in the weak to strong currency spectrum, the Euro will lie and we could see a very strong pound. In the longer term, assuming that Britain is in it, transactional flow still be easier. But it will also be easier for goods coming in. Hopefully a strong and stable currency will emerge so that exchange rate fluctuations will be less of an issue. In the long term there will be significant benefits, but there will also be more standardisation of pricing and transparency which will sort out the inefficient producers.

Sunderland attributes the group's success to a clear strategy in two distinct markets and positive commitment to strong brands worldwide, in whose franchise over £700 million was invested last year.

I believe very strongly in the importance of innovation. We place a great premium on innovation in both streams of our business, not just in products, but packaging and route to market too.

We seek to continue to grow our business through acquisition and have a very clear strategy essentially to find companies which can be bolted on to existing businesses to create critical mass and leadership in various markets.

The international soft drinks business operates to a powerful franchising formula that has been the driving force of some of the world's most successful companies – Coca-Cola and Pepsi.

Examples of the focused strategy of Cadbury Schweppes come with the acquisition of the Crush brand in Chile in 1989, for which an international marketing strategy has been developed, and Dr Pepper in the US in 1995, providing the group with its biggest selling and most profitable soft drinks brand. 'We see opportunities with the States, and also outside, to develop the soft drinks markets and out brand within it,' said Sunderland. 'Soft drinks only account for four per cent world-wide of the amount of liquid people consume, so there's 96 per cent to go! After a decade of developing our business globally, we are now moving from an era which was previously scale-driven to one that is now value-driven. It is about extracting better returns, and being more rigorous about a process of acquisitions and capital expenditure in the future. Growth in shareholder value is our primary objective.'

The biggest potential, and largest pitfalls, lie in the new underdeveloped markets:

We have to find a way round different tastes and local consumer franchises. It is always difficult, but the new markets where we have greenfield operations are the most challenging.

For decades they have been closed to Western manufacturers. In the space of five years in the early 1990s, the whole of Eastern Europe, China and India has suddenly opened up. Two-thirds of the world's consumers became accessible to Western manufacturers. These are markets which are politically, economically and culturally very different, and very volatile. All the traditional conditions for doing business that we are used to – stability, structured trade, company law and infrastructure – don't exist in the way we know them.

Poland has been one of our great templates for greenfield development. From nothing three years ago we have built a factory, developed a route to market, and a whole commercial infrastructure which has given us nearly ten per cent of the market. Being profitable in year two and operating on a ten per cent trading margin is very unusual, believe me. (Interview by Janet Tibble with John Sunderland of Cadbury Schweppes, *Food and Drink Exporter*, May/June 1998)

ACTIVITY

1. Critically evaluate the marketing approaches used by Cadbury Schweppes in marketing their products worldwide.

2. To what extent do you think Cadbury Schweppes is practising cross-cultural marketing?

3. How do you think Cadbury Schweppes could improve their performance?

4. Based on indigenous competition, what are the options open to companies like Cadbury Schweppes?

Contemporary issues in cross-cultural marketing

The final part of the text, Part 4, concentrates on the contemporary and futuristic aspects of cross-cultural marketing. Chapter 14 presents what is often referred to as individual or one-to-one marketing. This chapter on cross-cultural perspectives to e-marketing begins by discussing the origins of the Internet, and the challenges of moving from place to space. The chapter ends by discussing the nature of the digital divide between and within countries, as well as the inhibitors to the adoption of the Internet and e-commerce in emerging economies.

Chapter 15 tackles the issue of multicultural marketing. The chapter argues that a rich cultural diversity within a society such as Australia presents a valuable resource in recognizing and responding to the opportunities presented in international markets, particularly in Asia. Chapter 16 examines the various types of SMEs and the barriers that pose challenges for them in cross-cultural marketing practice. The chapter concludes by providing alternative strategic approaches to cross-cultural customer segmentation and an understanding of how these influence the targeting and positioning strategies of SMEs.

Chapter 17 provides a challenging insight into the futuristic effects of culture on business by examining the concept of globalization in terms of the factors driving it as a worldwide trend. The chapter discusses the consequences of globalization in terms of its capacity to produce counter trends such as market fragmentation and tribalization of global consumer groups. The chapter concludes by challenging readers to consider how these counter trends might influence consumer marketing in specific areas in the future. Chapter 18 provides a fitting conclusion to the text by presenting arguments that build on and sum up many of the issues presented in the various chapters, as well as projections into the future of global marketing.

CHAPTER 14

Cross-cultural perspectives on e-business

Byron Keating and Robert Rugimbana

14.1 Introduction

> Cyberspace is the homeland of the Information Age – the place where the citizens of the future are destined to dwell. (John Perry Barlow, 1991)

Hoffman and Novak (1997) assert that this new homeland is revolutionizing business processes. They suggest that e-business provides a new paradigm for marketing, where firms and consumers can interact to deliver superior economic and social outcomes. Ghosh (1998) adds that the benefits of e-business are particularly profound for marketers that have an eye to doing business across borders. However, the potential of undertaking cross-cultural e-business is severely influenced by the disparate adoption of e-business. In short, not all citizens dwell equally in this new homeland.

The purpose of this chapter is to explore how the dynamics of e-business have, and continue to, impact on global business and cross-cultural marketing. In achieving this aim, the chapter will be divided into three parts. The first provides an overview of the e-business environment, including a discussion of the origins of the Internet, the challenges of moving from the traditional physical world to the new cyberspace, and the various definitions of e-business terms. The second section examines the application of e-business to the cross-cultural context and looks at the broad benefits of using the Internet as a cross-cultural marketing tool, as well as some of the statistics regarding the application of the innovation–diffusion process to e-business. The final section investigates the special circumstances associated with applying e-business to developing countries.

14.2   Overview of the E-business Environment

Brief History of the Internet

The Internet has existed since the late 1960s, when a limited number of computers were connected in the United States to form the ARPAnet. This was mainly used to enable academics and military personnel to exchange defence information. The recent growth and expansion of the Internet has been because of the development of the World Wide Web, a network within the network.

The WWW became a commercial proposition in 1993 after development on the original concept by Tim Berners-Lee, a British scientist working at CERN in Switzerland in 1989. The WWW changed the Internet from a difficult-to-use network that required advanced technical skills and knowledge, to an easy-to-use graphical interface that requires relatively little technical proficiency. In general, the advent of the WWW has resulted in the creation of an international publishing medium for the display, storage and transfer of data. This data is stored on powerful computers referred to as servers, which are interconnected via telephone networks and modems.

Consumers and businesses can find this data by performing intricate searches, and can access the data with a computer program called a web-browser. While early emphasis of the WWW was on sharing information, more recent attention has focused on the use of the infrastructure to perform commercial exchanges. The following timeline (adapted from UNDP, 2001) illustrates the technological developments that provided the foundation to the information revolution:

- *1975:* First personal computers introduced – programmable machines, small and inexpensive enough to be used by individuals.
- *1979:* First computer modem introduced by Hayes.
- *1982:* Basic networking protocol adopted as a standard, leading to one of the first definitions of the Internet.
- *1989:* Concept of the World Wide Web developed by CERN.
- *1993:* Mosaic introduced – the first popular graphical interface for the WWW.
- *1995:* Public Internet with high-speed backbone service, linking supercomputing centres, established by the US National Science Foundation.
- *1995:* MP3, Real Audio and MPEG enable distribution of audio and video content over the Internet.
- *1997:* Wireless Application Protocol (WAP) introduced.
- *Future:* High speed connection to every home, merger of cellular phones and personal digital assistants.

Industrial economy (marketplace)	Digital economy (marketspace)	
▶ Manufacturing dominates	▶ Knowledge and relationships dominate	
▶ Barrier: physical distribution	▶ E-distribution is new barrier	**Table 14.1**
▶ Barrier: lack of capital	▶ Capital is a commodity	Marketplace versus
▶ First-mover advantage is years	▶ First-mover advantage is months	marketspace.
▶ Innovative ideas contained internally	▶ Innovation is in the public domain	
▶ Relationships constrained by human capital	▶ Relationships can be established electronically	

Moving from Place to Space

The Internet is a powerful business tool that has transformed the fundamental dynamics of many social and commercial interactions. The barriers and obstacles that often accompanied traditional commerce are giving way to new business approaches. Consumers, producers and distributors can now have access to flexible, fast and inexpensive ways of participating in the global marketplace. Individual and corporate customers can approach this same marketplace differently, and gain access to previously unseen levels of information and variety.

The Internet's impact on the way the world does business is the result of the way in which it has altered basic business dynamics. The dynamics that have shaped economic practices since the early nineteenth century are being replaced by a new set of fundamental principles, based on a digital economy. In the previous industrial economy, exchange was dominated by manufacturing, supported by complex supply chains. However, in the new digital economy, there is an emphasis on information and ideas, where knowledge and relationships dominate.

In the industrial economy, the barriers of distribution and capital in a largely manufacturing-oriented economy often resulted in big advantages to the early movers. However, these advantages are often not as significant in the digital economy, where early mover advantages are rationalized. Rather, there are new barriers centred on integration of virtual and real world technologies, as well as the creation of competitive advantage where unanimity is so prevalent. The resolution of these challenges is seen as the purpose of e-business.

Electronic Business Defined

Electronic business is the exchange of business information and transactions, the development of customer relationships and service, and the creation of new business relationships using electronic methods (Chaffey, 2000). Though e-business had its origins in the electronic data interchange (EDI) phenomenon, it has taken on a new and broadened meaning through its use of the Internet, intranets and extranets (Kleindl, 2001).

Chaffey (2000) adds that the term 'e-business' is often interchanged with terms such as 'e-commerce' and 'e-marketing'; however, he insists that it is broader than these and can incorporate elements of both. He also contends that e-business transcends functional boundaries, and has relevance to all business functions from human resources to marketing to corporate strategy. Table 14.2 provides insight into some of the terminology.

Term	Meaning
Internet	This is a global network of computers that use a common interface for communication. The World Wide Web uses graphic based Internet standards, and has allowed easy access to information and communication around the world.
Extranet	An Internet-based connection between a business and its suppliers, distributors and partners and extranet is not open to the general public. These systems are replacing older electronic data interchange (EDI) systems.
Intranet	This is an internal private network that uses the same types of hardware, software and connections as the Internet. It can link divisions of a business around the world into a unified communications network.
e-business	This is the process of using information technology (IT) to support a fuller operation of the business. This could include generating leads, providing sales support, integrating partners and linking aspects of the business operation to suppliers and distributors through extranets, which are internal communications controlled through intranets.
e-commerce	E-commerce consists of using electronic information-based systems to engage in transactions or commerce online. This includes automating website purchases.
e-marketing	The application of the Internet and related digital technologies to achieve marketing objectives and support the marketing concept.

Table 14.2
Key e-business definitions.

Kleidl (2001) adds that the effective application of e-business requires an understanding of how consumer behaviour differs in the online world, and a commitment to developing the skills required to respond and prosper in this new marketspace. The next section of this chapter will examine how e-business applies to the cross-cultural marketing situation.

14.3 Cross-cultural E-business

E-Business as a Cross-cultural Marketing Tool

There are many possible implications for electronic business within cross-cultural marketing. The new, more global, medium gives customers access to more information, more competition, and inevitably more power. However, there are also significant opportunities available to firms wishing to undertake expansion into global markets. Sterne (1999) suggests that firms can use e-business to generate tangible benefits, e.g. greater market opportunities and profitability, as well as intangible benefits, such as an improved reputation and brand. Some of the main perceived benefits of using e-business to compete across cultures are listed in Table 14.3 below:

Business benefits	Customer benefits
▶ Global presence	▶ Global choice
▶ Improved competitiveness	▶ Quality of service
▶ Mass customization and consumerism	▶ Personalized products and services
▶ Shorten or eradicate supply chains	▶ Rapid response to needs
▶ Substantial cost savings	▶ Substantial price reductions
▶ Novel business opportunities	▶ New products and services

Table 14.3
Cross-cultural marketing benefits.

However, Rosen and Howard (2000) add that firms also need to be cautious when undertaking e-business as there are a number of factors that can confound potential online success. These include the burden of delivery, high start-up costs, difficulty in differentiating, need to continually upgrade technology and skills, as well as the lack of human contact. Perhaps the greatest challenge to firms wishing to utilize e-business as a tool for cross-cultural marketing is the uneven global diffusion of the Internet and related e-business practices.

Global Diffusion of E-business

The innovation–diffusion process has been applied to such disparate fields as management, sociology, marketing and medicine (Rai *et al.*, 1998), and is governed by two behavioural theories. First, the diffusion of innovation theory helps to explain how innovations diffuse through some social system (Rogers, 1983). Second, the value of adopting the innovation increases along with the number of adopters, also referred to as the theory of network externalities. Both theories suggest that the diffusion of any given innovation (such as e-business) over time is a bell-shaped, normal distribution (Rai *et al.*, 1998).

In the marketing context, the adoption process places adopters into categories and explores how the earlier adopters influence the later adopters. Marketers can then use this information to segment markets and design marketing campaigns. Figure 14.1 below highlights a typical adoption curve, and associated adopter categories.

From Figure 14.1 it can be seen that the innovators are first to adopt, followed by early adopters, early majority, late majority, and laggards. Kleindl (2001) contends that the innovation–diffusion process fails to acknowledge those that do not adopt for reasons of circumstance or choice. Czinkota *et al.* (1998) identify three prerequisites for adopting technology: (a) the availability of technology; (b) social and economic conditions suitable for diffusion of technology; and (c) the willingness and ability of receiving party to use and adapt technology. These prerequisites reflect the effectual e-readiness of a host community to adopt a new technology such as the Internet and e-business. However, as indicated previously, the diffusion of e-business will also be brokered by the current intensity and impact of e-business. Figure 14.2 represents the three steps of e-business diffusion.

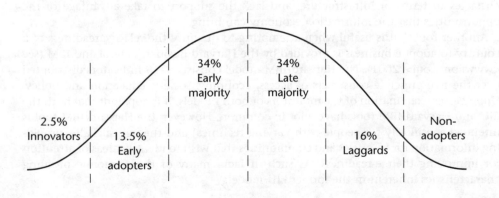

Figure 14.1
Typical adoption curve.

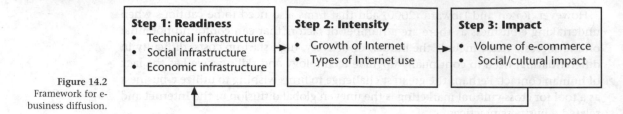

Figure 14.2
Framework for e-
business diffusion.

From Figure 14.2, we can see that readiness refers to the technical, commercial and social infrastructure necessary to support e-business. The main indicators are infrastructure take-up and the economic conditions of host communities. Intensity refers to the level of Internet usage, including frequency of use and the type and scope of activities undertaken over the Internet. Impact broadly refers to how the Internet and the information economy changes the host society, particularly the willingness to use the technology to undertake day-to-day work, and interact socially and economically. Some impact indicators include the value of this electronic commerce, and the perceptions of the benefits from use of the Internet.

Step 1: Readiness for E-business

The Economist Intelligence Unit (EIU, 2001) in the United States publishes a comprehensive ranking of countries on the basis of their measured e-readiness. The ranking categorizes countries on the basis of their overall e-readiness as calculated from 89 indicators across the six weighted dimensions: connectivity; business environment; consumer and business adoption; legal and regulatory environment; supporting services; and social and cultural infrastructure (see HREF1, 2001). The consequence of the calculations is the classification of the world's 60 largest economies on the basis of their perceived adopter category.

In Table 14.4 below, leaders are countries that have most of the elements of e-readiness in place. Contenders have both a satisfactory infrastructure and business environment, but are lacking in some of the other areas. Similarly, followers also lack the sophistication of the leader and contender, but have seen the importance of the Internet and are moving towards establishing the necessary infrastructure to support it. Laggards are the countries who are at risk of being left behind. They have serious obstacles in terms of infrastructure, and lack the support to take advantage of the opportunities that the information economy can bring.

Another tool that is useful when attempting to quantify the relative readiness of a country to adopt e-business is provided by the Harvard Business School and IBM (see <www.ibm.com>, 2001). The Harvard/IBM model consists of 19 indicators distributed over the five principle constructs of access, economy, society, education and policy. Upon closer examination of the indicators of both models, it is apparent that both the EIU and Harvard/IBM tools have a lot in common. However, the Harvard/IBM tool is intended specifically for people with varying technical and theoretical skills, providing information for countries and communities that wish to identify areas of attention for improving their e-readiness. As such, it lacks many of the economic profiling characteristics inherent in the former EIU model.

Leaders (Innovators)	Contenders (Early adopters)	Followers (Early majority)	(Late majority)	Laggards (Laggards)
United States	Ireland	Greece	Philippines	Bulgaria
Australia	France	Czech Repub.	Egypt	China
United Kingdom	Austria	Hungary	Peru	Ecuador
Canada	Taiwan	Chile	Russia	Iran
Norway	Japan	Poland	Sri Lanka	Romania
Sweden	Belgium	Argentina	Saudi Arabia	Ukraine
Singapore	New Zealand	Slovakia	India	Algeria
Finland	South Korea	Malaysia	Thailand	Indonesia
Denmark	Italy	Mexico	Venezuela	Nigeria
Netherlands	Israel	South Africa		Kazakhstan
Switzerland	Spain	Brazil		Vietnam
Germany	Portugal	Turkey		Azerbaijan
Hong Kong		Columbia		Pakistan

Table 14.4
e-Readiness rankings.

Source: Adapted from EIU, 2001.

Step 2: Intensity of E-business

In addition to the existence of adequate infrastructure and support mechanisms to facilitate the adoption of e-business, economic theory suggests that the rate of adoption will also be brokered by the economies of network externalities. In other words, adoption is very much influenced by the current intensity of Internet use, including the number of existing users and the type and nature of their use. Table 14.5 shows existing users on the basis of regions.

From Table 14.5 and the United Nations Development Report (2001), we can see that developed countries currently contribute around 88% of the current Internet user population, despite only representing 14% of the actual global population. Likewise, various online research firms report that developed countries are currently responsible for more than 90% of global e-commerce in both the B2B and B2C markets (see eMarketer, 2001a; eMarketer, 2001b).

In line with the economies of network externalities, Forrester Research (2000) assert that after the initial establishment of the information infrastructure, countries will experience only moderate growth until online trade reaches a critical mass of around 10% of its ultimate potential. After this mark is reached, the country will experience what they refer to as 'hypergrowth'. They add that a nation's hypergrowth year is preceded by a commerce threshold, which is a 12- to 18-month building period followed by explosive growth. They further assert that hypergrowth is a result of a confluence of the four factors – regulatory openness, infrastructure, global supply

	1998	2000
North America	26.3	54.3
Europe	7.7	32.1
Asia Pacific	0.5	2.3
Latin America	0.8	3.2
Africa and Middle East	0.34	1.4
Total World	2.4	6.7

Source: UNDP, 2001.

Table 14.5
Internet use by region (as % of population).

chain linkages and trading bloc activity – and a window of opportunity for public and private sector action.

From the report, Forrester (2001) indicated that the United States entered their hypergrowth year in 2000, followed by Western Europe in 2001, and Asia Pacific in 2002, with the remaining regions predicted to experience substantial growth between 2004 and 2010. It can be seen that even the laggards identified in the e-readiness rankings will experience some degree of growth over the next decade. However, it is also relevant to acknowledge that the hypergrowth predictions relate to the net growth relative to total anticipated growth. That is, even though the developing countries are expected to experience more significant growth in the next decade, their comparative potential is still relatively small when compared to the developed nations.

Step 3: Impact of E-business

Corresponding to their hypergrowth predictions, Forrester (2000) also provides a breakdown of the projected growth in online sales in each of the main global regions over the next couple of years. As alluded to earlier, even though developing countries are expected to enjoy a larger slice of the e-commerce pie over the next decade, the leaders and contenders identified in EIU's readiness rankings are still likely to maintain their economies of scale and enjoy a competitive advantage due to their early move into the online marketspace.

However, measuring the social and cultural impacts of the Internet is inherently more difficult. Figure 14.3 below indicates that technological innovation affects human development in two ways. First, it can directly enhance human capabilities by directly improving people's health, nutrition, knowledge and living standards, and increasing people's ability to participate more actively in the social, economic and political life of a community. Second, technological innovation is a means to human development because of its impact on economic growth through the productivity gains it generates. It raises the crop yields of farmers, the output of factory workers and the efficiency of service providers and small businesses. It also creates new activities and industries – such as the information and communications technology sector – contributing to economic growth and employment creation.

Further, we see that there is a strong correlation between the diffusion of high technologies, such as the Internet and e-business, and the relative growth of a nation's

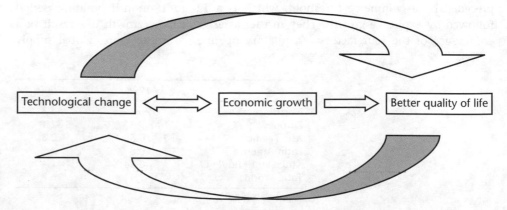

Technological change ⟷ Economic growth ⟹ Better quality of life

Figure 14.3
Link between technology and human development.

	Telephone lines (per 1000 people)		Internet hosts (per 1000 people)	
	1990	1999	1995	2000
Developing countries	22	69	0.1	1.0
Least developed countries	3	5	–	–
Arab states	34	69	0.1	0.6
East Asia	17	85	–	0.4
Latin America	63	131	0.2	5.6
South Asia	7	29	–	0.1
Africa	–	–	0.1	0.6
East Europe	125	205	0.3	4.7
OECD	392	509	8.4	75.0
High income OECD	473	594	11.0	96.9
High human development	416	542	9.0	80.5
Medium human development	28	79	–	1.0
Low human development	4	9	–	–
High income	470	591	10.8	95.2
Medium income	45	122	0.1	2.1
Low income	11	27	–	0.1
World	102	158	1.7	15.1

Source: UNDP, 2001.

Table 14.6
Relative impact of
Internet diffusion.

GNP (DOI, 2001). Also, when we examine the impact of Internet diffusion against the United Nation's Human Development Index (UNDP, 2001), we also find that countries with greater Internet diffusion enjoy greater social development. Table 14.6 below shows the relative impact of Internet diffusion in the developed and developing world.

From Table 14.6 it can be seen that countries with a lower e-business diffusion (as measured by the number of Internet hosts) perform worse under the United Nations Human Development Index. Therefore, given the generally accepted desire to raise the standard of living in the Third World, it prompts the question: what is preventing wider adoption of e-business in developing countries? The next section of this chapter will consider the specific factors that influence this question.

14.4   E-business in Developing Countries

The Digital Divide

As indicated in the previous section, despite the enormous benefits associated with adopting technologies such as e-business, there is a significant divide between the haves and the have nots. However, in addition to the obvious macro-divide between developed and developing countries, there is also an emerging micro-divide within countries. Though data is limited on the demography of Internet users, Internet use is clearly concentrated. The United Nations (UNDP, 2001) report that in most countries Internet users are predominantly:

- *Urban and located in certain regions*. In China, the 15 least-connected provinces, with 600 million people, have only 4 million Internet users – while Shanghai and Beijing, with 27 million people, have 5 million users. In the Dominican

Republic, 80% of Internet users live in the capital, Santo Domingo. And in Thailand 90% live in urban areas, which contain only 21% of the country's population. Among India's 1.4 million Internet connections, more than 1.3 million are in the five states of Delhi, Karnataka, Maharashtra, Tamil Nadu and Mumbai.

- *Better educated and wealthier.* In Bulgaria, the poorest 65% of the population accounts for only 29% of Internet users. In Chile, 89% of Internet users have had tertiary education; in Sri Lanka, 65%; and in China, 70%.

- *Young.* Everywhere, younger people are more apt to be online. In Australia, 18–24-year-olds are five times more likely to be Internet users than those above 55. In Chile, 74% of users are under 35; in China that share is 84%. Other countries follow the same pattern.

- *Male.* Men make up 86% of users in Ethiopia, 83% in Senegal, 70% in China, 67% in France and 62% in Latin America.

Some of these disparities are easing. For example, the gender gap seems to be narrowing rapidly – as in Thailand, where the share of female users jumped from 35% in 1999 to 49% in 2000, or in the United States, where women made up 38% of users in 1996 but 51% in 2000. In Brazil, where Internet use has increased rapidly, women account for 47% of users.

Benefits of E-business in the Developing World

In addition to the general benefits identified earlier in this report, the United Nations (UNDP, 2001) has also identified a number of distinct opportunities that are available to developing countries as a result of wider e-business adoption. The main four are discussed below:

- *Political participation.* The Internet delivers access to uncensored two-way communication, which has the ability to dramatically influence the outcome of the political process. For instance, in the Philippines the use of an e-mail petition was viewed to have a major impact on the recent impeachment trial of President Joseph Estrada (UNDP, 2001), where the gathering of over 150,000 signatures was believed to have encouraged Senators to vote with their consciences rather than politically-vested interests.

- *Greater transparency.* Greater access to information and technology has also helped developing countries to provide more accurate financial reporting. For instance, the Moroccan government has been able to halve the time required to prepare a national budget by using more efficient data management systems. The associated benefits have also been more accurate data and better economic planning.

- *Increased income.* Through the use of the Internet, developing countries are able to gain access to information that can help increase the productivity of their industry and the yields on their exports. For instance, in India the Swaminathan Research Foundation has been able to advise farmers on the best time to sell and the best price to sell at. Also, the technology has helped communities share information on different agricultural techniques and facilitate micro-trade.

- *Better health.* Perhaps the greatest benefit of Internet access has been the way the technology has allowed developing countries to access the latest health information, as well as open up new treatment options in situations where facilities and transport are always an issue. For instance, the global 'Healthnet' project has enabled health professionals in Africa, Asia and Latin America to procure equipment efficiently, and provide an accurate picture of the state of global epidemics.

Barriers to E-business in the Developing World

The benefits outlined above have been made possible predominantly via recent innovations in the area of mobile telephony. There are still significant barriers preventing the developing world from accessing the electronic marketing benefits that the developed world enjoys as a consequence of wider diffusion. Some of the main barriers are discussed below:

- *Infrastructure.* More widespread adoption of the Internet as a marketing tool is prohibited by restricted access to required infrastructure such as telephones and computers. For instance, the average diffusion per 1000 people of telephones and computers in the developing world is around 23 and 3 respectively, while this figure expands to 567 and 311 for the most developed countries. Furthermore, the low levels of infrastructure also act to keep access prices prohibitively high.
- *Affordability.* Unaffordable access is probably the single most important reason for low use of e-business in developing countries. For instance, Nnadozi (2001) asserts that the comparative costs and advantage preclude the adoption of e-commerce in countries where labour unit costs are low and technology costs are high. He contends that in developing countries, it makes better economic sense to invest in industries that are labour-intensive as the countries have a competitive advantage over the developed world where labour costs are much higher. Furthermore, national strategies are required in developing countries to overcome this barrier by providing subsidized Internet use, and reform measures that would lead to the reduction of costs and access charges.
- *Human capacity.* The low comparative levels of literacy in developing countries, along with the limitations in the area of technological skills, also act as a barrier to wider diffusion of electronic commerce and marketing. Furthermore, the World Wide Web is dominated by the English language, acting as a discriminatory barrier to the developing world. In many developing countries, problems arise because standard fonts for local languages are unavailable. In Russia, Internet use increased exponentially with the introduction of Cyrillic character sets (UNDP, 2001), illuminating the need to learn English.
- *Policy.* While the level of Internet diffusion is positively associated with the degree of transparency and political participation, the reverse is also the case. That is, in countries with restrictive governments and poor regulatory conditions, the opportunity for e-diffusion is limited. For instance, despite a desire to introduce a more liberal economic policy, a failure by China to open its economy to world trade has had a detrimental affect on foreign investment in telecommunications infrastructure (EIU, 2000).

- *Enterprise.* The current success of e-business in the developed world is largely attributable to private sector R&D, supported by a robust and entrepreneurial financial sector. In addition, there is a need to build applications that are focused on enhancing governance processes and specific development goals, including health, education, empowerment, environmental sustainability and support of employment and enterprise creation.

- *Content and application.* The ability to achieve development goals will not be effectively leveraged without content that is responsive to user needs and local conditions, in a language that is commonly understood, and with technical specifications that are sensitive to the actual use and working environment of users. For example, Arabization is currently considered to be a critical factor in developing information systems for countries in the Gulf region. There is also an unsatisfied demand for Arabic language educational materials in electronic format (<www.unesco.org>).

14.5 Conclusion

The purpose of this chapter has been to explore how the dynamics of e-business have impacted on global business and cross-cultural marketing. To achieve this aim, the chapter was divided into three parts. The first section provided an overview of the e-business environment, including a discussion of the origins of the Internet; the challenges of moving from the traditional physical world to the new cyberspace; and the various definitions of e-business terms. The second section examined the application of e-business to the cross-cultural context. It looked at the broad benefits of using the Internet as a cross-cultural marketing tool, as well as some of the statistics regarding the application of the innovation–diffusion process to the cyber-business context. The final section of the chapter investigated the special circumstances associated with applying e-business in developing countries.

REVIEW QUESTIONS

1. Discuss the origins of the Internet and identify the challenges of moving from place to space.
2. Define electronic business and distinguish it from other e-terms.
3. Describe the key strategic issues affecting the application of e-business as a cross-cultural marketing tool.
4. Discuss the framework e-business diffusion and the application of this process to the main regions of the world.
5. Identify the nature of the digital divide between and within countries, and identify and discuss the inhibitors to the adoption of the Internet and e-commerce in developing countries.

References

Chaffey, D., Mayer, C., Jonhston, K. and Ellis-Chadwick, F. (2000) *Internet Marketing*, Harlow: Pearson Education.

Czinkota, M. and Ronkainen, I. (1998) *International Marketing*, 5th edn., Orlando, FL: Dryden Press.

EIU (2001) *Ereadiness Rankings*, New York: Economic Intelligence Unit.

EMarketer (2000) *Internet Use by Region*, New York: Emarketer.

Fletcher, R. and Brown, L. (1999) *International Marketing: An Asia-Pacific Perspective*, Sydney: Prentice Hall.

Ghosh, S. (1998) 'Making business sense of the Internet', *Harvard Business Review*, March–April: 127–135.

Hoffman, D. L. and Novak, T. (1997) 'Marketing in hypermedia computer-mediated environments: conceptual foundations', *Journal of Marketing*, 60 (July): 50–68.

Hollensen, S. (2001) *Global Marketing: A Market Responsive Approach*, London: Prentice Hall.

HREF 1 (2001) <www.eiu.com>

HREF 2 (2001) <www.ibm.com>

HREF 3 (2001) <www.unesco.org>

Nnadozi, E. (2001) 'Why e-commerce is underdeveloped in Africa and what can be done about it'. IAABD conference proceedings, Atlantic City, NJ, pp. 402–5.

Rai, A., Ravichandran, T. and Subhashish, S. (1998) 'How to anticipate the Internet's global diffusion', Communications of the ACM, 4(10), 97–106.

Rogers, E. (1983) *Diffusion of Innovations*, 3rd edn., New York: Free Press.

Rosen, K. and Howard, A. (2000) 'E-retail: gold rush or fool's gold', *California Management Review*, 42—3): 72–100.

Sanders, M. and Temkin, B. (2001) *Global eCommerce Approaches Hypergrowth*, Amsterdam: Forrester Research.

Sterne, J. (1999) *World Wide Web Marketing*, 2nd edn., New York: John Wiley and Sons.

UNDP (2001) *Human Development Report 2001*, New York: United Nations.

CHAPTER 15

Multicultural marketing

Ian Wilkinson and Constant Cheng

LEARNING OBJECTIVES

At the end of this chapter readers will be able to:

► Explore a framework for analyzing multicultural marketing in terms of the inter-relations between three types of factors, i.e. the multicultural marketplace in Australia; international markets; and the multicultural resources that exist in Australia.
► Examine Australia's cultural diversity, as well as that of other multicultural societies, as a valuable resource for recognizing and responding to the opportunities presented in international markets.
► Identify a number of case studies to illustrate the ways in which opportunities in the domestic and international marketplace can arise and be responded to as a result of the multicultural dimensions of a society.

15.1 Introduction

Among the key issues facing all countries is the increasing internationalization of the world economy. International competition is being faced both at home and abroad as tariffs are reduced, markets deregulated and commerce transcends national borders. An important challenge for Australia is how it carves out its destiny in the fast-growing Asia-Pacific region. This presents many opportunities for business, but also many challenges and difficulties in conducting business across diverse cultures and business systems. Here we will argue that Australia's rich cultural diversity is a valuable resource in recognizing and responding to the opportunities presented in inter-national markets, particularly in Asia.

Australian society is culturally very heterogeneous because it is the product of a migrant population and its descendents. It has become home for people from many different cultural and geographic backgrounds and their descendants. Until the 1970s, the waves of migrants came mainly from Europe, particularly the United Kingdom, although there was a wave of migrants from China in the 1850s, during the gold rush. In the last decade or so there has been an increasing number of migrants from Asia, adding to the multicultural make-up of the society.

Multiculturalism was often seen as a problem in the past. Indeed, attempts were made to reduce cultural heterogeneity by restricting immigrants to white Europeans –

the so called 'White Australia' policy. In general, emphasis was placed on the problems and costs involved in migrants adapting to Australian customs and practices, and learning to speak English if that was not their mother tongue. Another type of problem is that of tensions and conflicts between ethnic communities of historical origin being introduced into Australia, such as the rivalry among Serbs and Croatians from the former Yugoslavia, or the attitudes of Chinese and Korean people towards the Japanese as a result of wartime and occupation experiences.

More recently the focus has shifted to a greater emphasis on the benefits and opportunities that may arise in a multicultural society (e.g. Harris, 1997; Office of Multicultural Affairs, 1995). We propose a framework for analyzing how multiculturalism can play a role in boosting the domestic and international competitiveness of firms – how synergies arise out of the cultural diversity. The framework is not only applicable to Australia, although the examples used to illustrate and support it are drawn from there. It is relevant to any society seeking to evaluate and better utilize the strengths and contributions of its cultural resources.

15.2 Australian Society and Multicultural Marketing

People born overseas, or with either parent born overseas, constitute a significant group in the Australian population. In 1995, 22.7% of Australia's population was born overseas, which is more than any other Western country (OECD, 1995). Forty per cent of Australians are migrants or the children of migrants, 13.7% of Australians were born overseas in non-English speaking countries, and people from 160 countries live in Australia (Federal Race Discrimination Commissioner, 1997). Finally, the 1995 Australian Census shows that, of people aged five years and over, 2,487,073 or 15.6% of the population speak a language other than English at home.

The economic, political and social implications of this cultural mix cannot be ignored, and has begun to be more widely recognized in recent times. For example, Woolworths, one of the major supermarket chains in Australia, developed a campaign to promote its fresh food products and wished to feature their own employees in the advertisements. They did not start out to feature people from various ethnic backgrounds, but this happened naturally a result of the ethnic composition of their workforce. Moreover, in appealing to all sections of the Australian population in their nationwide campaign, 'Woolworths the Fresh Food People', they began to feature the way fresh produce was used as part of various ethnic cuisines served in contemporary Australia. A match between the cultural diversity of the workforce and the population served became apparent, and was taken up and emphasized in various ways in subsequent versions of the campaign. Now Woolworths has audited the language and cultural knowledge and skills of their workforce, and made use of this in serving customers and in their campaigns. This is one example of the way a firm has come to recognize, respond to and value the cultural diversity of its staff.

The term 'multicultural marketing' is used here to refer to the ways firms use and respond to opportunities and challenges arising from a multicultural society in serving domestic and international customers. Such marketing is increasingly becoming part of mainstream marketing campaigns and business strategy in Australia, because of the multicultural make-up of Australian society and because, as business becomes more internationalized, it is called on to meet the demands of the multicultural world in which we live. Some other examples of how multicultural themes have entered mainstream marketing campaigns are as follows. The Australian Meat and Livestock Corporation, an industry sponsored promotion and research organization, won an award in 1996 for its campaign to promote lamb as the multicultural meal. It featured Greek, Indian and Thai lamb dishes as part of modern Australian cuisine. Culturally-diverse families were seen at mealtime serving these dishes. A corporate advertising campaign by the National Australia Bank (a 1997 award winner) included people of various ethnic backgrounds striving to achieve success in business. Lastly, the Australian Broadcasting Commission, an award winner in 1998, runs a series of national identification promotions that include people engaged in ethnically-related activities such as religious celebrations, weddings, dancing, music events and education. To begin with it is not clear the activity is taking place in Australia, but it is and each clip ends with someone declaring the Australian Broadcasting Commission is their television station by writing the station sign in the air.

In the following sections we provide a framework for analyzing the relationships between Australia's ethnic diversity and business performance in domestic and international markets. We illustrate our arguments by drawing primarily on cases from the Australian Multicultural Marketing Awards. These awards were established in 1991 to recognize and reward business, government and community organizations for excellence in serving the needs arising from Australia's cultural diversity, and in utilizing this diversity to succeed in international markets. The awards are administered by the Ethnic Affairs Commission of the state of New South Wales, a statutory body handling issues related to multicultural affairs which reports directly to the Premier of the State. Although they began in one State, the awards have become a national event with entries from all over Australia. A panel of judges comprising industry, government and academic representatives judges awards in five categories: Export, Commercial–Big Business, Commercial–Small Business, Government, Community and Advertising. The winner in each category receives a plaque plus prizes and the overall winner each year receives a special trophy plus a major prize. Certificates of Commendation are sometimes issued to other outstanding entries. These awards are announced at a gala dinner presided over by the Premier of the State. Each year around 50 entries are received and the numbers of entries are increasing.

15.3 Framework

Figure 15.1 depicts the basic conceptual framework used in our analysis, in terms of the interrelations between three components: the multicultural domestic market, multicultural international markets and the multicultural resources of a society. The *multicultural domestic market* refers to the culturally heterogeneous population and the way it affects the demand for products and services in Australia. *International markets* refer to the culturally-diverse societies that shape the demand for products and services internationally. The arrow from domestic to international markets indicates the way multicultural domestic markets can serve as a testing and learning ground for other markets – a kind of window on international markets. The reverse arrow indicates the way international market demand affects domestic demand through migration and through diffusion of the demand for products and services via cultural networks and identifications.

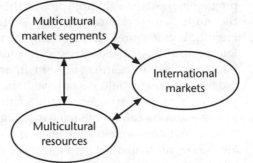

Figure 15.1
The three components of multicultural marketing.

The third component is the *multicultural resources* of Australia. This refers primarily to the skills and resources of its multicultural workforce, but also to other resources that have resulted from the multicultural heritage, such as cultural knowledge and understanding, ethnic organizations and institutions, material artifacts like churches and mosques, and international links and bonds. These resources help Australian-based firms to better understand and serve the multicultural domestic and international marketplace, and attract international businesses to Australia where they will make use of this resource. These interactions are indicated by the arrows linking multicultural resources to the other two elements of the framework. The following sections discuss each of these components and use case studies to show how they are interrelated.

15.4 Multicultural Market Segments in Australia

Cultural diversity affects the demand for products and services in Australia, requiring both the adaptation of existing products and services as well as the development of new ones. Opportunities and problems are created for industry and government.

Two types of needs arising in a multicultural domestic market may be distinguished. First, there are the needs of people from different cultural backgrounds to understand and adapt to the economic and social systems of Australia, including what Chan (1995) has referred to as 'settlement needs'. Attempts to serve these needs are reflected in programmes to introduce and explain to different ethnic communities' various government services, legal systems and the products and services offered in the marketplace. The second type of need results from the values, tastes and preferences of cultural groups and the variations in the role products and services play in their lives. This leads to demand for new types of products and services and the need to adapt existing products and services. These two types of need result in the existence of a rich assortment of customer groups to be satisfied in the domestic marketplace. A single 'ethnic market' does not exist but there are many diverse markets.

There are many examples of the different types of products and services developed in response to this multicultural marketplace. In the area of community services, perhaps the best example is the Special Broadcasting System (SBS) Radio and Television Broadcasting Channel, which was established by the Federal government in the 1970s to cater directly for the needs of the many cultural groups in Australia. The best programmes were sought from around the world and teams of translators, drawn from the Australian workforce, provided subtitles for any programmes not already in English. Furthermore, each morning the main news programmes from a number of European and Asian countries were broadcast (without subtitles), which allowed locals, as well as tourists, to keep in touch with their country of origin. Some programmes that would never have been seen on other channels, became generally popular, such as soap operas from South America. And the nightly SBS news programme quickly gained the reputation for the best coverage of international news – even though they were taking much of their feed from the leftovers of other stations. SBS is now supplemented by numerous community radio stations targeting particular ethnic communities and staffed by locals.

The New South Wales State Department of Fair Trading was the grand winner in the 1997 Multicultural Marketing Awards for its education campaign, introducing the Consumer Credit Code to various ethnic communities (*The Australian*, 1997). The code, launched in 1996, which protects people who borrow money or lease goods, is not the most interesting or easy of topics to communicate. The code operates nationwide but in NSW a campaign was developed to educate five communities that research had shown could most benefit from the code, i.e. Arabic, Chinese, Koori (Aboriginal), Vietnamese and Turkish. As the director of the campaign observed: 'We couldn't just do the mainstream campaign translated into different languages, we had to evaluate needs and then target a community' (*Ibid*.). Through research with the targeted communities, advertising materials were rewritten with culturally relevant concepts, images and designs. Community forums, local radio and the ethnic press were used, with native speakers from the different communities featured. As a result of the campaign, awareness in the community rose from 10% to 53%, especially in the Arabic and Vietnamese communities. Other campaigns designed to educate particular communities about government services include: WorkCover Authority's occupational health and safety information programme directed at the Vietnamese community; an Agricultural Education and Training programme targeted at the Aboriginal community; a School enrolment programme targeting a variety of non-English speaking communities; and a local council library that developed a Chinese language catalogue system.

Health-care services and education programmes have been strongly represented among the Multicultural Marketing Award winners. There have been several anti-smoking campaigns targeting communities such as Greek, Italian and Vietnamese. In each case, culturally-relevant themes and messages were developed. For middle-aged Greek males the theme was 'Someone is Missing', which focused on important family events such as the marriage of children, or the birth of a grandchild, at which the father/grandfather was not present because they had died of smoking-related causes. This family-based motivation was shown to be stronger than a personal health message. For the Vietnamese community, the theme of 'Health is Gold' was used and resulted from the government agency working closely with the community over five years, building links and conducting research (Ethnic Affairs Commission of NSW, 1995a).

In 1996 the grand award winner was the National Childhood Immunization Scheme, designed by the Department of Community Services in conjunction with a specialist marketing agency, Cultural Perspectives. Research identified language, pre-migration experience and socioeconomic access barriers as factors hindering the take-up of immunization in multicultural societies. For example, some children were not being immunized because the schedule in Australia differed from that in the country of origin. A nationwide multimedia campaign in 12 languages was used to reach key communities and was picked up in local ethnic press, with demonstrated success. A public relations campaign working with high profile people who spoke several languages was used as well (*The Australian*, 1996a). Another award winner in the same year was the Kidsafe Child Restraint Programme, targeting migrant communities that had low compliance rates with regulations requiring use of child restraints in cars. Other health campaigns include the HIV/AIDS Education and Support Service, which targeted 16 language groups, and a Sydney-based breast X-ray programme aimed at 50–60 year-old Chinese women.

Banking and financial services are other areas in which a number of successful multicultural marketing campaigns have been developed. The grand award winner in 1995 was the Advance Bank for their Cantonese Quickphone strategy, which was tailored to the needs of the 280,000 Chinese speakers in Australia (Ethnic Affairs Commission of NSW, 1995b). The service is a 24-hour, 7-day-a-week complete banking service. Focus groups and shadow shoppers were used to identify the needs of these customers and the deficiencies in current services. In addition, research was carried out in Hong Kong and Singapore to see how banks were advertised and to identify the types of services offered. Cantonese speakers were commissioned to write copy and key figures from the Australian-Chinese Community were used in the launch.

Another interesting example is the Korean Community Credit Union Incubator project, which resulted in the first new credit union to be established in Australia for decades. The origins of this was the difficulty migrants have in obtaining loans and financial services, because they lack a domestic credit rating. Instalment accounts and small loan accounts were developed by the Korean founder to cater for the needs of the community. The project was closely watched by Korean communities in Chile and China for possible adoption (*The Australian*, 1996b). Other winning campaigns include: the AMP Society targeting savings for children's education in the Chinese community; Westpac Bank's 1996 Lunar New Year campaign targeting the Chinese and Vietnamese communities, making use of numbers that symbolized assured prosperity and the custom of giving money gifts during Chinese New Year celebrations. More generally, banks and other service organizations have become more sensitive to the needs of different communities and have introduced staffing policies designed to match branch staff more with the cultural make-up of the local community. As a final example, the National Australia Bank (NAB) established the annual Ethnic Business Awards to both recognize and celebrate the efforts of non-Australian-born people achieving business success. (*Multicultural Marketing News*, 1991).

Telecommunications services have been adapted to the cultural composition of the marketplace in various ways. In 1995–1996 Optus telecommunications research showed that two-thirds of people born outside Australia make an international phone call at least once a month, which is a sizeable market. Drawing on the expertise of their workforce and working with a specialist ethnic marketing agency, Mosaica, they developed a campaign targeted at the Greek community. Ethnic press and television commercials featuring Greek staff were used to reach the community and a Greek-born local artist was commissioned to do the artwork. In the same year Global One focused on the ethnic community and won an award in 1996 for its campaign targeted at the Chinese community, 'Now Your World is One', which was designed to promote international direct dial services and build brand image (*The Australian*, 1996a). The decision-makers in the community were studied and use made of community organizations and ethnic media to reach target audiences. Support services were also provided, including a customer telephone centre with operators speaking many languages.

Various other types of products and services have been developed or adapted for the multicultural domestic market. One is the introduction of Middle Eastern recipes for dairy products by Chtaura Dairy Products. Starting as a small shop in a Sydney suburb, it carved out a niche making products that cannot be bought anywhere else in Australia, including kishk, a wheat-based yoghurt, drinking yoghurts, dips and exotic cheeses. These products appeal to communities other than the Arabic. The NSW Lotteries agency, the grand award winner in 1993, has developed a series of campaigns targeting various communities, especially the Chinese community, with instant scratch ticket designs and promotions featuring the Chinese Lunar Calendar. Qantas adapted the promotional campaign for its regular flights to Shanghai and Beijing to the Chinese community, featuring lucky number prices and media campaigns adapted to that community.

In education, a high school in a Sydney suburb with many non-English speaking communities teaches its Australian curriculum in science and other subjects in various languages. This is done because language problems can often prevent students achieving their full potential in these subjects, whereas, once they master English, the knowledge they have gained is just as relevant as if it were taught in English in the first place. Lastly, a recently published book provides an inventory of many of the products and services available to meet the needs of different ethnic communities in Australia, and demonstrates how the multicultural domestic marketplace has spawned a rich variety of market responses (Collins and Castillo, 1998). Its subtitle is 'Explore the World in One City'.

Of course, not all attempts at multicultural marketing are successful. Chan (1996) describes a number of examples where firms have used simplistic, inappropriate and mechanical translations of concepts from the Chinese culture in their campaigns. These include the use of particular numbers and colours in everything, however remote. When the Sydney Casino opened a free shuttle bus service for gamblers it used black coloured buses. The unfortunate symbolic significance of this to various ethnic groups, particularly the Chinese, soon became apparent and the colours were changed to gold. The colour black symbolizes bad luck because it is the colour worn during periods of mourning. The promotion of lottery tickets as gifts during Chinese New Year, as has been done by NSW Lotteries, is also questionable, as you are in effect giving away your good fortune (if the ticket is a winner) or giving bad fortune (if the ticket is a loser), both of which are not really sympathetic to the spirit of Chinese New Year. Other examples include crude and inappropriate translations of English language promotions and themes that have no real meaning in the Chinese context. These are the same kinds of mistakes that have been described by Ricks (1993) in international business.

The foregoing examples show how government and private business have recognized and responded to opportunities generated by Australia's multicultural society. They also show how the multicultural workforce plays an important role in helping organizations to recognize, understand and respond. In many cases, existing staff drawn from relevant cultural groups have been instrumental in shaping marketing strategy and use has been made of specialist marketing agencies skilled in researching and developing marketing strategies for various cultural communities. Lastly, the examples show how international market demand influences domestic demand through the introduction of new types of products and services from other cultures, and through research carried out in international markets being used to inform marketing planning in Australia.

In all cases we see the way in which an understanding of the habits, customs and values of a culture leads to the adaptation of marketing strategies in much the same way as occurs in international markets. This includes all elements of marketing: the design and features of the core product or service; packaging design and colours; promotion and advertising media and themes; prices and payment methods; distribution channels; and organizational design. Communication strategies assume particular significance in reaching cultural and language groups. Indeed, the provision of information is itself often the product, as when existing government, community or banking and financial services have to be communicated, or when community health education campaigns are devised for particular cultural groups. Marketing is not just about telling people what you can do for them, but about doing for them what they want done. This involves understanding the needs of the market and developing and adapting products and services to meet them as the cases demonstrate.

15.5 International Markets and Multiculturalism

Multiculturalism in Australia can contribute to the achievement of competitiveness in international markets. Serving multicultural needs at home can play a valuable role in understanding, entering and developing international markets, and the multicultural workforce is a source of direct insight into international markets, as well as a source of social and business links to those markets.

Australia's population is about 18 million, which is a small and isolated market, and this limits the ability of firms to achieve scale efficiencies in production and research operations domestically as a basis for international competitiveness. But while the scale of the domestic market as a whole may be limited, particular market segments can be significant, such as sectors of the mining and agricultural industry. Serving these markets domestically can be a source of international competitiveness and there are many successful international Australian firms operating in these industries. In a similar way, the rich cultural diversity and the associated needs form a special type of market in Australia of significant size. Moreover, there are links between satisfying these needs and developing products and services with international potential, because they provide a window through which firms can learn about the needs and customs of customers in other countries and how best to serve them.

A second reason why the small size of the domestic market may not be such an impediment to achieving international competitiveness is that international competition involves more than price competition. It involves creating and delivering value to customers, and being able to continually upgrade the quality of the products and services offered. This often means working closely with intermediate and final customers. Through the research, feedback and interaction that occurs, competitive products and services are created and improved. In this sense the *quality of demand* is more important than the quantity (Porter, 1990).

It is difficult to work closely with customers in foreign markets because of the physical and cultural distances that exist. However, the demands arising from Australia's multicultural society allow firms to better understand and work closely with customers in Australia who resemble in many ways customers in international markets.

Two types of opportunities may be distinguished here. First, there are the opportunities in international markets for firms that develop, produce and supply products and services to meet the needs of similar cultural communities domestically. For example, public education campaigns, television and radio programmes, English language programmes, health-care systems and other products and services designed for various cultural groups are likely to have potential in their countries of origin. Of course, there is an important caveat, as care must be taken to ensure that the international market does not differ in important ways from the domestic counterpart. Local cultural and environmental contexts affect the character of the market and migrants are not chosen in order to be a representative group of their country. For example, taste tests on migrants coming from particular countries may not always give the same results as those conducted in the home country, due to differences in dietary habits and cooking and eating situations. Furthermore, second and third generation migrant families become assimilated into the local culture, while at the same time helping to shape it. Hence they take on different characteristics from people in their country of origin.

The second type of opportunity relates to the people and firms that supply specialist inputs to those that directly serve multicultural domestic markets, including suppliers of specialist materials, components and services. An interesting example is the case of the subtitling services of SBS, the multicultural television channel, which has been mentioned already. In order to provide subtitles for all the programmes it screens from around the world, it made use of the multicultural domestic workforce to develop a high quality subtitling unit that has gained an international reputation. This led to opportunities to add value to non-English language films and programmes for sale in other English-speaking countries. Another example is the specialist firms that have emerged in Australia to undertake various research and marketing planning activities for clients serving domestic multicultural markets. These include language and translation services, education and training services, and specialist marketing agencies such as Cultural Perspectives, Mosaica, Emigre and 1A Communications. The skills and experience developed in Australia are opening up opportunities in other countries to produce similar campaigns and are attracting international firms to establish regional headquarters in Australia to serve their markets in Asia and elsewhere.

American Express, Cathay Pacific and DEC established operations in Sydney, in part because of the ready access to native speakers of all the languages in the region and the availability of other culturally-relevant services and expertise. Another example is Prestige International, a Japanese company that set up a call centre in Sydney to cater for tourist companies and others needing to handle calls in Japanese. Research indicated the demand for a multilingual call centre service for inbound customer service calls and for outbound telemarketing campaigns. They were able to broaden their operation to include other languages by drawing on the language abilities of the local population. Lastly, Cultural Perspectives, a specialist marketing agency focusing on multicultural marketing, was asked to develop a multicultural communication campaign for the New Zealand Inland Revenue freephone service because of the expertise and experience gained in the Australian market.

15.6   International Relations and Networks

Australia's multicultural society is not only a means of learning about opportunities in foreign markets and honing offers and strategies, it also provides ways of contacting and accessing international markets. Having the right product or service is only part of the problem of succeeding in international markets. There is also the need to develop and manage relations with overseas counterparts in business and government organizations. Research suggests that issues and problems related to this aspect of international marketing are often cited as factors inhibiting or preventing the development of international markets (Cavusgil and Zhou, 1994; Ford and Rosson, 1982; Barrett and Wilkinson, 1985). These include: relations with agents and distributors who are involved in promoting, distributing, and servicing products in the foreign market; relations with government organizations that are involved in approving and regulating commercial activity; and relations with final customers.

Australia's multicultural society creates opportunities for forging stronger international links within Australia and with counterparts overseas. The language and intercultural communication skills, the experience and cultural understanding that exists and the international networks of professional and personal contacts that have been built up cannot be easily duplicated. These help build bridges between Australia and other markets and facilitate intercultural communication, understanding and trade. Examples of this include: a clothing manufacturer considering approaching the Indonesian market used Indonesian staff in Australia to help identify the type of clothes to focus on; Qantas Flight Catering using local chefs drawn from different ethnic backgrounds to prepare food to meet the needs of different international carriers; Qantas employing Japanese native speakers from Australia on Japanese routes and native Chinese speakers on Taiwan and China routes; a Vietnamese migrant with legal training and experience in Vietnam and Australia using his knowledge and contacts to facilitate a major contract with the Vietnamese government.[1]

Universities have be able to build on the strengths and opportunities that arise as a result of the multicultural composition of their staff and students. For example, UWS Nepean has been able to establish a strong reputation in the area of international marketing and business in both teaching and research because of this. The links that have been forged with researchers and universities in other countries support the existing programmes and open up new possibilities for research and teaching collaboration. They also contribute to the internationalization of the university as a whole.

15.7   International Marketing Cases

The Export Category of the Multicultural Marketing Awards provides several cases illustrating the way domestic multicultural resources, networks and markets have led to international market success. For instance, the Lucky Monkey, Lucky Dog, Lucky Ox, etc. 'instant scratchy' lottery tickets, developed by the aforementioned NSW Lotteries to target Chinese and Vietnamese communities in Australia, has been taken up in Hong Kong and other Asian markets.

Techmeat Australia, an award winner in 1994, was started by a Korean immigrant who realized that Australian butchers and abattoirs were discarding cuts of meat considered as delicacies in his home country. He now exports $2 million worth of meat to Korea a year. Established Australian operators could or would not understand what was needed and refused to enter the market. However, Mr Kim was able to take advantage of his Korean meat industry contacts and education to begin exporting. Additional products were later added to the range, including using kangaroo meat offal.

An excellent example of the way different cultures can come into contact and build relations in Australia which eventually translates into export success is Gateway Pharmaceuticals (Ethnic Affairs Commission of NSW, 1995). Gateway is a trading company that contracts the manufacture of various pharmaceutical products to other firms in Australia. One hundred per cent of their business is export. The story of how the company came to be and its subsequent growth illustrates how the skills and experience gained overseas and in Australia, together with Lebanese and Vietnamese networks and good fortune, produced a successful business in Vietnam.

The founders migrated from Lebanon in the 1960s and, early on, arranged for some exports of pharmaceuticals to a relative in Lebanon who was a pharmacist. Later, through the local Lebanese community, they were introduced to a Lebanese pharmacist who operated a large pharmacy located in a suburb of Sydney with a high concentration of Vietnamese migrants. He had observed that many Vietnamese were buying over-the-counter medications, such as vitamin pills, in large quantities. They told him that they were shipping them back to Vietnam for use by friends and relatives and for sale on local markets. With some finance and expertise related to international trade, provided by Gateway, they explored the market potential in Vietnam through Vietnamese community networks, by participating in trade missions and through personal visits to the market.

To begin with, they relied heavily on their contacts within the local Vietnamese community, including how products should be manufactured and packaged and the colours to use. A young Vietnamese lady was employed to do the accounts, export invoicing and many other things. 'A lot of the times we would run things off her and her family. What do you think of this product? Is the packaging okay? We always delved into that pool of resources locally, to launch new products, or to freshen up something old – that resource locally was crucial for us.'[2] She also helped them to understand Vietnamese customs and practices and how to deal with some of the problems that arose.

From humble beginnings the business has grown into a successful export company with a range of products and an established distribution system in Vietnam. In 1998 they had four offices in Vietnam, two in Ho Chi Minh city and two in Hanoi, that together employed 60–65 people. They recently entered a joint venture with the Vietnamese Ministry of Health, that will enable them to manufacture their own products as well as contract manufacture and package the products of multinationals.

The Lebanese background of the directors was perceived as providing certain advantages in developing relations and negotiating with the Vietnamese. 'A lot of times we have to put on our Lebanese cap when we can't do things and purely analyze points of view. You have to go around the situation, you can't confront it head on. I think they have got the charm aspect involved in negotiations. It is not putting the hard word into an order initially, or things like this. You have got to make them truly feel comfortable in your presence and I think a lot of the Anglo-Saxon businessmen . . . come in very hard.'[3]

Hip Hang Trading is a partnership of a seventh-generation Australian and two Chinese-born partners, which resulted in the successful export of building products to China. They were able to capitalize on their complementary skills, understanding and contacts to identify and adapt products and marketing strategies to serve particular markets in China.

The winner of the 1997 export category was the Macquarie investment bank, which developed the China Housing Investment Fund to invest in low-to-medium-cost housing projects in China. The concept was conceived and developed by a multicultural management team, based in Sydney, who speak English, Mandarin and Cantonese, and additional staff were recruited with strong links to the target region in China. Links were established with the Australian-Chinese investment community to source investment funds through a targeted promotion and networking campaign, including a series of dinners and presentations in the community. This campaign had limited success in attracting investment funds from the Chinese community in Australia, in part because the links of the local Chinese community were predominantly with regions of China other than the target region. But the bank's experience in dealing with these communities in Australia, and the contacts made, helped them in later moves into Asia to find investors. Out of a total fund of $35 million, 40% has come from outside Australia, 20% from Asia and 20% from the USA. The Asian crisis at this time limited investment from Asia which would have been much higher. The first joint venture to build houses in China was signed with the State-owned Tianjin Housing Fund Management Centre and funds have been invested in six housing projects in the city with a total floor space of half a million square metres.

JNA Telecommunications designs and develops infrastructure for telecommunications carriers and supplies networks in China, Thailand, Vietnam, Egypt and Syria. In its award-winning entry in 1996, it stressed how it had made use of the skills of its ethnically-diverse workforce to identify business opportunities and market new products. For example, a manager originally from China was moved from another section of the company to make use of her knowledge and language skills. The company has subsequently won significant business in China, and exports have increased from a small proportion to $11 million in 1995. They bring engineers from client companies to Sydney for training, and the ability of a number of staff to offer both technical understanding and language skills makes this training possible.

Cultural diversity has also proved significant in attracting and catering for international tourists in Australia (Office of Multicultural Affairs, 1995). As already noted, the SBS Television Channel broadcasts news programmes each day from many countries. In addition, native speakers, restaurants, shops and organizations catering to the needs of different ethnic groups are easy to find (see Collins and Castillo, 1998).

15.8 Multicultural Resources

As firms in Australia have begun to recognize the potential contributions ethnic diversity can make to their business, they have had to deal with the issues and challenges of identifying, nurturing and rewarding these contributions in appropriate ways. This requires the development of culturally-sensitive managers with cross-cultural communication skills and associated management systems (Shaw, 1995; Elashmawi and Harris, 1998). In the past the focus was often on the problems associated with managing a culturally-diverse workforce, rather than the benefits – and there *are* problems due to variations in customs, practices and the associated communication difficulties. The challenge is to recognize and effectively build on the strengths and opportunities that also arise. Coping with these problems can have indirect benefits, since it leads to improved cultural sensitivity and intercultural communication, both of which are essential ingredients for successful international business operations. Firms that can cope well with cultural diversity at home should be able to cope with it abroad.

However, there are dangers in valuing people too narrowly – in terms only of their cultural background and potential economic contribution. This ignores other aspects of a person's personality and contribution. Another problem is that it is easy to assume that people from particular cultural backgrounds have intrinsic advantages in dealing with their country of origin, when in fact they may face special problems as well. Migrant communities in Australia may stem from particular subgroups or regions in their country of origin, who may be disaffected and persecuted minorities with limited and negative contacts and limited knowledge of other groups in the country. This may inhibit their ability to conduct trade with their mother country. For example, Vietnamese refugees include a number of well-educated and successful business people and professionals, but they came primarily from the South and have closer links with groups associated with the previous US-backed regime. This may limit their freedom of movement and affect the way they are regarded by the current leaders. In addition, people from particular cultural backgrounds may face problems in dealing with other cultures because of the history of relations between them. The relations between the Japanese and various Asian nations, as a result of wartime experiences, is one example of this, as are the hostile relations among various communities of the former Yugoslavia.

15.9 Conclusions

The preceding discussion has focused on the business and market opportunities that arise from Australia's multicultural composition. Particular emphasis has been placed on the value that comes from interrelating different cultures both in Australia and overseas, rather than the value of the diversity itself. In the past, firms in Australia tended to focus more on the problems arising from such cultural heterogeneity. Now they are beginning to value the benefits, particularly in a world that is becoming increasingly internationalized. There are many other nations with distinctive sub-groups, cultures and long histories of migration which have called for marketing strategies adapted to their needs (see, for example, Rossman, 1994). Thus, the framework developed and the examples given should be seen as examples of a far more general phenomena of both practical and academic interest, rather than the next 'buzzword' in marketing education (Nicastro, 1993).

There is a need for more research to be done to examine the relationship between multiculturalism and firms' performance. This article has served to focus attention on the area and provide a framework for thinking about it. While the award-winning cases described serve to demonstrate the nature and role played by multiculturalism in boosting a firm's competitiveness at home and abroad, further research is needed to more systematically measure the nature and impacts of cultural diversity on a firm's behaviour and performance. Also, additional case studies are needed to examine the processes by which multicultural resources are recognised, evaluated and activated within a firm, together with the effects these have on the firm and its performance.

Since the Multicultural Marketing Awards were established in 1991, several developments have taken place in the quality and characteristics of the entries, which we think reflects a growing sophistication and expertise in this area. These developments include:

- A shift away from simple adaptations of predominantly advertising messages as the mainstay of multicultural marketing strategies. This includes a shift from simple linguistic translations of media messages to true cultural adaptations, and to the development, *de novo*, of culturally-targeted campaigns and strategies.

- A shift from simple representations and even stereotypes of some ethnic communities in marketing campaigns to a more sophisticated understanding of the rich cultural diversity that exists among and within ethnic groups.

- A shift from monoculturally-focused marketing strategies to multiculturally-focused strategies which engage a larger slice of society. These include campaigns that have a sophisticated mix and integration of features designed for different, but related, ethnic groups and cultural dimensions, and campaigns, such as Woolworth's and the Australian Broadcasting Commission's station promotion, that celebrate and value aspects of multiculturalism as an essential and natural part of an overall campaign.

- A move away from multicultural marketing as a marginal add-on to a campaign or strategy, to one in which it is either automatically considered or is built directly into the fabric of the overall campaign.

- An increasing appreciation of the benefits that come from harnessing multicultural resources for both domestic and international business development. In fact, the distinction between domestic and international markets is becoming increasingly irrelevant as we come to live our lives in an ever more internationalized and interconnected economy and society.

- A shift from recognizing and adapting to diversity, to one of valuing, appreciating, celebrating and offering the fruits of this diversity. By this we mean offering to the community at large products, services and resources that stem from cultural diversity. These include multicultural products and services (e.g. Chinese massage and acupuncture services), cuisines, music, entertainment and lifestyles that characterize contemporary Australia.

Living and working in a multicultural society like Australia has a fundamental role to play in the nation's future well-being. Despite the associated problems, the everyday interaction of different cultures with different ideas, values, perceptions, customs and practices, produces a kind of 'synergy in diversity'. It helps to broaden our horizons. It acts as an antidote to the dangers of ethnocentrism and helps Australia to become more international and tolerant in its understanding, appreciation of and ability to deal with the world's rich cultural diversity.

REVIEW QUESTIONS

1. What other nations would you describe as multicultural?

2. Find an example of an advertising or marketing campaign targeting different ethnic groups.

3. What factors make people from a particular ethnic or cultural group similar and what factors make them different?

4. How would you develop an anti-smoking advertising campaign for Indian, Chinese and Italian ethnic groups? What type of advertising themes would you use and why? What communication channels would you use?

5. A food company is considering using a panel of Japanese migrants to test a product it is considering launching in Japan. What would you advise?

Notes

1. These examples are drawn from the Australian Trade Commission's Ethnic Communities Programme, which aims to develop exports through ethnic communities.
2. Personal interview, Director of Gateway Pharmaceuticals.
3. *Ibid.*

References

The Australian (1996a) 'Global One focused on ringing in the changes', 21 November: 17.
—— (1996b) 'The community comes first', 21 November: 17.
—— (1997) 'A case of credit where credit's due', 5 December: 19.
Barrett, N. J. and Wilkinson, I. F. (1985) 'Export stimulation: a segmentation study of the exporting problems of Australian manufacturing firms', *European Journal of Marketing* 19(2): 53–72.
Cavusgil, S. T. and Zou, S. (1994) ' Marketing strategy-performance relationship: an investigation of the empirical link in export market ventures', *Journal of Marketing* 58 (January): 1–21.
Chan, A. M. (1995) 'Multicultural marketing in Australia' in K. Grant and I. Walker (eds), *Proceedings of 7th Bi-Annual World Marketing Congress*, Volume 2, Melbourne: Monash University, July 6–10, pp. 71–6.
—— (1996) 'Marketing to Chinese Australians', paper presented at the Multicultural Marketing Conference, Virginia, USA, October 16–19.
Collins, J. (1997) 'Productive diversity: implications for global and local markets', paper presented at Ethnic Affairs Commission of NSW Multicultural Marketing Seminar, Wentworth Hotel, May 1.
Collins, J. and Castillo, A. (1998) *Cosmopolitan Sydney: Explore the World in One City*, Sydney: Pluto Press.
Elashmawi, F. and Harris, P. R. (1998) *Multicultural Management 2000*, Houston, TX: Gulf Publishing Company.
Ethnic Affairs Commission of NSW (1995a) *1994 Multicultural Marketing Awards Report*, Sydney: Ethnic Affairs Commission of NSW.

—— (1995b) *1995 Multicultural Marketing Awards Special Report*, Sydney: Ethnic Affairs Commission of NSW.

Federal Race Discrimination Commissioner (1997) *Face the Facts*, Canberra: Australian Government Printing Service.

Ford, D. I. and Rosson, P. J. (1982) 'The relations between export manufacturers and their overseas distributors', in M. Czinkota (ed.), *Export Management*, New York: Praeger, pp. 257–275.

Harris, F. (1997) *Productive Diversity – Employer Perspectives*, Sydney: NSW Migrant Skills and Qualifications Branch of the NSW Department of Training and Education Coordination.

Multicultural Marketing News (1991) '1991 National Australia Bank Ethnic Business Award Winners – from Italy, Taiwan, South Africa and Holland', October: 4–5.

Nicastro, M. L. (1993) 'Multiculturalism: the next "buzzword" in marketing education?', *Marketing Educator*, Summer: 7.

OECD (1995) *OECD Continuous Reporting System on Migration*, Paris: OECD.

Office of Multicultural Affairs (1995) *Productive Diversity in the Tourism Industry*, Canberra: Australian Government Publishing Service.

Porter, M. E. (1990) *The Competitive Advantage of Nations*, New York: Free Press.

Ricks, D. A. (1993) *Blunders in International Business*, London: Blackwell.

Rossman, M. L. (1994) *Multicultural Marketing: Selling to a Diverse America*, New York: American Management Association.

Shaw, J. (1995) *Cultural Diversity at Work*, Sydney: Business & Professional Publishing.

CHAPTER 16

Cross-cultural marketing for SMEs

Isobel Doole and Robin Lowe

LEARNING OBJECTIVES

At the end of this chapter readers will be able to:

▶ Recognize the various types of SMEs and their role in the economy.
▶ Appreciate the different characteristics of firms that lead to alternative methods of market entry.
▶ Understand the barriers that pose challenges to SMEs in cross-cultural marketing.
▶ Examine the alternative strategic approaches to cross-cultural customer segmentation and understand how these influence the targeting and positioning strategies of SMEs.

16.1 Introduction

There is an apparent dichotomy in the development of small and medium-sized firms (SMEs). For a few of the most successful, growth rates seem to be accelerating as they pursue opportunities across the world at an ever faster pace, driven and supported by the latest advances in information and communications technology. For many other SMEs, no matter where in the world they are situated, competition seems to increase. SMEs that have had a traditional and secure niche in the local business community are increasingly coming under attack from worldwide competition. It seems that no matter how small and specialized the local grocery or bookstore is, it has to compete with the global giants, such as Wal-Mart and Amazon.com.

SMEs have always been of great importance to the local or national economy because they create wealth and employment and frequently initiate innovation, but the majority of smaller firms are a less powerful force outside their home territory. Indeed, many SMEs, despite what may be competitive advantage in the product and service on offer, and significant marketing capability, never move into international markets at all. However, the changes in the international trading environment are increasing the opportunities for SMEs to become considerably more important in the future global economy, both in fast growing business sectors, and in specific market niches, where innovation in mature industry sectors can lead to new opportunities for the smaller firm.

In this chapter, we look at the nature and types of SMEs, the importance of SMEs to their local economy and why it is important to encourage them to market across cultures. In doing this, we explore why and how they become involved in cross-cultural markets and seek to understand the barriers that pose challenges to their internationalization. Finally, we examine the alternative ways SMEs expand internationally and the type of cross-cultural competitive strategies they adopt.

16.2 What is an SME?

A number of definitions of the small and medium-sized firm sector exist, but the most commonly-used terms relate to the number of employees in the company. The European Union, for example, defines a small firm as employing between 0 and 49 employees and a medium firm as employing between 50 and 249 employees.

According to recent UK Government estimates, there were 3,657,885 active businesses in the UK. Of these, 99% employed less than 250 and these small and medium-sized businesses accounted for 56% of employment and 52% of GDP. However, because this classification includes sole operators as well as quite sophisticated businesses, it is not particularly useful for segmenting the smaller firms sector.

In this chapter, therefore, the review of smaller firm strategies is not restricted to firms with a specific number of employees, but, instead, to those businesses in general which think and act like small and medium-sized enterprises. Typically, their strategies are closely linked to their owners' knowledge, capability and ambition. Indeed, they often become the very personification of their owner and are thus strongly influenced by the home country culture. This is something we will be discussing later in the chapter.

The reason for adopting this stance is that, for example, a garment-making firm with 250 employees has a very restricted capacity to internationalize, whereas a 250 employee financial services or computer software company could be a significant international player. Many quite large businesses have operated in the same way for decades, perhaps exporting to the same customers in the same countries for years. They are unwilling or unable to seek out new markets and stick to what and who they know. Such firms take business decisions within the 'inner' management group as they have done for years and in much the same way that family owners of small firms take decisions.

Many of the fastest growing international firms grow very rapidly through the 250 employee ceiling without making significant changes to their international strategic approach. Our discussion in this chapter therefore relates to issues affecting firms which could not be described as multinationals with any real global power. With these factors in mind, SMEs can be categorized as follows.

Marginal/Lifestyle Firms

The vast majority of SMEs provide lower income per hour than is possible from employment in another organization. Examples of this are the small convenience store where the whole family might be involved in the enterprise. When all the hours that are needed to run the business are set against its total income it is not the basis of dreams or riches!

The impact of this segment on the economy is limited because over the long term the number of births of new companies is often cancelled out by the number of deaths. Over shorter periods, however, the segment can be dramatically affected by changes in the national economy in general, and the local economy in particular (for example, if a major local employer closes down and this has a knock-on effect on dependent businesses). New businesses in this sector can have a high displacement effect on the existing business base. For example, there are a relatively fixed number of hairdressers, local shops, car mechanics and market traders that are needed in the local economy and, in order to succeed, the new local businesses have to take customers from the existing firms, so putting them at risk.

Cross-cultural marketing, therefore, has little relevance to the majority of these businesses other than where it poses the threat of competition. In practice, however, a few lifestyle firms find a business formula, sometimes by accident, that is viable in cross-cultural markets, and so the firm becomes more ambitious as the opportunity for growth is realized.

Community Enterprises

Within the community context there is a further issue that is worth consideration in a discussion of cross-cultural marketing. In regions where there are high levels of deprivation or inequality, there are typically particular barriers preventing conventional business starts and growth, such as insufficient demand, shortage of capital, a workforce lacking the right skills and unattractive locations, etc. Increasingly, in these regions government policy is moving towards encouraging self-help activity, for example, by setting up community enterprises that respond to a whole range of community needs. These include: overcoming the barriers to work; inclusion of ethnic minorities into the workforce; training in valued skills; and simply 'getting people off the streets' and away from the temptation of crime. Community enterprises are typically supported by public funds because they are seen as not simply providers of employment, but also as change agents in achieving greater social inclusion, better health, and improved education and housing.

There have been many excellent examples of success in community enterprise, but the main challenge is to overcome the limitations to their growth that is the result of the context in which they have been set up. The challenge for them, as they achieve success in economic regeneration, is how to convert from their initial 'social funding dependency' to become businesses within the mainstream business community.

There are examples of community enterprises that are involved in cross-cultural marketing, both as suppliers to multinationals, as will be discussed later, and, for example, as part of cooperative marketing schemes, but typically community enterprises can be at a significant disadvantage. Whilst they often have first-hand experience of the need for cultural sensitivity in day-to-day operations, they typically lack international management experience.

Attractive Small/Medium Company

A percentage of firms develop a particular competence or capability that allows a stable input of resources, limited growth and a degree of security. Perhaps customers are relatively loyal within the firm's niche, competition may be predictable and modest growth may be possible. Consequently the firm may have the potential to provide significant salaries, employment benefits and a flexible lifestyle. The owner may find the main advantage being 'his/her own boss'. However, the owner typically has limited ambition and capability for managing business growth and may be content with a predictable, but comfortable lifestyle. The danger, of course, with this type of business is that the 'safe' niche may be attacked by a much more aggressive competitor, especially as business becomes even more globalized through e-business.

This segment of SMEs, therefore, faces the challenge of how to develop a sustainable, attractive small/medium business model either by targeting business sectors that are unlikely to be significantly affected by cross-cultural marketing, or by developing a niche product or service for those business sectors that are served by cross-cultural marketers.

High Growth Potential Firms (Entrepreneurship)

Many writers argue that the term 'entrepreneurship' should be applied only to the type of firm that has the potential for rapid growth of sales and profits, and thereby ultimately become a large corporation. A relatively small number of businesses fall into this category. As few as 4–5% of SMEs generate 50% of SME employment growth. It is this type of organization that will be the main focus of our comments on SMEs in this section.

Within this segment are hypergrowth firms that typically experience growth in turnover and employees in excess of 100% over a three-year period. Typically, they identify and exploit a unique and defendable niche in the market and develop products and services that are 'leading edge'. These are the firms that tend to make the news. In the last few years many technologically-based businesses have found it necessary to be extremely ambitious in order to survive and grow and are 'born global'. These companies market their products and services around the world, and thus face the challenges of cross-cultural marketing from the first days of their existence. However, it is likely that the majority of new technology innovations will be relatively less culturally-sensitive, and thus require a less locally-adapted marketing approach than products and services that are competing in more traditional business sectors.

16.3 The Importance of SME Activity in CCM

Of the huge number of SMEs, only a small percentage, perhaps less than 5 per cent, have the ambition and capability to grow significantly. It is difficult to estimate how many of them are likely to be involved in cross-cultural marketing.

The British Chamber of Commerce suggest that 25% of small and medium-sized firms export occasionally and 38% frequently, but only 21% export over half of their turnover. Oldfield (1997) researched the 100 fastest growing firms in the UK and concluded that 50% of these firms did not show evidence of any export activity. He also found that less than 15% of the firms achieved more that 50% of their turnover from exports. Atherton and Sear (1997), in a three-year study investigating the regional competitiveness in the North-eastern region of the UK, estimated that the percentage of SMEs that were internationally active in this region was possibly only 2–3%.

The role and contribution of small and medium-sized firms in the exports of an economy has, however, received increasing attention. The interest reflects both a national government concern with generating greater exports and the increasing focus on competitiveness in cross-cultural markets by SMEs themselves. Government policies, it seems, are geared to improving performance of SMEs on international markets, as a means by which they can generate growth in their economies. In the USA, a significant trade deficit with Japan has signalled the resurgence of political interest. In Australia, where only 11% of small businesses export (Graham, 1999), cross-cultural markets are perceived as offering unlimited scope for SMEs to grow. Austrade, the Australian government trade department responsible for international trade, identified the development of cross-cultural marketing by small businesses as a priority area for support in encouraging growth in Australian SMEs. SMEs which market their products and services in the domestic economy often grow at the expense of other domestic SMEs because of the relatively limited home market, whereas export markets offer seemingly unlimited scope for SMEs to grow.

This is also the case in the UK. In the 1995 *Competitiveness White Paper*, the UK government set a target of achieving 30,000 new exporters in the UK by the year 2000. Despite the best efforts of the authors, it has not been possible to ascertain whether this objective was achieved, or whether its success or otherwise was evaluated. Whether the target was achieved or not, it did serve the purpose at the time of focusing attention on the need for public policy initiatives to enhance the competitiveness of SMEs on cross-cultural markets. This was reaffirmed by the current Prime Minister Tony Blair, who prioritized the need for British firms to improve their capabilities to compete effectively on cross-cultural markets and benchmark themselves against the best in the world.

The SME sector has also become more important as a creator of wealth and employment due to the downsizing in global firms. Large global firms are reducing their workforces across the world, and increasingly concentrating on out-sourcing their non-core components, often to smaller firms. Employment in the public sector has been decreasing during this same period due to the extensive privatization of public sector-owned utilities and agencies, such as gas, electricity, water and telephones. Further, an increased volume of public sector services, such as cleaning and catering, has been contracted out to private organizations. In many countries this has left the small and medium-sized firms sector as the only significant growing source of wealth and employment.

However, despite this many SMEs ignore the potential of their products and services to be marketed across cultures and concentrate instead on their domestic markets. A conclusion of a study carried out in the UK (Doole, Stokell and Lowe, 1996) was that many SMEs regarded exporting as an *add on activity* and so withdrew from international markets when orders in the home market improved or conditions on international markets became unfavourable. By contrast, a small but significant minority succeeded on international markets and showed a strong commitment to further expansion in their international activities. There was little recognition by a number of SMEs of the potential growth through international opportunities. This was again evidenced by Grimes (1998) in a study of 600 SMEs in the Yorkshire and Humber regions. This study found that 13% of firms withdrew from export activity due to the strong appreciation in the value of sterling at the time of the study.

16.4 The Internationalization Process: Motivations and Barriers

As stated above, many SMEs never become involved in cross-cultural marketing activities. A series of research studies has found that it is often a great deal easier to encourage existing exporters to increase their involvement in international markets than to encourage those who are only involved in their domestic markets to begin the process. The reasons given by companies for not pursuing cross-cultural marketing are numerous. The biggest barrier seems to be a fear by some companies that their products are not marketable overseas, and they consequently become preoccupied with the domestic market. Important areas which firms have identified as barriers centre around:

- fear of bureaucracy;
- trade barriers in foreign markets;
- transportation difficulties;
- lack of trained personnel;
- lack of incentive to move out of the domestic market;
- lack of coordinated government assistance;
- unfavourable conditions in international markets;
- slow payment by buyers;
- lack of competitive products;
- payment defaults;
- language barriers.

For many firms, exporting is the first significant step in cross-cultural marketing. It is the stage in the internationalization process where firms recognize that cross-cultural markets provide the advantage of considerably expanded market potential with relatively little commitment and limited associated risk. In many cases, the SME will have overcome significant attitudinal barriers as they begin to look on cross-cultural marketing as akin to looking for new customers in the next town, next state or on another coast. Cross-cultural marketing, when defined as the marketing of goods and/or services across national and political boundaries, becomes the means by which SMEs can seek market expansion.

The recognition by an SME of the need to seek market expansion through cross-cultural marketing may well be a result of proactive searching for market expansion by the firm or, as is often the case, a reaction to potential customers in international markets seeking out the firm as a possible supplier. Katsikeas (1994) identified the following reactive stimuli:

- adverse domestic market conditions;

- an opportunity to reduce inventories;
- the availability of production capacity;
- favourable currency movements;
- the opportunity to increase the number of country markets and reduce the market-related risk;
- unsolicited orders from overseas customers.

Proactive stimuli include market diversification. If a company sees only limited growth opportunities in the home market for a proven product, it may well see market diversification as a means of expansion. This could mean new market segments within a domestic market, but it may well mean geographic expansion in foreign markets. Thus, companies try to spread risks and reduce their dependence on any one market. For example, BF Rail, a firm in the north of the UK, traditionally obtained 90% of its sales from one customer – the company controlling the coal mines in the region in which it was located. When many of the coal mines began to close, BF Rail soon realized that if they were to survive they needed to pursue a strategy of market diversification through international expansion.

Alternatively, the firm may identify market gaps. The proactive company with a well-managed marketing information system may identify foreign market opportunities through its research system. This could, of course, be by undertaking formal structured research or by identifying opportunities through a network of contacts scanning international markets for potential opportunities. Katsikeas (1994) identifies the following proactive stimuli:

- attractive profit and growth opportunities;
- the ability to easily modify products for export markets;
- public policy programmes for export promotion;
- foreign country regulations;
- the possession of unique products;
- economies resulting from additional orders.

And certain managerial elements including:

- the presence of an internationally-minded manager;
- the opportunity to better utilize management talent and skills;
- management beliefs about the value of cross-cultural marketing.

16.5 The Levels of International Development

Firms competing in cross-cultural markets can be categorized by examining the level of international development that they have achieved and their attitudes to competing internationally. The characteristics that they exhibit are as follows:

- *Passive* exporters tend to lack an international focus, perceive export markets to have a high hassle factor, and have little direct contact with foreign customers.

Cross-cultural marketing tends to come from unsolicited orders, but these are rarely followed up by the passive exporter.

- *Reactive* exporters, whilst preferring not to market to different countries, will expend effort on key export accounts. They have only a basic knowledge of their markets and are still undecided on their approach to cross-cultural marketing. Unsolicited orders account for most of their international business.

- *Experimental* exporters are those companies that are beginning to structure their organization around international activities. They make regular contacts with key accounts and offer modest adaptations to their products to meet the needs of different cultures. They tend to actively seek customers in a small number of key markets and are beginning to see cross-cultural marketing as an important part of the business.

- *Proactive* exporters are focused on key cross-cultural markets and devote management time and resources to developing and entering new export markets. Senior management regularly visit different countries to maintain and build relationships with customers. The company will make significant concessions to accommodate the differing cultural needs of the markets. These companies routinely collect and use information to develop long-term strategies and manage risk in international markets. They are used to winning repeat business in key markets and actively seeking to expand their customer base across cultures.

- *Committed* exporters have a strong customer base in a variety of different cultures across the world. This business accounts for the vast majority of annual turnover and is seen to be the cornerstone of the organization. These companies understand what makes their products special in cross-cultural markets and are committed to exploiting their competitive advantage. They often build close relationships with a variety of stakeholders, including key customers, and are willing to make major adaptations to accommodate the cultural needs of foreign markets.

In the early stages of international development, SMEs may treat cross-cultural markets as purely short-term economic opportunities to be pursued in order to maximize short-term profit. As firms become more involved in international markets they treat the resulting business opportunities as strategic to company development. Successful firms invariably build a distinctive competitive position across a range of cross-cultural markets. In examining cross-cultural marketing in SMEs, the type of strategies pursued and how firms build a competitive advantage across a range of markets are therefore important areas of consideration.

16.6 Cross-cultural Marketing Strategies

In exploiting cross-cultural market opportunities to generate revenue from international markets, SMEs have a number of alternative market development strategies that provide a means by which they can develop their marketing strategies in cross-cultural markets. The main alternatives we will consider in this section are as follows:

- *Domestic purchasing*, where an organization purchases the product from the SME locally, then markets or sells the products on cross-cultural markets for them.

- *Exporting*, where the SME is primarily concerned with selling domestically developed and produced goods in cross-cultural markets.

- *Marketing services across cultures*. For small firms a major area of development in cross-cultural marketing is the marketing across different cultures of services that are delivered from the home location.

- *Importing and re-exporting*, where the SME may import goods, add value to them and then re-export.

- *Participation in the international supply chain* of a larger organization. The SME may ride piggyback, using a larger organization to market their products by means of their supply chain partners.

- *Direct marketing*, allowing the firm to market products and services globally from a domestic location. The growth of this area of cross-cultural marketing has accelerated as a result of e-business development.

- *International niche marketing*, where a firm with a highly differentiated product or service overseas is able to maximize its performance in a very small and limited market by targetting a large number of geographical locations.

Domestic Purchasing

Some firms or individuals do not realize that their products or services have potential value on cross-cultural markets until they are approached by the buyer from a foreign organization. The foreign buyer may make the initial approach, purchase the product at the factory gate or from the community enterprise, and take on the task of exporting, marketing and distributing the product in international markets.

Anita Roddick used this approach to source naturally occurring ingredients for Body Shop's ranges of toiletries and cosmetics and make domestic purchasing a feature of Body Shop's marketing activity. Taking a moral stance and demonstrating environmental concern, however, can make the firm a target for detractors and, moreover, relatively unsophisticated suppliers are often difficult to manage.

Whilst for the manufacturer or supplier, domestic purchasing could hardly be called a cross-cultural marketing strategy, it does provide the firm with access to and limited knowledge of international markets. However, the supplying organization is able to exert little control over the choice of markets and the strategies adopted in marketing its products. Small firms find that this is the easiest method of obtaining foreign sales but, being totally dependent on the purchaser, they are unlikely to be aware of the purchasing firm's intention to terminate the arrangement because of competitor activity or a change in consumer behaviour. This can have serious consequences for the community enterprise. If an SME is intent upon seeking longer-term viability for its cross-cultural marketing strategy, it must adapt a more proactive approach which will inevitably involve obtaining a greater involvement in, and understanding of, the markets in which their products are selling. Vignette 16.1 illustrates the impact of a variety of economic factors on community-based enterprises.

VIGNETTE 16.1: Stitching footballs in Pakistan

Sialkot is a major centre for producing soccer balls and it received bad publicity when a journalist exposed local manufacturers who were employing child labour to stitch the balls. In 1997, the Atlanta Agreement was signed and 66 local manufacturers volunteered to stop child labour and allow monitors to check on their production. Now the charity, Save the Children believe that there is almost zero child labour.

Before the agreement most of the cutting and laminate printing was done in factories whereas stitching was outsourced from families around the villages. Now stitching is done by full-time adults in special centres. This had a number of beneficial effects. Saga Sports, which makes 4–5 million balls a year for Nike and other brands now has better control systems, shorter delivery times and lower inventory.

However, the balls are now more costly to make and consumers are not willing to pay extra for adult-only certified products. Chinese machine stitched balls are cheaper and their machine stitching is now suitable for more expensive balls. Indeed, Saga are setting up a factory there. Pakistan's share of the soccer ball market dropped from 65% to 45% between 1996 and 1998. Some smaller producers went out of business and family incomes fell by about 20%.

Exporting

The traditional model of SME international development is exporting, in which goods are manufactured in one country and transferred to buyers in other countries. For many firms exporting is the first significant stage in the internationalization process. It provides the advantage of considerably expanded market potential with relatively little commitment and limited associated risk. For many firms exporting is a temporary stage in the process of internationalization, because they rapidly realize that manufacturing is becoming increasingly less sustainable as a source of competitive advantage. With few exceptions, someone somewhere will always offer an acceptable version of the product at a lower price. Therefore, later stages of internationalization usually involve other market entry methods (Doole and Lowe, 2001).

However, other firms, both large and small, never progress beyond the stage of relatively limited involvement in international markets, and so will always simply follow a strategy of exporting goods to other markets without significantly increasing their involvement.

Marketing Services across Cultures

In the past, the marketing of services across different cultures has largely been the province of the tourism industry, with domestic firms such as hotels, tour operators and leisure attractions generating foreign earnings for the country by attracting visitors. However, with increased international travel and improved access to worldwide communications, a much wider range of services is available to visiting customers across different cultures. Examples include the provision of education, specialized training, health-care, sports, cultural and leisure events and specialist retailing of, for example, luxury goods.

Clearly, these activities lead to wealth and jobs being generated in the local economy in much the same way as exporting and niche marketing. The international marketing strategy processes and programmes are similar too, in that the products and services must meet the requirements of cross-cultural customer segments. Consequently, the issues of adaptation of the marketing mix elements are equally important. The additional challenge is to ensure that the benefits obtained from the service provided must be unique and superior, and thus outweigh the benefits to the consumer of locally-available services in their own culture, as well as the cost of travel that the customers may incur in the purchase process.

Importing and Re-exporting

Superficially, importing appears to be the opposite process to exporting, and as such might be seen by governments as 'exporting' jobs and potential wealth. However, the purpose of raising this issue here is to highlight the nature of international trade as it is today. Rarely do supply chains for products and services involve solely domestic production and delivery. More usually, 'exporting' and 'importing' become inextricably linked, and so the challenge becomes one of adding value to imported components and services, no matter from where they are sourced, so that they can then be re-exported in order to effectively and profitably meet the international customers' needs. Often it is by importing products from another country, or even through outward investment, that a SME is able to achieve a competitive advantage on international markets, as in the case of Flybait.

Supply Chain Internationalization

The pattern of internationalization of firms that are part of the supply chain of a multinational is usually determined by the international strategy that is adopted by that firm. For example, if the multinational company decides to begin manufacturing in a new location, its component and service suppliers may be encouraged to set up new facilities close to the new location in order to ensure continuity of supply. The downsizing that has occurred in many global firms as a response to the global slowdown since 2001 has led firms to think about what was their core competence and answer the question what business are we in? The response to this question led a number of firms operating globally to identify those components and services which were part of the overall product offer, but which they regarded as being peripheral to their business. As a result of this, many of these large corporations have decided to outsource more of their supplies.

Direct Marketing and Electronic Business (e-business)

For smaller firms with limited resources available to set up international operations, direct marketing and, in particular, e-business, offer tremendous opportunities to overcoming many of the barriers associated with developing cross-cultural marketing strategies.

VIGNETTE16.2: Flybait

Flybait produce and distribute a range of fishing tackle products specifically for the game and fly-fishing markets. The company sells exclusively to retailers and specialist distributors. Their principal communication vehicle in cross-cultural markets is their catalogue. They supply a large number of product lines including, fly fishing materials, tools and equipment, floatants and sinkants, fly boxes and tackle bags and a range of rods, reels, lines, nets and fishing products. Their flagship product line is a vast range of over 1500 exotically coloured fishing flies.

One of the main foundations on which Flybait built their international success was a cheap but effective distribution to international markets. The establishment of an alliance has further enhanced this with an assembly operation in Kenya for the production of their *Flies Collection*. This was the range of exotically coloured fishing flies which are now assembled in Kenya and imported to the UK before being sold across international markets. This allowed Flybait access to cheaper raw materials and meant the cost of the assembly of the flies was far less than if the process was carried out in the UK. The flies once assembled are shipped to the UK and then distributed worldwide. This allows the company to achieve a competitive edge internationally in the supply of specialist fishing flies.

Direct marketing offers the benefits of cutting out other distribution channel members, such as importers, agents, distributors, wholesalers and retailers, by using a variety of communications media, including post, telephone, television, networked computers and web-based facilities. All these allow country borders to be crossed relatively easily and at modest cost, without the SME having to face many of the barriers highlighted earlier in this chapter.

Doole and Lowe (2001) suggest direct marketing also has a number of disadvantages. Despite the range of media available, communicating can still be problematic and there is always the danger of cultural insensitivity. Because of the need to manage customers at long distances, it is necessary to use databases which must be up-to-date, accurate and be capable of dealing with foreign languages and cultural complexities. Even an incorrect name can be insulting to the recipient.

It is e-business, based on Internet and intranet trading, which is expected to grow fastest over the next few years. The Internet provides firms with a shop window to the world without a member of staff needing to leave the office. It can provide the means of obtaining payment, organizing and tracking shipment and delivery. For some products and services it can provide the means by which market information can be accumulated; new ideas can be collected, developed and modified by customers and other stakeholders.

E-business has also led firms to redefine their marketing strategies. Many e-business services take the form of information transfer and this forms the basis of the product or service itself; for example, specialist advice on personal finance, travel and hobbies. As well as being a route to market in its own right, in the form of direct commerce, the Internet as an interactive marketing information provider is having an increasingly important role in an integrated communications strategy by supporting face-to-face relationship building.

As an increasing number of SMEs establish relationships with international suppliers, partners, agents, etc., supported by electronic communications, it is becoming clear that those SMEs that are not connected face being shut out of the international business network. The Internet offers the benefits to SMEs of real time communications across distances, and the leveling of the corporate playing field leading to more rapid SME internationalization. It also allows SMEs to build competitive advantage by:

- creating new opportunities;
- erecting barriers to entry;
- making cost savings from online communications;
- providing online support for inter-firm collaboration, especially in research and development;
- enabling lower-cost information search and retrieval;
- the establishment of company websites for marketing and sales promotion; and
- the transmission of any type of data including manuscripts, financial information and CAD/CAM (computer aided design, computer aided manufacture) files.

Small companies offering specialized niche products can find the critical mass of customers necessary to succeed through the worldwide reach of the Internet. Low-cost Internet communications permit firms with limited capital to become global marketers at an early stage in their development.

However, there are some disadvantages, especially the relative ease with which it is possible to become flooded with electronic messages. Moreover, e-business is at early stages of development and many firms are simply trying it to see if it generates sales. Whilst this may be manageable for certain products and services where production volumes can be easily increased or decreased, sales feasts and famines can cause havoc where production capacity is less flexible.

As more firms use e-business it is becoming more sophisticated. For example, search engines are now designed to find the 'best deal' rather than identify every single offer. The implications of this are that instead of marketing being an essentially passive activity for many SMEs using e-business, the marketing input required in designing websites will need to become increasingly sophisticated in promoting the products, providing interactive product design development and safe payment arrangements. Technical and customer service support and initial customer segmentation and targeting are becoming increasingly important to the delivery of an effective, focused business. Thus, whilst many SMEs have, up until now, seen e-business as a low cost distribution channel, in the future greater competition and more sophisticated versions of e-business may well make it more difficult for SMEs to compete.

Niche Marketing

Cross-cultural niche marketing occurs where firms become a strong force in a narrow specialized market of one or two segments across a number of country markets. This means that the market segment in which they operate is often too small or specialized to attract large competitors. Thus, an SME operating in such a segment needs to find many such segments across a range of countries and cultures in order to build a viable marketing strategy. If an SME is targeting a small niche across a number of different cultures, the product or service must be distinctive (highly differentiated) and be recognized by consumers and other participants in the international supply chain as having a clear and distinct positioning.

In order to sustain a niche marketing strategy over the longer term the SME will need to have a good knowledge base of the cross-cultural segments and a clear understanding of the success criteria in the different cultures. It will need to provide high levels of service, carry out small-scale innovations and maintain a separate focus, perhaps by being content to remain relatively small in any one culture. If the firm's objective is to concentrate on profit margin rather than building market share in any one country, this may be the most appropriate strategy. However, this can sometimes mean a firm can face difficult decisions as in the case of Stadium Forgings.

VIGNETTE 16.3 : Stadium Forgings

In 1996 Stadium Forgings was awarded a major contract in Japan, for which the company had beaten a Japanese competitor. This, in the view of the management, was a major achievement and followed eighteen months of hard work and a considerable investment made in both time and resources by the company. They had to undergo rigorous inspection checks as well as make many visits to Japan in order to convince the new client of their credentials. The first 18 months of the contract were highly successful and resulted in a number of repeat orders.

However, in 1998, the strong appreciation of the Sterling currency against the growing weakness of the Yen led the Japanese customer to ask Stadium to readjust its prices for the renewal of the contract due in 1999. Stadium worried this could lead to a loss situation soon developing.

They negotiated, but, in the end, were unwilling to reduce prices to the level required. The reason they were unwilling to lower prices to secure the contract was that they saw themselves as being in the business of supplying high quality precision forgings around the world. This was a small and specialist niche market in which they felt they had built a competitive position world-wide. Their international strategy was based on the principle of focusing only on those markets where they could distinguish themselves from more low priced competitors, and so achieve high margins. Stadium were willing to be flexible, but they were not willing to compromise on this principle and thus responded to the demands of the Japanese, not by reducing prices, but by aggressively seeking new opportunities in other countries where their experience in Japan and the lessons learnt, could be profitably applied.

16.7 The Strategy Development Process

Having considered the various categories of SME cross-cultural marketing strategies, we now turn to the factors which influence the strategic development of SMEs. Whilst there are an infinite number of strategies that an SME might adopt, depending on its particular situation, the principal approach to cross-cultural strategy development follows three stages (normally referred to as segmentation, targeting and positioning – STP marketing):

■ Identification of the various consumer *segments* that exist within the business sector, using the various segmentation methods. It is important for SMEs to define cross-border segments with clearly identifiable requirements that they are able to serve.

■ The firm must then *target* the segments which appear to be most attractive in terms of their size, growth potential, the ease with which they can be reached and their likely purchasing power.

■ In seeking to defend and develop its business the firm needs to *position* its products or services in a way that will distinguish them from those of its local and international competitors and build up barriers which will prevent those competitors taking its business.

International Marketing Segmentation

Market segmentation is the strategy by which a firm partitions a market into submarkets or segments that are likely to manifest similar responses to marketing inputs. The aim is to identify the markets on which a company can concentrate its resources and efforts. In this way, it can achieve maximum penetration of that market, rather than going for perhaps a market-spreading strategy where the company aims to achieve a presence, however small, in as many markets as possible. The two main bases for segmenting international markets are by geographical criteria (i.e. countries) and transnational criteria (i.e. individual decision-makers).

The traditional practice is to use a country-based classification system as a basis for selecting international markets to enter. The Harrell and Kiefer matrix (see Harrell and Kiefer, 1993; cited in Doole and Lowe, 1997) encourages companies to make an assessment of potential cross-cultural markets on an evaluation of both the attractiveness of the country market and the compatibility of that market to the company's strengths. Potential target countries can then be classified into three types:

■ *Primary* markets are the best opportunities for long-term strategic development. Companies may want to establish a permanent presence in these countries and so conduct a thorough research programme. Firms expect to earn at least 30% of export turnover in primary markets.

■ *Secondary* markets are where opportunities are identified, but political or economic risk is perceived as being too high to make long-term irrevocable commitments. As a result, these markets would be handled in a more pragmatic way due to the potential risks identified. A comprehensive marketing information system would be needed to continually monitor the situation. Usually secondary markets account for between 10–30% of export turnover.

■ *Tertiary* markets are the catch-what-you-can markets. These markets will be perceived as high risk and so the allocation of resources will be minimal. Objectives in such countries would be short-term and opportunistic; companies would give no real commitment and would not carry out significant research.

It has long been recognized that SMEs, when operating in cross-cultural markets, identify their primary markets as the ones where they feel most culturally at ease. Thus, the perception of the firm is that the psychological distance between the international market and their home market (known as the psychic distance) is relatively small. In cross-cultural marketing the psychic distance effect is usually a function of the firm's perception of risk and their knowledge of foreign market conditions. Firms will reduce the degree of commitment and risk exposure in markets where the gap is perceived to be much wider and these they term as tertiary markets.

The approach is a particularly useful device for a company operating in a portfolio of markets to prioritize market opportunity. Once the prime country markets have been identified, companies usually use standard techniques to segment the markets within countries, using such variables as demographic/economic factors, lifestyles, consumer motivations, geography, buyer behaviour, psychographics, etc. The problem, however, is that depending on the information base, it may be difficult to fully formulate secondary segmentation bases and achieve consistency across markets. The approach can run the risk of leading to a differentiated marketing approach, which may leave the company with a very fragmented international strategy.

Transnational Segmentation

Doole and Lowe (2001) suggest that if a company is to try and achieve a consistent and controlled marketing strategy across all its international markets, it needs a transnational approach to its segmentation strategy. To achieve a transnational segmentation approach, the country as a unit of analysis is too large to be of operational use. An alternative approach is to examine the individual decision-maker (Walters, 1997) using such variables as demographic, psychographic and behavioural criteria.

Demographic variables have obvious potential as cross-national segmentation criteria. The most commonly used variables include sex, age, income level, social class and educational achievement. Psychographic segmentation involves using 'lifestyle' factors in the segmentation process. Appropriate criteria are usually of an inferred nature and concern consumer interests and perceptions of 'way of living' in regard to work and leisure habits and include activities, interests and opinions. Objective criteria, normally of a demographic nature, may also be helpful when defining life segments. Research International, when researching the transnational segments of young adults, globally divided them into four broad categories. 'Enthusiastic materialists' are optimistic and aspirational and to be found in developing countries and emerging markets like India and Latin America. 'Swimmers against the tide', on the other hand, demonstrate a degree of underlying pessimism and tend to live for the moment and are likely to be found in southern Europe. In northern Europe, the USA and Australasia are the 'new realists', looking for a balance between work and leisure with some underlying pessimism in outlook. Finally, the 'complacent materialists' defined as passively optimistic, are located in Japan.

Behavioural variables also have a lot of potential as a basis for global market segmentation. In particular, attention to patterns of consumption and loyalty in respect of product category and brand can be useful, along with a focus on the context for usage. Variables such as the benefit sought or the buying motivations may be used.

Behaviourally-defined segments may be identified in terms of a specific aspect of behaviour that is not broad enough to be defined as a 'lifestyle'. An example of this is the extremely wealthy travellers who tend to buy the same fashion brands, stay at the same hotels and buy the same luxury products. This group not only includes the wealthy from traditionally wealthy nations, but also those newly rich entrepreneurs from previously closed economies.

Despite the attractiveness of using individualistic characteristics, it is apparent that there is strong potential for significant differences in the patterns of consumer behaviour within global segments derived using this method. Also, international similarities in lifestyle and behaviour do tend to be specific, and relevant primarily to specialist products and niche markets.

Hierarchical Country–Consumer Segmentation

To overcome some of the above problems, a compromise approach would be to implement a procedure for global segmentation which integrated features of both processes. Kale and Sudarshan (1987) have outlined a process to formulate strategically equivalent segments (SES) that transcend national boundaries. On this basis, the marketing strategy would follow the premise that world markets consist of both similarities and differences, and that the most effective strategies reflect a full recognition of similarities and differences across markets rather than within markets. They argue that companies competing internationally should segment markets on the basis of consumers, not countries. Segmentation by purely geographical factors leads to national stereotyping. It ignores the differences between customers within a nation that result, for example, from a greater recognition of the existence of increasingly multicultural communities, and also ignores similarities across boundaries.

It is argued that this approach would enable marketers to design strategies at a cross-national segment level and so take a more consumer-orientated approach to international marketing. In prioritizing markets, companies would use consumers as their primary base. Some writers argue that companies still need a secondary segmentation stage to identify the key countries where these transnational segments can be found and that country environments (legal, political, social and economic) necessitate different marketing mix strategies, such as promotion and distribution, see Vignette 16.4.

Targeting Approaches

For SMEs, the key decision of targeting will therefore largely result from the methodology they have used to segment their international markets. If they have used a culturally- or geographically-based methodology, the major targeting decision will relate to which country markets they are going to select and then how they should develop a market share within each country. Given the limited resources of SMEs and the narrow margin for failure, it is vital that their method of targeting country markets is effective.

Firms that establish a domestic base first, before selecting further country market involvement, develop either through an incremental process of country market diversification, or by concentrating in a few countries following an initial expansion period. In this case, the SMEs may concentrate their activities in a small number of

VIGNETTE 16.4: **Williamson**

Sometimes SMEs may start by segmenting their markets using cultural or geographic criteria and then as they develop their international markets also develop more sophisticated criteria for segmenting their markets. As Europe moved closer towards economic integration, Williamson, a manufacturer of specialist kitchen knives found that retailers were increasingly buying on a European-wide basis. The diversity of brand names and product lines they had built up in order to meet the specific cultural needs of individual markets was becoming increasingly difficult to sustain in a cohesive cross-cultural strategy. They decided they could no longer defend their competitive position in these markets on their existing strategy, and had to refocus their thinking.

Traditionally, in order to develop a strategy to satisfy the varying demands of each market they had segmented the European market on a country-by-country basis. They now started working towards reorienting their international strategy to develop a more integrated approach with a more cohesive and unified brand image: As Mark Darcy, the Managing Director said,

> As Europe becomes more and more integrated then whatever is happening in one market is vitally important to what is happening in another market. You can't consider, for example, Belgium as existing on an island and having nothing to do with what's happening, say in Sweden. You have got to make sure that you're making a similar offering in your policies, they have got to be relevant to the country involved but you do need to be aware of what is happening in other markets.

The first building block of the change in orientation was to move to a customer-based segmentation approach across Europe. Through this process, they identified four clusters across their European markets. At the same time, they undertook a rationalization exercise in the number of brands and product lines offered. The result meant that for each market cluster identified they competed on three price points for each product line:

> Broadly speaking we look for a good, better and best offering in whatever market in which we're operating. In the Iberian cluster, for example, there is a good, better and best offering appropriate to the needs of the market where the best offering is on a par with the good offering in Northern Scandinavia.

The stimulus for the change in their strategy came from critical changes taking place in international markets. They had however, built a knowledgeable understanding of those events and assessed the implications of market changes rather than simply accepting them. They had then reoriented their strategic thinking in the light of those changes and developed a potential solution.

markets in which a significant market share can be built. SMEs often select countries because of the close psychic distance, the network of contacts they have made there or because they are able to piggyback on a larger organization in that market.

Following a market-concentration strategy enables a firm to achieve market specialization, economies of scale, market knowledge and a high degree of control. For these reasons, government support agencies often recommend that small firms follow a market concentration strategy in order to concentrate resources and achieve a greater market share. However, this conflicts with the views of the SME following a niche marketing strategy, where with such a small potential market share in any one market, greater profitability is viewed as being best achieved by spreading across a number of markets.

Many SMEs successfully operating across a number of cross-cultural markets see themselves as operating as international niche marketers, not necessarily as exporters to a particular foreign country market. Consequently, once they have exploited that particular niche, they look elsewhere in order to develop, and for this reason they follow a market diversification strategy. Thus customer development in a number of cross-cultural markets is more important than market share acquisition in the country already entered.

If a firm has used other than geographic or cultural methods to segment their markets, they may well expand into many cross-cultural markets as they only aim to gain a superficial presence in each one and build only a low overall market share. This market diversification approach reduces market risks, enables firms to exploit the economies of flexibility and be more adaptable to different market needs.

Katsikeas and Leonidou (1996) compared the profiles of SME firms that pursued a market concentration strategy with those who followed a market diversification strategy amongst a sample of SME food manufacturers in Greece. They concluded, in their study, that the firms following a market diversification strategy were much more proactive and attached greater importance to the pursuit of building a strong portfolio of international business, whereas market concentrators tended to follow a reactive, or passive, export approach. Thus SMEs operating successfully across cross-cultural markets view their international markets in terms of customers, not necessarily in terms of countries, and so seek those customers in as many countries as possible. This is important as it gives them the means of focusing their strategies towards the needs of their customers and a much clearer view of how their products should be positioned in those markets.

Generic Positioning Strategies

Having identified the target segments, the SME must then develop its unique and distinct positioning by building upon its source of competitive advantage. In order to create competitive advantage, Porter (1985) suggested that firms should adopt one of three generic strategies: cost leadership, which requires the firm to establish a lower cost base than its local or international competitors; a focused strategy, where the firm concentrates on one or more narrow segments and thus builds a specialist knowledge of the target segment; or differentiation, where the firm emphasizes particular benefits in the product, service, or marketing mix, that customers might perceive to be both important and a significant improvement over competitive offers.

It is very difficult in cross-cultural marketing for SMEs to follow a cost leadership strategy or even entertain aspirations of being the cheapest in their markets. Those SMEs that adopt a low-cost strategy to achieve cost leadership can be potentially vulnerable to price competition, either from local firms in the foreign country market or larger multinationals temporarily cutting prices to force the SME out of that market. Usually, successful firms will choose to build competitive advantage by avoiding price competition and focusing on the achievement of margins through focus or differentiation.

This notion was supported by the findings of Pelham and Wilson (1996). Their study, investigating the link between small firm performance and marketing orientation in a longitudinal sample of 65 firms, proposed that small firms that pursued a low-cost strategy tended to emphasize an internal orientation based on cost containment and production efficiencies rather than delivering superior value in the market. Given the limited ability of small firms to pursue a low-cost strategy, superior performance was viewed as being best achieved by delivering superior customer value through differentiated products for carefully selected market niches. Thus, it is not the product strength alone that is a critical factor in cross-cultural markets, but how the firm builds competitive advantage by creating superior value for its customers through its total product and service offer, supported by effective use of the marketing mix.

VIGNETTE 16.5: Trigem

One of the characteristics of fast growth companies is their willingness to innovate, take risks and adapt to a new situation. South Korean company Trigem, a personal computer maker, is a typical example.

Trigem launched its eMachines onto the US market at less than $600 per machine and took 14% of the US market in August 1999. It was able to sell at this price by persuading component suppliers to cut prices in return for bulk orders and faster growth.

In Spring 1999 it launched an Apple iMac look-alike and was promptly sued by Apple in the US and Japan for trademark infringement. This followed a Compac law suit claiming infringement of 13 patents, nine belonging to Intel and coincided with an investment bank report which said that eMachines 'has not even remotely created a business model that is sustainable'. The challenge Trigem faces is whether it can learn fast enough to survive in a sophisticated market such as the US.

Firms seek to differentiate their products from competitors in cross-cultural markets either by product innovation or by adding value through additional services; for example, by offering high levels of customer support and technical advice. SMEs competing in international markets do so with limited resources, and so any cross-cultural marketing strategy they pursue must be developed within that context. Successful firms will invest resources either in developing the capability to add value to their product offering to targeted customers worldwide or in ensuring they maintain superior product performance ahead of competitors worldwide in specific targeted cross-cultural niches.

Many SMEs base their cross-cultural marketing strategy on the generic strategy that has given them competitive advantage in domestic markets, and then attempt to apply this same successful strategy in international markets. Again, however, their limited resources often force them to make a change to their strategy. They may have largely used a pull strategy in their domestic marketing, and thus directed much of their promotional activity at their ultimate customers, whereas in international markets they frequently adopt a less costly push strategy. This means the firm promotes only to the intermediaries in the distribution channel and expects them to promote (or push) the products and services to the final customer.

Of fundamental importance to the development of an effective cross-cultural marketing strategy for some SMEs is having a very strong position in the home country. US firms have benefited from having a huge potential domestic market. By contrast, SMEs from emerging markets, and from countries with smaller domestic markets, often have to export merely to survive. There can, however, be some dangers in entering sophisticated markets without a robust business model as shown in the Trigem case.

16.8   Further Considerations

The primary focus in this chapter has been examining the cross-cultural marketing strategies of SMEs. So far we have examined the varying levels of involvement SMEs have in cross-cultural markets and discussed the need for an SME to select an appropriate segmentation approach to target priority customer groups across cultures. We have also looked at how SMEs establish a competitive positioning. However, central to the achievement of a viable long-term cross-cultural marketing strategy is the way the SME manages it organizational activities across international markets. SMEs have very limited resources to build any organizational structures, and so rely heavily on developing a network of partners across markets in order to implement their cross-cultural strategies. Research has shown that successful SMEs appear to exhibit particular competence in their ability to build and utilize a series of relationships as a cost-effective (time and resources) way of identifying new market opportunities and reducing the risk of entering unknown markets.

A relational strategy is often central to the firm's long-term objective of maintaining their competitiveness in cross-cultural markets over time. Research carried out by Doole (2000), amongst a sample of SME exporters, found such strategies gave the firm a number of strategic advantages by:

- providing access to markets;

- building barriers to entry by competitors;

- improving the level of support to the end-user,

- tying in customers to longer-term commitments to market development;

- improving the speed of access to and accuracy of information on market changes;

- building repeat business;

- providing the connections to hold the cross-cultural marketing strategy together;

- improving the effectiveness of communication links.

Firms build partnerships of varying degrees of intensity and use these relationships to enhance their capability to compete in different cultures. These relationships are valuable for a number of reasons. They help the SME to quickly gain the knowledge and information needed for cost-effective market entry, to build barriers to competition by establishing a locally-responsive, adaptable and flexible distribution channel, as well as ensuring their customers in different markets around the world obtain effective service. The relationships can, therefore, be the firms' major communication link to their cross-cultural markets, both in relaying communications to the market to help build the firm's competitive advantage and relaying information back from the market, which provides input into the decision-making processes of the firm. Relationships are the process by which the strategy is built, organized and implemented; they are the glue, vital pieces of the jigsaw.

Asian firms are typically most committed to relationship development as a central element of their cross-cultural marketing strategy. Indeed, it appears that some Asian firms develop their segmentation strategy around selecting target markets where there are strong cultural ties, as the case below shows (see Vignette 16.6).

VIGNETTE 16.6: **Cross-cultural marketing Chinese style**

Chinese entrepreneurs are developing their cross-cultural marketing strategies by using existing networks of contacts. They operate through a network of family and 'clan' relationships in different geographies, political and economic systems. This approach reflects the Chinese culture and the Confucian tradition of hard work, thrift and respect for one's social network.

This provides the rationale for retaining a small business approach to cross-cultural marketing that is capable of a variety of business solutions at relatively low risk. However, Chinese management recognize the need for innovation and growth, and to encourage greater openness to outsiders if they wish to compete effectively in cross-cultural markets.

Relationship development plays an important role in enabling firms to build the capability to achieve sustainable competitive advantage over the long term. Central to this is that through their relationships firms develop their knowledge base of the changes occurring in cross-cultural markets, thus enabling them to anticipate and deal with the challenges and changes in the marketplace. They use relationships to improve the quality of their decision-making by seeking assurances that the decisions that they make are valid and appropriate for the culture of the market in which they are competing. As the managing director of a firm operating in many different international markets remarked,

> Our information comes from customers around the world, but it's not just customers. Your contacts are in banking and in shipping, and they enable you to actually draw up a picture of what is really happening so you understand the culture of the country, not just what people want you to know.

Networks and relationships can therefore be critical to the success of SMEs all over the globe competing across different cultural markets.

16.9 Conclusion

Traditionally, explanations for the success of SMEs in cross-cultural markets have been sought in the marketing mix paradigm. This has meant the focus of research studies has been on explaining marketing transactions and exchanges, rather than a long-term strategic focus on competitiveness. Thus, traditionally, the literature on cross-cultural marketing for smaller firms has generally viewed marketing as being treated as a tactical issue by the firms, and has neglected concern for such things as strategic positioning, the importance of developing a sustainable competitive advantage, quality issues, customer retention and customer service.

In practice, successful firms develop strategies based on delivering customer satisfaction to their target segments, thus ensuring high levels of customer retention by providing a high quality total product and service offer. In this way, they are able to establish clear positioning that is distinctive compared to local and other multinational competition. Central to the achievement of these objectives is the relational strategy developed by the SME and the success they have in developing an integrated network of partners across the cross-cultural markets in which they operate.

REVIEW QUESTIONS

1. How can the smaller business compensate for its lack of resources and expertise in cross-cultural marketing?

2. Why is niche marketing likely to be a superior approach to export selling?

3. There is a view that success in cross-cultural marketing is determined more by the SMEs' senior management ambition and capability than external barriers, such as bureaucracy, transport difficulties and late payment. What are the arguments for and against this proposition?

4. Explain the advantages and disadvantages of the alternative approaches to cross-cultural market segmentation.

5. Identify the key components of a successful cross-cultural marketing strategy for a SME.

References

Atherton, A and Sear, L. (1997) 'Support for the Exporting SME: current configuration of provision in the North East of England', *20th ISBA National Conference Proceedings*. Sheffield.

Doole, I. (2000) 'How SMEs learn to compete effectively on international markets'. Ph.D.thesis, Sheffield, Hallam University.

Doole, I. and Lowe, R. (2001) *International Marketing Strategy, Analysis, Development and Implementation*, 3rd edn, Thomson Learning

Doole, I., Stokell, N. and Lowe, R. (1996) *The Performance and Perceptions of Exporters*, DTI Publication Report (A) Sheffield; (B) Rotherham.

Graham, P. G. (1999) 'Small business participation in a global economy', *European Journal of Marketing* 33(1–2).

Grimes, A. (1998) *A Study of Export Activities*, DTI.

Harrell, G. D. and Kiefer, R. D. (1993) 'Multinational market portfolio in global strategy development,' cited in I. Doole and R. Lowe (1997) *International Marketing Strategy, Analysis, Development and Implementation*, Thomson Learning.

Kale, S. H. and Sudharsen, D. A. (1987) 'A strategic approach to international segmentation', *International Marketing Review*, Summer.

Katsikeas, C. S. (1994) 'Export competitive advantage: the relevance of firm characteristics', *International Marketing Review*, 11(3): 33–53.

Katsikeas, C. S. and Leonidou, L. C. (1996) 'Export market expansion: differences between market concentration and market diversification', *Journal of Marketing Management* 12: 113–34.

Oldfield, C.(1997) 'Eyretel is leading the charge', *The Sunday Times*, 7 December.

Pelham, A. M. and Wilson, D. T. (1996) 'A longitudinal study of the impact of market structure, firm structure, strategy and market orientation culture on dimensions of small-firm performance', *Journal of the Academy of Marketing Science* 24(1): 27–43.

Porter, M. E. (1985), *Competitive Advantage: Creating and Sustaining Superior Performance,* New York: The Free Press.

Walters, P. G. P. (1997) Global market segmentation: methodologies and challenges', *Journal of Marketing Management* 13: 165–77.

CHAPTER 17

The future of global consumer cultures

Michael Dailey and Susan Carley

> ### LEARNING OBJECTIVES
>
> At the end of this chapter readers will be able to:
>
> ▶ Understand the concept of globalization and its impact on consumer marketing.
> ▶ Understand the factors driving globalization as a worldwide trend.
> ▶ Comprehend that globalization is expected to produce countertrends, namely fragmentation and tribalization of global consumer groups.
> ▶ Grasp how these countertrends might influence consumer marketing in such areas as branding, new product development and market segmentation.

17.1 Introduction

Consider the following real-life scenario: on a recent visit to Guadalajara, Mexico, a Mexican-born colleague and I made a quick stop at the *Gigante Supermercado* near our hotel, hoping to secure an authentic Mexican souvenir for each of our children, and some samples of local candies for our students back in the States. My colleague fondly recalled favourite candies and snack foods from her childhood, describing flavours and textures unfamiliar to the typical American palate. Meanwhile, my sights were set on locating a unique plaything to delight my son's classmates at their next session of 'show-and-tell'. To the disappointment of my companion, the guava candy of her childhood was not to be found among the rows of Hershey bars and Reese's Peanut Butter Cups. The toy aisle was equally disenchanting, containing nothing of local colour or manufacture. We skipped the candy, but settled for a 'Hawaiian Barbie' doll and a Spiderman action figure. For my adolescent daughter, I selected a Spanish recording of (American) Christina Aguilara's latest CD.

Globalization as a fundamentally significant high-level trend is no longer news. The experience recounted above is now commonplace in a world in which sociocultural differences in tastes, behaviour and lifestyles appear to be converging, transforming consumers and their patterns of consumption. Globalization has become a driving force in marketing, leading to growing standardization of products, promotions and distribution to meet the requirements of 'the global consumer'. With this trend unfolding, one might anticipate the marketer's job as becoming less complex as consumer differences subside and homogeneity increases.

The likely reality is more complicated than that. While undeniably a force rapidly altering the world as we know it, globalization is tempered by countertrends less apparent to the casual observer. These countertrends may initially produce smaller ripples, but early detection and understanding of the emerging interactions within this system should prove crucial to global marketers in the years to come.

This chapter explores the interactions and implications of these trends for a probable future, with special emphasis on near- and long-term influences on consumer culture. We will discuss the major trend of globalization and the countertrends of fragmentation and tribalization, then examine a range of implications for marketing in this emerging world. Our approach is one of informed speculation, as is appropriate when discussing the future – which is inherently unpredictable.

17.2 Globalization

Globalization is a broad long-term trend affecting consumer cultures and a majority of social institutions. At the micro-level, globalization is transforming everyday living in such areas as gender relationships, clothing and fashion, the availability and use of time, and the pursuit of material goods. At the other end of the spectrum, globalization influences macro-level institutions, including politics, economics and religion. Save a major wildcard (e.g. nuclear warfare on a worldwide scale, a global ecological disaster or a virulent pandemic), globalization should prove to be an inexorable trend.

A number of factors are driving this trend, foremost of which is the growth of interconnectivity. With each communications innovation – telegraph, telephone, radio, fax, mobile telephony and now the Internet – the pace of globalization has quickened and the world has become 'smaller'. As a result of this increasingly pervasive and broadband interconnectivity, cultural memes (i.e. individual cultural elements, analogous to genes within a gene pool) are spreading further and faster than previously possible.

Demographic trends are likewise contributing to globalization. Migration brings consumers of widely-ranging backgrounds together physically, providing ready opportunities for cross-cultural fertilization (as well as conflict). Migration from less-developed to more developed nations is a common pattern, as people from the former flock to the latter in search of employment and what they perceive to be a better quality of life. In the United States, for instance, immigrants coming across the border from Mexico are beginning to have a noticeable effect on Americans' tastes in music and food preferences, similar to the reverse influence noted in the Guadalajara scenario cited above. On the national scale, the increasing urbanization of populations is further concentrating opportunities for cross-fertilization. The globalization of consumer culture is also driven by increasing rates of marriage outside of traditional ethnic, cultural and religious groupings, a natural occurrence as people have greater exposure to those from other cultural and national backgrounds.

Consumer changes brought on by globalization can also be attributed to the historical spread of market capitalism trade practices, especially since the waning of national communism. Capital markets seek cheap labour, as well as foreign investment opportunities, to a greater extent than ever before. This is exemplified by the considerable international investment in *maquiladora* manufacturing sites near the USA–Mexico border, and the routine outsourcing by US firms of software development and customer service call centres to India. Workers in less-developed countries have benefited from contract manufacturing plants providing employment and better wages, which have permitted them to buy television sets and Internet-enabled computers. The forces of market capitalism and interconnectivity thus interact, further driving the trend toward globalization as consumers in these markets are exposed via various media to the consumption value patterns of seductive, once far-off 'promised lands'.

17.3 Countertrends

Fragmentation

Globalization will probably never reduce the complex human system to a state of homogeneity. Although interconnectivity is increasingly enabling access to information from anywhere on the globe, a common knowledge-base does not necessarily yield a common set of values and common social, economic and political structures.

To this point, increasingly distributed access to information is also driving the countertrend of fragmentation, the breaking down of existing social and consumer groupings. Modern media have fuelled a growing global awareness of alternative sociopolitical arrangements. Television coverage of the war in Vietnam in the 1960s helped polarize public opinion in the United States. Repressive traditional governments and political systems have been liberalizing or falling, to be replaced by increasingly democratic and market-oriented ones. Local and regional insurrections and conflicts, such as those in Tiananmen Square and the former Yugoslavia, have been partially fuelled by fax and e-mail communications, abetted by electronically-enabled solidarity with distant sympathizers.

Fragmentation is a long-term historical trend as well. Many varieties of human systems have been fragmenting for centuries. The old European colonial empires of Africa have fractured, and continue to subdivide along ethnic and religious fissures, as have been governments in Eastern Europe. Major world religions and political parties have also experienced fragmentation; as examples, fundamentalist strains of Islam and Christianity have flourished in recent years.

Tribalization

However, fragmentation, like globalization, does not inevitably proceed toward maximum entropy. If fragmentation may be compared to biological catabolism – the tearing down of tissues – a countervailing anabolic, or building up, trend may be termed tribalization, the re-forming of social and consumer groupings along new axes.

Tribalization, like fragmentation, is also driven by increasing interconnectivity. The Internet allows individuals with shared interests, goals or perspectives to find one another anywhere in the world. The basic human need for affiliation is an important force fuelling this countertrend. Through websites, chat rooms and electronic bulletin boards, the Internet has permitted geographically-separated people to form friendships, romances and even marital partnerships that would not otherwise occur. Users with an interest in genealogy find distant kin in other parts of the globe. Workers converse on a daily basis via office e-mail with colleagues they have never physically met, but with whom they're well acquainted. In ways such as these, fragmentation gives rise to new social groupings based on common purpose or interests, rather than geographical proximity. Unlike their traditional counterparts from days past, these new groups are more likely to be based on achieved, rather than ascribed, elements.

Figure 17.1 illustrates the interrelationships among the three major trends under discussion here. The high-level trend of globalization serves as a broad backdrop to a dynamically counterbalancing complex of fragmentation and tribalization. Driven partly by interconnectivity, fragmentation describes the breaking down of existing groups and institutions. Tribalization can be seen as a dynamic, anti-entropic countertrend to fragmentation, as the constituents of old groupings reform into new patterns and collectivities.

The dynamic cycling of this subsystem of fragmentation and tribalization is not uniform across the global stage. Different geographic regions and cultural systems may proceed at different paces. Fragmentation may overshadow tribalization for considerable periods of time, especially in the geopolitical arena. It is unrealistic to expect stable new political groupings to emerge quickly from the disintegrating Balkan region or postcolonial African states. On the other hand, the United States has been the source of much of the overt pressure toward globalization, and partially as a consequence may reflect more of a balance between fragmentation and tribalization.

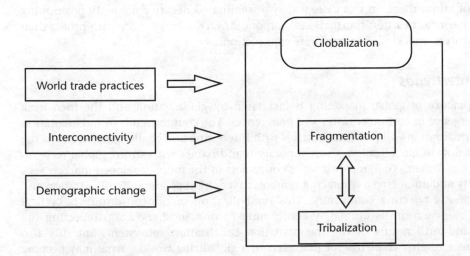

Figure 17.1
Interrelationships between globalization, fragmentation and tribalization.

17.4 Implications for Marketing

Globalization

Now that we have laid the groundwork for a general model integrating the trends and countertrends of globalization, fragmentation and tribalization, driven by interconnectivity and demographics, let us consider the implications for marketing and consumer culture.

As an homogenizing influence, globalization is producing some obvious effects that have been widely discussed elsewhere. As a major overarching trend, it is creating truly global mass markets for certain industries and products (e.g. apparel, consumer electronics and entertainment). Due to its influence, marketers will find more opportunities for global branding and the advantages it delivers (e.g. greater economies of scale and broad appeal to globetrotting consumers). In a globally integrated world, products with strong brand equity will more easily find consumer acceptance, challenging marketers to master the skills of global product/brand management. To the extent that a true 'global consumer' does or soon will exist, positioning strategies for a particular brand will tend to become more uniform. This approach is most relevant now, with the rapidly developing global youth culture. In many ways, young people around the world are more similar to one another than they are to their parents, especially in the area of lifestyle-oriented consumption (e.g. music, clothing and consumer electronics).

For the international marketer, globalization also brings unique challenges, along with opportunities. Consumer interconnectivity and global travel create more problems in the pricing arena, as consumers find it increasingly easy to shop for products employing price as a major criterion. One clear effect of the broad availability of product information and supply via the Internet is downward pressure on price. Widely sought-after global brands also attract the attention of counterfeiters. Intellectual property, patent and copyright issues are providing corporations with growing headaches – witness the legal and public relations problems experienced by global pharmaceutical manufacturers in their attempts to enforce their patents (and thus their high prices) on AIDS medications in relatively disadvantaged nations that cannot afford them. In this case, widely-disseminated negative publicity positioning 'Big Pharm' as heartless transnational corporations, concerned more with profits than saving lives, quickly led to corporate capitulation.

Countertrends

The practice of global marketing is facilitated by globalization and the increasing convergence in consumer tastes and preferences. The countertrends of fragmentation and tribalization will present marketers with interesting and challenging eddies in the broad flow of globalization. Contemporary brand names with strong global recognition (e.g. Armani, Gap) may wither as consumers in the more developed markets seek novelty and uniqueness, embracing symbols that exhibit greater individualization and consciously rejecting conformity. This symbolization of nonconformity is cyclical (with nonconformists ultimately conforming to one another), again reflecting the back-and-forth nature of the fragmentation–tribalization subsystem. But this also produces another challenge for marketers in a globalizing world – what may become an increasingly difficult search for novelty in the face of broadly increasing cultural homogeneity. Research teams for Philips Consumer Electronics, Reebok International, PepsiCo and other transnational corporations are already scouting on the global front, looking for interesting regional variations and cultural memes that can be developed into new marketing themes, styles and products. The producers of the *Sputnik Mindtrends Report* send crews of young researchers armed with microphones and videocameras into the streets of America, searching for emerging cultural memes among diverse youth tribes such as 'club kids', 'body morphers' (piercing and tattoos), 'technoshamanists' and 'new conservatives'. This type of activity will likely become more important as globalization – and the threat of boring uniformity – proceeds toward a greater degree of cultural homogeneity.

One current problem facing those wishing to benefit from globalization is the burgeoning tribalization of those philosophically opposed to the concept, or perhaps its economic enactment. Again, assisted by interconnectivity, numerous constituencies are organizing to resist what is perceived to be the neocolonialism of market capitalism through the actions of the World Trade Organization, the World Bank and the International Monetary Fund. Fears are that developing nations will be used simply as sources of cheap labour and markets for goods and services controlled by and reflecting the particular values of developed – especially Western – nations. This movement is directed against the economic and, to a lesser degree, the cultural and environmental implications of globalization. Concerns involve replacement of local economies with the perceived hegemony of hyperkinetic and impersonal market capitalism, the loss of traditional social support systems, and the exporting of sources of pollution to developing nations.

The dynamic interplay of fragmentation and tribalization will always produce new niche markets and opportunities. Even the social groups arrayed against the perceived evils of globalization represent new tribes with distinctive predilections and needs that will be addressed by marketing in the near future. The business of marketing to the evolving global consumer culture will not involve a simple, mass-market approach. It will be challenging in its requirements for broad environmental scanning to detect emerging icons, styles and 'tribal markets'. But it should also be highly rewarding for those with foresight and a deep appreciation for the dynamics of the interplay of these trends.

REVIEW QUESTIONS

1. What factors have contributed to, or been driving forces behind, globalization?

2. Discuss how globalization might affect each of the following marketing practices: (a) the introduction of new products or services; (b) promotional strategy; (c) pricing decisions; (d) market segmentation; and (e) branding.

3. The authors predict that globalization as a worldwide trend will result in some unanticipated countertrends. Discuss these countertrends and why they might occur.

4. Imagine the world as it might appear in 2020. In your opinion, will global consumers be more homogeneous or more heterogeneous than they are today? How about in the year 2050? Why do you feel this way?

CHAPTER 18

The future and challenges of cross-cultural and multicultural marketing

C. P. Rao

LEARNING OBJECTIVES

At the end of this chapter readers will be able to:

▶ Understand the challenges to cross-cultural and multicultural marketing in the face of changing macro environmental factors, domestically and internationally.

▶ Trace the evolution of multicultural and cross-cultural marketing from an historical perspective.

▶ Explain the complexity of multicultural and cross-cultural issues as applied to marketing and consumer behaviour.

▶ Identify the underlying dimensions of consumption and societal culture and their implications for marketing and consumer behaviour.

▶ Appreciate the nexus between social responsibility and cross-cultural business opportunity.

▶ Explore the pros and cons of integrated approaches to the emerging macro and micro issues in cross-cultural and multicultural arenas.

▶ Understand the relevance of the micro marketing concept to the advancement of information and communication technology.

▶ Appreciate the emerging issues in cross-cultural and multicultural areas and their implications for marketing and consumer behaviour both in domestic and global markets.

18.1 Introduction

In recent years, the marketing discipline has been going through a number of major paradigm shifts. The traditional transaction-oriented marketing is being replaced by relationship marketing. In recent times, segmentation marketing with emphasis on viable segments as target markets is progressively replaced by micro marketing facilitated by the advances in the information, communication and production technologies. As the international trade barriers break down under the World Trade Organization (WTO) regime, global marketing is replacing the dominance of domestic marketing. The global marketing possibilities are also greatly facilitated by the globalization, privatization and liberalization forces sweeping the world economies. In addition to these emerging trends in the marketing discipline, the dominant cultural paradigm in marketing has shifted from dominance of majority culture to multi-cultural and/or cross-cultural marketing.

For both domestic marketing and global marketing, marketers all over the world are being forced to recognize the fact of cultural diversity of marketplaces and how to make their marketing efforts effective in such culturally diverse contexts. From this perspective, this book makes a significant contribution to both cross-cultural market-ing theory and practice. The major purpose of this concluding chapter is to forecast the future and challenges of cross-cultural marketing in the coming years. Any attempts at forecasting the future of a field of study should be based on a critical assessment of the emerging trend in the past. Hence, in the first part of this chapter an attempt will be made to identify and discuss the major streams of research that have emerged in the past with regard to cross-cultural marketing and/or multicultural marketing. Following this, the key issues which need to be addressed to enable the marketers to face the future challenges of cross-cultural and/or multicultural market-ing will be identified and discussed.

18.2 Past Trends

In understanding, analyzing and predicting consumer behaviour for marketing man-agement purposes, the role of culture has always been given a prominent role in consumer behaviour studies, which in turn are expected to facilitate the effectiveness of marketing management efforts. In the post-Second World War years, with the adoption of marketing concepts, marketers started imparting greater consumer ori-entation to their marketing efforts. As a result, consumer behaviour has emerged as a sub-field of marketing discipline. Initially, consumer behaviour research mainly focused on the behavioural aspects of consumers of the majority culture, and that too was limited to domestic country context. Historically, this was the case in the USA, the home of the marketing discipline. However, the marketing phenomenon spread to other parts of the world, either through increasing international trade or through the expanding operations of multinational corporations worldwide. This often led to comparisons between the behaviours of foreign consumers with those of the USA, and thus the initial research efforts into cross-cultural marketing came into existence.

In this type of research study, the emphasis has always been to point out the differences between the consumers of the USA and other Western industrialized countries and the non-Western countries. Concurrently, by the 1960s another trend emerged, especially in the USA, where marketing academicians started paying atten-tion to the consumer behaviours of minority groups in that country. Although subcultures were recognized as a part of any cultural investigation of consumer behaviour, the 1960s and 1970s witnessed significant research dealing with minority groups in the USA, especially the African-Americans (Alexis, 1972; Andreasen, 1975, 1978; Bauer, Cunningham and Wortzel, 1965; Bullock, 1961; Bush, Gwinner and

Solomon, 1974; Surdivant, 1969). This trend of comparing and contrasting the majority culture with specific minority cultural groups, such as the African-Americans, was extended to other minority groups such as Hispanic-Americans and Asian-Americans in subsequent years (Cohen, 1992; Cui and Vanscoyoc, 1993; Czepiec and Kelly, 1983; Delenerand and Neelankavil, 1990; Deshpande, Hoyer and Donthu, 1986; Donthu and Cherian, 1994; Faber, O'Guinn and Meyer, 1987; Mulhern and Williams, 1994; Saegert, Hoover and Hilger, 1985; Valencia, 1983).

In such research studies, there were two dominant research streams. The first research stream dealt with comparing the majority culture with minority cultures. The second research stream dealt with investigating the consumer behaviours of minority groups. The ethnicity and its impact on consumption, and hence its implications for marketing, has been the dominant research theme of many research studies in recent years (Costa and Bamssy, 1993; Cui, 1995, 1997; Green, 1992, 1996; Kaufman, 1991; Rao and Kurtz, 1993; Rossman, 1994). These streams of research continue to be pursued and these facets of marketing have been recognized in recent years under the broad umbrella of multicultural marketing.

Multicultural marketing emphasizes the need for recognizing the cultural diversity in each country when formulating marketing efforts. Similarly, in the global context, cross-cultural marketing emphasizes the need to recognize the cultural diversity across countries. Cross-cultural marketing research forms a significant part of international marketing research. Because of the conceptual similarities between multicultural and cross-cultural marketing and their potential for integration in the future, it is worth noting the significant past trends in this field of study. Inherently, international marketing requires marketing across cultures.

As the international trade started expanding in the post-Second World War years, international marketers started paying greater attention to the cultural dimension of international marketing. Cultural aspects of each country become significant environmental forces that need to be clearly understood by international marketers to effectively market their products and services to consumers and intermediaries in overseas markets.

As the multinational companies expanded their direct marketing involvement in many foreign markets, the cultural dimension of managing their sales organizations has become a major challenge. Historically, cultural anthropologists pointed out the implications of global cultural diversities for international business and marketing (Hall, 1960, 1977, 1990). The early research efforts were primarily directed at pointing out the cultural differences between the Western countries, particularly the USA, and countries in different parts of the world from the perspectives of their implications for international marketing in different country markets or global regions. The early international marketing literature is replete with such 'foreign markets are culturally different' type of research investigations. Such emphasis on cultural differences also resulted in focusing on issues of how to adjust and adapt international marketing efforts to the cultural nuances of diverse global markets.

With increasing international trade and fast-paced expansion of multinational corporations, business operations on a global scale made the experts assert that globalization of markets is taking place, and hence focusing on cultural diversity is not a fruitful approach to effective international marketing (Levitt, 1983). The globalization of markets school of thought emphasized the advantages of standardization of marketing strategies and operations across countries. The proponents of globalization of markets propounded that, because of fast-paced changes in global travel and communications, cultures are converging, especially in the arena of consumption. However, in the following years significant work by Hofstead (Hofstead, 1980, 1984, 1994) revived the cultural diversity issue. Utilizing Hofstead's conceptual schema, numerous empirical studies were conducted in international marketing, whose main theme was that significant differences exist with regard to a variety of consumer, intermediary and employee behaviours across cultures. These opposing points of view of globalization of markets and persistence of cultural diversity resulted in an ongoing debate about standardization versus adaptation in the field of international marketing. After protracted debate and related research on the standardization versus adaptation controversy, the contemporary wisdom in international marketing is 'plan globally and act locally'.

Research into both the fields of multicultural and cross-cultural marketing continues with great vigour. Marketers, both domestic and global, are faced with several dilemmas, such as standardization versus adaptation in international marketing or whether to take an integrated versus separate approach to marketing in multicultural domestic markets. The challenges of cultural diversity both in domestic and international markets continue to daunt marketers. Considerable academic attention has been paid to both the fields of multicultural and cross-cultural marketing. Much of the research in international marketing is devoted to cross-cultural marketing. Some authors suggested that international marketing should be dealt with purely from the perspectives of cross-cultural analyses (Usuner, 1993; Mooiji, 1998).

Concurrently, academic attention to the various issues of multicultural marketing has increased greatly in recent years. Specialized conference series by the Academy of Marketing Sciences have been devoted to the theme of multicultural marketing. There have been several books published in recent years on various aspects of multiculturalism and its marketing implications (Costa and Bamossy, 1995; Seelye and Seelye-James, 1996; Rossman, 1994; Howes, 1996). Given the past research trends as briefly enumerated earlier, what are the future challenges facing these fields of research, so that they can make a significant contribution to the relevant research streams and to related managerial practice? The following pages are devoted to discussing the future and challenges of cross-cultural marketing.

18.3 Integrating Multicultural and Cross-cultural Marketing

In the past, the fields of multicultural and cross-cultural marketing proceeded as separate fields of research investigation. However, given the manner in which marketing practice is carried out, the distinction between domestic versus international marketing is fast disappearing. Domestic markets are becoming increasingly multicultural. Cultural diversity and the marketing challenges posed by such diversity in domestic markets are in no way different from those long experienced in global markets. Unlike in the past, the culturally diverse markets cannot be treated as fringe markets with limited market attractiveness. From the perspectives of both economic opportunity as well as social responsibility, cultural diversity issues in marketing need to be addressed by marketers.

The importance and challenges of multiculturalism are likely to increase in future as political and social identity of various groups in a multicultural society is asserted in democratic societies. Given the similarities between multicultural domestic markets and cross-cultural international markets, researchers should explore the scope for transferability of knowledge gained in one field to the other field. Experiences gained in effectively marketing to a diversity of cultural groups in domestic marketing will be beneficial when extending operations to overseas markets, where marketers also have to deal with a diversity of cultures. Recently, some researchers have started paying attention to this potential of interrelationship between multicultural and cross-cultural marketing (Pires, 1999; Cui, 1997; Wilkinson and Cheng, 1999).

Since the cross-cultural marketing research stream is extensive, there is much opportunity to extend its conceptual and methodological frameworks to the investigation of multicultural marketing issues. Interfacing and integrating these two fields of consumer behaviour studies is bound to yield significant synergistic results for both theory and practice.

18.4   Converging Commonality or Diverging Diversity

In the context of both cross-cultural and multicultural marketing research studies, researchers have been faced with a dilemma for a long time. This is related to the key issue of whether the contemporary consumer behaviour, both in a single country and multiple country context, reflects a converging commonality or diverging diversity. In cross-cultural marketing, the protagonists of emerging global markets have long argued that with growing middle classes in each country as it goes through successive stages of economic development and modernization, common consumption patterns and cultures are emerging worldwide. On the other hand, the culture-driven consumer behaviour proponents vehemently argue that cultural disparity among the countries should form the basis for effective global marketing. In practice, global marketers seem to blend and balance these two extreme points of view and let the situational and contextual considerations dictate the pragmatic marketing actions.

From a research perspective, the field of cross-cultural marketing currently emphasizes cultural diversity more than the evolving cultural homogeneity in global markets. Given this dichotomy between theoretical research and managerial practices, the future research efforts in this field should pay more attention to isolating the effects of converging commonality and persisting heterogeneity of cultures in global markets. As a result of globalization, privatization and liberalization forces create progressively emerging 'global villages'; it therefore behooves researchers to more realistically attribute the impact of culture on consumption, rather than over-emphasizing cultural diversity and attributing every conceivable difference among the diverse global markets to cultural differences.

The dilemma of converging commonality and diverging diversity confronts the field of multicultural marketing too. Historically, the cultural identity of minority groups and its impact on their consumption patterns has been ignored, and in the USA the 'melting pot' theory, whereby all minority groups are presumed to assimilate into the majority culture, has predominated. However, as the minority groups started asserting their identity and gained political and economic significance, the 'melting pot' theory was gradually discarded in favour of ethnic diversity, with an emphasis on difference among diverse ethnic groups in a country. Obviously, ethnic diversity is more pronounced in some countries, such as the USA, Canada, Malaysia, Australia and South Africa. The emerging field of multicultural marketing emphasizes ethnic cultures as distinct and dominant forces shaping consumption patterns of their members.

With this point of view, research in multicultural marketing often emphasizes ethnic differences, especially with majority culture. The effects of cultural assimilation inherent to the 'melting pot' theory are usually ignored in contemporary multicultural marketing research. With increasing emphasis on the ethnic diversity paradigm, other causal factors which effect consumption patterns of ethnic minorities are often ignored. Especially in many developed countries, ethnic minorities are also often economically disadvantaged groups. The latter attribute significantly impacts on the consumption pattern of these groups. But much of the research in multicultural marketing ignores these important economic aspects of consumption and attributes the minority consumption patterns to their ethnic cultural orientations.

Just as in the case of cross-cultural marketing, there seems to be too much emphasis on the role of cultural forces in explaining consumer behaviour of ethnic groups. Just like the emerging middle class in different global markets exhibiting common consumption patterns irrespective of their cultural orientation, the same phenomenon can be postulated in countries with ethnic diversity. A judicious assessment of the realistic role of ethnic cultures, along with other larger forces of cultural assimilation, economic and social status and other possible causal factors should be incorporated in multicultural marketing investigations. As in the case of cross-cultural marketing, future research efforts in multicultural marketing should take into account both the converging commonality forces and the persistent cultural diversity in assessing consumer behaviour in multicultural marketing contexts.

18.5 Consumption Culture versus Social Culture

As argued above, in both the fields of cross-cultural and multicultural marketing, a dominant role is assigned to culture to explain consumption behaviours of national or ethnic groups. However, there is mounting research evidence to indicate that consumption culture is emerging all over the world as a distinct phenomenon apart from the social culture of national and ethnic societies. One may attribute various factors to the development of consumption culture worldwide in recent years. As countries and societies develop economically, material comforts and conveniences are desired and can be afforded by increasing numbers in each group. Consumption of various goods and services becomes a sign of well-being and modernization and members of all societies strive to emulate global consumption patterns. This spread of consumption culture is further facilitated by modern communications, worldwide travel, free trade and expansion of the operations of world's multinational corporations. Also, modern marketing efforts by marketers all over the world, both domestic and foreign, accelerates the spread of this consumption culture.

Obviously, for economic reasons, the extent and strength of consumption culture as a motivating force by itself varies from country to country, and among various ethnic groups within a country. The spread of consumption culture on a global scale has been accelerating in recent years and it is fast spreading from developed industrial nations to less developed countries. The forces of modernism and consumption culture may become stronger motivating forces for behaviour than the forces of tradition, social cultural values and norms. Such transformation from traditional social cultural rigidities to more consumption-oriented behaviours has taken place in highly urbanized and industrialized societies of the world. The same trend can also be observed in different degrees in other parts of the world today.

This emerging consumption culture may be compatible with the traditional norms and values of social culture, or there could be potential conflicts between the two. To the extent that consumption culture is compatible with social culture, marketers do not experience major difficulties in marketing their goods and services. In a sense, the emerging consumption culture reinforces the traditional social culture. But there will be situations where the consumption culture could potentially conflict with traditional social cultural norms and values. These types of situations are often faced by international marketers when they attempt to introduce a variety of products and services in traditional societies.

While the international marketing literature is full of episodic examples of the blunders committed by international marketers (Ricks, 1993), it is known that through their marketing efforts marketers also transform societies to adapt a wide variety of products and services. The spread of fast foods and soft drinks worldwide is just one concrete example of this phenomenon. The result of the spread of consumption culture in a society is that it could prove stronger than the traditional social culture. Of course, both coexist. The potential conflict between the two pointed out earlier may be resolved by keeping them apart. In other worlds, it may be postulated that as societies economically advance and modernization spreads, consumption culture may predominate over traditional social cultures. This does not mean that traditional social cultures will be discarded. But behaviours by people will be compartmentalized, wherein for social behaviour traditional cultural values and norms will be observed, but for buying and consumption of goods and services consumption culture may prevail. In a sense, it can be further postulated that traditional social cultural values and norms may become irrelevant when it comes to consumption-related behaviours.

The growing dominance of consumption culture is further evidenced by the fact that consumption culture promoted by multinational corporations is often resisted by conservative groups in some countries, who feel strongly that their traditional culture is being diluted. What is observed in the global marketing context is also relevant in multicultural country contexts. Given these trends, researchers of both cross-cultural and multicultural marketing have to clearly define the role and strength of culture in relation to a wide variety of consumption-related behaviours. One may surmise that the role of traditional cultural values and norms as forces shaping consumption behaviour, whether in the context of nations or ethnic groups within a nation, is declining.

18.6 Multiculturalism beyond Ethnicity

The rise of consumption culture and its implications for both cross-cultural and multicultural research were discussed earlier. Concurrently, another trend which is resulting in a diversity of consumption cultures which cut across the traditional social cultural groups is emerging. In consumer behaviour research, such consumption subcultures are called 'lifestyle' groups. The emergence of these diverse 'lifestyle' groups, with their distinctinctive consumption orientations, have been initially identified in mass consumption-oriented, industrially advanced countries. However, as the consumption patterns in the rest of the world emerge on the same lines as in the industrially advanced countries, the emergence of 'lifestyle' groups can be observed in many parts of the world. Thus, the members of these 'lifestyle' groups form a variety of ethnic subcultures in the same country and on a global basis from across diverse world cultures. Purely from the marketing management perspective these 'lifestyle'-based multicultural groups are more important for both domestic and international marketers.

'Lifestyle' consumption cultures are typically identified and measured based on traditional economic and demographic characteristics, as well as distinct 'lifestyle' orientations, rather than traditional social–cultural values and norms. The contemporary focus in marketing on such groups as youth market, mature market, singles market, young urban upwardly mobile market, double income no kids market, etc. clearly shows the growing importance of such 'lifestyle'-based consumption cultures.

Traditional cultural values and norms which identify family formation and family life cycle stages as important means for analyzing markets are proving to be inadequate, if not irrelevant. For example, as per the latest census data in the USA, less than 20 per cent of households qualify as a traditional family, if a family is defined as consisting of wage-earning husband, home-making wife and two children. Thus, more than 80 per cent of the household fall into different categories of 'lifestyle' consumption groups. The members of each such 'lifestyle' consumption group are drawn from various ethnic cultures within a country and from diverse cultures across the world.

This emergence of such 'lifestyle'-based consumption groups raises some interesting research issues for both cross-cultural and multicultural marketing researchers. First, are the 'lifestyle' orientations stronger than cultural values and norms in consumption-related behaviours of each 'lifestyle' consumption group? Second, would there be significant differences among different ethnic subcultures within a country and across cultures globally with regard to adoption of the emerging 'lifestyle' consumption orientations? Third, if there is conflict between 'lifestyle' consumption orientation and traditional social cultural values and norms, how do individuals resolve such conflicts in either resisting or adopting the 'lifestyle' consumption orientations? Addressing these and other related research issues in the context of 'lifestyle' consumption groups will significantly contribute to the literature on cross-cultural and multicultural marketing. In a sense, this approach advocates consciously linking consumption subcultures with cultural diversity issues.

18.7 Business Opportunity or Social Responsibility?

Most of the research in both cross-cultural and multicultural marketing fields is typically conducted from the perspectives of facilitating effective marketing to culturally diverse groups of consumers. Focus on business opportunity rather than on social responsibility aspects of both cross-cultural and multicultural marketing has increased in recent years. Most of the research is aimed at investigating the differences across subcultures and cultures so that marketers can adapt their marketing efforts to effectively market goods and services to various cultural groups. But social welfare and social responsibility aspects are important dimensions of both cross-cultural and multicultural marketing.

Early on during the development of literature on multicultural marketing, the importance of the social responsibility dimension was recognized (Andreasen, 1972, 1975; Goodman, 1968; Sexton, 1971; Sturdivant, 1969; Sturdivant and Wilhelm, 1968). This was due to the economic and social disadvantages of the minority groups which were the focus of minority marketing in the 1960s and 1970s in the USA. However, in recent years the focus of multicultural marketing has shifted more towards the issues of exploring and exploiting the marketing opportunities. However, since some of the economic and social disadvantages of a large portion of some ethnic subcultures still continue to persist, the social responsibility dimensions of multicultural marketing need to be brought back into focus.

Similarly, in the context of cross-cultural marketing research the market opportunity dimensions predominate over social responsibility dimensions. But some of the experiences of multinational corporations, such as the Nestlé corporation experience with baby formula in developing countries, point out that cross-cultural marketing research exclusively focusing on business opportunity to the exclusion of social welfare and social responsibility issues could be detrimental, especially in the developing countries. In the light of the growing disparity between the rich and poor countries in recent years, the social welfare and social responsibility dimensions of cross-cultural marketing research should receive equal focus along with the market opportunity dimensions.

18.8 Integrated or Separate Approach to Marketing?

The conventional wisdom in both the fields of cross-cultural and multicultural marketing is that marketers should always adapt to the cultural uniqueness of cultural groups, either in the domestic market or in the global market. But this conventional wisdom can be challenged by the fast-emerging consumption culture which seems to cut across diverse cultural settings. In addition, costs of adapting to a diversity of cultures, in either domestic or global markets, may often result in competitive advantage.

This dilemma of whether to standardize or adapt to each cultural setting has been going on for more than a quarter of a century in the field of international marketing. In international marketing, the contemporary wisdom seems to be 'think globally and act locally'. The emergence of consumption culture, which was discussed earlier, supports the opportunity and the need for greater standardization of marketing plans and programmes, both in the domestic and international markets.

In multicultural marketing research, there was some concern about mixing diverse cultural groups because either the majority or the minority cultural groups may get alienated by such integrated approaches (Block, 1972; Bush, Hair and Solomon, 1974, 1979; Cohen, 1992). However, as cultural diversity increases and as the middle class segment of each cultural group grows, there will be increased acceptance of cultural diversity and simultaneously a decrease in cultural prejudice. These emerging trends of cultural empathy, tolerance and appreciation are further promoted by intensified global communications and international travel. Taking advantage of these trends of 'cultural co-existence', both in domestic and international contexts, some companies, e.g. British Airways, are opting for more integrated marketing efforts. This argument does not preclude the relevance of certain cultural traits such as langauge, religion and symbolic communications for effective marketing purposes. But past and current research in the fields of cross-cultural and multicultural marketing mainly focuses on cultural differences to the total exclusion of consumption commonalities.

As consumption culture spreads and the middle class grows, one may hypothesize that there will be increased 'cultural integration'. Considerable research in cross-cultural sociology clearly shows the commonality of motivations, attitudes, aspirations and lifestyles of middle-class people across societies. Such emerging common consumption cultures provide expanding market opportunities for both domestic and international marketers. Research needs to focus on these emerging commonalities of consumption. At the same time, the proper role of cultural subtleties and nuances should be assessed and their proper role for practical marketing purposes determined. Merely seeking and emphasizing differences across cultures may not be consistent with emerging trends of consumption culture, and the marketers need to find possible commonalities for pursuing standardization strategies and cost reductions. From these perspectives it is suggested that future research efforts in cross-cultural and multicultural marketing should be focused more on integrative aspects of consumption culture rather than exclusively focusing on the separateness of social cultural identities.

18.9 Multicultural Micro-marketing

Advances in information technology (IT) and communication technologies are enabling marketers to resort to more direct marketing. Historically, mass marketing was replaced by segmentation marketing. But contemporary marketing practice is moving in the direction of replacing segmentation marketing by direct marketing. Data-based marketing and Internet marketing are enabling marketers to reach customers directly across the globe. Such technology-driven marketing, both in domestic and international markets, has interesting implications for cross-cultural and multicultural research studies. First, if the customers are willing to utilize IT and communication technologies as a means to interact with marketers in the purchase of goods and services, they are likely to exhibit common consumption behaviours, irrespective of their cultural contexts. Of course, there will be individual differences with regard to their motivations, attitudes, preferences and brand loyalties, etc. But under database and Internet direct marketing, the unit of analysis is the individual customer rather than a cultural segment, either within a country or across the globe.

This is not to say that individuals are not affected by their cultures. Certain aspects of the use of information and communication technologies, such as confidence to use, privacy, security, perceived risk, etc. will vary across cultures. But the marketers will be able to assess the individual differences with regard to these behavioural traits with the vast amount of information they gather and process about individual customers across cultures. If such direct marketing, based on information technology and communications technologies, is going to the future wave of marketing, research needs to carefully assess what should be the role of cross-cultural and multicultural studies aimed at helping marketers both domestically and internationally. The opportunity for multicultural micro-marketing opens up new vistas for research in both cross-cultural and multicultural marketing areas.

18.10 Conclusions

In recent years, marketing discipline has gone through significant paradigm shifts. Consumer behaviour has emerged as a subdiscipline within the marketing discipline (Sheth and Parvatiyar, 2002). Culture is always considered a very important aspect of consumer behaviour. The cultural dimension of marketing and consumer behaviour resulted in two distinct streams of research – cross-cultural research across world cultures and multicultural research within specific countries. In the past, both these streams of research mainly emphasized the differences among the cultural groups researched, either in the global context or within a country, and the implications of such intercultural differences for marketing management purposes.

However, there is growing evidence that increasing integration across cultures both within a country and across countries is creating an emerging common consumption culture. Such a consumption culture is exhibiting greater commonalities, especially among the middle-class segment, across all cultural groups. These developments call for greater integration of cross-cultural marketing and multicultural marketing research streams. By integrating these fields of research, greater synergy can be achieved to benefit the development of more relevant research for the benefit of marketing practice, both at the domestic and international levels.

In the past, in both cross-cultural and multicultural marketing research studies, there was undue emphasis on cultural diversity and on emphasizing the implications of such diversity for suggesting adaptive marketing. But cultural integration, especially at the consumption level, seems to take place both in global markets and in domestic markets. Hence, future research needs to look carefully into the extent of such converging commonalities and clearly specify of the extent of divergence which is still relevant for marketing management purposes.

In most of the earlier research into cross-cultural and multicultural studies, the assumption was that social cultural values and norms strongly impact consumer behaviour in various cultural groups. But 'consumption culture' seems to emerge as distinct from social culture. People in different cultural groups may be compartmentalizing their consumption and social behaviours separately. In a sense, 'consumption culture' seems to develop across the world independently of social cultures. This dichotomy between consumption and social behaviours needs to be taken into account in future research studies dealing with cross-cultural and multicultural marketing.

Within the emerging 'consumption culture', diversity of 'lifestyle' groups seems to impact consumer behaviour rather than ethnic orientation. This development calls for deviation from a strictly ethnic orientation to a more 'lifestyle' orientation in future cross-cultural and multicultural marketing studies. At the very least, the relative roles of each of these forces need to be critically evaluated before making recommendations based on research mainly premised on ethnicity.

In most of the literature on cross-cultural and multicultural marketing, the major emphasis has been to investigate the cultural differences and point out the implications for exploiting the market opportunities. But the social responsibility and ethical issues are equally, if not more, important for cross-cultural and multicultural marketing, especially with regard to socially and economically disadvantaged ethnic groups within a country and diverse cultural groups in less developed countries of the world. It is suggested that future research efforts should pay greater attention to the social responsibility and ethical dimensions of the issues involved.

Finally, the advances in information technology and communication technologies are enabling marketers all over the world to reach customers on an individual basis through their micro-marketing strategies. Because of such direct micro-marketing opportunities, researchers concerned with cross-cultural and multicultural marketing should explore the implications of these technology-driven marketing practices in both domestic and global markets.

REVIEW QUESTIONS

1. How would you describe the roles and importance of cross-cultural and multicultural marketing in the face of changing macro environmental factors domestically and internationally?

2. What would you consider to be the most important underlying dimensions of consumption and culture and their implications for marketing and consumer behaviour?

3. Identify and discuss the most important pros and cons of integrated approaches to the emerging macro and micro issues in the cross-cultural and multicultural arenas.

4. How relevant are micro-marketing concepts to the advancement of information and communication technology?

5. What do you feel are the most critical emerging issues in cross-cultural and multicultural arenas? And what implications do they have for marketing and consumer behaviour in both domestic and global markets?

References

Andreasen, A. R. (1975) *The Disadvantaged Consumer*, New York: Free Press.

Andreasen, A. R. (1978) 'The ghetto marketing life cycle: a case of underachievement', *Journal of Marketing* 15 (February): 20–28.

Andreasen, A. R. (ed.) (1972) *Improving Inner-City Marketing*, Chicago: American Marketing Association.

Bauer, R. A., Cunningham, S. M. and Wortzel, L. H. (1965) 'The marketing dilemma of Negroes', *Journal of Marketing* 29: 1–6.

Block, C. E. (1972) 'White backlash to Negro ads: fact or fantasy?', *Journalism Quarterly* 49 (Summer): 258–262.

Bullock, H. A. (1961) 'Consumer motivations in black and white, I and II', *Harvard Business Review* 39 (May–June): 89–104; (July–August): 11–24.

Cohen, J. (1992) 'White consumer response to Asian models in advertising', *Journal of Consumer Marketing* 9 (Spring): 17–27.

Costa, J. A. and Bamossy, G. J. (eds) (1995) *Marketing in a Multicultural World: Ethnicity, Nationalism and Cultural Identity*, Thousand Oaks, CA: Sage Publications.

Cui, G. (1997) 'Marketing strategies in a multi-ethnic environment', *Journal of Marketing Theory and Practice*, Winter: 120–127.

Delener, N. and Neelankavil, J. P. (1990) 'Information sources and media usage: a comparison between Asian and Hispanic subcultures', *Journal of Advertising Research* 30(3): 45–52.

Deshpande, R., Hoyer, W. and Donthu, N. (1986) 'The intensity of ethnic affiliation: a study of the sociology of Hispanic consumption', *Journal of Consumer Research* 13: 214–220.

Donthu, N. and Cherian, J. (1994) 'Impact of strength of ethnic identification on Hispanic shopping behavior, *Journal of Retailing* 70(4): 383–393.

Faber, R. J., O'Guinn, T. C. and Meyer, T. P. (1987) 'Television portrayals of Hispanics: a comparison of ethnic perceptions', *International Journal of Intercultural Relations* 11: 155–169.

Gentry, J. W., Jun, S. and Tansuhaj, P. (1995) 'Consumer acculturation processes and cultural conflict: how veneralizable is a North American model for marketing globally?', *Journal of Business Research* 32(2): 129–139.

Glazer, N. and Moynihan, D. P. (1963) *Beyond the Melting Pot*, Cambridge, MA: Harvard University Press.

Goodman, C. S. (1968) 'Do the poor pay more?', *Journal of Marketing* 32: 18–24.

Green, C. L. (1992) 'Ethnicity: its relationship to selected aspects of consumer behavior', *Southern Marketing Association Conference Proceedings*, New Orleans, pp. 4–7.

Hirschman, E. C. (1981) 'American Jewish ethnicity: its relationship to some selected aspects of consumer behavior', *Journal of Marketing* 45: 102–110.

Hofstead, G. (1984) *Culture Consequences: International Differences in World Related Values*, Beverly Hills, CA: Sage Publications.

Howes, D. (ed.) (1996) *Cross-cultural Consumption: Global Markets, Local Realities*, London: Routledge.

Hui, M., Joy, A., Kim C. and Loroche, M. (1993) 'Equivalence of lifestyle dimensions across four major subcultures in Canada', *Journal of International Consumer Marketing* 5(3): 15–35.

Kaufman, C. J. (1991) 'Coupon use in ethnic markets: implications from a retail perspective', *Journal of Consumer Marketing* 8 (Winter): 41–51.

Laroche, M., Kim, C., Hui, M. K. and Joy, A. (1996) 'An empirical study of multidimensional ethnic change: the case of the French Canadians in Quebec', *Journal of Cross Cultural Psychology* 27(1): 114–131.

Levitt, T. (1983) 'The globalization of markets', *Harvard Business Review*, May–June: 92–102.

Paranjpe, A. C. (1986) *Ethnic Identities and Prejudices: Perspectives from the Third World*, Leiden, The Netherlands: Brill.

Rao, C. P. and Kurtz, D. L. (1993) 'Marketing strategies for reaching minority markets', in R. L. King (ed.), *Minority Marketing: Research Perspectives for the 1990s*, Chicago: Academy of Marketing Science, pp. 1–7.

Ricks, D. A. (1993) *Blunders in International Business*, Cambridge, MA: Blackwell Publishers.

Rossman, M. L. (1994) *Multicultural Marketing: Selling to a Diverse America*, New York: American Management Association.

Schaninger, C. M., Bourgeois, J. B. and Buss, W. C. (1985) 'French–English Canadian subcultural consumption differences', *Journal of Marketing* 48 (Spring): 82–92.

Seelye, N. H. and Seelye-James, A. (1995) *Culture Class: Managing in a Multicultural World*, Chicago: NTC Business Books.

Sexton, D. E. (1971a) 'Do blacks pay more', *Journal of Marketing Research* 8: 420–426.

Sexton, D. E. (1971b) 'Comparing the cost of food to blacks and to whites – a survey', *Journal of Marketing* 35 (July): 40–46.

Sexton, D. E. (1972) 'Black buyer behavior', *Journal of Marketing* 32(10): 36–39.

Sturdivant, F. D. (1969) *The Ghetto Market Place*, New York: Free Press.

Sturdivant, F. D. and Wilhelm, W. T. (1968) 'Poverty, minorities and consumer exploitation', *Social Science Quarterly* 49: 643–650.

Tse, D. K., Belk, R. W. and Zhou, N. (1989) 'Becoming a consumer society: a longitudinal and cross-cultural content analysis of print ads from People's Republic of China, Hong Kong and Taiwan', *Journal of Consumer Research* 16 (March): 457–472.

Wallendorf, M. and Reilly, M. (1983) 'Ethnic migration, assimilation and consumption', *Journal of Consumer Research* 21 (December): 293–302.

Williams, J. D. and Qualls, W. J. (1989) 'Middle class black consumers and intensity of ethnic identification', *Psychology and Marketing* 6(4): 263–368.

Cultural values in retailing

Ogenyi Omar and Charles Blankson

C7.1 Introduction

International airport retailing and the air transport industry have undergone significant change over the past three decades. The total number of passengers travelling by air has continued to rise, and there has also been a significant change in the demographic composition of those travelling (Freathy and O'Connell, 1998). Air travel no longer represents the exclusive preserve of the privileged few. Charter airlines and discount operators have entered the market seeking to provide a low-cost air transportation service. In response to the increasingly competitive nature of the airline industry, the way in which airports are managed and operated has also fundamentally changed (Omar and Kent, 2001). In Europe in particular, a greater ascendancy has been given to the role of commercial activities within the international airport environment.

Retail has been at the forefront of this development and the number and types of retail unit found in international airports such as London Heathrow has increased dramatically. Many airports retailers have sought to expand their product range beyond the traditional categories of liquor, tobacco, perfume and confectionery. International airport retailers have found themselves having to purchase products for a diverse range of consumer groups and negotiate with suppliers over a wider portfolio of product categories.

The value of fashion to most consumers is to develop a sense of personal identity through a contrast between their perceived fashion orientation and that of others in their culture and social settings. This self-identity construct constantly helps to define and measure self-image through perceived contrast to others. This chapter explores the ways that air-travelling consumers within the airport environment use fashion values to inscribe their fashion purchase behaviour in a complex ideological system of self and society. Phenomenological interviews with outward air-travellers concerning their perceptions and experiences of fashion are interpreted, with specific consideration given to cultural issues. We found that by appropriating fashion perceptions, consumers generate personal fashion values that express dominant fashion norms in their social milieu, and in consumer culture at large. We therefore concluded that consumers also transform culturally-based fashion values to fit the circumstances of their specific social settings and their sense of personal history, interests and lifestyles.

C7.2   Contextual Background

Airport retailing is relatively new and is growing rapidly due to increases in passenger movements, higher average spend per passenger, and a large increase in the amount of retail floor-space. The market could be segmented into two sectors: duty- and tax-free, which account for nearly 80 per cent of sales, and 'tax and duty paid' (including catering), which represent the balance. This research is conducted entirely on the 'airside', where passengers are exposed to duty- and tax-free goods. Outward travellers' purchasing of fashion accessories is restricted to airside stores.

Airport shopping centres to a large degree follow the well-established urban speciality shopping centre role model (Wash, 1992), with specialist branded anchor stores and retail stores providing a homogeneous mix of tenants and their merchandise, tuned to the needs of their travelling customers. The British Airport Authority (BAA), that operates and manages Heathrow, is determined to create a shopping area that looks and feels like a shopping centre, rather than a collection of shops (Newman *et al.*, 1995). Such an environment with large comfortable seating areas ensures customer relaxation – the assumption being that relaxed customers quickly get in the mood to shop.

Kent and Omar (1996) found several limitations surrounding airport purchasing of fashion items, including the ability of travelling customers to carry what they bought as hand luggage on board; the ability of the customer to try on the item before purchase; the ability to pay for purchases quickly and easily (no long queues); and the ability of sales staff to understand the customers (some foreigners speak English with pronounced accents). They observed that tight customer targeting is implicit and essential, noting that these limiting factors are accompanied by increased costs in terms of staff training, security and opening hours.

Despite these limiting factors, there is a force operative in the determination of an airport store's customer body besides the obvious factors of airport environment, duty- and tax-free price ranges and merchandise. Kotler (1974) identified this force to be the store personality, referring to the way in which an airport store is defined in the minds of travelling customers (Doganis, 1992), partly by its functional qualities and partly by an aura of psychological attributes (Newman *et al.*, 1995). Although airport retailers must be concerned with the more concrete factors, intangible features play a crucial role in attracting fashion purchasing and operationally differentiate cultural values in fashion selection within the airport environment.

In keeping with their different personalities, airside stores attract different types of fashion clientele (Doganis, 1992), and customers choose the store whose overall image best fits the image they hold of themselves (Newman *et al.*, 1992). For example, shoppers who identify themselves with various social classes may choose to shop at stores of different fashion status from others. Thus, while the purpose of this article is to analyze the meanings that consumers use to interpret their experiences and conceptions of fashion which provide entry into a complex system of cultural meanings encoded in conventional ways of talking about fashion (fashion discourses), an important part of the study deals with some assumptions about cultural values which prompted the purchase of fashion at Heathrow.

Rather than reflecting a solely culturally-dominant view of fashion purchasing, current cultural values present a multitude of countervailing interpretative positions that reflect the historical legacy of an ongoing social dialogue over the societal consequences of fashion phenomena. And, because they are democratic, pluralistic and multicultural sites, airport stores are most suited for this investigation. Through this legacy, the concrete issues of dress, clothing tastes and public appearances have been encoded in a panoply of theories, concerning topics such as the morality of consumption, conditions of self-worth, the pursuit of individuality, the relation of appearance to deeper character traits and the dynamics of social relationships (gender role, sexuality, standard of taste, economic equality and social class standing).

C7.3 Theoretical and Conceptual Framework

In view of their diverse associations, and diverse perceptions of the airport environment, the perception of fashion values provide travelling consumers with a plurality of interpretative positions which can enable them to compare opposing values and beliefs. Outward-bound consumers use these countervailing values of fashion to address a series of paradoxes existing between their sense of individuality and their sensitivity to sources of social prescription in their lifestyles (Kent and Omar, 1996).

Hetrick and Lozada (1994), analyzed the historically-established cultural meanings manifested in consumers' interpretations of fashion phenomena, and noted that the ways in which consumers use these countervailing values to create personal understandings of fashion vary widely between individuals with the same cultural background. According to Pitta *et al.* (1999), culture and expectations within cultures affect all business transactions in that different cultures have different rules of conduct. However, as the authors put it, one problem in dealing with cultures is that it is difficult to define universally. The authors claim that culture represents the values and patterns of thinking, feeling and acting in an identifiable group. Within the international context, culture represents how people in a civilization interact with one another. The Western fashion pattern and its corresponding images diffused by mass media (Sparke, 1995) and television advertising (Lury, 1996) has often been interpreted as an important basis of the ideology of fashion consumption throughout the world. This is despite diversities in cultural attire usually based on profession, religion and ethnicity.

However, Rubenstein (1995), basing her argument on this critical perspective, observed that fashion perceptions and values indoctrinate consumers in the ideology of fashion consumption. Faurschou (1987), on the other hand, commented on fashion as 'the logic of planned obsolescence, which is not just a necessity for market survival, but the "cycle of desire" itself, the endless process through which the body decoded and recoded, in order to define and inhibit the newest territorial space for capital expansion.' Both Jameson (1991) and Bordo (1993) argued that the ideological process discussed by Faurschou immerses consumers' self-perceptions in cultural meanings and social ideals that foster a depthless, materialistic outlook, and a perpetual state of dissatisfaction over a particular current lifestyle and physical appearance.

In contrast to this indoctrinating view, Thompson and Haytko (1997) posit that fashion discourses are used by consumers in a number of creative and proactive ways that do not reproduce a single, hegemonic outlook. Arthur's (1993) hypothesis was that the countervailing meanings manifest in complex patterns of social relationships, such as gender roles, enable consumers to engage in novel juxtaposition and creative reworking of dominant values. In a similar spirit, it could be inferred that the airport store consumers' use of fashion discourses are intertextual (de Certeau, 1984), and incorporate a wide array of cultural views, including those that express countervailing tendencies to the ideology of consumption. By juxtaposing and combining these countervailing values, travellers shopping at the airport stores may construct interpretations of fashion phenomena that often run against the doctrine of ideological influences frequently attributed to the high-fashion ethos of glamour and celebrity.

Social theorists (Belk and Pollay, 1985; Leach, 1991; Bocock, 1993) have argued that the ethos of glamour has facilitated the emergence of the consumer-driven capitalist economy by widely diffusing an image of 'the good life' based on the attainment of material affluence. The supposition here is that this high-fashion glamourization may have contributed to the celebrity status ascribed to leading fashion models. Within the context of the airport environment, however, high fashion offers a salient image of the extraordinary and glamorous world of fashion that passengers distinguish from the ordinary and practical nature of everyday wear. The extraordinary quality and glamour attributed to the airport stores' fashion accessories (Kent and Omar, 1996) encourage impulse purchasing.

A significant range of scholarly activities (Wolf, 1991; Lague, 1993; Nemeth, 1994; Ingrassia, 1995) have implicated the fashion industry in the United States and in Western Europe in a plethora of societal problems afflicting women, including eating disorders (Fallon, 1990), reduced self-esteem (Probyn, 1987), body image distortion (Richins, 1995), and increased predilections for cosmetic surgery interventions (Stephens *et al.*, 1994). According to Thompson and Hytko (1997), these critical narratives have now attained widespread circulation through newspapers and popular women's magazines that present stories revealing the inner workings of fashion imagery, such as the manipulation of appearances through make-up, lighting and photo retouching. As discussed by Rabine (1994), women's magazines usually present conflicting ideologies instead of functioning as a seamless web of oppression. However, it can be argued that the advertising images of women's fashion magazines reproduce the traditional perceptions about the importance of women's appearance and the imperative to enhance attractiveness through clothing, cosmetics and dietary regimes.

C7.4 Sources of Information

Data were generated by means of phenomenological interviews (Thompson *et al.*, 1989) at Heathrow airport with 50 outward travellers who purchased items of fashion at the airport stores located on the airside. Only the outgoing passengers were interviewed for this study. It was not deemed necessary to interview the inward passengers because many of them would have shopped at the departing airport stores. Any traveller who did not purchase items regarded as fashion accessories was not interviewed. Interviews were conducted in August 1998. All participants in the study were assured of anonymity. Participants' pseudonyms and their residential status (UK or overseas) formed the base for analytical evaluation and discussion. The participants were travellers (i.e. consumers) of varying age groups and nationalities. They were simply classed as UK or overseas residents (see Figure C7.1).

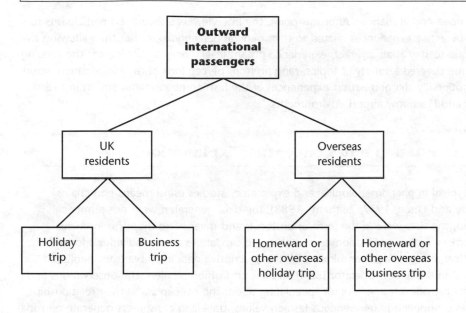

Figure C7.1
The structure of
passenger domicile
and purpose of
travel.

The interviews were characterized by a conventional quality in which the participant set the sequence of the interview dialogue. Rather than following a predetermined format, the interviewer's questions were formulated in concert with a participant's reflections and were directed at bringing about more thorough descriptions of specific fashion and airport experiences (Zeithaml, 1988). The interviewer's probes and follow-up questions were informed by a general familiarity with the research domain and insights gained through the process of interviewing. However, the primary aim of the interviews was to allow each participant to articulate the network of meanings that constituted his or her personal understanding of fashion and the airport shopping phenomena (Thompson and Haytko, 1997).

Participants were informed prior to each interview that the purpose of the study was to gain an understanding about their feelings, experiences and perceptions related to choice of fashion at the airport stores. Each interview was audiotaped and transcribed verbatim. The length of the interviews ranged from twenty to forty-five minutes. Each interview was conducted in a departure waiting area on the airside. Interviews were conducted separately by two researchers (one male and one female), who were experienced in this interview technique. Each of the interview dyads had the same gender pairing, on the assumption that this matching would facilitate personal discussions about positive and negative experiences of airport fashion shopping phenomena.

The interviewers sought to create a context in which the participants felt comfortable and at ease in discussing their experiences and perceptions of fashion at Heathrow. The interviews began by attaining general background information about the participants (their occupations, personal interests, destinations). Following this, the interviewer shifted to the topic of fashion with the questions: 'When you think of fashion, what comes to your mind?' and 'Is buying an item of fashion at the airport stores of any significant meaning to you?' In keeping with phenomenological interview techniques (Thompson et al., 1989), these opening questions were designed to begin the dialogue in an open-ended manner. After this point, the interviewers encouraged participants to describe actual experiences related to their general perceptions, rather than allowing the dialogue to stay at an abstract, experience-distant level. For each participant the ensuing dialogue covered a variety of topics, ranging from perceptions of the high-fashion world to emotionally-charged airport experiences of the fashion phenomena arising in their social and Heathrow airport environments.

C7.5   Evaluation and Conceptual Explanations

As is typical in phenomenological and exploratory studies using means-end chains (Jacoby and Olson, 1977; Zeithaml, 1988), the data generated were not numerical. Instead, the data were in the form of protocols and means-end maps for individual consumers. Patterns of responses and observed similarities across individuals form the analytical results. When combined with the descriptive data available from published sources on the airport operator (BAA) and airport fashion retailers, the observations and insights provide a framework for speculating about the concepts and their relationships .

By appropriating heterogeneous fashion values, travelling consumers generate personal fashion narratives and metaphoric and metanymic references that negotiate key existing tensions and often express resistance to dominant fashion norms in their social milieu. Consumers' interpretative uses of fashion perceptions create emergent values that reflect a dialogue between their personal objectives, lifestyles, fashion-specific interests and the multitude of countervailing cultural values associated with fashion phenomena.

Using the passenger domicile structure and the purpose of travel categorization (Figure C7.1), airport fashion purchasers were grouped into fashion conformists and anticonformists, and their fashion purchase behaviour was reconciled through the contrasting interpretations of fashion in terms of glamour or triviality. While fashion conformists are highly sensitive to the opinions of peers and are fashion followers rather than leaders (Joy and Venkatesh, 1994), anticonformist narratives express a theme of autonomy and independence (Webb, 1994). The anticonformists tend to moderate the paradox that the desire to be a self-directed individual is usual and normal in the UK (Lewis and Hawksley, 1990). This mythic idea of identity construction through the uniqueness of one's consumption choices has long served as a promotional theme for mass-produced items of fashion. Heathrow Airport has taken this aspect of fashion retailing seriously by expanding fashion retailing opportunities (allowing more and varied retailers) and limiting environmental constraints (creating a pleasing and conducive shopping atmosphere).

The Residents of the United Kingdom (Domestic Residents)

Items of fashion sold at Heathrow reflect the dramatic, exciting and stimulating space of the airport shopping environment and the preferences of air passengers. The UK residents travelling overseas, either on holiday or on business, were able to compare airport prices with those of high street stores. They bought mainly British items of fashion deemed suitable for use abroad, including swimwear, sportswear, T-shirts, shorts and underwear. Leisure (holiday) travellers exhibit impulse (unplanned) purchase behaviour and tend to start their holiday spending at Heathrow. It is obvious that the items of fashion that sell well at the airport are those that cross the cultural boundaries.

Most business travellers tend to buy items of fashion as gifts for overseas friends and business colleagues. They were more likely to buy jewellery (brooches, rings, wristwatches, bracelets), scarves and hankies. A large majority of business travellers are familiar with the merchandise sold at Heathrow. The motive for buying these items of fashion at the airport varied, but the general motivating force included the duty- and tax-free prices; as one traveller responded: 'I understand and I can compare the prices of items sold at the airport. But you can't go wrong when you buy this stuff in a duty- or tax-free store. They're worth the money. Every sensible person bought something even if they don't need them just yet.' A female traveller emphasized the 'Englishness' (British culture) in her response when she said: 'I always like to show my foreign friends that I am English through the clothes I wear while I am there. So if I find fashionable summer wear at Heathrow I always buy it. The prices are reasonable for the quality. I'll say fashion here is very good value for money.' It could be inferred from these responses that both cultural association and price (value for money) are among the key motivating factors for fashion purchasing at Heathrow Airport.

Overseas Residents

These are passengers that are either travelling home (place of origin), or to other overseas destinations on holiday or on business. The items of fashion purchased by these groups of travellers appeared to be culturally and/or religiously based. For example, it is possible that some African and Arab males prefer to wear their traditional attire, while women wear clothes that symbolize their faith. Similarly, Asians purchase items of fashion that reflect their customary accepted fashion. Although these groups of travellers will buy fashion oriented to their culture, they also buy British attire for special or occasional wear abroad.

Cultural Dimensions

Cultural analysis of fashion (Finklestein, 1991) has often emphasized its psychological role in fashioning the 'self-concept'. Admissions by some respondents (mainly overseas residents) suggest that the type of fashion (colour and style) they buy reflects their cultural value and societal acceptance of what is fashionable. On the other hand, a statement from one of the respondents that 'when you are around people who really place emphasis on fashion and they are all looking good, it sharpens your skills, you can become a critic and you can take criticism', demonstrates that fashion plays a prominent role in creating an entire sphere of social relationships, even if the material is purchased at the airport. This particular customer in an airport environment seems to have interpreted the sense described by Jenkins (1992), in which fashion sensibilities were discussed within a socially negotiated set of rules of interpretation and aesthetic standards.

Another passenger, an African woman, described fashion as an interpretation of social practices centred on dress which provides a set of meanings that encode a history of social relationships significant to her self-identity. In her words, 'if you see me, you should know which part of the world I come from by the nature, colour and style of my dress. People usually dress to suit their culture. I wear what is acceptable and expected of a woman of my age.' Her statement demonstrates that the sense of dressing for oneself is not so much a matter of being a strong-willed, inner-directed individual, as it is dressing to fit into a culture that is symbolically present, but distant from her current airport environmental setting. Similarly, a Chinese gentleman remarked that 'what I am wearing now is good for English weather and environment, it is also good for travelling. It is not really a Chinese type of clothing, so I do not wear this at home.' One may infer from his statement that fashion response represents a relevant community of interest that can transcend a temporary and spatial setting. Theoretically, a subject can therefore sustain a valued sense of social identity by dressing in accord with fashion norms and standards relevant to a phenomenologically defined reference group that may be far removed from the national peer group.

The Role of Gender

The fashion-specific manifestations of general cultural predisposition are always more complex than can be represented by general descriptions of the social construction of femininity and masculinity alone (Stern, 1993). Several of the male respondents (both UK and overseas residents) in this research expressed a definite interest in fashion and appearance, and had purchased one or more items of fashion from the duty- and tax-free stores.

Nevertheless, airport fashion purchasing did invoke gender distinction that expressed differing relationships. Thus, a number of issues that were focused in the interviews with female respondents simply did not arise in those with male respondents. While female respondents were concerned with issues related to fashion, physical appearance and the potentially negative consequences of the 'beauty myth', men were not sensitive to beauty ideals of fashion – at least, not conventionally.

Whereas male airport fashion purchasers insistently treated the representation of masculinity in fashion imagery as a non-issue, women interpreted fashion's beauty ideals as being far more consequential to their self-identity. They also expressed a multitude of differing and ambivalent interpretative relationships to these images. These differing gender relations with respect to airport fashion purchasing are consistent with social dimensions of masculinity and femininity in English culture. Whereas girls socially acquire sensitivity to appearance and fashion (Cooke, 1996), boys socialize within a system of cultural meanings that do not forge such a strong and direct link between physical attractiveness, fashionability and self-identity (Bordo, 1993).

C7.6 Discussing the Main Issues

This study has focused attention on fashion purchasing behaviour at Heathrow Airport, basing the argument/comments on a consideration of countervailing cultural values. It has assessed the ways in which travellers derive personal perception and subsequent behaviours of items of fashion purchased and evaluated through the countervailing fashion norms. Through this value appropriation, travellers compare self-image and societal norms in making their purchase.

Fashion-specific interest consumers usually associate the world of everyday fashion with a nexus of professional and family obligations, constraints and societal pressures to conform to a particular lifestyle mould. At Heathrow Airport, this social contrast seemed to have enabled young travellers to associate items of fashion with a rebellious, youthful and unencumbered identity. Their narrative of youthful differentiation offers a personal expression of Lakoff's proposal that an underlying general motivation for fashion consciousness is a desire to sustain a sense of personal uniqueness in the relatively depersonalizing milieu of modern social life (Lakoff, 1987). This desire is not a generic form of uniqueness, but rather a specific sign of distinction within a particular social typification, such as being a 'suit-and-tie' family person. A number of airport high-fashion purchasers express this desire to be unique, autonomous and independent, though the wish is not formulated in terms of nonconformity. For non-UK residents, fashion purchasing is uniquely associated with what is acceptable within their native or adopted cultural environment.

In its project of glamorization, the world of high fashion provides an image of success that can be used to generate enjoyable moments of fantasy and dreams for the future (Holbrook and Hirschman, 1982). On the other hand, in trivializing the interpretation of fashion, shoppers at Heathrow can assume a moralistic, inner-directed stance by appropriating a set of anti-fashion meanings that paradoxically have often been incorporated into the promotional themes of fashion merchandising (Davis, 1992). The rejection of fashion (anti-fashion styles) is a sign of positive moral virtues, such as seriousness of purpose, sensibility and rational self-directedness. The rejection of 'fashion' in this way differs in its motivation from the rejection of fashion due to its non-compliance with a native culture. Cultural rejection is based on traditional values (Firat and Venkatesh, 1995), while anti-fashion style is based on personality traits or a traditional nonconformity of 'protestant' groupings (Borgmann, 1992).

The purchasing of fashion in an airport environment is the action of an individual traveller organized in a manner that allows for at least some sense of collective identity and the maintenance of some degree of social order. Although ideologies (held beliefs) can reproduce social inequities (Sparke, 1995), they can also benefit the individual (de Certeau, 1984) by providing rules that enable them to negotiate the complexities of social life. As the evidence of these interviews might be seen to suggest, fashion ideologies emerge through a conscious or unconscious dialogue between shoppers, who interpret the conditions of their everyday lives and the countervailing cultural norms. In their purchase decisions for use in Britain, overseas residents tend to be influenced more by the value of everyday wearable and stylish fashions than by price.

The fashion values and the stated reasons for fashion purchase at Heathrow, as expressed in these interviews, encoded tensions among historically-predominant traditional beliefs and contemporary views that exist in response to fashion changes. This uneasiness included issues relating to traditional and non-traditional gender segmented roles, socially recognized class and race barriers to social mobility within British society.

Travelling consumers' purchase of fashion items at Heathrow was therefore related to complex interpretations, due to different frameworks of perception, from which they ascribed meanings to their fashion behaviour and different choice motivating factors – identified as 'value for money', 'brand quality' and 'suited to cultural norms'. For both UK and overseas residents (men and women), the interpretation of fashion value in relation to countervailing culture serves as a tool for resisting the perceived pressure of conformity exerted by cultural norms. Retailers, for their part, tend to use this interpretation as a goal for fashion advertising and marketing efforts. For most British women, however, the comparison of fashion values based on cultural acceptability is almost a thing of the past. Prominent cultural ideals are no longer compatible with modern feminine appearance and fashion projected by the media. On the other hand, women of other nationalities interviewed for this study strongly adhere to their culture in purchasing items of fashion, despite the radically changing culture.

The British women's fashion image interpretation cultivates a sense of defiance towards the culturally-accepted fashion style in Britain. But most women did not see this feminine resistance as a radical transformation in their fashion perception that reflected an escape from the influence of their cultural beliefs. Their opposition is simply conforming to countervailing cultural values. Thus, young people may refuse to wear what was once regarded as culturally-accepted wear.

In general, some travellers' conformity to the interpretation and understanding of fashion is suggested by culturally-dominant fashion perceptions, while other travellers attribute critical oppositional meanings to those selected aspects of fashion they deem relevant to an everyday (casual) lifestyle. These diverse interpretations do not express a view independent of the overall ideological structure of fashion, which can and does include them. Rather, juxtaposing and combining countervailing fashion values form resistance or submission to fashion. In this way, travellers who spend little time at Heathrow make use of the ideological tensions among culturally available fashion perceptions to articulate a personal sense of fashion that may even run against the norm of what they see as a dominant fashion orientation of their social setting. Conversely, the use of ideological meanings enables their own engagement in the world of fashion through preferred styles, body aesthetics or social identification to be interpreted as an anti-fashion and self-directed orientation.

The purchases of those air travellers who bought on impulse could be described as conforming to an ethos of modernity representing the sanctity of individuality and self-direction. These travellers had expressed a demonstrable preference for a modernist design aesthetic by rejecting unrealistic fashion styles. It is this rejection which segmented fashion purchase behaviour into those who buy for everyday use (for example, professional, religious or national wear), and the glamourized (impractical) fashion as seen in the fashion shows. However, fashion purchase at Heathrow is associated with the Heathrow retail environment being perceived by travellers as an iconic home of fashion modernity. The atmospherics and the affective environment all simultaneously create a tantalizing imaginary world of high but practical fashion, resulting in impulse purchasing.

Finally, the travelling participants in this study exhibited a fair degree of diversity in terms of their ethnic, socioeconomic and geographical profiles, and were all grappling with a number of issues typical of airport travellers, such as anxiety, anxious waiting and impulse shopping. These localized Heathrow considerations were useful to the researchers because they served to heighten the relevance of airport fashion shopping phenomena. The Heathrow environmental setting is also conducive to the aim of analyzing how airport fashion choice may be based on the appropriation of countervailing cultural values, and influenced by impulse buying, but without marketing input considerations (because advertising, etc. is less of a factor). Meanwhile, the applicability of this airport-based account to other retail contexts remains a question that will have to be addressed by future research.

C7.7 Management Implications

Despite creating a relaxed shopping environment, airport retail managers and strategists will probably have to offer more merchandise which are multiculturally based in the mid- to higher ranges, and less in the highest range. Value for money is very important as travellers look for famous brand name quality, but at the 'right' price. The importance of effective management in the multicultural environment has recently been echoed by Pitta *et al.* (1999), who stated that: 'it is vital for Western marketers to understand the expectations of their counterparts around the world . . . understanding cultural bases can arm a marketer with knowledge needed to succeed in cross-cultural business'. Airport retail management will have to adopt a strategic collaborative approach with their concessions, and share more of the risk and less of the reward. BAA must bring interesting and innovative retailers into Heathrow shopping centre, to avoid the risk of ultimately boring the customers. New entrants into airport retailing will have to tune their fashion offers accordingly. However, as airports and retailers are just beginning to get their tenant and merchandising mix right in the airside shopping centres, a new conduit for air travel retail distribution is emerging, including the onboard innovative, integrated, interactive entertainment system.

C7.8 Conclusion

Travellers in this study have described Heathrow as an upmarket shopping centre without the value-added tax (VAT). Although it is the world's busiest international airport, Heathrow is renowned for traffic delays and for being crowded. Nevertheless, it is perceived as a shoppers' paradise. After the passport and security check, Heathrow resembles the classiest shopping mall, with high-quality branded merchandise at duty- and tax-free prices. For most holiday travellers, duty-free shopping represents an added holiday saving.

Heathrow as a fashion-retailing environment with iconic status is a place imbued with symbolic images capable of evoking influential emotions. Thus, the notion of flying from Heathrow has undisputed elements of luxury and glamour, even for regular travellers. This favourable customer state-of-mind generates excitement, resulting in a positive mood to shopping. The actual fashion-purchasing act is dependent on cultural and fashion factor acceptability within the countervailing traditional norms. Thus, the Heathrow shopping environment is particular in terms of the effect it has upon individual travellers. Persons of UK residency exhibit differentiated fashion purchase behaviour at Heathrow, depending on the purpose of the journey (holiday or business). Overseas residents purchase items of fashion to wear while in Britain or to take home as a sign of having been to Britain.

ACTIVITY

1. The British Airport Authority (BAA) that operates and manages Heathrow Airport is determined to create a shopping area that looks and feels like a shopping centre rather than a collection of shops. Comment with suitable retail examples on why it is necessary for BAA to create a shopping centre rather than a collection of shops.

2. What do you consider to be the major limitations surrounding the purchase of fashion items at Heathrow airport?

3. A match between customers' self-image and the store perceived image is one of the key determinants of store choice at Heathrow Airport. With the aid of suitable examples from the retail industry, explain the role of social class as a factor for an airport store choice for fashion purchasing.

4. The type of fashion which air-travellers buy at Heathrow reflects their cultural values and societal acceptance of what is fashionable. Explain and expand on this statement using suitable examples.

5. Apart from the categorization of airport fashion purchasers into fashion conformists and anticonformists, what other segmentation methods could you recommend for classifying airport fashion shoppers?

6. 'Cultural analysis of fashion usually emphasized its psychological role in fashioning the self-concept.' Explain this statement with suitable examples.

7. 'People usually dress to express or suit their culture.' Discuss with suitable examples.

References

Arthur, L. B. (1993) 'Clothing, control, and women's agency: the mitigation of patriarchal power', in S. Fisher and K. Davis (eds), *Negotiating at the Margins*, New Brunswick, NJ: Rutgers University Press, pp. 66–86.

Belk, R. W. and Pollay, R. (1985) 'Images of ourselves: the good life in twentieth century advertising', *Journal of Consumer Research* 11 (March): 887–897.

Bocock, R. (1993) *Consumption*, London: Routledge.

Bordo, S. (1993) *Unbearable Weight: Feminism, Western Culture, and the Body*, Berkeley, CA: University of California Press.

Borgmann, A. (1992) *Crossing the Post-modern Divide*, Chicago: University of Chicago Press.

Cooke, K. (1996) *Real Gorgeous: The Truth about Body and Beauty*, New York: Norton.

Davis, F. (1992) *Fashion, Culture and Identity*, Chicago: University of Chicago Press.

de Certeau, M. (1984) *The Practice of Everyday Life*, Berkeley, CA: University of California Press.

Doganis, R. (1992) *The Airport Business*, London: Routledge.

Fallon, A. (1990) 'Culture in the mirror: sociocultural determinants of body image', in T. F. Cash and T. Pruzinsky (eds), *Body Images*, London: Guilford Press, pp. 80–109.

Faurschou, G. (1987) 'Fashion and the cultural logic of post-modernity', in A. Kroker and M. Kroker (eds), *Body Invaders. New World Perspectives*, Macmillan: Montreal, pp. 78–94.

Finklestein, J. (1991) *The Fashioned Self*, Oxford: Polity Press.

Finklestein, J. and Venkatesh, A. (1995) 'Liberatory post-modernism and the re-enchantment of consumption', *Journal of Consumer Research* 22 (December): 239–267.

Freathy, P. and O'Connell, F. (1998) 'The role of the buying function in airport retailing', *International Journal of Retail & Distribution Management* 26(6): 247–256.

Hetrick, W. P. and Lozada, H. R. (1994) 'Constructing critical imagination: comments and necessary diversions', *Journal of Consumer Research* 21 (December): 548–558.

Holbrook, M. B. and Hirschman, E. C. (1982) 'The experiential aspects of consumption: consumer fantasies, feelings, and fun', *Journal of Consumer Research* 9 (September): 132–140.

Ingrassia, M. (1995) 'The body of the beholder', *Newsweek* (April 24): 66–67.

Jacoby, J. and Olson, J. C. (1977) 'Consumer response to price: an attitudinal, information-processing perspective', in Y. Wind and P. Greenberg (eds), *Moving Ahead with Attitude Research*, Chicago: American Marketing Association.

Jameson, F. (1991) *Postmodernism, or, the Cultural Logic of Late Capitalism*, Durham: Duke University Press.

Jenkins, H. (1992) *Textual Poachers: Television Fans and Participatory Culture*, London: Routledge.

Joy, A. and Venkatesh, A. (1994) 'Post-modernism, feminism, and the body: the visible and the invisible in consumer research', *International Journal of Research in Marketing* 11 (August): 333–357.

Kent, A. and Omar, O. (1996) 'The UK airport retailing: positioning using price, quality, and assortment variables', University of Strathclyde, Scotland: Marketing Education Group.

Kollat, D. T. and Willet, R. P. (1967) 'Customer impulse purchasing behaviour', *Journal of Marketing Research* 4 (February): 21–31.

Kotler, P. (1974) 'Store atmospherics as a marketing tool', *Journal of Retailing* 49 (Winter): 48–65.

Lague, L. (1993) 'How thin is too thin?', *People* , 20 September: 74–80.

Lakoff, G. (1987) *Women, Fire, and Dangerous Things: What Categories Reveal About the Mind*, Chicago: University of Chicago Press.

Leach, W. (1991) *Land of Desire*, New York: Pantheon.

Lewis, B. R. and Hawksley, A. W. (1990) 'Gaining a competitive advantage in fashion retailing', *International Journal of Retail & Distribution Management* 18 (4): 21–31.

Lury, C. (1996). *Consumer Culture*, New Brunswick, NJ: Rutgers University Press.

Nemeth, M. (1994) 'Body obsession', *Maclean's*, 2: May 45–49.

Newman, A. J., Davies, B. J. and Dixon, G. (1995) 'A theoretical model approach to terminal shopping syndrome: a future challenge for UK airport operators?', 24th European Marketing Academy Conference, ESSEC, Paris (May).

Omar, O. and Kent, A. (2001) 'International airport influences on impulsive shopping: trait and normative approach', *International Journal of Retail & Distribution Management* 29 (5): 226–235.

Pitta, D. A., Hung-Gay, F. and Isberg, S. (1999) 'Ethics issues across cultures: managing the differing perspectives of China and the USA', *Journal of Consumer Marketing* 6(3): 240–256.

Probyn, E. (1987) 'The anorexic body', in K. Arthur and M. Kroker (eds), *Body Invaders: New World Perspectives*, Macmillan: Montreal, pp. 201–212.

Rabine, L. W. (1994) 'A woman's two bodies: fashion magazines, consumerism, and feminism', in B. Shari and S. Feriss (eds), *On Fashion*, New Brunswick, NJ: Rutgers University Press, pp. 59–75.

Richins, M. L. (1991) 'Social comparison, advertising, and consumer discontent', *American Scientist* 38 (February): 593–607.

Rubenstein, R. P. (1995) *Dress Codes: Meanings and Messages in American Culture*, Boulder, CO: Westview Press.

Sparke, P. (1995) *As Long as it's Pink: The Sexual Politics of Taste*, San Francisco: Pandora.

Stephens, D. L., Hill, R. P. and Hanson, C. (1994) 'The beauty myth and the controversial role of advertising', *Journal of Consumer Affairs* 28 (Summer): 137–153.

Thompson, C. J. and Haytko, D. L. (1997) 'Speaking of fashion: consumers' uses of fashion discourse and the appropriation of countervailing cultural meanings', *Journal of Consumer Research* 24 (June): 15–42.

Thompson, C. J., Locander, W. B. and Pollio, H. R. (1989) 'Putting consumer experience back into consumer research: the philosophy and method of existential phenomenology', *Journal of Consumer Research* 16 (September): 133–147.

Walsh, S. J. (1992) 'Opportunities in airport retailing', in *Retailing in the 1990s – Responding to the Challenge of Change*, Financial Times Conferences, 28–29 September, London.

Webb, A. (1994) 'The starvation demons', *Maclean's*, 2 May: 50.

Wolf, N. (1991) *The Beauty Myth*, New York: Anchor.

Zeithaml, V. A. (1988) 'Consumer perception of price, quality, and value: a means-end model and synthesis of evidence', *Journal of Marketing* 52 (July): 2–22.

CASE 8

Super 12s rugby union: Comparing the information content and infotainment usage in Australian, New Zealand and South African Super 12s websites

Jamie Carlson, Phillip J. Rosenberger III and John Paynter

C8.1 Introduction

This study examines 10 professional team sport website homepages in the Super 12 Rugby Union Football Competition (in Australia, New Zealand and South Africa) in order to determine the information content of the sites and to determine how the content relates to the elements of the marketing mix. The results indicate a 'Price' and 'Product' focus by the websites examined, which suggest that these team websites are failing to take full advantage of the Web's interactive capabilities. Furthermore, the website homepages were found to be 'Information-oriented', requiring a low-level degree of interaction by the user.

The Internet and sport are a perfect match for success in web-based marketing (Brown, 1998). Professional sport can provide rich information content and also establish a dialogue with its fans through interactive features (Caskey and Deply, 1999; Deply and Bosetti, 1998), for example, in-depth product information, venue information and interactive experiences, which bolster 'insider knowledge' and add to the connection between the sport and the fan (Moses, 1997). Furthermore, US professional sport websites experienced a 5.93% increase in Internet usage globally by mid-2000, and revenues from advertising, ticket sales and merchandising will make sports websites among the most profitable Internet ventures by 2005 (Netratings, 2000; NUA, 2000).

However, little is known about what sporting organizations are actually doing on their websites and how these websites augment marketing through the World Wide Web (Beech, Chadwick and Tapp, 2000). The research that does exist, however, focuses upon successful website management (Pope and Forrest, 1997), how the Internet can be used as a promotional tool in sport (Johns, 1997) and the information content of North American Major League Baseball websites (Brown, 1998). The study reported here expands on this by utilizing a content analysis technique to identify and examine the presence of information content of the Tri-nations Super 12 Rugby websites. Information content is what will be communicated and how it will be expressed through words, pictures and even animation and audio (Deply and Bosetti, 1998). Furthermore, these websites are also classified according to the *infotainment* framework, which combines the ideas of 'information' and 'entertainment' (Paynter and Chung, 2001). The framework (see Figure C8.1) uses a two-by-two matrix with the axes of degree of information and interaction to evaluate websites.

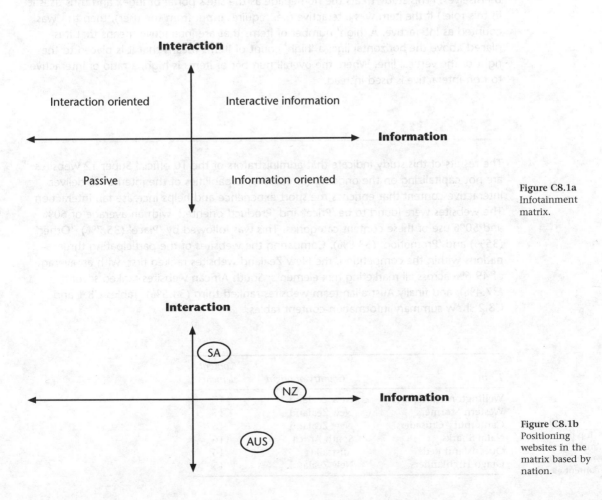

Figure C8.1a
Infotainment matrix.

Figure C8.1b
Positioning websites in the matrix based by nation.

C8.2 Methodology

The population for this study comprised the 10 official team websites of the Tri-nation Rugby Union sporting competition (2 of the 12 teams did not have official websites). A content analysis technique was used to identify and examine the presence of information content in a website, utilizing an organization's homepage as the basis of analysis (Dholakia and Rego, 1998). Categories of content are based on the four P's of the marketing mix: (a) *product*, which included the physical team, club and related merchandise; (b) *price*, information on ticket pricing; (c) *promotion*, information related to team promotions and web-based promotional activities; (d) *place*, information related to pre-season or in-season game location and stadium arrangements; and (e) *other*, website information not belonging in one of the previous categories. Scoring was done by a '0' and '1', representing the absence or presence of a link for a category element, and then summed to form an index score.

The websites were then examined from an infotainment perspective, whereby the number of elements in the site were counted. Where possible, the site map or index was used as a proxy for this, as it represented the types of items present, not the items themselves. (This study treats the homepage as the site's portal or index and thus uses it in this role.) If the item was interactive (i.e. requires input from the user), then this was counted as interactive. A 'high' number of items that are interactive means that it is placed above the horizontal line; a 'high' count of items means that it is placed to the right of the vertical line. Where the overall number of items is high, a ratio of interactive to non-interactive is used instead.

C8.3 Results

The results of this study indicate that administrators of the 10 official Super 12 websites are not capitalizing on the ongoing (interactive) capabilities of the Internet to deliver interactive content that enriches the sport experience and helps increase fan interaction. The websites were found to be 'Price' and 'Product' oriented, with an average of 60% and 50% use of these content categories. This was followed by 'Place' (35.7%), 'Other' (35%) and 'Promotion' (33.8%). Comparing the websites of the participating three nations within the competition, the New Zealand websites ranked first, with an average of 49.6% across all marketing mix elements; South African websites ranked second (37.4%); and finally Australian team websites ranked third (34.5%). Tables C8.1 and C8.2 show summary information-content tables.

Table C8.1
Top five websites ranked by number of information content elements.

Team	Country of origin	Content elements
Wellington Hurricanes	New Zealand	17
Western Stormers	New Zealand	17
Canterbury Crusaders	New Zealand	16
Natal Sharks	South Africa	16
Queensland Reds	Australia	16
Otago Highlanders	New Zealand	15

Classification	Category	%
Product	News releases	100
Promotion	Email subscription	90
Product	Player information	90
Promotion	Multimedia	90
Other	External links	80
Other	Contact	70
Other	Hyperlinked ads	70

Table C8.2
Most frequently
used information
content categories.

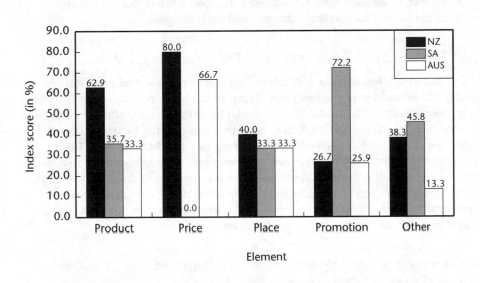

Figure C8.2a
4P information
content
comparison (by
nation).

The overall results suggest that the 10 Tri-nation Rugby Union website homepages examined are primarily utilized as a distribution channel for ticket-related information and player- and club-related information. Further, the results also suggest that the majority of websites are information-oriented, requiring a low-level degree of interaction

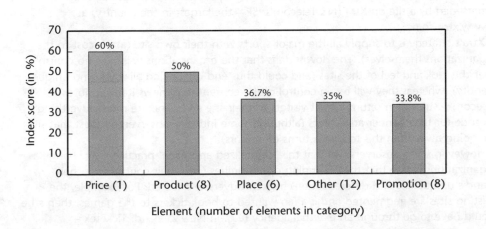

Figure C8.2b
4P information
content index.

by the user. Figure C8.2 shows the websites positioned in the infotainment matrix based on nation of origin.

C8.4 Cross-cultural Managerial Considerations for the Super 12s

Super 12s marketing managers presumably aim to build awareness for their respective teams, grow the brand, and strengthen fan identification and loyalty to the respective team. However, recent developments and observations of the administration of the individual Super 12 websites have highlighted a number of issues that should be of concern to the Super 12 marketing managers seeking these goals.

Super 12 Branding Considerations: The Local Perspective

In New Zealand, the five teams are all composites representing several provinces. In Australia, ACT was added to the two original representative teams (rugby is only a minor code in the other states). In South Africa there has been bitter rivalry and infighting even within the four franchises – the provincial teams that make up the franchises have changed over time so it has been difficult for the teams on and off the field. This exacerbates the problem of ensuring good branding, and of ensuring brands that do not conflict with individual provincial sponsors. All major organizations are expected to have a strong brand image and this is to be reflected in a website. The organizations must compete against other codes (both summer, e.g. cricket, and winter, e.g. NRL) for the sponsors' and fans' attendance, television rights and news coverage.

The Changing Role of Website Administration in New Zealand

It has been observed that the New Zealand teams have moved away from maintaining their own websites to an outsourcing situation. It is often difficult for organizations to bear this expense, especially as rapid changes in technology and telecommunications render the hardware obsolete and, therefore, the content that is capable of being delivered. In-house staffing costs must also be considered. To illustrate this, the Auckland Blues website is no longer being maintained as a separate website, but has been superseded by a site on Xtra (NZ Telecom's ISP – the largest in the country) at <www.xtra.co.nz>.

Xtra's strategy is to supply all the major sports with their own site (at no cost to the organizations themselves). The downside is that the organizations will have no control over the look and feel of the sites (and could thus end up looking alike with no unique identity), whereas they will retain control of the content (e.g. news items, photos). Telecom's Xtra will in return attract visitors to their site and generate more advertising revenue for their banner advertisers (although some industry observers suggest that sites are going away from this too, as it turns off visitors).

However, some observers feel that this 'centralized approach' practice may change as organizations realize that their branding opportunities (and their control over their brand's uniqueness and differentiation) may be adversely affected. For example, the existing sites are fragmented and if a fan wanted to book tickets to the games, then s/he would have to go through an external agency (e.g. in New Zealand, Ticketek –

<www.tickettek.co.nz>), and pay a booking fee. There is also no link between the sites, although during the season the booking agency will feature stories about the major events for which they handle the bookings. This is just one example of a way in which New Zealand Super 12 organizations are not maximizing the returns available from the Web.

Seasonal Nature of the Product

Another factor about the Super 12s competition is the seasonal lifecycle of the product, i.e. the Super 12 games are from March–June (Winter in the southern hemisphere); then there is the test and club season; then the international tours for the respective national Rugby Union sides (e.g. the Wallabies (Australia), All Blacks (New Zealand) and Springboks (South Africa)). Hence, the Super 12s competition itself is limited to 12 weeks of rounds and two weeks of finals and semi-finals. These are preceded by warm-up games in February, but the core fan interest is over a period that lasts for only three months of the year. This is when the merchandising, ticket sales and any other items of interest will be at maximum potential as well. Therefore, it can be hard to sustain interest (and underwrite the costs of supporting a website, too) when the season is limited. On the merchandising side, unlike the fashion industry, it is difficult to have end-of-season sales (especially with the trend to change team stripes every year, at the expense of the fans).

The Role of Unofficial Websites in South Africa

Finally, there is the role of unofficial sites for each team, which especially predominate in South Africa. These unofficial sites also add to the problem of diluting a team's branding, as the individual teams have little or no control over these sites. When searching on the Internet for a team's website, it is often difficult to ascertain just which are the 'official' websites (especially if dedicated, web-savvy Super 12 fans maintain them). If a team wishes to sell tickets or merchandise or generate exposure to sponsor-related ads/ messages, then these unofficial sites compound the difficulty of getting the customer 'in through the front door'.

C8.5   Conclusion

The results of this study indicate that administrators of the Super 12 Rugby websites are not capitalizing on the ongoing interactive capabilities of the Internet to deliver interactive content that enriches the sport experience and helps increase fan interaction. Whilst the Super 12 Rugby websites are currently deficient in an interactive sense, this can represent a significant opportunity to enhance their e-business prospects, such as better managing the interaction with and the creation of new 'customer communities' (Williams and Cothrel, 2000).

Customer communities, which include virtual communities in the case of the Web, are best suited to high-involvement brands, such as those related to sports (Chaffey et al., 2000). Customer communities can be a powerful force, both in terms of influencing the market as well as in being mobilized by a Super 12 Rugby team to help achieve its goals.

Community members derive a variety of benefits from community participation, including need fulfilment, inclusion, mutual influence and shared emotional experiences (Rayport and Jaworski, 2001: 135).

Super 12 Rugby teams that create communities which satisfy both relational and transactional needs will likely reap the benefits of greater customer loyalty and gain important insights into the nature and needs of their customer/fan base (Armstrong and Hagel, 1996). This sense of community (belonging) could thus help encourage Super 12 Rugby users to return to the team's website (Rayport and Jaworski, 2001). For example, Beech *et al.* (2000) found that UK soccer clubs' use of the Internet for community building was seen by the clubs as 'a winner', so the potential for Super 12s virtual communities is promising.

To conclude, there are many, many websites on the Internet. In the same way, there is much competition for the entertainment dollar and for the fans to attend different events. For example, there are major competing Winter sporting codes in the three countries. In Australia, Australian Rules Football and Rugby League are the most popular; in South Africa it is soccer and only in New Zealand is Rugby Union the most popular sport. Even in New Zealand, for instance, the Auckland Blues do not have sell-out crowds, despite the larger population base compared to smaller centres, as they have to compete against the Football Kingz (soccer) and the Auckland Warriors (Rugby League). There is an overlap in all three countries, too, with the end of the Summer season, as international cricket is still being played at the same time as the Super 12s competition gets under way. This is exacerbated as there is even conflict in obtaining playing venues, especially in New Zealand with its smaller population, where the grounds are multi-purpose, and in catering for both rugby and cricket are not ideally suited for either. As can be seen, the intensity of the competition extends well beyond the playing field.

ACTIVITY

1. How does the Super 12s competition fit within the GLOCAL ('think global and act local') paradigm? How can (or does) the Web help the Super 12s competition?

2. Why do you think there are differences in the websites across the three different countries?

3. What are the advantages and disadvantages to both parties of a third party maintaining similar sites (e.g. as Xtra is now doing in New Zealand)? Would this practice work be desired in Australia or South Africa? Also, what are the branding implications for this practice for the individual teams by not having direct control over their own website?

4. Where should the Super 12s websites fit on the infotainment framework and why? Do you think it would vary for the three countries? What could marketing managers do to shift their team's website from where it is to a different location in the infotainment matrix?

5. Have a look at the websites for a league/sporting competition in your own area/country. How does it differ from the Super 12s situation described here?

References

ABS (1999) *Sporting Attendance, Australia*, Report No. 4174.0, Canberra: Australian Bureau of Statistics.

Armstrong, A. and Hagel, J. III (1996) 'The real value of on-line communities', *Harvard Business Review* 74 (May–June): 134–141.

Beech, J., Chadwick, S. and Tapp, A. (2000) 'Emerging trends in the use of the Internet – lessons from the football sector', *Qualitative Market Research: An International Journal* 3(1): 38–46.

Brown, M. T. (1998) 'An examination of the content of official major league baseball team sites on the World Wide Web', *Cyber-Journal of Sports Marketing*, <http://www.cjsm.com/Vol.2/brown.htm>.

Caskey, R. J. and Deply, L. A. (1999) 'An examination of sport websites and the opinion of Web employees toward the use and viability of the World Wide Web as a profitable sports marketing tool', *Sports Marketing Quarterly* 8(2): 13–24.

Chaffey, D., Mayer, R., Johnston, K. and Ellis-Chadwick, F. (2000) *Internet Marketing*, Harlow: Pearson Education.

Delpy, L. and Bosetti, H. A. (1998) 'Sport management and marketing via the World Wide Web', *Sport Marketing Quarterly* 7 (March): 21–28.

Dholakia, U. and Rego, L. (1998) 'What makes Web pages popular? An empirical investigation of Web page effectiveness', *European Journal of Marketing* 32 (7/8): 724–736.

Johns, R. (1997) 'Sports promotion on the Internet', *Cyber-Journal of Sports Marketing* 1(4), <http://www.cjsm.com/vol1/johns.html>

Moses, W. J. (1997) 'Sports in the digital age: digital choices and challenges', *Business of Sport* 2(2): 10–11.

Netratings (2000) 'Apparel and sports categories led internet traffic gains in August, according to Nielsen//NetRatings', available at <http://www.corporate-ir.net/ireye/ir_site.zhtml?ticker=NTRT&script=411&layout=-6&item_id=116865>

NUA Internet Surveys (2000) 'Internet usage statistics', available at <http://www.nua.ie/nkb/>

Paynter, J. and Chung, W. (2000) 'Infotainment', *Conference Proceedings of the 3rd Australasian Services Marketing Workshop*, Dunedin, New Zealand, 2000, pp. 31–33.

Pope, N. and Forrest, E. (1997) 'A proposed format for the management of sports marketing websites', *Cyber-Journal of Sports Marketing* 1(4), <http://www.cjsm.com/Vol1/Pope&Forrest.htm>

Rayport, J. F. and Jaworski, B. J. (2001) *e-Commerce*, New York: McGraw-Hill/Irwin.

Shilbury, D., Quick, S. and Westerbeek, H. (1998) *Strategic Sport Marketing*, New York: Paul & Company Publishers Consortium.

Williams, R. L. and Cothrel, J. (2000) 'Four smart ways to run online communities', *Sloan Management Review* 41 (Summer): 81–91.

Index

Page numbers in *italics* refer to illustrations and tables; page numbers in **bold** refer to main discussion.